Applied
Software
Measurement

Other McGraw-Hill Books in Software Engineering

Applied Software Measurement

Assuring
Productivity and Quality

Capers Jones
Software Productivity Research, Inc.
Burlington, Massachusetts

McGraw-Hill, Inc.
New York   St. Louis   San Francisco   Auckland   Bogotá
Caracas   Hamburg   Lisbon   London   Madrid
Mexico   Milan   Montreal   New Delhi   Paris
San Juan   São Paulo   Singapore
Sydney   Tokyo   Toronto

Library of Congress Cataloging-in-Publication Data

Jones, Capers.
   Applied software measurement : assuring productivity and quality /
Capers Jones.
      p.   cm.   —(Software engineering series)
   Includes bibliographical references and index.
   ISBN 0-07-032813-7
   1. Computer software—Quality control. 2. Function point
   analysis. I. Title. II. Series: Software engineering series (New York, N.Y.)
   QA76.76.Q35J66   1991
   005—dc20   91-4762
                                                                    CIP

   3 4 5 6 7 8 9 0   DOC/DOC   9 7 6 5 4 3 2

ISBN 0-07-032813-7

*The sponsoring editor for this book was Jeanne Glasser, the editing
supervisor was Galen H. Fleck, and the production supervisor was
Suzanne W. Babeuf. This book was set in Century Schoolbook. It was
composed by McGraw-Hill's Professional Book Group composition unit.*

Printed and bound by R. R. Donnelley & Sons Company.

*Subscription information to BYTE Magazine:
Call 1-800-257-9402 or write Circulation Dept.,
One Phoenix Mill Lane, Peterborough, NH 03458.*

Contents

QA76.76
Q35
J66
1991

MAY 27 1993

Preface

Measurement has been the basis of all science and engineering progress except for software. Although software is a creature of the mid-twentieth century, when both economic metrics and other engineering metrics are well developed, it has followed a strange path all on its own and has existed for almost 50 years with very little quantification of either productivity or quality or the factors which influence them.

The book's title, *Applied Software Measurement*, defines the book's intent: to demonstrate that software is in fact capable of accurate measurements, and that the measurements have notable practical value to both the management and the technical community within the software industry.

Software has made some progress without measurement, of course, but its progress has been essentially that of an art form or craft rather than an engineering discipline. How has it happened that a major industry can exist without basic knowledge of the factors which influence it?

First, both computers and modern software originated in the closing years of World War II to aid the military in solving certain mathematical problems. Mathematics has never been a marketed commodity, nor has it ever been easy to measure either mathematical results or the work of mathematicians. Therefore, software had its origin as a subdiscipline of a science which was interested primarily in final results, but which had no history of measuring the speed or effort required to achieve those results. Mathematical solutions of military problems were obviously so time-consuming that both calculators and computer technology were desirable, but the original need for speed was based more on military necessity than on economics.

Second, the initial wave of software applications in the late 1940s and early 1950s tended to be complex ballistic and scientific calculations which had four significant characteristics: (1) Solving the problems themselves required substantial mental effort but not much in the way of paperwork. (2) The problems were fairly small and self-contained, so only one, or perhaps two persons were involved. (3) Both machine language and primitive assembly languages were so tedious and difficult to use that coding became both a focal point of and a bottleneck to moving problem solutions onto a computer. (4) Once the problems were solved and the solutions were encoded, they did not change very much afterward.

Thus, when measurement of early software projects did occur, it was fairly reasonable to express the measurements in the crude terms of "lines of code." There were no measurements that encompassed the pure mental work of programming, and the enormous volumes of specifications and user documents were not part of the first generation of software projects. Nor was maintenance a major consideration for the first 10 years or so of software production.

It should be noted that, as a commodity, software lagged behind computers by more than 10 years. For vacuum-tube-based computers and the early discrete transistor computers, the bulk of the costs were associated with the computer itself, and the software was normally bundled with the hardware and given away. There is certainly very little business incentive to measure a commodity that is given away, so there was no economic pressure for improved software metrics. When computers began to move into the dormain of business applications and outside the solution of specialized military and systems problems, software began to break away from hardware and move toward becoming a separate subindustry.

Unfortunately, the subindustry carried with it the mindset from the 1940s and 1950s that measurements were either intrusive (derived from software's mathematical origins) or should be based on lines of code (derived from the exhaustion and frustration of working with machine language and primitive assembly languages). Thus, the origins of software and the nature of the early work neither demanded measurements nor supplied any overwhelming economic reasons to explore and improve measurement.

What happened next was the explosion of software and computing in the 1960s, 1970s, and 1980s. Computers evolved from being specialized military and academic curiosities into being the main driving force of modern business, industry, and government. The demand for computers exceeded the early IBM prognostications by more than a 1000 to 1, and the demand continues to grow. Software production changed from being the province of obscure and esoteric specialists into one of the largest occupations in human history.

With the enormous growth in the demand for software and the similar growth in the number of software professionals, economic necessity has made measurements imperative. The president of a large company might not have been greatly concerned about measuring the performance of a computer and a few specialists in the late 1950s. But by 1990, the company could not operate or compete successfully without computers and software, and the employed software professionals might constitute 10 percent of company's work force. The annual budgets for computers, peripherals, and professional staff might exceed $1 billion!

It is obvious that the need for accurate measurements of software productivity and quality is directly related to the overall economic importance of software to industry, business, and government. That means that measurement is now a mainstream software activity, and it is one that is on the critical path to corporate and national success.

The contents of the book are intended to cover all of the broad and most of the specific topics associated with starting a full corporate measurement program that encompasses productivity, quality, and human factors. Chapter 1, the Introduction, is an overview of all aspects of applied software measurement in modern corporations, including on-going project measures, annual baselines, productivity measures, quality measures, demographic measures, and production library measures. It introduces standard economic concepts and points out the advantages of functional metrics for economic studies.

Chapter 2, The History and Evolution of Functional Metrics, starts by explaining in detail the economic fallacies of lines-of-code metrics. It then discusses all of the major variations in functional metrics since the first public announcement of function points in 1979. Topics covered include function points, DeMarco bang metrics, feature points, the British Mark II function point method, the IFPUG method, and several others.

Chapter 3, United States Averages for Software Productivity and Quality, attempts to carve out the current overall national rates for all key software productivity and quality topics. It uses the backfire function point technique to create U.S. averages for software productivity and quality. It also discusses the reasons for productivity variations between MIS, systems, and military projects. It includes a retrospective historical study of software productivity at 10-year intervals from 1950 to 1990, with projections forward to 2000.

Chapter 4, The Mechanics of Measurement, discusses the work of starting a corporate software baseline for the very first time. It deals with both sociological and technical issues of introducing applied software measurements. A baseline must contain both accurate "hard" data and also reliable "soft" data to determine why projects vary.

Chapter 5, Measuring Software Quality and User Satisfaction, discusses the business significance of quality for international competition of high-technology products. It then discusses the closely intertwined topics of quality control and user satisfaction. The chapter introduces the measurement of defect origins, defect severities, and defect removal efficiency. Also discussed is the measurement of user-reported defects after release of software to customers. The chapter includes cautions about paradoxical measurements, such as "cost per defect," that are economically unsound.

Appendix A, Rules for Counting Procedural Source Code, gives the detailed rules devloped by Software Productivity Research to ensure consistent counting of source code size.

Appendix B, Rules for Counting Function Points and Feature Points illustrates and discusses the detailed rules necessary to ensure consistent counting of function points and feature points.

Appendix C, Example of a Fully Measured Software Project, shows the total volume of information that must be recorded to fully measure a project. The volume of information approximates recorded for a human patient undergoing a complete medical examination. This appendix illustrates and discusses all of the salient data types, including soft data on the environment and methods, hard data on the tangible deliverables, and normalized data using functional metrics.

Appendix D, Example of an Annual Baseline Report, shows a full annual corporate software baseline report for a medium-size company. Such a baseline will be about the same size, and require about the same kind of effort, as the production of a corporate annual report to shareholders and investors. The appendix illustrates and discusses the kinds of aggregation and analysis needed to show productivity and quality trends at the corporate level.

Appendix E, Example of an Executive Briefing on a New Baseline, shows a typical report to senior management. Not only are baseline reports printed for management distribution but special executive summaries are normally prepared for senior management. The appendix illustrates and discusses a typical executive-level presentation on software strengths and weaknesses, productivity, and quality.

Acknowledgments

Special appreciation to my wife, Eileen Jones, not only for her support of the book but also for her outstanding ability to make Software Productivity Research an enjoyable place in which to do research. Our thanks to our family for their support over the years. Appreciation is due to Dana Jones, my mother, and to Cliff and Maggie Provonsil, Eileen's parents.

Appreciation is also due to the staff of Software Productivity Research for building the tools that collected much of the data, for carrying out much of the data collection work, and, of course, for keeping the company running and supporting our clients. Thanks to Debbie Chapman, Chas Douglis, Scott Goldfarb, Jane Greene, Wayne Hadlock, Shane Hartman, Dave Herron, Eileen Jones, Mark Pinis, Elaine Sutherlin, Richard Ward, and John Zimmerman. Thanks also to Ken and Christine Bowes.

The author was fortunate for being present in both IBM and ITT when their corporate software measurement programs were gearing up. Appreciation is due to the late Ted Climis of IBM, whose executive support of measurement did much to incorporate metrics into the IBM mainstream. Appreciation is also due to the many IBM managers and metrics researchers, including Al Albrecht, Ken Christensen, Jim Frame, Harlan Mills, Horst Remus, and Claude Walston.

Appreciation is due to the Chairmen of ITT, Harold Geneen, Lyman Hamilton, and Rand Araskog, for their recognition that software is a critical corporate asset. Appreciation is also due to the ITT metrics researchers, including Bert Albert, Donn Combelic, Phil Crosby, Bill Curtis, Robert Dunn, Bob Kendall, Yuan Liu, Richard Margo, John Vossburgh, Fred Sayward, and Ray Wolverton.

Appreciation is also due to the measurement teams at the companies whose data helped in preparation. Thanks to the software measurement teams at AT&T, Bell Northern Research, Bendix, Church of the Latter Day Saints, CODEX, DEC, Ford Motors, General Electric, GTE, Du Pont, Hartford Insurance, Hewlett-Packard, JC Penney, Motorola, NCR, Pacific Bell, Ralston Purina, Sears Roebuck of the U.S. and Canada, Sun Life Insurance, Tandem, TRW, UNISYS, US West, Wang, and Westinghouse.

Appreciation is due to the many metrics and software engineering colleagues whose work provided some of the concepts discussed here: Al Albrecht, Jay Arthur, Vic Basili, Barry Boehm, Deborah Caswell, Samuel Conte, Bill Curtis, Tom DeMarco, Brian Dreger, Bob Grady, Watts Humphry, Chris Kemerer, Tom Love, Tom McCabe, Ben Porter, Roger Pressman, Larry Putnam, Charles Symons, Jerry Weinberg, and Ellie Williamson.

Thank to Galen Fleck for his fine editing.

Capers Jones

Applied
Software
Measurement

Introduction

Software development and maintenance have become major corporate concerns in the last half of the twentieth century. Although most companies could not survive or compete successfully without software and computers, senior executive management remains troubled by a set of chronic problems associated with software applications: long schedules, major cost overruns, low quality, and poor user satisfaction.

These problems have occurred so widely that it is fair to characterize them as a "corporate epidemic." Yet software is not out of control in every company. The companies that have been most successful in bringing software under control tend to share most of these six characteristics:

1. They measure software productivity and quality accurately.
2. They plan and estimate software projects accurately.
3. They have capable management and technical staffs.
4. They have good organization structures.
5. They have effective software methods and tools.
6. They have adequate staff office environments.

All six characteristics are important, but the first is perhaps the most significant of all, since it tends to permeate and influence the others. Let us consider each of the six in turn.

Applied software measurement

Measurement is the basis of all science, engineering, and business. Unfortunately, software developers lagged far behind other professionals in establishing both standard metrics and meaningful targets. The phrase "applied software measurement" refers to the emerging discipline associated with the accurate and meaningful collection of information which has practical value to software management and staffs. The goal of applied software measurement is to give software managers and professionals a set of useful, tangible data points for sizing, estimating, managing, and controlling software projects with rigor and precision.

For many years, measuring software productivity and quality was so difficult that only very large companies such as IBM attempted it. Indeed, one of the reasons for IBM's success was the early emphasis the company put on the applied measurement of quality and productivity, which gave IBM the ability to use the data for corrective purposes. But stable metrics and accurate applied measurement of software have been possible since 1979, and now every company can gain the benefits and insights available from applied software measurement.

The problem today is not a deficiency in software measurement technology itself; rather, it is cultural resistance on the part of software management and staff. The resistance is due to the natural human belief that measures might be used against them. This feeling is the greatest barrier to applied software measurement. The challenge today is to overcome this barrier and demonstrate that applied software measurement is not harmful, but as necessary to corporate success as standard financial measurements.

What tends to separate leading-edge companies from trailing-edge companies are not only technical differences but cultural differences as well. Project managers in companies at the leading edge, such as IBM, Du Pont, and Hewlett-Packard, may have 10 times as much quantified, historical information available to them to aid in project planning as their peers in companies at the trailing edge.

Managers in leading-edge companies also have accurate demographic and morale information available, which is largely missing at the trailing edge. Not only is such information absent at the trailing edge, but the managers and executives within trailing-edge companies are often deluded into thinking their companies are much better than they really are!

Planning and estimation

Planning and estimation are the mirror images of measurement. The factors and metrics that were recorded during project development are now aimed toward the future of uncompleted projects. There is a perfect correlation between measurement accuracy and estimation accuracy: Companies that measure well can estimate well; companies that do not measure cannot estimate either. Commercial-grade estimation tools have been available since the middle 1970s, and they are now becoming widely deployed. Here too measurement is significant, since only companies with accurate historical data can validate estimates and judge their accuracy. Leading-edge enterprises normally do not attempt to estimate large projects by hand; instead, they use either proprietary tools based on their own history or commercial estimating tools based on general industry data.

Management and technical staffs

Leading-edge companies tend to attract and keep good managers and good technical staffs. What attracts such people appears to be exciting projects, excellent working conditions, and the pleasure of working with capable colleagues. Although it is outside the scope of this book, leading-edge companies such as IBM tend to go out of their way to measure employee satisfaction by means of annual corporate opinion surveys. Trailing-edge companies have trouble keeping capable management and staff. What causes the dissatisfaction are poorly conceived or canceled projects, inadequate working conditions, primitive tools and methods, and the lack of stimulating colleagues and effective project management. Trailing-edge companies are seldom aware of these problems because they lack any form of measurement or opinion survey.

Organization structures

Software in the 1990s is becoming specialized just as medicine and law have become specialized. As special technical skills are needed, such as those of database administrators, quality assurance specialists, human factors specialists, and technical writers, it becomes more and more important to plan organization structures carefully. Indeed, among the hallmarks of the larger leading-edge corporations are measurement specialists and measurement organizations. One of the useful by-products of measurement is the ability to judge the relative effectiveness of organization structures such as hierarchical vs. matrix management for software projects and centralization vs. decentralization for the software function overall. Here too, measurement can lead to progress and the lack of measurement can lead to expensive mistakes.

Methodologies and tools

The labor content of software projects is extraordinarily high. Very few artifacts require as much manual labor as a large software system. Many software methodology, tool, language, and CASE vendors claim to displace human effort through automation with 10- or 20-to-1 improvements in productivity. Are such claims justified? Generally, they are not. Only companies that measure software productivity and quality can find their way through the morass of conflicting assertions and pick a truly effective path. As it turns out, heavy investment in tools prior to resolving organizational and methodological issues is normally counterproductive and will improve neither quality nor productivity. Only accurate measurements can navigate a path that is both cost-effective and pragmatic.

The office environment

The final aspect of leading-edge companies is a surprising one: The companies tend to have adequate office space and good physical environments. It appears that, for knowledge workers such as software professionals, the impact of physical office environments on productivity may be as great as the impact of the tools and methods used. Open offices and overcrowding tend to lower productivity, whereas private offices and adequate space tend to augment it. Findings such as that are possible only from accurate measurements and multiple-regression studies of all the factors which influence human endeavors.

Art is normally free-form and unconstrained; business is normally under management control. In companies with no measurement practices, software projects are essentially artistic rather than business undertakings. That is, there is no way for management to make an accurate prediction of the outcome of a project or to exert effective control once the project has been set in motion. That is not as it should be. Software should be a normal business function with the same rigor of planning, estimating, risk, and value analysis as any other corporate function. Only measurement, carefully applied, can convert software production and maintenance from artistic activities into business activities.

Although many different sociological and technological steps may be needed to bring software under management control in a large company, all of them require accurate measurement as the starting point. That is true of all physical and social systems: Only measurement can assess progress and direction and allow feedback loops to bring deviations under control.

The Essential Aspects of Applied Software Measurement

Three essential kinds of information must be considered when dealing with applied software measurement, or the measurement of any other complex process involving human action:

1. Hard data
2. Soft data
3. Normalized data

All three kinds of information must be recorded and analyzed in order to gain insights into productivity or quality problems.

Hard data

The first kind of information, termed "hard data," refers to things that can be quantified with little or no subjectivity. For the hard-data elements, high accuracy is both possible and desirable. The key hard-data elements that affect software projects are:

- The number of staff members assigned to a project
- The effort spent by staff members on project tasks
- The schedule durations of significant project tasks
- The overlap and concurrency of tasks performed in parallel
- The project document, code, and test case volumes
- The number of bugs or defects found and reported

Although hard data can in theory be measured with very high accuracy, most companies are distressingly inaccurate in the data they collect. Factors such as unpaid overtime by professional staff members, management costs, user involvement, and frequent project accounting errors can cause the true cost of a software project to be up to 100 percent greater than the apparent cost derived from a normal project-tracking system. That fact must be evaluated and considered when starting a serious corporate measurement program: It will probably be necessary to modify or replace the existing project cost-tracking system with something more effective.

The solution to inaccurate tracking accuracy is not technically difficult, although it may be sociologically difficult. It is only necessary to establish a standard chart of accounts for the tasks which will normally be performed on software projects and then collect data by task.

The sociological difficulty comes in recognizing that current tracking systems tend to omit large volumes of unpaid overtime, user effort on projects, managerial effort, and often many other activities. Senior executives and software project managers must have access to an accurate accounting of what the true cost elements of software projects really are.

One of the most frequent problems encountered with project historical data that lowers data accuracy is a simple lack of granularity. Instead of measuring the effort of specific activities, companies tend to accumulate only "bottom line" data for the whole project without separating the data into meaningful subsets, such as the effort for requirements, design, and coding. Such bottom-line data is essentially worthless because there is no real way to validate it.

For purposes of schedule and management control, it is common to break software projects into somewhere between 5 and 10 specific phases such as "requirements, design, coding, testing, and installation." Such phase structures are cumbersome and inadequate for cost measurement purposes. Too many activities, such as production of user documentation, tend to span several phases, so accurate cost accumulation is difficult to perform.

Table 1.1 is an example of the standard chart of accounts used by Software Productivity Research[1] when collecting the project data shown in the later sections of this book. It illustrates the kind of granularity by activity needed for historical data to be useful for economic studies. This chart of accounts is based on activities rather than phases. An "activity" is defined as a bounded set of tasks aimed at

TABLE 1.1 Example of a Standard Software Chart of Accounts

Cost accumulators	MIS projects	Systems projects	Military projects
1. Requirements	X	X	X
2. Prototyping		X	X
3. Architecture		X	X
4. Formal project plans		X	X
5. Initial analysis and design	X	X	X
6. Detail design	X	X	X
7. Formal design reviews		X	X
8. Coding	X	X	X
9. Reusable code acquisition		X	X
10. Purchased code acquisition	X		X
11. Formal code inspections		X	X
12. Independent verification and validation			X
13. Formal configuration management			X
14. Formal integration		X	X
15. User documentation	X	X	X
16. Unit testing	X	X	X
17. Function testing	X	X	X
18. Integration testing		X	X
19. System testing	X	X	X
20. Field testing		X	X
21. Acceptance testing	X		X
22. Independent testing			X
23. Formal quality assurance		X	X
24. Installation and training	X	X	X
25. Project management	X	X	X
Average number of activities	12	20	25

completing a significant project milestone. The milestone might be completion of requirements, completion of a prototype, or completion of initial design.

Although Table 1.1 uses 25 standard activities, that does not imply that only 25 things must be done to develop a software project. The 25 activities are accounting abstractions used to accumulate costs in a convenient manner. Any given activity, such as "requirements," obviously consists of a number of significant subactivities or specific tasks. Indeed, even small software projects may require hundreds of specific tasks in a full work breakdown structure; large projects may require many thousands. A task-level chart of accounts, although capable of high precision, tends to be very cumbersome for cost accumulation, since project staff must record times against a very large number of individual tasks.

The 25 activities listed in Table 1.1 illustrate the level of granularity needed to gain economic insights into the major costs associated with software.

Unless a reasonably granular chart of accounts is used, it is difficult to explore economic productivity in ways that lead to insights. For example, it has been known for many years that military software projects typically have lower productivity rates than civilian software projects of the same size. One of the key reasons for that can easily be seen by means of a granular chart of accounts.

MIS projects normally perform only 12 of the 25 standard activities; systems software projects perform about 20; and military projects normally perform all 25. The need to perform almost twice as many activities explains why military projects are usually quite low in productivity compared to civilian projects.

Soft data

The second kind of information, termed "soft data," comprises topics in which human opinions must be evaluated. Since human opinions will vary, absolute precision is impossible for the soft data. Nonetheless, it is the soft data, taken collectively, which explains variations in project outcomes. The key soft data elements that affect software projects are:

- The skill and experience of the project team
- The constraints or schedule pressures put on the team
- The stability of project requirements over time
- User satisfaction with the project
- The expertise and cooperation of the project users

- Adequacy of the tools and methods used on the project
- The organization structure for the project team
- Adequacy of the office space for the project team
- The perceived value of the project to the enterprise

Although soft data is intrinsically subjective, it is still among the most useful kinds of information that can be collected. Soft data is the major source of information that can explain the variations in productivity and quality without which a measurement program cannot lead to insights and improvements. Therefore, in a well-designed applied software measurement program, much effort and care must be devoted to selecting the appropriate sets of soft factors and then developing instruments that will allow this useful data to be collected and analyzed statistically. That is the most difficult intellectual task associated with measurement programs.

Normalized data

The third kind of information, termed "normalized data," refers to standard metrics used for comparative purposes to determine whether projects are above or below normal in terms of productivity or quality. This form of information was very troublesome for the software industry, and more than 40 years went by before satisfactory normalization metrics were developed.

The historical attempts to use lines of code for normalization purposes failed dismally because of the lack of international standards that clearly defined what was meant by a "line of code" in any common language and because of serious mathematical paradoxes. Indeed, lines-of-code metrics are technically impossible for studying economic productivity, which is defined as the "goods or services produced per unit of labor or expense." Lines of code are neither goods nor services, and for many large software projects less than 20 percent of the total effort is devoted to coding.

The mathematical paradoxes and the reversal of apparent economic productivity associated with lines-of-code metrics totally negate the validity of such data for statistical analysis. The most troubling aspect of the paradox is the tendency for lines-of-code productivity rates to penalize high-level languages. The reason for this paradox was first described by the author in 1978 in the *IBM Systems Journal*.[2] However, the fundamental mathematics of the paradox had been worked out during the industrial revolution, and the basic reason for the problem has been known by economists and industrial engineers for more than 200 years!

In any manufacturing process in which fixed costs are significant, a

TABLE 1.2 Example of the Mathematical Paradox Associated with Lines-of-Source-Code Metrics

	Assembler version	Ada version
Lines of source code in project	7500	2500
Noncoding effort in person-months	3	3
Coding effort in person-months	3	1
Total project effort in person-months	6	4
Net source lines per person-month	1250	625

reduction in the number of units constructed will raise the average cost per unit. For software, more than half of the project costs can go to noncoding tasks such as requirements, specifications, documentation, and testing. These noncoding tasks tend to act like fixed costs, raise the cost per source line, and lower the source lines per person-month rates for projects written in high-level languages.

Table 1.2 illustrates the paradox of an increase in real economic productivity but a decline in source lines per person-month for high-level languages. Assume that two projects are identical in functionality, but one is written in a low-level language such as Assembler and the second written in a high-level language such as Ada. The noncoding tasks stay constant between the two examples and tend to act as fixed costs. The reduction in the number of source code statements in the Ada example, therefore, tends to act like a reduction in manufactured units.

Note that although the Ada version required only 4 person-months of total effort and the Assembler version required 6 person-months, the lines-of-code metric appears to be twice as good for the Assembler version. That violates the standard economic definition of productivity and common sense as well.

Since October 1979, when A. J. Albrecht of IBM first publicized function points,[3] the new function-based metrics, such as function points for MIS projects and feature points for systems software, are becoming the preferred choice for software normalization. They have substantially replaced the older lines-of-code metric for purposes of economic and productivity analysis.

Function points will be described in detail in Chap. 2. The function-based metrics are derived from counts of the externally visible aspects of a software project that are significant to its users. The basic IBM function point metric uses weighted counts of five parameters: inputs, outputs, inquiries, logical files, and interfaces. (The feature point metric, developed for real-time and systems software, uses the same five parameters and also enumerates the number of algorithms. Other pa-

TABLE 1.3 **Example of Basic Function Point Counts**

Element	Number		Weights		Total
Inputs	2	×	4	=	8
Outputs	2	×	5	=	10
Inquiries	0	×	4	=	0
Logical files	1	×	10	=	10
Interfaces	1	×	7	=	7
Total					35

Note: Chapter 2 will discuss adjustments to the basic counts.

rameters, such as counts of entities and relationships, also are used by some of the function-based metrics.)

The essential aspects of function points apply empirical weights to the five Basic factors that comprise an application. For example, the function point total for the projects shown in Table 1.2 might be as shown in Table 1.3.

Note that function points are independent of lines of code, so the function point total for both the Assembler and the Ada versions would be the same: 35 function points in this case. Measures based on function points, such as cost per function point and function points per staff-month, are much more reliable than the older lines of code for economic purposes.

Functional metrics are artificial business metrics equivalent perhaps to cost per square foot in home construction or the Dow Jones stock indicator. Contractors do not build houses a square foot at a time, but nonetheless cost per square foot is a useful figure. Software professionals do not build software one function point at a time, but cost per function point is a useful economic metric.

As mentioned, both function points and feature points are totally independent of the number of source code statements, and they will stay constant regardless of the programming language used. Table 1.4 il-

TABLE 1.4 **Example of the Mathematical Validity Associated with Function Point Metrics**

	Assembler version	Ada version
Number of function points in project	35.0	35.0
Noncoding effort in person-months	3.0	3.0
Coding effort in person-months	3.0	1.0
Total project effort in person-months	6.0	4.0
Net function points per person-month	5.83	8.75

lustrates the same pair of example programs as shown in the previous Table 1.2, only this time productivity is expressed in function points per person-month. Since both the Assembler version and the Ada version are identical in functionality, assume that both versions contain 35 function points.

Observe how the function point metric agrees with both common sense and the economic definition of productivity, since the same quantity of an economic unit (35 function points) has been produced for less labor in the Ada example.

Now that function points have been in use for more than 10 years, some surprising new findings have occurred, and indeed whole new kinds of studies that were previously impossible can now be carried out. To illustrate the economic advantages of using the function point metric for large-scale studies, it is now possible to assert that the current national average for software productivity at the project level in the United States appears to be about five function points per staff-month. The range, however, runs from a fraction of a function point for large and complex systems developed traditionally to more than 140 function points per person-month for small applications with a high volume of reusable components. This average is derived from the most of more than 4000 projects evaluated by the author from 1965 forward, and more recently by the members of the staff of Software Productivity Research.[1]

Figure 1.1 illustrates the use of function points and shows the current U.S. ranges for software productivity rates at the project level. Expressed in an alternative way, an average function point for software in the United States will require about 32 hours of human effort, but the range is more than 15 to 1 on either side of that norm for rea-

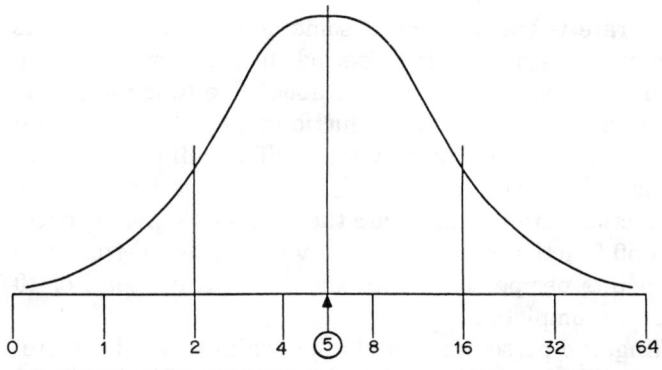

Figure 1.1 Average U.S. software project productivity expressed in function points per staff-month.

sons that can be explained by variations in the tasks performed and by careful analysis of the soft factors.

MIS projects typically are the most productive in the United States and average about eight function points per person-month; systems software averages about four function points per person-month; and military software averages only about three function points per person-month because of the large number of tasks and the enormous volume of paperwork required by military specifications.

Assignment scopes and production rates

Two secondary measures that are extremely useful are those termed "assignment scope" and "production rate." An assignment scope is the amount of some deliverable for which one person will normally be held fully responsible. For new development projects, programmers are normally assigned between 50 and 100 function points, or 5000 to 10,000 code statements, as typical workloads.

For the purposes of maintaining existing software (fixing bugs and making small changes), an ordinary programmer will normally be responsible for perhaps 300 to 500 function points if the application is in a normal language such as Cobol. That is a particularly useful statistic, because most large companies have production libraries that total from 200,000 to more than 1 million function points. The average maintenance assignment scope is a key factor for predicting future maintenance staffing requirements.

Once assignment scope data is collected, the assignment scope is a key metric in determining how many technical staff members will be needed for both development and maintenance projects. Dividing the total size of a new project by the average assignment scope derived from a historical project will generate a useful estimate of the average staff size to be required.

The production rate is the amount of some deliverable which one person can produce in a standard time period such as a work-month. The previously mentioned U.S. average of about five function points per staff-month is an example of a production rate. The production rate is a key metric in determining how much effort will be needed in terms of person-months, since the total size of the project divided by the average production rate will generate the amount of effort needed. Thus a project of 50 function points in size divided by an average rate of five function points per person-month should require a total of 10 person-months to be completed.

Once the staffing and person-month of effort values have been created for a project, the approximate schedule can quickly be determined by simply dividing the effort by the staff. For example, a 24-

person-month project to be completed by a staff of four people should take about 6 calendar months. Once their logic has become assimilated, assignment scopes and production rates lead to very useful quick-estimating capabilities.

Strategic and Tactical Software Measurement

In military science, strategy is concerned with the selection of overall goals or military objectives, whereas tactics is concerned with the deployment and movement of troops toward those goals. There is a similar dichotomy within corporations that affects the measurement function. A corporate strategy will concern the overall business plan, target markets, competitive situations, and direction of the company. Corporate tactics will concern the specific steps and movement taken to implement the strategy.

For the purposes of measurement, strategic measurements are normally those which involve the entire corporation and the factors which may influence corporate success. Tactical measurements are those which concern specific projects, and the factors which can influence the outcomes of the projects (Table 1.5).

A full applied software measurement program will include both

TABLE 1.5 Strategic and Tactical Software Measures

Kind of data	Strategic measures	Tactical measures
Hard	Total staff size	Staffing by activity or task
	Occupation groups	Effort by activity or task
	Portfolio size	Costs by activity or task
	User support	Project deliverables
	Market share studies	Defect rates and severities
	Profitability studies	Function or feature points
	Cancellation factors	Staff assignment scopes
	Annual software costs	Staff production rates
	Annual hardware costs	Project risk analysis
	Annual personnel costs	Project value analysis
Soft	Morale surveys	User satisfaction
	Incentive plans	Effectiveness of tools
	Annual education	Usefulness of methods
	Corporate culture	Appropriate staff skills
	Executive goals	Environment adequacy
	Competitive analysis	Project constraints
Normalized	Total function points	Project size
	Annual function points	Productivity rate(s)
	Function points per	Defect rate(s)
	user (consumption)	Cost rate(s)

strategic and tactical measurements. Some of the more common forms of strategic measurement include an annual survey of total data processing expenses vs. competitive companies, an annual survey of staff demographics and occupation groups vs. competitive companies, and an annual survey of the size, mix, quality, current status, and backlog associated with the corporate portfolio.

For productivity itself, sometimes the differences between the strategic concept of productivity and the tactical concept can be surprising. For example, when companies start to think in terms of productivity measurement, most of them begin tactically by measuring the efforts of the direct staff on a set of successfully completed projects. That might generate a number such as an average productivity rate of perhaps eight function points per person-month for the projects included in the tactical study. Tactical project measures are a reasonable way to measure successfully completed projects, but what about projects that are canceled or not successfully completed? What about indirect staff such as executives, administrators, and secretarial people whose salaries are paid by the software budget but who are not direct participants in tactical project work?

A strategic or corporate productivity measurement would proceed as follows: The entire quantity of function points delivered to users in a calendar year by the software organization would be counted. The total software staff effort from the senior software vice president down through secretarial support would be enumerated, including the efforts of staff on canceled projects and the staff on incomplete projects that are still being built. Even user effort would be counted if the users participated actively during requirements and project development. The strategic or corporate productivity metric would be calculated by dividing the total quantity of delivered function points in a calendar year by the total number of person-months of effort expended by the whole organization. This, of course, will generate a much lower number than the previous tactical rate of eight function points per person-month, and a normal strategic corporate rate might be only from one to three function points per person-month. The current average is about 1.5.

Both strategic and tactical measurements are important, but they tend to give different insights. The strategic measures tend to be very important at the CEO and senior executive levels; the tactical measures tend to be very important at the group, unit, and project levels.

Plainly, a corporation must pay the salaries and expenses of its entire software organization from the vice presidents downward. It must also pay for canceled projects and for projects that are under development but are not yet complete. The strategic form of productivity measurement tends to be a very useful indicator of overall corporate effi-

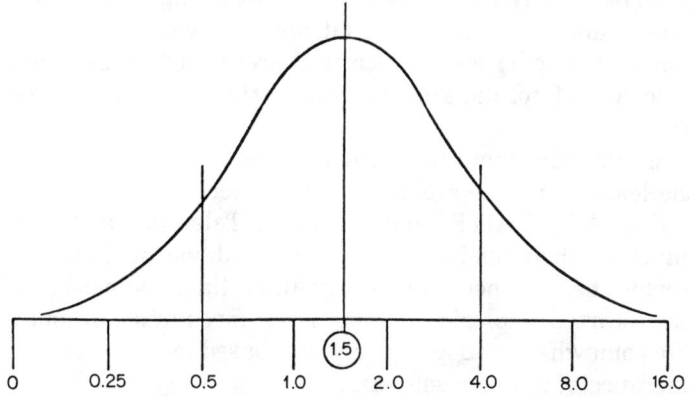

Figure 1.2 Average U.S. software enterprise productivity expressed in function points per staff-month.

ciency in the software domain. Figure 1.2 shows average U.S. productivity at the strategic or enterprise level.

It cannot be overemphasized that both the strategic and tactical forms of measurement are useful, but each serves its own purpose. The strategic form is of great interest to senior executives, who must pay for all software staff and expenses. The tactical form is of great interest to project and divisional managers.

Prior to the advent of function points, it was not technically possible to carry out large-scale strategic measurement studies at the corporate, industry, or national level. Now, however, the functional metrics have been widely deployed, and it is possible to make at least the first steps in exploring productivity differences by company, by industry, and by nation.

Current Measurement Experiences by Industry

The leading high-technology companies that produce both computers and software, such as IBM, Hewlett-Packard, Tandem, UNISYS, Wang, and DEC, tend to measure both software productivity and quality and to use the data to make planned improvements. They are also very good at measuring user satisfaction and they are comparatively good at project estimating. The trailing companies within this segment produce only partial quality measurements and little or nothing in the way of productivity measurement. Sociologically, quality tends to receive greater emphasis in high-technology companies than elsewhere because the success of such companies' products demands high quality.

There seems to be a fairly good correlation between high technology and measurement, and the companies that have active research and development programs under way in technical areas, such as Du Pont, General Electric, and Motorola, are often innovative in software measurements too.

The telecommunications manufacturing business, on the whole, has been one of the leaders in software measurement technology. Companies such as ITT, AT&T, GTE, and Northern Telecom have long known that much of their business success depends on quality, and they have therefore been pioneers in quality and reliability measures. Most have also started exploring productivity measures, although they tend to lag somewhat in adopting function-based metrics because of the preponderance of systems software.

The telecommunication operating companies such as Pacific Bell, on the other hand, have tended to be quite sophisticated with productivity measurements and were early adopters of function points, perhaps because, with thousands of software staff members, productivity is a pressing concern.

When airlines and automotive manufacturers were extremely profitable, neither software productivity nor measurement tended to be emphasized. In the wake of deregulation and reduced earnings for airlines, and in the wake of enormous overseas competition in the automotive segment, both kinds of manufacturers are now attempting to make up for lost time by starting full quality and productivity measurement programs. Airlines such as Delta, American, Quantas, and British Air are taking active steps to enter the software measurement arena, as are automotive manufacturers such as Ford.

Energy and oil production companies, also in the wake of reduced earnings, are now starting to move quickly into the domain of productivity measurement and are beginning to move toward measures of quality and user satisfaction as well. Companies such as Exxon and Amoco were early students of software productivity measurement, and they have been moving into quality and user satisfaction as well.

The pure software houses have lagged behind the computer manufacturers in measurement of productivity and also in measures of quality in terms of defect rates. There are exceptions such as MSA, however; MSA has a very sophisticated quality measurement program under way and is also moving into productivity measures. The software houses, by and large, tend to do an acceptable job of measuring user satisfaction. Their estimating is often spotty and imperfect, as both Lotus and Microsoft have demonstrated by their recent slippages of announced delivery dates.

Management consulting companies such as Software Productivity Research; DMR Group; Peat, Marwick & Mitchell; Nolan, Norton &

Company; and Ernst & Young have often been more effective than universities both in using metrics and in transferring the technologies of measurement throughout their client base.

The defense industry has long been active in measurement, but in part because of government requirements, often attempts to both measure and estimate productivity by using the obsolete lines-of-code metric with unreliable results. Even the measurement initiatives in defense research establishments such as the Software Engineering Institute (SEI) tend to lag behind the civilian sectors. SEI has not yet adopted any of the economically sound function-based metrics, although Watts Humphrey of SEI's attempts to measure the stages of software maturity are attracting much attention.[7] The defense segment is also spotty and incomplete in terms of quality measurement. That is unfortunate, given the size and resources of the defense community. The defense community is among the world leaders in terms of estimating automation, however, and most large defense contractors have professional estimating staffs supported by fully automated software-estimating packages. That does not, of course, mean that the defense industry has an excellent record of estimating accuracy, but it does mean that estimating is taken seriously.

The leading insurance companies, such as Hartford Insurance, UNUM, USF&G, John Hancock, and Sun Life Insurance, tend to measure productivity, and they are now stepping up to quality and user satisfaction measures as well. The trailing companies within the insurance segment seem to measure little or nothing. There is a general correlation with size, in that the larger insurance companies with several thousand software professionals are more likely to use measures than the smaller companies. Insurance is a very interesting industry because it was one of the first to adopt computers and one of the few in which there have been significant correlations between effective measurements and overall corporate profitability.

Banking and financial companies for many years tended to lag in terms of measurement, although there were some exceptions. In the wake of increased competition and dramatic changes in banking technology, the financial institutions as a class are attempting to make up for lost time, and many are mounting large studies in attempts to introduce productivity, quality, and user satisfaction measures as quickly as possible. Interestingly, Canadian banks such as CIBC and the Bank of Montreal may be ahead of U.S. banks such as the Bank of America in software measurement.

In the manufacturing, energy, and wholesale-retail segments, the use of software productivity measurement appears to be proportional to the size of the enterprise: The larger companies with more than 1000 software professionals, such as Sears Roebuck and J.C. Penney, measure productivity, but the smaller ones do not. Quality and user satisfaction measurements are just beginning to heat up within these industry segments.

Such public utilities as electric, water, and some telephone operating companies have started to become serious students of measurement in the wake of deregulation, and they are taking productivity measurement quite seriously. Such companies as Consolidated Edison, Florida Power and Light, and Cincinnati Gas and Electric are becoming fairly advanced in those measurements. Here too, however, quality and user satisfaction measures have tended to lag behind.

In the publishing business, the larger newspapers such as *The New York Times* have tended to be fairly active in both estimating and measurement, as have publishers of specialized documents such as telephone directories. Book publishers, on the other hand, have tended to be very late adopters of either measurement or estimation. It is surprising that some of the leading publishers of software engineering and measurement books are not in fact particularly innovative in terms of their own software methods and metrics!

Federal, state, and local government agencies have not as a rule spent much energy on measuring either software productivity or quality. That is perhaps due to the fact that they are not in a competitive environment. There are some interesting exceptions at the state level, where such government agencies as Human Resources in Florida are starting to measure and estimate well, but by and large government tends to lag behind the private sector in these concepts. At the national or federal level, it is interesting that the internal revenue services in both the United States and Australia tend to be fairly active in both software measurement and software estimating technologies.

Academic institutions and universities are distressingly far behind the state of the art in both intellectual understanding of modern software measurements and the actual usage of such measurements in building their own software. The first college textbook on function points, Dreger's text on *Function Point Analysis,*[8] was not published until 1989, a full 10 years after the metric was placed in the public domain by IBM. Even so, the author is employed by Boeing and is only a part-time faculty member. The number of major U.S. universities and business schools that teach software measurement and estimation concepts appears to be minuscule, and for the few that do the course materials appear to be many years out of date. The same lag can be observed in England and Europe. Interestingly, both New Zealand and Australia may be ahead of the United States in teaching software measurement concepts at the university level.

Using function-based metrics for large-scale industrial studies

A final illustration of how function-based metrics can be used for large-scale studies is illustrated by Table 1.6, which shows a provisional ranking of strategic or corporate software productivity rates for some 40 industrial and governmental segments. The data in the table has a high margin of error and does not actually support two decimal place precision. Table 1.6 is included to show the kinds of large-scale studies that can now be accomplished. Although partial data from more than 400 companies and government agencies is included, that is not a sufficient sample. Also, the raw data itself is highly suspect, since many of the enterprises had notable gaps and errors in their available data. The normalized data is derived primarily by backfiring from source-code metrics to feature points.

The rates in Table 1.6 are based on the total number of person-months for all direct and indirect software staff including executives, administrators, and nonproject support. Rates were estimated by dividing the total delivered feature points by the total accumulated number of person-months for all staff from vice presidents downward. Both direct technical staff and indirect workers such as secretarial support and administrative support are included. The effort amounts also include work expended on canceled projects and on projects which were still under development but not yet ready for delivery. The data in Table 1.6 is not derived from individual projects; it reflects the gross output of an industry divided by the total number of person-months employed by the software functions.

The sequence of industries in Table 1.6 is interesting, but it is quite likely to change as more data becomes available. The general attributes of the industries in the higher third of the productivity range suggest a correlation between overall profitability and the ability to invest substantial amounts of money in adequate tooling and support. For at least two of the high-productivity industries (commercial software and software consulting groups) it is also a known fact that unpaid overtime may exceed 15 h/week. This phenomenon may well cause their productivity rates to be artificially high.

Factors associated with midrange industries tend to be mixed. Some of these industries may be short of discretionary capital; others may not have compensation rates or environments that attract sufficient quantities of top professionals. For the industries in the lower third of the productivity range, there are at least three possible correlations: (1) unavailability of funds for adequate tooling and support because of low profitability of the industry, (2) excessive volumes of paperwork caused by government or military requirements, (3) industries in which unpaid overtime is not present in any significant amount.

TABLE 1.6 Provisional U.S. Software Productivity Rates Expressed as Feature Points per Person-Month

	FP/PM
Above-Average Industry Segments	
1 Commercial software houses	3.50
2 Software consulting groups	3.45
3 Insurance companies	3.40
4 Computer manufacturers	3.38
5 Oil and gasoline production	3.35
6 Telecommunications operating companies	3.20
7 Banking and finance	3.20
8 Entertainment (TV, films, etc.)	3.00
9 Sports (pro football, baseball, etc.)	3.00
10 Security and commodity brokers	2.80
11 Chemical and plastic production	2.75
12 Hotel chains	2.65
13 Restaurant chains	2.65
Average Industry Segments	
14 Electronics manufacturing	2.50
15 Pharmaceutical manufacturing	2.35
16 Aerospace manufacturing	2.25
17 General manufacturing	2.15
18 Agricultural production	2.00
19 Metals fabrication	1.85
20 Wholesale and retail	1.65
21 Conglomerates	1.50
22 Automotive manufacturing	1.35
23 Office equipment manufacturing	1.30
24 Appliance manufacturing	1.25
25 Airlines	1.25
26 Metals and mining	1.20
Below-Average Industry Segments	
27 Universities and academic institutions	1.10
28 Public utilities (water/gas, etc.)	1.05
29 Railroad transportation	1.00
30 Trucking and warehousing	1.00
31 Hospitals and health care	0.90
32 Paper and allied products	0.85
33 Telecommunications manufacturing	0.65
34 Food processing	0.60
35 Printing and publishing	0.55
36 Defense contractors	0.50
37 City and county governments	0.50
38 State governments	0.45
39 Federal government (civilian)	0.40
40 Federal government (military)	0.30

Measurement and the Software Life Cycle

An effective project measurement system adds value to all of the major phases of software lifecycles. Figure 1.3 illustrates the major kinds of measurements associated with each phase. For projects that are enhancements or replacements of existing systems, which in the 1990s comprise the majority of all projects, the structure, complexity, and defect rates of the existing software should be analyzed. It is at this point that the normal project cost tracking system should be initialized for enhancements.

During the requirements phase, function or feature points are enumerated and then the first formal cost estimate is normally prepared. For new projects, the requirements phase is the normal point at which the project cost tracking system should be initialized. It is also appropriate to initialize the project defect and quality tracking system, since requirements problems are often a major source of both expense and later troubles.

As the requirements are refined, the next aspect of measurement deals with whether the project should be in the form of a custom application or in the form of a package that is acquired and modified. The risks and value of both approaches are considered.

If the decision is to construct the project, then a second estimate should be prepared in conjunction with the logical design of the application. Since from this point on defect removal can be the most expensive element, it is imperative to utilize reviews and inspections and record defect data. A second and more rigorous cost estimate should be prepared at this time. During physical design, reviews and inspections are also valuable and defect data will continue to accumulate.

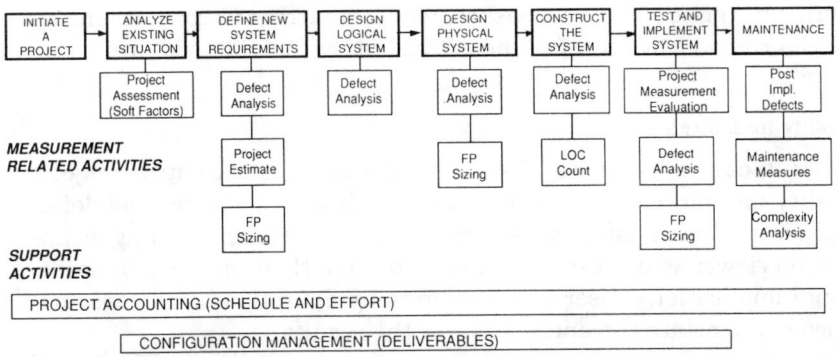

Figure 1.3 Measurement activities and the software lifecycle.

The coding or construction phase of an application can be either troublesome or almost effortless depending upon the rigor of the preceding tasks. A third formal cost estimate should be prepared; it will be very rigorous in accumulating costs to date and very accurate in estimating costs to the completion of the project. Defect and quality data recording should also be kept during code reviews or inspections. Complexity measures of the code itself can now be performed as well.

The testing phase of an application can range from a simple unit test by an individual programmer to a full multistage formal test suite that includes function test, integration test, stress test, regression test, independent test, field test, system test, and final acceptance test. Both the defect data and the cost data from the testing phase should be measured in detail and then analyzed for use in subsequent defect prevention activities.

During the maintenance and enhancement phase, both user satisfaction measures and defect measures should be carried out. It is at this point that it becomes possible to carry out retrospective analyses of the defect removal efficiencies of each specific review, inspection, and test and of the cumulative efficiency of the overall series of defect removal steps. A useful figure of merit is to strive for 95 percent cumulative defect removal efficiency. That is, when defects found by the users and defects found by the development team are summed after the first year of usage, the development team should have found 95 percent of all defects.

The Structure of a Fully Applied Software Measurement System

A fully applied software measurement system for an entire corporation or government agency is a multifaceted undertaking that will include both quality and productivity measures and produce both monthly and annual reports. Figure 1.4 shows the overall schematic of a full enterprise software measurement system. Let us consider the essential components of a full measurement system for software.

Quality measures

Starting at the left of Fig. 1.4, there are two major components of a quality measurement program: user satisfaction measures and defect measures. User satisfaction is normally assessed once a year by means of interviews; actual users are asked to give their opinions of operational applications. User satisfaction is by definition a soft measure, since opinions are the entire basis of the results.

The second quality factor or defect counts are continuously recorded

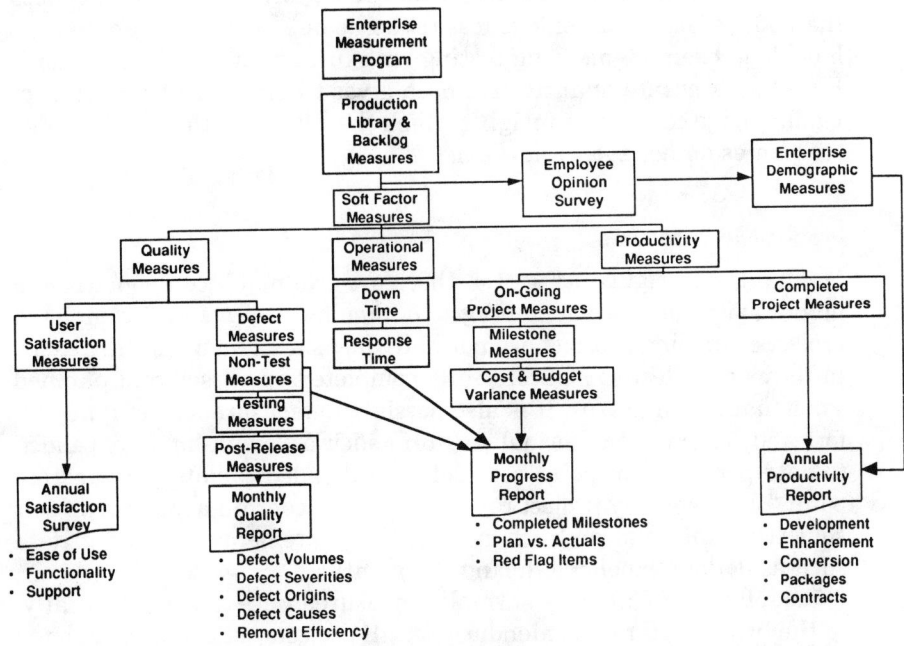

Figure 1.4 Enterprise software measurement system.

during project life cycles starting as early as requirements reviews and continuing through maintenance. Defect measures are normally reported on a monthly basis. In a well-planned measurement program, defect counts are one of the key hard-data measures. In trailing-edge companies, either quality in terms of defects is not measured at all or the measurements start so late that the data is woefully incomplete.

One of the most useful by-products of defect measurement is termed "defect removal efficiency." This is defined as the ratio of bugs found prior to installation of a software application to the total number of bugs in the application. Leading-edge enterprises are able to find in excess of 95 percent of all bugs prior to installation, whereas trailing-edge enterprises seldom exceed 70 percent in defect removal efficiency. There appears to be a strong correlation between high defect removal efficiency and such other factors as user satisfaction and overall project costs and schedules, so this is a very important metric indeed.

The measurement of defect removal efficiency is a sure sign that a company is at the leading edge, and only a handful of major corporations such as IBM and AT&T have carried out these powerful measures. Such companies are aware that most forms of testing are less than 30% efficient or remove less than one bug of every three, so they have long been augmenting testing with full reviews and inspections. Here too, accurate quantitative data gives the managers and staff of leading-edge companies insights which their peers in the trailing-edge companies do not even know exist!

Productivity measures

Moving to the right in Fig. 1.4, there are two major components of a productivity measurement program: ongoing projects and completed projects. Ongoing projects are normally measured, on a monthly basis, in terms of milestones successfully completed or missed and planned vs. actual expenditures. It is also possible to measure accumulated effort and cost in some normalized form such as "work-hours expended to date per function point" or "dollars expended to date per function point." The monthly project reports normally contain a mixture of soft subjective information such as problem statements and hard data such as dollars expended during the month.

Completed projects are normally measured once a year. Typically, in the first quarter of a calendar year all projects that were completed and installed in the previous year will be measured and analyzed. This annual measurement of completed projects provides an ever-growing database of historical data and becomes the heart of the enterprise measurement program. Once an enterprise completes its first annual productivity report, it can use that as the baseline for judging improvements over time.

In producing an annual productivity report, all of the relevant soft factors need to be included, and the hard data for the project in terms of deliverables, schedules, staffing, and so forth should be extremely accurate. It is also desirable to convert the hard data into normalized form, such as cost per function point, for comparative purposes.

The annual productivity report will contain both strategic and tactical data, just as a corporate annual report will contain both. Indeed, companies such as IBM, ITT, and Pacific Bell tend to create their annual software productivity reports on the same schedules as the corporate annual reports to stockholders and even to adopt similar formats and production techniques such as the use of high-quality paper, professional graphics, and excellent layouts.

Because new development projects, enhancement projects, maintenance projects (defect repairs), package acquisition projects, and projects involving contract personnel tend to have widely different productivity profiles, it is desirable to segregate the annual data very carefully. This is the area where normalization is most important and where function-based metrics are starting to provide new and sometimes surprising insights into productivity and quality topics.

Production library and backlog measures

Large corporations tend to own many thousands of small programs and some hundreds of large systems. ITT, a major international corporation, surveyed its production library in the early 1980s and found that it owned some 65 million lines of source code, which was equivalent to about 520,000 function points. This software was spread over more than 100 subsidiary corporations and was apportioned among some 28,000 small programs and 2000 large systems. The replacement cost for the production library was in excess of $2 billion.

The ITT backlog of potential applications awaiting development consisted of approximately 65 large new systems and more than 3500 small new programs. In addition, more than 150 large systems and about 5000 small programs were awaiting updates and enhancements. The backlog size was equivalent to about 18 million source code statements or 170,000 function points. This backlog would have taken about four calendar years to implement and about 8500 labor-years. The costs for building the backlog would have approximated $600 million.

An interesting but seldom performed form of production library measurement study is that of the usage patterns of programs and systems, as described by Kendall and Lamb.[5] From a year-long analysis of IBM's data centers, they found that less than 5 percent of the company's applications used more than 75 percent of its machine capacity. Not only that, but standard packages such as the operating systems, sorts, and commercial databases utilized more machine capacity than all custom applications put together. An even more surprising finding was that, of the custom applications owned by IBM, more than two-thirds appeared to be dormant and were not executed at all in the course of the year.

That kind of strategic information is becoming increasingly vital as companies all over the world depend upon computing and software for their operational control and their new products as well. Production library and backlog analyses should become standard strategic measures in all medium-size to large corporations and should be performed on an annual or semiannual basis.

Soft-factor measures

Even accurate recording of quality and productivity data cannot answer questions about why one project is better or worse than another. To answer such questions, it is necessary to come to grips with one of the most difficult aspects of measurement: how to capture soft factors or subjective opinions in a way that can lead to useful insights. Soft-data collection is a necessary adjunct to both quality and productivity measures, and it can be stated that without effective soft-data measurement, the hard data will be almost useless.

This topic of measuring soft factors devolves into two related subtopics: (1) What soft factors should be measured? (2) What is the best way to collect soft data?

Every known factor that can influence software productivity and quality, of which there are more than 200, is a potential soft factor for measurement purposes. The primary soft factors are those which have the greatest known impacts, and this set of primary factors includes the skill and experience of staff, the cooperation of users during requirements and design, schedule or resource constraints, methods employed on the project, tools available, appropriate choice of programming language(s), problem complexity, code complexity, data complexity, project organization structures, and the physical environment.

Although the soft data is subjective, it must be recorded in a way that lends itself to statistical analysis. Since free-form text responses are difficult to analyze, this requirement normally leads to the creation of a multiple-choice questionnaire, so that all of the recorded information can be analyzed by computer. Following is an example of a typical soft-factor multiple choice question to illustrate the principle:

User involvement during development?

1. User involvement is not a major factor
2. Users are heavily involved during early stages
3. Users are somewhat involved during early stages
4. Users are seldom involved during early stages
5. User involvement is not currently known

A normal soft-factor questionnaire will contain from 10 to more than 200 questions, such as the one developed by Software Productivity Research.[4]

Operational measures

Operational measures are those which concentrate on the adequacy and responsiveness of the computing environment. They normally include measures of (1) computer availability and downtime, (2) response time for users and development staff, (3) data storage volumes, (4) data storage access, and (5) telecommunications traffic, if any.

Operational measures have traditionally been the first form of metrification used by companies, because computer room efficiency has been studied since the 1950s. Most of the operational measures consist of hard data, but the more sophisticated companies augment simple monthly reports with personal interviews of users to collect soft data on user satisfaction with turnaround and computer room performance. Operational measures are normally considered to be tactical.

Enterprise opinion survey

Leading-edge companies are aware that taking good care of employees pays off in both higher productivity and lower voluntary attrition rates. A normal part of taking good care of employees is an annual opinion survey, which is normally conducted by a personnel group. This, of course, is one of the purest forms of soft data, since it deals primarily with subjective opinions. Opinion surveys are also strategic measures, since staff feelings and opinions have a wide and pervasive influence. It is important that, once such a survey has been conducted, change should follow swiftly. Nothing is more debilitating to morale than an opinion survey followed by inaction. Some of the kinds of topics included in the opinion survey include satisfaction with salary and benefits plans, physical office environments, company policies, and overall management direction. Although by their nature opinion surveys deal with soft or subjective opinions, they differ from the project-related tactical soft-factor studies in that they concentrate on issues that are general or corporate in nature.

Enterprise demographic measures

Now that software is approaching 50 years of age as an occupation, the same kind of specialization is occurring for software professionals that manifested itself for other knowledge workers such as doctors, attorneys, and engineers. It is highly desirable to perform an annual census of the kinds of software specialists needed and employed by the enterprise. This is one of the most useful kinds of strategic hard data that a company can collect for long-range planning purposes.

Some of the kinds of specialists that might be included are quality assurance specialists, technical writers, database administrators, estimating specialists, maintenance specialists, systems programmers, application programmers, human factors specialists, performance specialists, testing specialists, and planning specialists.

In all human activities that have been measured accurately, specialists tend to outperform generalists. Among large corporations with more than 1000 software professionals employed, those with generalists often lag behind those with specialists in terms of software productivity. An annual demographic survey can become a significant tool leading to improvement.

The Sociology of Software Measurement

Establishing an applied measurement program for software requires sensitivity to cultural and social issues. The normal reaction to a measurement program by both project management and staff is apprehension, and only when it is shown that the data will be used for beneficial purposes rather than punitive purposes will the apprehension subside.

The sociology of measurement implies a need for high-level corporate sponsorship of the measurement program when the program is first begun, since the normal reactions of subordinate managers whose projects will actually be measured are dismay, resistance, and apprehension. Normally, either the CEO or an executive vice president would be the overall measurement sponsor and would delegate responsibilities for specific kinds of measures to those lower down in the hierarchy. Indeed at such companies as IBM in the 1960s, ITT in the 1970s, and Hewlett-Packard in the 1980s, it was the demand for accurate measures from the CEO level that started the corporate measurement programs in the first place. The IBM corporate software measurement program has not yet been fully described for external publication, but a description of the Hewlett-Packard software measurement system has been published by Grady and Caswell.[6]

In a well-designed applied measurement program, staff and management apprehension or opposition is very transitory and lasts for only a month or so prior to start-up, after which the real value of accurate measures makes the system expand spontaneously. At Hewlett-Packard, for example, a small experiment in software project measurement was so useful and so successful that over a period of several years it expanded on a voluntary basis into a major international study including virtually all of Hewlett-Packard's software development laboratories. Indeed, the internal measurements have proved to be so valuable that in 1989 Hewlett-Packard began to offer the same kind of software project measurement services to their customers.

What causes the transition from apprehension to enthusiasm is that a well-designed applied measurement program is not used for punitive purposes and will quickly begin to surface chronic problems in a way that leads to problem solution. For example, excessive schedule pressures, inadequate office space, and insufficient computer turnaround may have been chronic problems for years and yet been more or less invisible. But a good measurement program can spot the impact of such problems and quantify the benefits of their solution.

The sociology of data confidentiality

In many companies, corporate politics have such prominence that project managers and some executives will be afraid to submit their data to a corporate measurement group unless the confidentiality of their data is guaranteed by the measurement group. That is, each manager will want to find out personally how his or her data compares to the corporate or group average but will not want that data distributed to other project groups or to "rival" managers.

Although it is sometimes necessary for reasons of corporate culture to start a measurement program on a confidential basis, the approach is both sociologically and technically unsound. In a mature and well-managed enterprise, software productivity and quality measurements are normal business tools and should have about the same visibility and the same security classification as corporate financial data. A branch sales manager, for example, could hardly insist on the confidentiality of the branch's quarterly profit-and-loss data.

Group, divisional, and corporate executives should receive productivity and quality reports on all projects and units within their scope of responsibility, just as they receive profit-and-loss reports or normal financial reports. A well-designed software measurement program will not be a punitive weapon; it will identify all weaknesses that need correction and point out all strengths that need encouragement.

Another disadvantage of data confidentiality is that it tends to lower the credibility of the measures themselves. For the first year of ITT's corporate measurement program in 1980, the data was held in confidence. The consequence was that no one really cared about the results. In the second year, when the projects were explicitly identified, acceptance of the measurements as important to managers and executives increased dramatically.

The sociology of using data for staff performance targets

Once a company begins to collect software productivity and quality data, there is a natural tendency to want to use the data to set staff performance targets. That, of course, is one of the reasons for apprehension in the first place. Leading-edge companies such as IBM and Hewlett-Packard do set performance targets, but for sociological and business reasons the targets should be set for executives at the director and vice presidential level, rather than for the technical staff.

The major reason for that is that executives are in a much better position to introduce the changes necessary to achieve targets than are technical staff members or first line managers. Neither the technical staff nor subordinate managers are authorized to purchase better tools and workstations, stop work and receive necessary education, or introduce new practices such as full design and code inspections. Executives, on the other hand, can do all those things.

A secondary reason for establishing executive targets is likely to become more and more important in the future: Corporate officers have a legal and fiduciary duty to achieve professional levels of software quality, and if they do not, both their companies and themselves may find expensive lawsuits and perhaps even consequential damages in their futures!

Perhaps the single event that more than any other made IBM a leader in software quality for many years was the establishment in 1973 of numeric quality targets for software executives and the inclusion of those targets in their performance and bonus plans. Prior to that time, IBM, like many other companies, talked about achieving high quality, but when the pressure of business caused a choice between opting for high quality or skipping something like inspections to try to shorten delivery dates, quality seldom won. Once IBM's vice presidents and directors had quality goals in their performance plans, however, quality was no longer just being given lip service but became a true corporate incentive.

The sociology of measuring one-person projects

More than half of all software projects in the world are small projects that are carried out by a single programmer or programmer-analyst. This situation requires special handling, since it is obvious that all data collected on one-person projects can easily be used for appraisal purposes. The delicacy of measuring one-person projects is especially sensitive in Europe, where some countries prohibit the measurement of an individual worker's performance either because of national law, as in Sweden, or because the software staffs are unionized and such measurements may violate union agreements, as in Germany.

The normal solution to this problem in large companies such as IBM and ITT can be one or more of several alternatives: The basic alternative is to establish a cutoff point of perhaps two person-years and simply not measure any project that is smaller. This solution tends to concentrate the measurements on the larger and more costly projects, where, indeed, the value of measurement is greatest. A second solution is to collect one-person project data on a voluntary basis, since many programmers are perfectly willing to have their work measured. It is, however, tactful to ask for volunteers. A third solution, possible only in very large companies, is to aggregate all small one-person projects and then create an overall set of small-project statistics that does not drop below the division or laboratory level.

Of course, it is also possible to bite the bullet and use one-person project data for appraisal purposes, and some companies indeed do that. It is, however, very likely to lead to morale problems of a significant nature and perhaps even to lawsuits by indignant staff members who may challenge the measurements in court.

The sociology of MIS vs. systems software

Many large high-technology corporations produce both management information system (MIS) projects and also systems software, such as operating systems or telecommunication systems. Some also produce other kinds of software as well: process control, scientific software, mathematical analysis, and so on.

Generally speaking, the MIS staffs and the systems software staffs have such difficulty communicating and sharing technical ideas that they might as well inhabit different planets. The dichotomy will affect measurement programs too, especially since systems software productivity is normally somewhat lower than MIS productivity because of the larger number of tasks performed and the effect of the soft factors. The natural reaction by the systems software groups to this fact is to assert that systems software is much more complex than MIS applications. Indeed, many systems software producers have rejected function-based metrics for two reasons: Function points originated in the MIS domain, and MIS projects normally have higher productivity rates.

This kind of dispute occurs so often that companies should plan remedial action when beginning their measurement programs. There are several possible solutions, but the most pragmatic one is simply to segregate the data along clear-cut lines and compare MIS projects primarily to other MIS projects and systems software primarily to other systems software. A more recent solution is to adopt the feature point metric for systems software productivity measures, since the built-in assumptions of feature points about algorithmic complexity tend to generate higher totals for systems software than for MIS projects.

Whatever solution a company decides on, the problem of needing to be sensitive to the varying software cultures needs attention right from the start.

The sociology of measurement expertise

The managers and technical staff workers who embark on a successful measurement project are often surprised to find permanent changes in their careers. There is such a shortage of good numerical information about software projects and such enormous latent demand by corporate executives that, once a measurement program is started, the key players may find themselves becoming career measurement specialists. This phenomenon has affected careers in surprising ways. From informal surveys carried out by Software Productivity Research, almost half of the measurement managers are promoted as a result of their work. About a third of the managers and technical staff workers who start corporate measurement programs work in the measurement area for more than 5 years thereafter. Both A. J. Albrecht and the author began their measurement careers with short measurement projects intended to last for less than 2 months. In both cases, the demand for more measurement information led to long-term careers.

Justifying and Building an Applied Software Measurement Function

For most U.S. companies other than those at the very leading edge such as IBM, Hewlett-Packard, AT&T, and a few others, a software measurement program will be a new and perhaps exotic concept. It will be necessary to justify the costs of measurement and to plan the staffing and sequence of establishing the measurement function with great care. The following are the major topics that must be considered.

The value of applied software measurement programs

It is, of course, not possible to perform direct productivity or quality comparisons between companies that measure and companies that do not, since only the ones that measure have any data. This phenomenon creates a trap of circular reasoning within companies that do not measure: Executives tend to say "prove to me that measurements will bε valuable." But since the same executives have no idea of their current levels of productivity, quality, or user satisfaction, there is no baseline against which the proofs can be made.

Project managers and executives in companies that do not measure software numerically actually have a vested interest in preventing measurements from occurring. They suspect, rightly, that their performances will not be shown in a favorable light if measurements occur, and so they tend to obstruct metrics work rather than support it.

To make an initial case for the value of measurements, it is often necessary to depend on such indirect factors as market share, user satisfaction, and profitability. It is also necessary to gain the support of executives high enough in the company, or secure enough in self-esteem, that they will not feel threatened by the advent of a measurement program.

Let us consider the value of measurement to a specific major corporation that has measured for many years: IBM. It is often said that "knowledge is power," and perhaps no other company in history has had available so much knowledge of its software. One of the major reasons for IBM's long dominance of the computer industry is that its founder, Thomas Watson, Sr., was personally insistent that IBM strive for the highest levels of quality and user satisfaction possible, and he introduced quality measures very early in the corporation's history. Both Watson, his son Thomas Watson, Jr., and the other IBM chairmen have continued that trend. It is revealing to consider some of the kinds of measurement data available within IBM but not necessarily available to most of IBM's major competitors.

IBM's quality data includes full defect recording from the first requirements review through all forms of inspection and all forms of testing and then all customer-reported bugs as well. IBM probably knew the measured efficiencies of every kind of software review, inspection, and test before any other corporation in the world, and it was able to use that data to make net corporate software quality improvements of about 5 to 1 during the late 1960s and early 1970s. Although IBM put much of this data into the public domain, very few competitors bothered to replicate IBM's findings! Of course, even IBM puts out some low-quality products and makes mistakes. But in terms of the percent of all products in the market that have high quality, few companies can equal IBM's overall rates.

IBM was also the first company to discover that software quality and software productivity were directly coupled and that the projects with the lowest defect counts by customers were those with the shortest schedules and the highest development productivity rates. This phenomenon, discovered by IBM in the early 1970s and put in the public domain in May 1975, is still not understood by many other software-producing enterprises that tend to think that quality and productivity are separate issues.

IBM's customer-reported defect database is so powerful and sophisticated that IBM can produce reports showing the origins and severities of defects for any product, for any month of any year, in any country, and in every major city. The data can also be sorted by industry as well. Software managers and senior executives in IBM receive such data monthly, and they also receive cumulative trends that show long-term progress for each product, each laboratory, each division, and the corporation as a whole.

IBM's user satisfaction surveys also revealed, long before most other companies realized this point, that user satisfaction and numeric defect rates were directly correlated. Projects with low defect counts tended to be high in user satisfaction; projects with high defect counts tended to be low in user satisfaction. This discovery also was made in the early 1970s.

IBM's employee demographic and opinion survey data can identify all technical occupation groups within the company and both the current and past morale history of every laboratory, branch office, and manufacturing location within the corporation. It is also possible for IBM executives to gain other kinds of useful information, such as the annual attrition rates of each location by occupation group within the company.

In addition to these software and demographic measurements, IBM managers and executives have an enormous quantity of economic and market data available to them, including the histories of the economic trends of all countries, demographic and population statistics of all cities in more than 100 countries, and the sales statistics of every IBM product in every geographic region of the world, every industry, and every time period for more than 15 years in the past and projected forward for more than 10 years in the future.

IBM's software productivity measures included systems, military, and MIS software projects. The multiple regression techniques used by Felix and Walston of IBM's Federal Systems Division[9] were published in 1977 as a landmark study which showed the factors that influenced software productivity. The analysis of the mathematical errors of lines of code was first published by the author in the *IBM Systems Journal* in 1978[2]; it proved conclusively that lines of code could never match economic productivity assumptions. Function points were invented within IBM for MIS projects by A. J. Albrecht of IBM's Data Processing Services Division and placed in the public domain in October 1979.[3] The insights and correlations based on that metric have been used by IBM to make far-reaching improvements in software methods and tools.

Of course, even with all of this data IBM can sometimes make mistakes and can sometimes be surprised, as by the success of the original personal computer or by the decline in large mainframe sales in the middle 1980s. Nonetheless, IBM managers and executives tend to have at least 10 times as much valid measurement-based data available to them as do equivalent managers and executives in most other companies, and IBM's long-term success is in large part due to that wealth of factual information.

So far as can be determined, there are few if any counterexamples to the IBM success story. In other words, companies without measurements and adequate data probably cannot replicate IBM's long-term successes.

The costs of applied software measurement programs

Accurate and complete measurements of software are not inexpensive; indeed, the costs can approximate the costs of a corporate cost accounting function. In the companies that have full applied measurement programs for software, the annual costs can sometimes exceed 4 to 5 percent of the total software budget, with about 2 percent being spent on measuring productivity and 2 to 3 percent spent on measuring quality and user satisfaction. By coincidence, the same breakdown often occurs in soft- and hard-data collection: about 2 percent for collecting the soft factors and about 2 to 3 percent for collecting the hard data from completed projects on an annual basis.

Very large corporations such as IBM, Hewlett-Packard, and AT&T can have permanent corporate measurement staffs in excess of a dozen individuals, regional or laboratory measurement staffs of half a dozen at each major site, and intermittent involvement in measurements by several hundred managers and staff members. The companies that have full software measurement programs are also the companies with the best track records of success in terms of both bringing software projects to completion and achieving high levels of user satisfaction afterwards. They also tend to be industry leaders in respect to morale and employee satisfaction.

The skills and staffing of a measurement team

Most universities and academic institutions have no courses at all in the measurement of software quality, productivity, or user satisfaction, so it is seldom possible to hire entry-level personnel with anything like an adequate academic background for the work at hand.

Business schools and MBA programs also are deficient in these topics, so most companies are forced to substitute on-the-job training and industry experience in software management for formal credentials.

Some of the skills available in measurement teams such as those at IBM, AT&T, Du Pont, Hewlett-Packard, and ITT include a good knowledge of statistics and multivariate analysis, a thorough grounding in the literature of software engineering and software project management, a knowledge of software planning and estimating methods and the more powerful of the available tools, a knowledge of forms design, a knowledge of survey design, a knowledge of quality control methods including reviews, walk-throughs, inspections, and all standard forms of testing, a knowledge of the pros and cons of all software metrics including the new function-based metrics, and knowledge of accounting principles.

The special skills and knowledge needed to build a full measurement program are so scarce in the United States as a whole that many companies begin their measurement programs by bringing in one or more of the management consultants who specialize in such tasks. Once the consulting group assists in the start-up phase, the corporate measurement team takes over the future studies and measurements.

The placement and organization of the measurement function

Measurement of software productivity, quality, and user satisfaction works best with a dedicated staff of professionals, just as cost accounting and financial measurement works best with a dedicated staff of professionals. Leading-edge companies that recognize this fact will normally establish a corporate measurement focal point under an executive at about the level of a director or third-line manager. This focal point will often report to someone at the level of a vice president, executive vice president, or chief information officer (CIO). The corporate measurement group will coordinate overall measurement responsibilities and will usually produce the annual productivity report. As with finance and cost accounting, the larger units and subordinate organizations within the corporation may have their own local measurement departments as well.

The raw data collected from tracking systems, in-depth studies, surveys, interviews, and other sources should be validated at the source prior to being sent forward for aggregation and statistical analysis. However, some wrong data seems to always slip by, so the corporate group must ensure that all incoming data is screened, and questionable or incorrect information must be corrected. The raw data itself can either be collected by local personnel on the scene, by traveling data collection specialists from the unit or corporate measurement function, or even by outside consultants if the enterprise is just getting started with measurement.

If the corporation has a formal quality assurance (QA) function, the defect-related data will normally be collected by QA personnel. Quality data can, of course, be reported separately by the QA staff, but it should also be consolidated as part of the overall corporate reporting system.

User satisfaction data for commercial software houses and computer companies is often collected by the sales and marketing organization, unless the company has a human factors organization. Here too, the data can be reported separately as needed, but it should be consolidated as part of the overall corporate reporting system.

If the company does not have either a sales and marketing organization or a human factors organization, it would be normal to bring in a management consulting group that specializes in user satisfaction measurements to aid during the start-up phase.

The sequence of creating an applied software measurement program

For sociological reasons, measurement programs are often established in a sequence rather than as an attempt to measure all factors simultaneously. As a rule of thumb, companies at the extreme leading edge such as IBM will have all nine measurements deployed. To be considered a leading-edge enterprise at all, a company will have at least five of the nine measurement classes operational. Trailing companies will usually have no more than the first two forms of measurement deployed. At the extreme rear of the trailing edge are the unfortunate companies that have no measurements at all. They tend to be short-lived organizations whose future is not likely to be happy, and they stand a good chance of failing or being acquired by better-managed competitors.

The time span for creating a full software measurement program will vary with the urgency and executive understanding of the value of measurement. IBM's measurement program tended to evolve naturally over many years, and it started with opinion surveys even before the computer era. IBM got into quality measures even before software and computers became prominent in its product line, and it was perhaps the first U.S. company to actually measure software quality. Its software quality measures were started in 1964 for commercial and systems software, and it added productivity measures in 1968. Function points were invented within IBM's DP Services Division in about 1975 and placed in the public domain in October 1979. Thus, for more than 20 years, IBM's management and executives have had useful data available to aid in improving software quality and productivity.

ITT, on the other hand, had very few software measures of any kind other than an annual demographic survey prior to 1980. In 1981, ITT entered into a crash measurement program and implemented both quality and productivity measurements in less than a single calendar year. That is about as fast as a large company can enter the measurement arena.

The observed sequence of measurement in successful large enterprises tends to follow this pattern:

1. *Operational measures:*   Historically, operational measures have been first. Most companies already record the key operational measures of computer utilization, downtime, and response time. These measures may be used for charge-backs, and they normally serve to keep tabs on the overall health of the computing complex. Operational measures have been common since the 1950s.

2. *Ongoing project measures:*   Many large companies already require monthly status reports from project managers on accomplished milestones or planned vs. actual expenditures. Informal monthly on-going project measures are common, but they are not always very effective as early warning indicators because of a natural human tendency to conceal bad news if possible. On-going project measures have been fairly common since the 1950s in large or very large corporations.

3. *Production library and backlog measures:*   When the CEO and senior executives of corporations begin to sense how much money is tied up in software, they naturally want to find out the true dimensions of the corporation's investment. When they ask the CIO or senior software vice president, the initial answer is likely to be "I don't know." This embarrassing exposure quickly tends to trigger a full production library and backlog study which will often be performed by an outside management consulting group that specializes in such tasks.

4. *User satisfaction measures:*   The next measurement that companies tend to implement is that of user satisfaction. It is a basic metric for enterprises that market software and an important metric for internal information systems as well. Effective measurement of user satisfaction normally requires actual interviews with users. Forms and questionnaires alone are seldom sufficient to find out what really needs to be known, although such information is certainly helpful. User satisfaction surveys for software and computing products started in the late 1950s and 1960s.

5. *Completed project measures:*   Now that function-based metrics

have become widespread, many companies have started counting the function point totals of completed projects and accumulating resource data as well. This form of measurement can be useful, but neither function points nor resource data alone can deal with the issue of why some projects succeed and others fail. Nonetheless, it is a sign of growing sophistication when a company begins to collect accurate hard data and functional metrics from completed projects. Although some companies such as IBM have been measuring since the 1960s, completed project measures have only started to become common during the 1980s as a by-product of the development of function-based metrics.

6. *Soft-factor measures:*   When a company begins to strive for leadership, it is natural to want to know everything that is right and everything that is wrong about the way it does business. At this point, such a company will start an in-depth survey of all of the soft factors that influence software projects. That is, it will perform a project-by-project survey of the methods, tools, skills, organization, and environment available for software development and maintenance. The soft factors can be used to eliminate weaknesses and augment strengths. The soft factors and the completed project data can be collected at the same time, and they can even be part of the same survey questionnaire or instrument. Soft-factor measures started to undergo serious study in the 1970s, and they matured in the 1980s.

7. *Software defect measures:*   Only the true industry leaders such as IBM have stepped up to the task of measuring software defect rates, and this is a partial explanation of IBM's long-term success. Since the cost of finding and fixing bugs has historically been the largest software cost element, quality control is on the critical path to productivity control. Also, there is a strong observed correlation between defect levels and user satisfaction; users seldom give favorable evaluations to software products with high defect rates. Only a handful of U.S. companies have accurate measures of software defect rates and defect removal, and they tend to dominate their industry segments. The leading-edge U.S. companies began their defect measures in the 1960s, but for many others, this will be a topic of the 1990s.

8. *Enterprise demographic measures:*   Very few companies realize how important their employees truly are to corporate success. Those that do tend to perform annual demographic surveys of exactly how many employees they have in the skill classes that are relevant to corporate goals. The data can then be used for long-range projections over time. Unfortunately, some otherwise very sophisticated companies have not been able to carry out demographic surveys because of their tendency to lump all staff members under such job titles as "member

of the technical staff." Since more than 40 kinds of specialists are associated with software, it will become increasingly important to include demographic measures as part of the overall corporate measurement program in the future. The military services and some government agencies have been keeping track of job categories since prior to World War II, but for many companies this will be a task for the 1990s.

9. *Enterprise opinion survey:* An opinion survey is last on the list not because it is least important, but because it requires the greatest amount of lead time and is the greatest change in corporate culture to begin implementation. Opinion surveys, of course, affect all employees and not just the software staffs, so it is necessary to have support and backing from the entire executive ranks. It is also necessary to have the survey instruments acquired or produced by personnel experts, or the results at best will be misleading and at worst may be harmful. Finally, it is necessary for the company to face reality and try to solve any major problems which the opinion survey uncovers. Opinion surveys are, of course, older than the computer era, and industry leaders have been using them since the 1950s. For many companies, opinion surveys must be a topic to be addressed in the 1990s.

Applied Software Measurement and Future Progress

Progress in all scientific and engineering work has been closely coupled to accurate measurements of basic phenomena. Without the ability to measure voltage, resistance, and impedance, there could be no electrical engineering. Without the ability to measure temperature, blood pressure, blood types, medical practice could scarcely exist. Without the ability to measure barometric pressure, wind velocity, and wind direction, meteorology would be even more imperfect than it is today.

Software is at a pivotal point in its intellectual history. For the first 45 years of existence, it achieved a notorious reputation as the worst-measured engineering discipline of the twentieth century. Now that accurate and stable software measures are possible, the companies that seize the opportunity to base their improvements on quantified, factual information can make tremendous progress.

The companies that wish to improve but do not measure are at the mercy of fads and chance. Progress may not be impossible, but it is certainly unlikely. Only when software engineering is placed on a base of firm metrical information can it take its place as a true engineering discipline rather than an artistic activity, as it has been for much of its history. Measurement is the key to progress, and it is now time for software to learn that basic lesson.

Suggested Readings

Arthur, Jay, *Measuring Programmer Productivity and Software Quality*, Wiley Press, New York, 1985. Jay Arthur is a software engineering researcher at U.S. West. In his book he discusses the pros and cons of various measurement techniques from the standpoint of how real companies are likely to use the information.

Conte, S. D., H. E. Dunsmore, and V. Y. Shen, *Software Engineering Metrics and Models*, The Benjamin/Cummings Publishing Company, Inc., Menlo Park, Calif., 1986, 396 pages. This book contains descriptions of most of the relevant metrics that can be used on software projects, together with suggestions for their applicability. It also contains discussions of statistical sampling, validation of data, and other useful information. Although aimed more at software engineering than at management information, it nonetheless covers the field in more depth than almost any other source. It is a good book for anyone getting started in metrics selection or evaluation.

Jones, Capers, *Program Quality and Programmer Productivity*, Technical Report TR 02.764, IBM Corporation, San Jose, Calif., 1977, 96 pages. This report reveals as much as IBM has ever chosen to reveal about the internal measurements of large systems software projects within the company. It includes data on a number of related topics, including productivity, quality, machine utilization, and the technologies which IBM had concluded were beneficial or harmful. For competitors of IBM, it is significant to note that the report, although published in 1977, contained more than 10 years worth of historical information which had already been available within the company.

———, *A History of Software Engineering in IBM from 1972 to 1977*, Software Productivity Research, Inc.; Burlington, Mass., 1989, 25 pages. This report is the history of a critical 5-year period in IBM, during which time software evolved from a relatively low-key support function for hardware devices into a true strategic product line. In 1972, software projects had grown enormously in size and complexity, but IBM's methods of managing and measuring progress were still groping with the changes. Each year during the period, a major problem was addressed and brought under control. In every case, the availability of measured data provided a background of facts which enabled IBM's senior management to make usually sound business decisions.

———, *A 10 Year Retrospective of Software Engineering within ITT from 1979 to 1989*, Software Productivity Research Inc., Burlington, Mass., 1989, 35 pages. This report shows the evolution of software engineering methods within a major corporation, and it illustrates how measurement data became one of the most powerful tools for making rapid improvements in both quality and productivity of software projects. It also discusses the creation and functions of the well-known ITT Programming Technology Center, which was one of the premier R&D laboratories for software in the United States prior to ITT's sale of several divisions to Alcatel.

Sayward, F. G., and M. Shaw, *Software Metrics*, MIT Press, Cambridge, Mass., 1981, 399 pages. Fred Sayward was one of the researchers at the well-known ITT Programming Technology Center. This book is yet another of the dozen or so written or edited by researchers of that organization. It contains a very useful discussion on the design of experiments and on ensuring that measured data is not biased by accident or poor collection techniques. It also contains useful discussions of many standard software engineering metrics.

References

1. Jones, Capers, *U.S. Industry Averages for Software Productivity and Quality*, Version 4.0, Software Productivity Research, Inc., Burlington, Mass., December 1989, 37 pages.

2. Jones, Capers, "Measuring Programming Quality and Productivity," *IBM Systems Journal,* vol. 17, no. 1, 1978, vol. IBM Corporation, Armonk, N.Y., pp. 39–63.
3. Albrecht, A. J., "Measuring Application Development Productivity," *Proceedings of the Joint SHARE, GUIDE, and IBM Application Development Symposium, October 1979.* Reprinted in Capers Jones, *Programming Productivity—Issues for the Eighties,* IEEE Press, Catalog Number EHO239-4, 1986, pp. 35–44.
4. Software Productivity Research, Inc., *CHECKPOINT® Questionnaire,* Version 1.2, Software Productivity Research, Inc., Burlington, Mass., 1989, 55 pages.
5. Kendall, R. C., and Lamb, E. C., "Management Perspectives on Programs, Programming, and Productivity," presented at *GUIDE 45,* Atlanta, Ga., 1977. Reprinted in Capers Jones, *Programming Productivity—Issues for the Eighties,* IEEE Press, Catalog Number EHO239-4, 1986, pp. 35–44.
6. Grady, R. B., and Caswell, D. C., *Software Metrics: Establishing a Company-Wide Program,* Prentice-Hall, Englewood Cliffs, N.J., 1987, 288 pages.
7. Humphrey, W., *Managing the Software Process,* Addison-Wesley, Reading, Mass., 1989, 489 pages.
8. Dreger, J. Brian, *Function Point Analysis,* Prentice-Hall, Englewood Cliffs, N.J., 1989, 185 pages.
9. Walston, C., and Felix, C. P., "A Method of Programming Measurement and Estimation," *IBM Systems Journal,* vol. 10, no. 1, 1977. Reprinted in Capers Jones, *Programming Productivity—Issues for the Eighties,* IEEE Press, Catalog Number EHO239-4, 1986, pp. 60–79.

The History and Evolution of Functional Metrics

The Invention and First Publication of Function Points

As noted in Chap. 1, function points were invented by A. J. Albrecht of IBM in the middle 1970s.[1] A function point is a synthetic metric that is comprised of the weighted totals of the inputs, outputs, inquiries, logical files or user data groups, and interfaces belonging to an application. Once an application's function point total is known, the metric can be used for a variety of useful economic purposes, including:

1. Studies of software production
   - Function points per person-month
   - Work-hours per function point
   - Development cost per function point
   - Maintenance cost per function point

2. Studies of software consumption
   - Function points owned by an enterprise
   - Function points needed by various kinds of end users
   - Build, lease, or purchase decision making
   - Contract vs. in-house decision making
   - Software project value analysis

3. Studies of software quality
   - Test cases and runs required per function point
   - Defects discovered per function point

To make an abstract topic concrete, Fig. 2.1 illustrates the essential

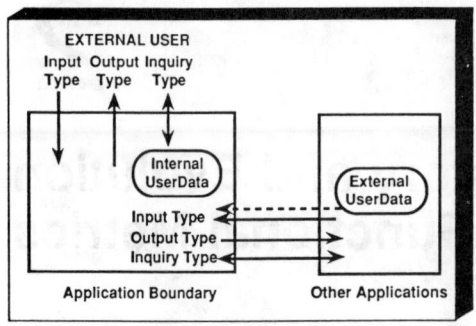

Figure 2.1 A basic application and its function point parameters.

topics that function points seek to enumerate. An average software application will normally have inputs and outputs that affect the end users, and many applications will also have inquiry capabilities. The application will normally also have data storage capabilities whereby information of interest to users can be kept and updated. Finally, the application may be part of a system, or it may share data with external applications.

After being used internally within IBM for several years, function points were discussed publicly for the first time in October 1979 in a paper which Albrecht presented at a joint SHARE/GUIDE/IBM conference held at Monterey, California.[2]

When he invented function points, Albrecht was working for IBM's Data Processing Services group. He had been given the task of measuring the productivity of a number of software projects. Because IBM's DP Services group developed custom software for a variety of other organizations, the software projects were written in a wide variety of languages: Cobol, PL/I, RPG, APL, and assembly language, to name but a few, and some indeed were written in mixed languages.

Albrecht knew, as did many other productivity experts, that it was not technically possible to measure software production rates across projects written in different levels of language with the traditional lines-of-code measures.

Other researchers knew the problems that existed with lines-of-code measures, but Albrecht deserves the credit for going beyond those traditional and imperfect metrics and developing a technique that can be used to explore the true economics of software production and consumption.

Albrecht's paper on function points was first published in 1979 in the conference proceedings, which had only limited circulation of several hundred copies. In 1981, with both IBM's and the conference organization's permission, the paper was reprinted in the IEEE tutorial entitled "Programming Productivity: Issues for the Eighties" by the author.[3] This republication by the IEEE provided the first widespread circulation of the concept of function point metrics outside IBM.

The IEEE tutorial brought together two different threads of measurement research. In 1978, the author had published an analysis of the mathematical problems and paradoxes associated with lines-of-code measures.[4] That article, also included in the 1981 IEEE tutorial, proved mathematically that lines of code were incapable of measuring productivity in the economic sense. Thus, it provided strong justification for Albrecht's work on function point metrics, which were the first in software history that could be used for measuring economic productivity.

It should be recalled that the standard economic definition of productivity is: "Goods or services produced per unit of labor or expense." A line of code is neither goods nor services in the economic sense. Customers do not buy lines of code directly, and they often do not even know how many lines of code exist in a software product. Also, lines of code are not the primary deliverables of software projects, so they cannot be used for serious studies of the production costs of software systems or programs.

The greatest bulk of what is actually produced and what gets delivered to users of software comprises words and paper documents. In the United States, sometimes as many as 400 English words will be produced for every line of source code in large systems. Often more than 3 times as much effort goes into word production as goes into coding. Words are obviously not economic units for software, since customers do not buy them directly, nor do they have any real control over the quantity produced. Indeed in some cases, such as large military systems, far too many unnecessary words are produced.

As already mentioned, customers do not purchase lines of code either, so code quantities have no intrinsic value to users. In most instances customers neither know nor care how much code was written or in what language an application is embodied. Indeed, if the same functionality could be provided to users with less code by means of a higher-level language, customers might benefit from the cost reductions.

If neither of the two primary production units of software (words and code) is of direct interest to software consumers, then what exactly constitutes the "goods or services" that make software a useful economic commodity? The answer, of course, is that users care about the functions of the application.

Prior to Albrecht's publication of the function point metric, there were only hazy and inaccurate ways to study software production, and there was no way at all to explore the demand or consumption side of the software economic picture.

Until 1979, the historical problem of measuring software productivity could be stated precisely: "The natural units of software production (words and code) were not the same as the units of software consumption (functions)." Economic studies require a standard definition of both what is produced and also of what is consumed.

Since neither words nor lines of code are of direct interest to software consumers, there was no tangible unit that matched the economic definition of goods or services that lent itself to studies of software's economic productivity.

A function point is an abstract but workable surrogate for the goods that are produced by software projects. Function points are the weighted sums of five different factors that are of interest to users:

- Inputs
- Outputs
- Logical files (also called user data groups)
- Inquiries
- Interfaces

Function points are defined by Albrecht to be "end-user benefits," and they are actually starting to serve as the economic units which customers wish to purchase or to have developed. That is, function points are beginning to be used in contract negotiations between software producers and their clients.

Clients and developers alike can discuss an application rationally in terms of its inputs, outputs, inquiries, files, and interfaces. Further, if requirements change, clients can request additional inputs or outputs after the initial agreement, and software providers can make rational predictions about the cost and schedule impact of such additions, which can then be discussed with clients in a reasonable manner.

Function points, unlike lines of code, can also be used for economic studies of both software production costs and software consumption. For production studies, function points can be applied usefully to effort, staffing, and cost-related studies. Thus, it is now known that the approximate U.S. average for software productivity at the project level is 5 function points per person-month. At the corporate level, where indirect personnel such as executives and administrators are included as well as effort expended on canceled projects, the U.S. average is about 1.5 function points per person-month. Function points can also be used to explore the volumes and costs of software paperwork production, a task for which lines of code were singularly inappropriate.

For consumption studies, function points are beginning to create an entirely new field of economic research that was never before possible. It is now possible to explore the utilization of software within industries and the utilization of software by the knowledge workers who use computers within those industries. Table 2.1 shows the approximate quantity of function points utilized by selected enterprises in the United States. The data was derived from studies of the production libraries of representative companies.

Although the margin of error in Table 2.1 is high, this kind of large-scale study of the volumes of software portfolios required by industries could not easily be performed prior to the advent of the function point metric. Although lines of code might be attempted, the kinds of companies shown in Table 2.1 typically use up to a dozen or more different languages: Cobol, C, Assembler, SQL, and so on.

Table 2.2 shows yet another new kind of consumption analysis possible from the use of function points. It illustrates the approximate number of function points required to support the computer usage of selected occupation groups in the United States. Here too the margin of error is high and the field of research is only just beginning. But research into information-processing consumption was not technically possible prior to the advent of the function point metric. It appears that function points may be starting to shed light on one of the most difficult economic questions of the century: how to evaluate the business value of software applications.

TABLE 2.1 Approximate Number of Function Points Owned by Selected U.S. Enterprises

Enterprise type	Function points in production library
Small local bank	125,000
Medium commercial bank	350,000
Large international bank	450,000
Medium-size life insurance company	400,000
Large life insurance company	550,000
Large telephone operating company	450,000
Large telephone manufacturing company	600,000
Medium-size manufacturing company	200,000
Large manufacturing company	375,000
Large computer manufacturer	1,650,000

TABLE 2.2 Approximate Number of Function Points Utilized by Selected Occupations in the United States

Occupation group	Function points used to support job performance
Airline reservation clerk	30,000
Travel agent	35,000
Corporate controller	20,000
Bank loan officer	15,000
Insurance claims adjuster	5,000
Aeronautical engineer	25,000
Electrical engineer	25,000
Telecommunications engineer	20,000
Software engineer	15,000
Mechanical engineer	12,500
First-line project manager (software)	3,500
Second-line project manager (software)	3,500

Since software economic consumption studies are only just starting, the information in Tables 2.1 and 2.2 must be regarded as preliminary and as containing a high margin of error. Nonetheless, it is a powerful illustration of the economic validity of function points that such studies can be attempted at all.

In conclusion, although function points are an abstract and synthetic metric, they are no less valid for economic purposes than many other standard economic metrics which also are abstract and synthetic, such as the Dow Jones stock indicator, British thermal units for heaters, accounting rates of return, internal rates of return, net present value, and the formulas for evaluating the net worth of an enterprise. Function points are starting to point the way to the first serious economic analyses of software production and software consumption since the computer era began.

Problems with and Paradoxes of Lines-of-Code Metrics

One of the criticisms sometimes levied against function points is that they are subjective whereas lines of code is objective. It is true the function point counting to date has included a measure of human judgment, and therefore includes subjectivity. (The emergence of a new class of automated function point tools is about to eliminate the current subjectivity of functional metrics.) However, it is not at all true that lines of code is an objective metric. Indeed, as will be shown, in all of human history there has not been a metric as subjective as a line of code since the days when the yard was based on the length of the arm of the king of England!

To understand the effectiveness of function points, it is necessary to understand the problems of the older lines-of-code metric. Regretfully, most users of lines of code have no idea at all of the subjectivity, randomness, and quirky deficiencies of this metric.

As mentioned, the first complete analysis of the problems of lines-of-code metrics was the previously mentioned study by the author in the *IBM Systems Journal* in 1978.[4] In essence there are three serious deficiencies associated with lines of code.

1. There has never been a national or international standard for a line of code that encompasses all procedural languages. (See Appendix A for an example of what such a standard might look like.)

2. Software can be produced by such methods as program generators, spreadsheets, graphic icons, reusable modules of unknown size, and inheritence, wherein entities such as lines of code are totally irrelevant.

3. Lines-of-code metrics paradoxically move backwards as the level of the language gets higher, so that the most powerful and advanced languages appear to be less productive than the more primitive low-level languages. That is due to an intrinsic defect in the lines-of-code metrics. Some of the languages thus penalized include Ada, APL, C++, Objective C, SMALLTALK, and many more.

Let us consider these problems in turn.

Lack of a standard definition for lines of code

The software industry will soon be 50 years of age, and lines of code have been used ever since its start. It is surprising that, in all that time, the basic concept of a line of code has never been standardized.

Counting physical or logical lines. The variation that can cause the greatest apparent difference in size is that of determining whether a line of code should be terminated physically or logically. A physical termination would be caused by the ENTER key of a computer keyboard, which completes the current line and moves the cursor to the next line of the screen. A logical termination would be a formal delimiter, such as a semicolon, colon, or period.

For languages such as Basic, which allow many logical statements per physical line, the size counted by means of logical delimiters can appear to be up to 500 percent larger than if lines are counted physically. On the other hand, for languages such as Cobol, which utilize conditional statements that encompass several physical lines, the physical method can cause the program to appear perhaps 200 percent larger than the logical method. From informal surveys of the clients of Software Productivity Research carried out by the author, it appears that about 35 percent of U.S. project managers count physical lines, 15 percent count logical lines, and 50 percent do not count by either method.

Counting types of lines. The next area of uncertainty is which of several possible kinds of lines should be counted. The first full explanation of the variations in counting code was perhaps that published by the author in 1986,[5] which is surprisingly recent for a topic almost 45 years of age. Most procedural languages include four different kinds of source code statements:

1. Executable lines (used for actions, such as addition)
2. Data definitions (used to identify information types)
3. Comments (used to inform readers of the code)
4. Blank lines (used to separate sections visually)

Again, there has never been a U.S. standard that defined whether all four or only one or two of these possibilities should be utilized. In typical business applications, about 40 percent of the total statements are executable lines, 35 percent are data definitions, 10 percent are blank, and 15 percent are comments. For systems software such as operating systems, about 45 percent of the total statements are executable, 30 percent are data definitions, 10 percent are blank, and 15 percent are comments.

From informal surveys of the clients of Software Productivity Research carried out by the author, it appears that about 10 percent count only executable lines, 20 percent count executable lines and data definitions, 15 percent also include commentary lines, and 5 percent even include blank lines! About 50 percent do not count lines of code at all.

Counting reusable code. Yet another area of extreme uncertainty is that of counting reusable code within software applications. Informal code reuse by programmers is very common, and any professional programmer will routinely copy and reuse enough code to account for perhaps 20 to 30 percent of the code in an application when the programming is done in an ordinary procedural language such as C, Cobol, or Fortran. For object-oriented languages such as SMALLTALK, C++, and Objective C, the volume of reuse tends to exceed 50 percent because of the facilities of inheritance that are intrinsic in the object-oriented family of languages. Finally, some corporations have established formal libraries of reusable modules, and many applications in those corporations may exceed 75 percent of the total volume of reused code.

The problem with measuring reusability centers around whether a reused module should be counted at all, counted only once, or counted each time it occurs. For example, if a reused module of 100 source statements is included five times in a program, there are three variations in counting:

1. Count the reused module at every occurrence.

2. Count the reused module only once.

3. Do not count the reused module at all, since it was not developed for the current project.

From informal surveys of the clients of Software Productivity Research carried out by the author, about 25 percent would count the module every time it occurred, 20 percent would count the module only once, and 5 percent would not count the reused module at all. The remaining 50 percent do not count source code at all.

Applications written in multiple languages. The next area of uncertainty, which is almost never discussed in the software engineering literature, is the problem of using lines-of-code metrics for multi-language applications. From informal surveys of the clients of Software Productivity Research, it appears that about a third of all U.S. applications include more than one language and some may include a dozen or more languages. Some of the more common language mixtures include:

- Cobol mixed with a query language such as SQL
- Cobol mixed with a data definition language such as DL/1
- Cobol mixed with several other special-purpose languages
- C mixed with Assembler
- Basic mixed with Assembler
- Ada mixed with Assembler
- Ada mixed with Jovial and other languages

Since there are no U.S. standards for line counting that govern even a single language, multilanguage projects show a great increase in the number of random errors associated with lines-of-code data.

Additional uncertainties concerning lines of code. Many other possible counting variations can affect the apparent size of applications in which lines of code are used. For example:

- Including or excluding changed code for enhancements
- Including or excluding macro expansions
- Including or excluding job control language (JCL)
- Including or excluding deleted code
- Including or excluding scaffold or temporary code that is written but later discarded

The overall cumulative impact of all of these uncertainties spans more than an order of magnitude. That is, if the most verbose of the line-counting variations is compared to the most succinct, the apparent size of the application will be more than 10 times larger! That is an astonishing and even awe-inspiring range of uncertainty for a unit of measure approaching its fiftieth year of use!

Unfortunately, very few software authors bother to define which counting rules they used. The regrettable effect is that most of the literature on software productivity which expresses the results in terms of lines of code is essentially worthless for serious research purposes.

Size variations that are due to individual programming style. A minor controlled study carried out within IBM illustrates yet another problem with lines of code. Eight programmers were given the same specification and were asked to write the code required to implement it. The amount of code produced for the same specification varied by about 5 to 1 between the largest and the smallest implementation. That was due not to deliberate attempts to make productivity seem high, but rather to the styles of the programmers and to the varying interpretations of what the specifications asked for.

Software functions delivered without producing code

A large-scale study within ITT[6] in which the author participated found that about 26 percent of the approximately 30,000 applications owned by the corporation had been leased or purchased from external vendors rather than developed internally. Functionality was being delivered to the ITT software users of the packages, but ITT was obviously not producing the code. Specifically, about 140,000 function points out of the corporate total of 520,000 function points had been delivered to users in the form of packages rather than being developed by the ITT staff. The effective cost per function point of unmodified packages averaged about 35 percent of the cost per function point of custom development. However, for packages requiring heavy modification, the cost per function point was about 105 percent of equivalent custom development. Lines-of-code metrics are essentially impossible for studying the economics of package acquisitions or for make-vs.-buy productivity decisions.

The advent of the object-oriented languages and the deliberate pursuit of reusable modules by many corporations is leading to the phenomenon that the number of unique lines of code that must actually be hand-coded is shrinking, whereas the functional content of applications continues to expand. The lines-of-code metric is essentially useless in judging the productivity impact of this phenomenon. The use of inheritance and methods by object-oriented languages, the use of corporate reusable module libraries, and the use of application and program generators makes the concept of lines of code almost irrelevant.

As the 1990 decade progresses, an increasing number of graphics or icon-based "languages" will appear, and in them application development will proceed in a visual fashion quite different from that of conventional procedural programming. Lines of code, never defined adequately even for procedural languages, will be hopeless for graphics-based languages.

The paradox of reversed productivity for high-level languages

Although lack of standardization is the most visible surface problem with lines of code, the deepest and most severe problem is a mathematical paradox that causes real economic productivity and apparent productivity to move in opposite directions! This phenomenon was introduced and illustrated in Chap. 1, but its importance makes it deserve a more elaborate explanation.

The paradox manifests itself under these conditions: As real economic software productivity improves, metrics expressed in both lines of source code per time unit and cost per source line form will tend to move backwards and appear to be worse than previously. Thus, as real economic productivity improves, the apparent cost per source line will be higher and the apparent lines of source code per time unit will be lower than before even though less effort and cost were required to complete an application.

Failure to understand the nature of this paradox has proved to be embarrassing to the industry as a whole and to many otherwise capable managers and consultants who have been led to make erroneous recommendations based on apparent productivity data rather than on real economic productivity data. The fundamental reason for the paradox has actually been known since the industrial revolution, or for more than 200 years, by company owners and manufacturing engineers. The essence of the paradox is this: If a product's manufacturing cycle includes a significant proportion of fixed costs and there is a decline in the number of units produced, the cost per unit will naturally go up.

For software, a substantial number of development activities either include or behave like fixed costs. For example, the applications requirements, specifications, and user documents are likely to stay constant in size and cost regardless of the language used for coding. This means that when enterprises migrate from a low-level language such as assembly language to a higher-level language such as Cobol or Ada, they do not have to write as many lines of source code to develop applications but the paperwork costs are essentially fixed. In effect, the number of source code units produced declines in the presence of fixed costs.

Since so many development activities either include fixed costs or behave like fixed costs, the cost per source line will naturally go up. Examples of activities that behave like fixed costs, since they are independent of coding, include user requirements, analysis, functional design, design reviews, user documentation, and some forms of testing such as function testing.

Table 2.3 is an example of the paradox associated with lines of source code metrics in a comparison of Assembler and Ada. Assume $5000 per month is the fully burdened salary rate in both cases. Note that Table 2.3 is intended to illustrate the mathematical paradox, and it exaggerates the trends to make the point clearly visible.

As shown in Table 2.4, with function points the economic productivity improvements are clearly visible and the true impact of a high-level language such as Ada can be seen and understood. Thus, function points provide a superior base for economic productivity studies than lines-of-code metrics.

To illustrate some of the more recent findings vis-à-vis the economic advantages of high-level languages as explored by function points, Fig. 2.2 shows the comparative productivity rates for a number of language categories. Data such as that shown in Fig. 2.2 is technically and mathematically impossible with lines-of-code metrics.

To summarize, economic productivity deals with the amount of effort required to produce goods or services that users consume or utilize. Studies of productivity, therefore, can be divided into those which

TABLE 2.3 The Paradox of Lines-of-Code Metrics and High-Level Languages

	Assembler version	Ada version	Difference
Source code size	100,000	25,000	– 75,000
Activity, in person-months:			
Requirements	10	10	0
Design	25	25	0
Coding	100	20	– 80
Documentation	15	15	0
Integration and testing	25	15	– 10
Management	25	15	– 10
Total effort	200	100	– 100
Total cost	$1,000,000	$500,000	– $500,000
Cost per line	$10	$20	+ $20
Lines per month	500	250	– 250

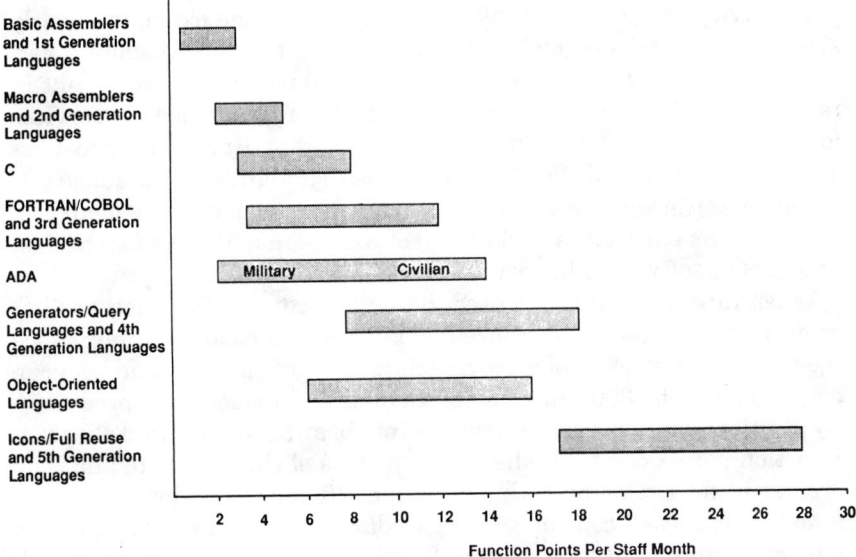

Figure 2.2 Productivity rates associated with language levels when measured with function points.

TABLE 2.4 The Economic Validity of Function Point Metrics

	Assembler version	Ada version	Difference
Function points	300	300	0
Activity, in person-months:			
Requirements	10	10	0
Design	25	25	0
Coding	100	20	−80
Documentation	15	15	0
Integration and testing	25	15	−10
Management	25	15	−10
Total effort	200	100	−100
Total cost	$1,000,000	$500,000	−$500,000
Cost per function point	$3,333	$1,666	−$1,667
Function points per person-month	1.5	3.0	−1.5

concentrate on production efficiencies and those which concentrate on demand or consumption.

Table 2.3 highlights the failure of lines of code to measure economic productivity or even to make common sense. As the examples clearly show, the Ada version took only half the effort of the Assembler version and cost only half as much. This is a 50 percent improvement in real economic productivity, or the ability to produce goods or services for a given level or labor and expense. But when lines-of-code metrics are used, the economic gains attributable to a high-level language disappear and the low-level language seems, erroneously, to be more productive. This paradox caused no end of confusion and error for the first 45 years of software's history.

When function points are used, however, economic productivity improvements are no longer concealed but become clearly visible. Since the two preceding examples provide the same functionality and both can be assumed to be 300 function points in size, consider their productivity results measured in function point form as shown in Table 2.4. Function points can be applied to both sides of the equation, and they are useful for exploring both production efficiencies and customer demand. The lines-of-code metric is paradoxical for studies of production efficiency, and it is essentially useless for studies of customer demand.

Albrecht's Original 1979 Function Point Methodology

When first published in October 1979,[2] Albrecht had created function points as a metric that could meet these five goals:

1. It dealt with the external features of software.

2. It dealt with features that were important to users.

3. It could be applied early in a product's life cycle.

4. It could be linked to economic productivity.

5. It was independent of source code or language.

When the function point metrics were first published, they consisted of four significant questions that could be answered easily for any software product, plus an adjustment for complexity. The 1979 function point method looked as shown in Table 2.5.

To use the 1979 IBM function point method, it was only necessary to count the number of inputs, outputs, inquiries, and logical master files that were associated with the application being measured. The counts were then multiplied by empirically derived weighting factors. The unadjusted total was then raised or lowered by as much as ±25 percent for complexity, and the final result was the adjusted function point total. The metric could be applied as early as the requirements phase, and compared to the older lines-of-code metric, function points were a much better indicator of economic productivity.

The 1979 IBM function point marked the first point in the history of software where the true economic value of high-level languages could be directly measured. The early studies of 24 projects by Albrecht himself and published at the October conference in 1979 contained the first tangible evidence in software engineering history that languages such as Cobol, PL/I, and RPG yielded higher economic productivity rates than assembly languages. Until that time, the whole issue of direct measurement of high-level languages had been virtually impossible other than by the circuitous method of converting the sizes of all projects studied into basic assembly language.

TABLE 2.5 The 1979 Version of the IBM Function Point Metric

Significant parameters	Weighting factors		Unadjusted total
Number of inputs	× 4	=	_____
Number of outputs	× 5	=	_____
Number of inquiries	× 4	=	_____
Number of master files	× 10	=	_____
Unadjusted total			_____
Complexity adjustment (up to ±25%)			_____
Adjusted function point total			_____

However, it soon became evident that the way complexity was handled by the early function point technique needed to be modified to solve two problems: (1) Complexity was totally subjective. (2) Plus or minus 25 percent was not a broad enough range for the observed impact of complexity on real-life projects.

As function points started to be widely used outside IBM, Albrecht and his colleagues next addressed the need to make the complexity adjustments more objective and more pervasive in impact. These changes would be released later, in the 1984 IBM revision.

Worldwide Publication of Function Points in 1981

At the joint IBM/SHARE/GUIDE conference in 1979, Albrecht's paper attracted considerable attention among the participants. One of the other speakers, the author, who had been carrying out complementary research in software measurement, recognized the economic validity of the function point metric and made plans to include the topic in a new book that was in planning.

In 1981, with both IBM's and the conference organization's permission, Albrecht's paper was reprinted in the IEEE tutorial entitled "Programming Productivity: Issues for the Eighties."[3] This publication by the IEEE provided the first widespread circulation of the concept of function point metrics outside IBM and began to attract users on a global basis.

The 1981 IEEE tutorial also included other research on the paradoxes associated with lines-of-code metrics. While working for IBM in 1978, the author had published an analysis of the mathematical problems and paradoxes associated with lines-of-code measures in the *IBM Systems Journal*.[4] That article, also included in the 1981 IEEE tutorial, proved that lines of code were incapable of measuring productivity in the economic sense. Thus the work of the author and Albrecht could be viewed as opposite sides of the same coin: the author was able to demonstrate the fallacy of lines of code for economic purposes; Albrecht was able to create an economically valid metric for the first time in software history. Albrecht's own external publication of the function point metric occurred in 1984 when IBM published his famous guidelines.[7]

DeMarco's 1982 Publication of the "Bang" Functional Metric

Albrecht and the author were certainly not the only researchers who were attempting to go beyond the imperfect lines-of-code metric and move toward functional metrics. In 1982, Tom DeMarco published a description of a different kind of functional metric which he initially termed the "bang metric."[8] This unusual name was derived from the vernacular phrase, "getting more bang for the buck." A less jocular name for the metric would be the "DeMarco functional metric."

Although DeMarco and Albrecht were acquainted with each other and their metrics were aimed at the same problem, the bang metric and the function point metric are somewhat different in form and substance. (The two appear to be totally independent inventions, incidentally.) DeMarco's consulting had often taken him into the domain of systems software and some of the more complex forms of software engineering, rather than pure MIS projects. His bang metric was the first attempt to apply functional metrics to the domain of systems and scientific software. In the metric, the basic elements to be counted are the following:

1. Functional primitives
2. Modified functional primitives
3. Data elements
4. Input data elements
5. Output data elements
6. Stored data elements
7. Objects (also termed "entities")
8. Relationships
9. States in a state transition model of the application
10. Transitions in a state transition model
11. Data tokens
12. Relationships involving retained data models

As can be seen, the DeMarco bang metric is a considerable superset of the Albrecht function point metric, and it contains such elements as data tokens and state transitions which are normally associated with the more complex forms of systems software such as operating systems and telecommunication systems.

The full set of things which can be counted by using the bang metric is of imposing if not intimidating length. However, DeMarco has pointed out that applications can be conveniently segregated into those that are "function strong" and those that are "data strong." That is, most applications will emphasize either functionality or files and data.

It is not impossible to relate the bang metric to function points. Since DeMarco has stated that subsets are acceptable, it is possible to select an exact match of bang and function point parameters. However, complexity adjustments of the two methods would still be different because the IBM adjustments are rule-driven and the DeMarco method is largely subjective.

Although the DeMarco bang metric is technically interesting and can lead to valuable insights when utilized, it fell far behind the Albrecht function point metric in terms of the numbers of users and practitioners once IBM began to offer function point courses as part of its data processing education curriculum. The metric also fell behind in convenience when numerous software packages that could aid in the calculation of IBM's function point metrics began to be marketed while the bang metric still required manual methods. Although the CADRE tool set contains support for the bang metric, there are now more than 20 vendors with tools which facilitate function point counting.

Finally, the DeMarco metric fell behind in the ability to evolve when the International Function Point User's Group (IFPUG) was formed. There is no equivalent for bang metrics to the IFPUG Counting Practices Committee, which serves to both enhance function points and provide standard definitions and examples. It would not be impossible, of course, to create a bang metric subcommittee within IFPUG, but that has not yet been done.

Albrecht's 1984 Revision of the IBM Function Point Methodology

In 1984, Albrecht and IBM published a major revision of the function point method[7] that significantly revised the technique. It is the basis of the current IBM function point methodology. Also in 1984, IBM started to include courses in function points as part of its data processing education curriculum, which created a quantum leap in overall utilization of the technique.

In the 1984 revision, the impact of complexity was broadened so that the range became approximately 250 percent. To reduce the subjectivity of dealing with complexity, the factors that caused complexity to be higher or lower than normal were specifically enumerated and guidelines for their interpretation were issued. Instead of merely counting the number of inputs, outputs, master files, and inquiries as in the 1979 function point methodology, the current methodology requires that complexity be ranked as low, average, or high. In addition, a new parameter, interface files, has been added. The current IBM implementation of function points looks as shown in Table 2.6.

With the 1984 IBM implementation, each major feature such as external inputs must be evaluated separately for complexity. In order to

TABLE 2.6 IBM's 1984 Revision of the Function Point Metric

Significant parameter	Low complexity	Medium complexity	High complexity
External input	× 3	× 4	× 6
External output	× 4	× 5	× 7
Logical internal file	× 7	× 10	× 15
External interface file	× 5	× 7	× 10
External inquiry	× 3	× 4	× 6

make the complexity evaluation less subjective, Albrecht developed a matrix for each feature that considers the number of file types, record types, and/or data element types. For example, Table 2.7 shows a matrix dealing with the complexity of external inputs.

The treatment of complexity is still subjective, of course, but it is now supported by guidelines for interpretation. Examples of inputs include data screens filled out by users, magnetic tapes or floppy disks, sensor inputs, and light-pen or mouse-based inputs. The adjustment table for external outputs is shown in Table 2.8, and it is similar to the input adjustment table.

Examples of outputs include output data screens, printed reports, floppy disk files, sets of checks, or printed invoices. The adjustment table for logical internal file types is shown in Table 2.9, and it follows the same pattern.

Examples of logical internal files include floppy disk files, magnetic tape files, flat files in a personal computer database, a leg in a hierarchical database such as IBM's IMS, a table in a relational database such as DB2, and a path through a net in a network-oriented database. Table 2.10 shows the adjustments for external interfaces, and it follows the same pattern as the others.

Examples of an interface include a shared database and a logical file addressable from or to some other application. The last parameter is inquiries, which is similar to the others but is divided into the two

TABLE 2.7 Adjustment Weights for External Inputs

File types referenced	Data element types		
	1–4	5–15	⇒ 16
0–1	Low	Low	Average
2	Low	Average	High
⇒ 3	Average	High	High

TABLE 2.8 Adjustment Weights for External Outputs

File types referenced	Data element types		
	1–5	6–19	⇒ 20
0–1	Low	Low	Average
2–3	Low	Average	High
⇒ 4	Average	High	High

TABLE 2.9 Adjustment Weights for Logical Internal Files

File types referenced	Data element types		
	1–19	20–50	⇒ 51
0–1	Low	Low	Average
2–5	Low	Average	High
⇒ 6	Average	High	High

TABLE 2.10 Adjustment Weights for Interface Files

File types referenced	Data element types		
	1–19	20–50	⇒ 51
0–1	Low	Low	Average
2–5	Low	Average	High
⇒ 6	Average	High	High

subelements of the input portion and the output portion, as shown in Tables 2.11 and 2.12:

Examples of inquiries include user inquiry without updating a file, help messages, and selection messages. A typical inquiry might be illustrated by an airline reservation query along the lines of "What

TABLE 2.11 Adjustment Weights for Inquiry Input Portions

File types referenced	Data element types		
	1–4	5–15	⇒ 16
0–1	Low	Low	Average
2	Low	Average	High
⇒ 3	Average	High	High

TABLE 2.12 Adjustment Weights for Inquiry Output Portions

File types referenced	Data element types		
	1–5	6–19	⇒ 20
0–1	Low	Low	Average
2–3	Low	Average	High
⇒ 4	Average	High	High

Delta flights leave Boston for Atlanta after 3:00 p.m.?" as an input portion. The response or output portion might be something like "Flight 202 at 4:15 p.m."

Function point abbreviations and nomenclature

The IBM 1984 revision of the function point counting rules introduced yet another change that is minor in technical significance but important from a human factors standpoint. It adopted a set of standard full-length descriptions and standard abbreviations for the factors and variables used in function point calculations. Since examples and discussions of function points by experienced users tend to make use of those abbreviations, novice users of function point should master them as soon as possible.

Inputs, outputs, inquiries, logical files, and interfaces obviously comprise many different kinds of things, so the generic word "type" was added to the 1984 full nomenclature. However, since it is necessary to use some of the terms many times when giving examples, the revision introduced standard abbreviations as well. The changes in nomenclature and abbreviations are shown below:

1979 nomenclature	1984 nomenclature	1984 abbreviations
Inputs	External input type	IT
Outputs	External output type	OT
Logical files	Logical internal file type	FT
Interface	External interface file type	EI
Inquiries	External inquiry type	QT

Other abbreviations that were created in the 1984 IBM revision include the following:

DET   Data element type
FTR   File types referenced

RET   Record types

L   Low (for complexity)

A   Average (for complexity)

H   High (for complexity)

The terminology of function points has tended to change frequently, although the fundamental concepts have been remarkably consistent. Unfortunately, novices tend to be put off by the complexity of the terms, even though the terms are no more difficult, for example, than those associated with stocks or corporate finance.

The 14 influential adjustment factors

Another significant change in the 1984 IBM revision was an expansion in the range of complexity adjustments and the rigor with which the adjustments are carried out. Recall that, in the original 1979 version, complexity was a purely subjective adjustment with a range that spanned ±25 percent. In the 1984 revision, it is derived from the overall impact of 14 influential factors, and the total range of adjustment of the complexity multiplier runs from 0.65 to 1.35.

The 14 influential complexity factors are evaluated on a scale of 1 to 5 (with a 0 being used to eliminate factors that are not present at all). The 14 influential complexity factors are assigned shorthand identifiers that range from C1 to C14 for accuracy and convenience when referencing them.

C1   Data communications

C2   Distributed functions

C3   Performance objectives

C4   Heavily used configuration

C5   Transaction rate

C6   On-line data entry

C7   End-user efficiency

C8   On-line update

C9   Complex processing

C10   Reusability

C11   Installation ease

C12   Operational ease

C13   Multiple sites

C14   Facilitate change

In considering the weights of the 14 influential factors, the general guidelines are these: score a 0 if the factor has no impact at all on the application; score a 5 if the factor has a strong and pervasive impact;

score a 2, 3, 4, or some intervening decimal value such as 2.5 if the impact is something in between. This is, of course, still subjective, but the subjectivity is now spread over 14 different factors.

IBM's tutorial materials[9] provide the following general suggestions for assigning weights to the 14 influential factors:

0	Factor not present or without influence
1	Insignificant influence
2	Moderate influence
3	Average influence
4	Significant influence
5	Strong influence

Let us consider the maximum ranges of the 14 influential factors and look in detail at the scoring recommendations for the first two:

C1 data communication.   Data communication implies that data and/or control information would be sent or received over communication facilities. This factor would be scored as follows:

0	Batch applications
1	Remote printing or data entry
2	Remote printing and data entry
3	A teleprocessing front end to the application
4	Applications with significant teleprocessing
5	Applications that are dominantly teleprocessing

C2 distributed functions.   Distributed functions are concerned with whether an application is monolithic and operates on a single contiguous processor or is distributed among a variety of processors. The scoring for this factor is as follows:

0	Pure monolithic applications
1	Applications that prepare data for other components
2	Applications distributed over a few components
3	Applications distributed over more components
4	Applications distributed over many components
5	Applications dynamically performed on many components

C3 performance objectives.   Performance objectives are scored as 0 if no special performance criteria are stated by the users of the application and scored as 5 if the users insist on very stringent performance targets that require considerable effort to achieve.

C4 heavily used configuration. Heavily used configuration is scored as 0 if the application has no special usage constraints and as 5 if anticipated usage requires special effort to achieve.

C5 transaction rate. Transaction rate is scored 0 if the volume of transactions is not significant and 5 if the volume of transactions is high enough to stress the application and require special effort to achieve desired throughputs.

C6 on-line data entry. On-line data entry is scored 0 if none or fewer than 15 percent of the transactions are interactive and 5 if all or more than 50 percent of the transactions are interactive.

C7 end-user efficiency. Design for end-user efficiency is scored 0 if there are no end users or there are no special requirements for end users and 5 if the stated requirements for end-user efficiency are stringent enough to require special effort to achieve them.

C8 on-line update. On-line update is scored 0 if there is none and 5 if on-line updates are both mandatory and especially difficult, perhaps because of the need to back up or protect data against accidental change.

C9 complex processing. Complex processing is scored 0 if there is none and 5 in cases requiring extensive logical decisions, complicated mathematics, tricky exception processing, or elaborate security schemes.

C10 reusability. Reusability is scored 0 if the functionality is planned to stay local to the current application and 5 if much of the functionality and the project deliverables are intended for widespread utilization by other applications.

C11 installation ease. Installation ease is scored 0 if this factor is insignificant and 5 if installation is both important and so stringent that it requires special effort to accomplish a satisfactory installation.

C12 operational ease. Operational ease is scored 0 if this factor is insignificant and 5 if operational ease of use is so important that it requires special effort to achieve it.

C13 multiple sites. Multiple sites is scored 0 if there is only one planned using location and 5 if the project and its deliverables are intended for many diverse locations.

C14 facilitate change. Facilitate change is scored 0 if change does not occur, and 5 if the application is developed specifically to allow end users to make rapid changes to control data or tables which they maintain with the aid of the application.

Using the 14 influential factors for complexity adjustment

When all of the 14 factors have been considered and scores assigned individually, the sum of the factors is converted into a final complexity adjustment by the following procedure:

1. Multiply the sum of the factors by .01 to convert the sum to a decimal value.

2. Add a constant of 0.65 to the decimal value to create a complexity multiplier.

3. Multiply the unadjusted function point total by the complexity multiplier to create the final adjusted function point total.

It can be seen that the 14 influential factors yield a multiplier that has a range from 0.65 to 1.35. If none of the factors were present at all, the sum would be 0, so only the constant of 0.65 is used as the multiplier. If all 14 factors were strongly present, their sum would be 70. Using the procedure of $70*.01 + .65 = 1.35$, the final multiplier in this case is 1.35.

Here is an example of the calculation sequence used to derive a function point total by using IBM's current method. Assume an average project with 10 inputs, 10 outputs, 10 inquiries, 1 data file, and 1 interface. Assume average complexity for the five primary factors and a range of weights from 0 to 5 for the 14 influential factors, so that the sum of the 14 influential factors total to 40 influence points.

Basic counts	Elements		Weights		Results
10	Inputs	×	4	=	40
10	Outputs	×	5	=	50
10	Inquiries	×	4	=	40
1	Logical file	×	10	=	10
1	Interface	×	7	=	7
Unadjusted total					147

The influential factor calculations are as follows:

Data communications	0
Distributed functions	0
Performance objectives	4

Heavily used configuration	3
Transaction rate	3
On-line data entry	4
End-user efficiency	4
On-line update	2
Complex processing	3
Reusability	0
Installation ease	4
Operational ease	4
Multiple sites	5
Facilitate change	4

The sum total of the influential factors is 40. Then,

$$40*.01 = .40 + .65 \text{ [constant]} = 1.05 \text{ [complexity multiplier]}$$

The final adjustment is:

147 [unadjusted total]*1.05 [complexity multiplier]

= 154 [adjusted function points]

Although the steps with the IBM method can be time-consuming, the calculation sequence for producing function points is fairly simple to carry out. Not quite so simple is reaching a clear agreement on the exact number of inputs, outputs, inquiries, data files, and interfaces in real-life projects. When first starting with function points by using the IBM method, users should be cautioned not to get to bogged down in rules and determinations of exact weights. If you think clearly about the application, your counts are likely to be acceptably accurate. In summary form, here are the basic concepts used when counting with function points.

1. *Inputs:* Inputs are screens or forms through which human users of an application or other programs add new data or update existing data. If an input screen is too large for a single normal display (usually 80 columns by 25 lines) and flows over onto a second screen, the set counts as 1 input. Inputs that require unique processing are what should be considered.

2. *Outputs:* Outputs are screens or reports which the application produces for human use or for other programs. Note that outputs requiring separate processing are the units to count: In a payroll application, an output function that created, say, 100 checks would still count as one output.

3. *Inquiries:* Inquiries are screens which allow users to interrogate

an application and ask for assistance or information, such as HELP screens.

4. *Data files:* Data files are logical collections of records which the application modifies or updates. A file can be a flat file such as a tape file, one leg of a hierarchical database such as IMS, one table within a relational database, or one path through a CODASYL network database.

5. *Interface:* Interfaces are files shared with other applications, such as incoming or outgoing tape files, shared databases, and parameter lists.

As can be seen, the current IBM function point methodology is substantially more rigorous than the original 1979 implementation, but the rigor has added considerably more work before an application's function points can be totaled. The effort involved to count the function points of a large system by using the current IBM methodology amounts to several days, sometimes spread out over several weeks.

Counting function points by using the current IBM method also requires trained function point specialists to ensure consistency of the counts. Both IBM and consulting companies such as Software Productivity Research are now providing both function point training and assistance in getting started with function points.

When first starting out with function points, formal training is definitely recommended; an example is the original function point workshop provided by IBM itself,[9] or the new function point workshop prepared by Albrecht for Software Productivity Research,[10] or one of the other consulting company offerings. It is interesting that most universities and academic institutions have not yet added courses in function point analysis to their curriculums and hence are some years behind the actual state of the art of software measurement.

Generally speaking, adopting the current IBM function point implies a serious commitment to good measurement and a willingness to devote staff, skills, and time. The payoff is the most reliable metric in software history, coupled with the ability to share productivity data with other enterprises.

The 1985 Software Productivity Research Method

In October 1985, Software Productivity Research introduced a new way to calculate function points as part of the SPQR/20 Software Productivity, Quality, and Reliability estimating model[11] and later as part of the SPQR SIZER/FP tool[12] and the CHECKPOINT® measurement and estimation tool.[13] The SPR function point variation simplified the way complexity was dealt with and reduced the human effort associated with counting function points. The SPR function point methodology yields function point totals that are essentially the same as those by the current IBM function point method. In repeated trials, it produced counts that averaged within 1.5 percent of the IBM method, with a maximum variation of about 15 percent.

The SPR function point methodology attempts to meet three additional goals over and above the five goals that the IBM method was intended to meet. The additional SPR goals are:

6. To create function point totals easily and rapidly and to be able to create function points prior to the availability of all of the IBM factors in a normal project life cycle

7. To predict source code size for any known language

8. To retrofit function points to existing software

The primary difference between the IBM and SPR function point methodologies is in the way the two deal with complexity. The IBM techniques for assessing complexity, discussed in the preceding section, are based on weighting 14 influential factors and evaluating the numbers of field and file references. The SPR technique for dealing with complexity is to separate the overall topic of "complexity" into three distinct questions that can be dealt with intuitively:

1. How complex are the problems or algorithms facing the team?

2. How complex are the code structure and control flow of the application?

3. How complex is the data structure of the application?

This simplification of the way complexity is treated allows the SPR method to backfire function points. If the source code size of an existing application is known, then the SPR function point technique and its supporting software can automatically convert that size into a function point total.

With the SPR function point method, it is not necessary to count the number of data element types, file types, or record types as it is with the current IBM method. Neither is it necessary to assign a low, average, or high value to each specific input, output, inquiry, data file, or interface or to evaluate the 14 influential factors as defined by the IBM method.

As a result of the reduced number of complexity considerations, the SPR method can also be applied somewhat earlier than the IBM method, as during the preliminary requirements phase. The effort required to complete the calculations also is reduced, and that can be significant for manual calculations. However, the effort-reduction aspect is less significant if function point calculation software is used.

The three SPR complexity parameters deal with the entire application rather than with the subelements of the application. Mathematically, the SPR function point methodology has a slightly broader range of adjustments than the IBM methodology (from 0.5 to 1.5), and it produces function point totals that seldom differ by more than a few percent from the IBM methodology. The three SPR complexity questions for a new application look like this:

Problem complexity?   _____

1. Simple algorithms and simple calculations
2. Majority of simple algorithms and calculations
3. Algorithms and calculations of average complexity
4. Some difficult or complex calculations
5. Many difficult algorithms and complex calculations

Code complexity?   _____

1. Nonprocedural (generated, spreadsheet, query, etc.)
2. Well structured with reusable modules
3. Well structured (small modules and simple paths)
4. Fair structure, but some complex modules and paths
5. Poor structure, with large modules and complex paths

Data complexity?   _____

1. Simple data with few variables and low complexity
2. Numerous variables, but simple data relationships
3. Multiple files, fields, and data interactions
4. Complex file structures and data interactions
5. Very complex file structures and data interactions

For fine tuning, the SPR complexity questions can be answered with decimal values, and answers such as 2, 2.5, and 3.25 are all perfectly acceptable.

TABLE 2.13 The 1985 SPR Function Point Method

Significant parameter		Empirical weight	
Number of inputs?	_____	× 4 =	_____
Number of outputs?	_____	× 5 =	_____
Number of inquiries?	_____	× 4 =	_____
Number of data files?	_____	× 10 =	_____
Number of interfaces?	_____	× 7 =	_____
Unadjusted total			_____
Complexity adjustment			_____
Adjusted function point total			_____

The SPR function point questions themselves are similar to IBM's 1979 questions in that only one set of empirical weights is used. The SPR function point questions are shown in Table 2.13.

Since the SPR function point method is normally automated, manual complexity adjustments are not required when using it. For those who might wish to use it manually, the SPR algorithm for complexity adjustment uses the sum of the problem complexity and data complexity questions and matches the results to the values shown in Table 2.14.

Note that Table 2.14 shows only integer values for the complexity sum. For decimal results between integer values, such as 3.5, the SPR software tools calculate a fractional adjustment factor. For example, if the complexity sum were in fact 3.5, the adjustment multiplier would be 0.75.

It may be asked why *code complexity* is one of the questions posed by the SPR method but omitted from the SPR adjustment calculations.

TABLE 2.14 The SPR Complexity Adjustment Factors

Complexity sum	Adjustment multiplier
1	0.5
2	0.6
3	0.7
4	0.8
5	0.9
6	1.0
7	1.1
8	1.2
9	1.3
10	1.4
11	1.5

The code complexity factor is not required by the logic of the function point metric when producing normal forward function point counts. However, for retrofitting or backfiring function points to existing software, code complexity is an important parameter, as will be seen later.

The SPR function point method attempts to meet the five goals of the original IBM function point method and three additional goals as well, as discussed below.

High-speed function point calculations

The SPR methodology is normally automated rather than manual, and in typical use, it does not require manual calculations at all. Because it deals with complexity in terms of only three discrete and intuitive parameters and does not require segmentation of individual factors into low, average, and high complexity, it can create function point totals very rapidly. Users who are generally familiar with function point principles and who also know an application well enough to state how many inputs, outputs, inquiries, data files, and interfaces are involved can generate function point totals in less than a minute by using the automated SPR methodology.

Source code size prediction
for any language

The SPR function point calculation method was released in October 1985, and it was the first available methodology to provide automatic source code size prediction. Although only 30 common languages were initially sized, the mathematical logic of the SPR size prediction technique can be applied to any or all of the 500 to 1000 or so existing languages and dialects.

Size prediction is based on empirically derived observations of the level of languages and on the number of statements required to implement a single function point. The history of source code size prediction is older than function points themselves, and the coupling of these two fields of research has been very synergistic. Prior to the invention of function points, the problems of using lines-of-code metrics had been explored by the author at IBM's San Jose programming laboratory in the late 1960s and early 1970s. This research led to a technique of normalizing productivity rates by expressing all values in terms of "equivalent Assembler statements." For example, if a project were coded in Fortran and required 1000 source code statements and 2 months of effort, the productivity rate in terms of Fortran itself would be 500 statements per month.

However, the same functionality for the application, had it been written in basic assembly language, would have required about 3000 source code statements, or three times as much code as was actually needed to do the job in Fortran. Dividing the probable 3000 assembly statements by the 2 months of observed effort generated a productivity rate of 1500 "equivalent Assembler statements" per month.

The purpose of this conversion process was to express productivity rates in a constant fashion that would not be subject to the mathematical anomalies and paradoxes of using lines of code with the languages of varying power. In a sense, basic assembly language served as a kind of primitive form of function point: The number of assembly statements that might be required to produce an application stayed constant, although the actual number would fluctuate depending upon which language was actually used.

In working with it, it was realized that the normalization technique provided a fairly rigorous way of assigning a numeric level to the power of a language. In the 1960s and 1970s, the terms "low-level language" and "high-level language" had become widespread but "level" had never been mathematically defined.

The level of a language was defined at IBM as the number of basic assembly language statements it would take to produce the functionality of one statement in the target language. Thus Cobol is considered to be level-3 because it would take about three assembly language statements to create the functionality of one Cobol statement. Fortran also was considered a level-3 language, since it took about three assembly language statements to encode functionality available in one Fortran statement. PL/I was considered a level-4 language because it took about four assembly language statements to replicate the functions of one PL/I statement.

The simple mathematics associated with levels allowed very rapid size conversion from one language to another. For example, if a program was 10,000 statements in basic assembly language, then dividing 10,000 by 3 indicated that the same application would have taken about 3333 Fortran statements. Dividing 10,000 by 4 indicated that about 2500 PL/I statements might have been required.

By the middle 1970s, the author, at IBM, had assigned provisional levels to more than 50 languages and could convert source code sizes back and forth among any of them. However, source code size conversion is not the same as source code size prediction. It was still necessary to guess at how many statements would be required to build an application in any arbitrary language. Once that guess was made, size conversion into any other language was trivial.

After the publication of the function point metric in 1979, the situation changed significantly. Several researchers, including Albrecht himself and the author, began to explore function point totals and source code size simultaneously. The research quickly led to a new definition of language level: "The number of source code statements required to encode one function point." Since function point totals can be enumerated as early as the requirements phase, the new definition implied that true source code size prediction would now be possible.

Software Productivity Research merged the new definition of "level" with the old definition and produced a list of some 300 common languages[14] that showed both the average number of source code statements per function point and the number of assembly statements necessary to create the functionality of one statement in the target language. Thus, for example, Cobol remains a level-3 language and two facts can now be asserted: (1) An average of three statements in basic assembly language would be needed to encode the functions of one Cobol statement. (2) An average of 105 Cobol statements would be needed to encode one function point.

Empirically, languages of the same level require the same number of source code statements to implement one function point, but the complexity of the application and its code have a strong impact. Although Cobol, for example, averages about 105 source statements per function point, it has been observed to go as high as 160 source code statements per function point and as low as 50 source code statements per function point.

Because of individual programming styles and variations in the dialects of many languages, the relationship between function points and source code size often fluctuates widely, sometimes for reasons that are not currently understood. Nonetheless, the relation between function points and source code statements is an extremely interesting and useful new form of research that no doubt will continue for many years. The average levels and ratios of source statements to function points for 50 general language categories are shown in Table 2.15.

For language classes that contain many different dialects and variations, such as "third generation," a default value is provided. The default is intended to be the approximate average level of languages within that class, and it is useful when attempting to place other languages within the table. The data in Table 2.15 comes from several sources. For common languages such as Cobol, many hundreds of projects have now been evaluated by actual counts in terms of both function points and source code size. For some languages, textbooks provide simultaneous implementations of the same algorithms in various languages. For other languages, only a few programs have yet been enumerated.

TABLE 2.15 Language Levels and Expansion Factors from Function Points to Source Code Statements for Selected Languages

Language	Level	Source statements per function point
1. Low-level default	1.0	320
2. Machine language	1.0	320
3. First generation default	1.0	320
4. Basic assembly default	1.0	320
5. Macro assembly default	1.5	213
6. C default	2.5	128
7. Interpreted Basic default	2.5	128
8. Fortran II	2.5	128
9. Fortran 66	2.5	128
10. Second generation default	3.0	105
11. Procedural language default	3.0	105
12. Fortran 77	3.0	105
13. Algol 68	3.0	105
14. Algol W	3.0	105
15. Chill	3.0	105
16. ANSI Cobol 74	3.0	105
17. Coral 66	3.0	105
18. Jovial	3.0	105
19. Strongly typed default	3.0	105
20. ANSI Cobol 85	3.5	91
21. Pascal default	3.5	91
22. Compiled Basic default	3.5	91
23. PL/S	3.5	91
24. High-level default	3.5	91
25. Third generation default	3.5	91
26. Report generator default	4.0	80
27. PL/I	4.0	80
28. Modula 2	4.0	80
29. Problem-oriented default	4.5	71
30. Ada	4.5	71
31. Weakly typed default	5.0	64
32. Prolog	5.0	64
33. Lisp	5.0	64
34. Forth	5.0	64
35. ANSI/Quick/Turbo Basic	5.0	64
36. English-like default	6.0	51
37. AI shell default	6.5	49
38. Simulation default	7.0	46
39. Decision table default	7.0	46
40. Database default	8.0	40
41. Nonprocedural default	9.0	35
42. Decision support default	9.0	35
43. Statistical language default	10.0	32
44. APL	10.0	32
45. Object-oriented default	11.0	29
46. Fourth generation default	16.0	20
47. Program generator default	20.0	16
48. Query language default	25.0	13
49. Spreadsheet default	50.0	6
50. Fifth generation default (graphic icons)	75.0	4

The range of statements per function point is quite broad: several hundred percent in some cases because of variations in individual programming styles and unknown causes. The data is presented to illustrate general trends, and it has a very large margin of error. In Table 2.15, the term "default" is used to show the generic value that should be considered when there are a number of languages approximately the same in level. For example, "third generation" or "fourth generation" has been an umbrella term for many languages.

It should be recalled that when Mendeleev first published the periodic table of atomic elements in 1869, some elements were in the wrong place and some had not even been discovered. The organizing principle of the periodic table, however, added considerably to the ability of chemists and physicists to explore useful relationships. Very likely some of the languages in Table 2.15 are in the wrong place, and it is obvious that hundreds of other languages could be added. Here too, the organizing principle may be useful enough to compensate for errors in the individual placements.

There are from 500 to more than 1000 programming languages in current usage in the world if all the dialects of languages such as Fortran, Cobol, and Lisp are counted separately. The sample of 50 generic languages shown above account for perhaps 95 percent of all software ever written. Cobol is by far the commonest programming language, and almost 50 percent of U.S. software is still written in it. A fairly new language, C, appears to have leapt into second place, and it is followed by Ada, Pascal, Fortran, Basic, and various generators in approximately that order.

Many applications are written in mixed languages, so the question that arises is how sizing might be performed in applications that are partially implemented in two, three, or any number of languages.

For example, suppose the application contains 1000 source code statements in Cobol and 1000 source code statements in a database development language such as DL1. Cobol is a level-3 language which will average about 105 statements per function point; DL1 is a level-8 language which will average about 40 statements per function point. To calculate a function point approximation for the combination, it is only necessary to divide the source code size by the average expansion factors, which will yield about 9.5 function points for the Cobol and 25 function points for the DL1. The application as a whole will contain 34.5 function points and will have an average expansion of about 58 source code statements per function point, giving the language combination an effective level of about 5.5.

The calculation sequence for mixed languages is shown below:

$$1000 \text{ Cobol statements}/105 = 9.5 \quad \text{Cobol function points}$$
$$\underline{1000 \text{ DL1 statements}/40 = 25.0 \quad \text{DL1 function points}}$$
$$2000 \text{ total statements} = 34.5 \quad \text{total function points}$$

$$2000 \text{ total statements}/34.5 = 57.97 \text{ statements per function point}$$
$$320 \text{ Assembler statements}/57.97 = 5.52 \quad \text{effective language level}$$

The calculations for mixed languages are tedious if carried out by hand or with a calculator for more than two languages. However, it is very easy to construct a spreadsheet or a simple program that can perform the calculations for any number of languages. (The maximum number of languages observed in one application in recent years is 11, so a tool that could calculate up to a dozen languages should be sufficient.)

Backfiring function points for existing software

Many enterprises have enormous portfolios of applications and systems written, in some cases, years before function points were even invented. For historical purposes and consistency, it is often desirable to be able to calculate function point totals for existing applications.

It is possible, of course, to count the function point parameters by hand in existing software. But those who have actually attempted to do that find that several days of effort may be required, and the work is often unpleasant. In extreme cases, even the documentation that describes the application may be missing or incomplete and the original programming staff no longer works at the enterprise.

The SPR function point method supports retrofitting of function points to existing software as its eighth goal beyond the five basic IBM function point targets. This retrofitting of function points is termed "backfiring." Backfiring of function points is possible because the SPR algorithms are bidirectional. If function points, code complexity, and the source language are the inputs, then the algorithms will predict source code size. If the inputs are source code size, code complexity, and source language, the algorithms will predict function points. The time required to retrofit function points to existing applications with the backfire method is usually less than a minute, assuming source code counts are available.

Once a relation between function points and source code size is established for a language such as Cobol, it becomes possible to backfire function points to older applications for which source code size is known by simply dividing the source code size by the appropriate function point expansion factor. For example, the function point total for an application of 10,000 Cobol source statements can be found by simply dividing 10,000 by the average expansion rate of 105 Cobol statements per function point, which yields a total of 95 function points.

However, it is at this point that *code complexity* becomes an important factor in function point calculations and rejoins *problem complexity* and *data complexity* in calculations. Highly complex code tends to require more source statements per function point than extremely simple code. Thus, very complex Cobol may require 150 statements to implement one function point, whereas very simple Cobol may require only 65 statements per function point.

The approximate range of adjustments in how many statements are required to implement one function point is illustrated by Table 2.16. For backfiring, first refer to Table 2.15 for the average number of statements per function point. For example, if you have 10,500 Cobol statements in your application, then dividing by the average expansion factor of 105 indicates that you have a total of 1000 function points for a project of average complexity. Next, divide the initial function point total by the adjustment factor shown in Table 2.16. Thus, if your application is of simple overall complexity, say a complexity sum of 6, divide by .85 to create a probable function point total of 1176.

If, on the other hand, your application is complex, say a complexity sum of 12, divide by 1.15 to create a probable function point total of 869. The implications of these calculations lead to a concept termed "the conservation of function points." In essence, it takes fewer statements to implement one function point for simple applications than it does for complex ones. This concept is also true in reverse: When function points are backfired, highly complex code will contain fewer func-

TABLE 2.16 Adjustment Factors for Source Code Size Prediction

Sum of problem, code, and data complexity	Code size adjustment multiplier
3	0.70
4	0.75
5	0.80
6	0.85
7	0.90
8	0.95
9	1.00
10	1.05
11	1.10
12	1.15
13	1.20
14	1.25
15	1.30

tion points than the same volume of simple code. This concept is counterintuitive, but it appears to be empirically correct.

For normal forward function point calculations, complexity adjustments also are desirable. To use the information in Table 2.16 in forward mode, first sum the values of the three SPR complexity factors (problem, code, and data), which will create a total that ranges from 3 to 15. Next refer to Table 2.15 for the language and average number of statements per function point that you are interested in. Third, refer to Table 2.16 and select the source code size multiplier that matches your complexity sum. Fourth, multiply the average number of statements per function point by the adjustment factor from Table 2.16.

For example, if you are interested in Cobol the average number of statements per function point can be seen to be 105 by referring to Table 2.15. If the sum of your complexity factors is 12, multiply 105 by 1.15 to create a new value of 120.75 as the probable number of source code statements per function point in your application, adjusted for complexity.

Although the adjustments in Table 2.16 seem to give good results, it should be noted that the overall impact of complexity on source code size is not yet an exact science. It is quite possible for projects to behave very differently from the results shown here.

Function Points for Maintenance and Enhancement Projects

In 1990, somewhat more than 50 percent of the programmers in the United States were working on maintenance and enhancement of existing software.[15] Plainly, function points should be useful for those projects too. Indeed, the need to use function points for maintenance adds a ninth goal:

9. The metric should be useful for maintenance and enhancements.

Albrecht's 1984 revision to the IBM function point technique added the capability for using function points on maintenance and enhancement projects. For such projects there are three steps in using function points: (1) The function point total of the project before the changes are made is calculated. (2) The function point total for the update itself is calculated. (3) The function point total for the new release after the revision is calculated.

When used for maintenance and enhancements, function points can provide some useful insights into overall costs. There is a useful figure of merit that is starting to receive serious study: the maintenance assignment scope. An *assignment scope* is the amount of work for which one person is normally responsible in the course of a year. For maintenance purposes, it is an interesting topic to discover how many function points one maintenance programmer can comfortably handle. For modern well-structured software in a language such as Cobol, a maintenance programmer can be responsible for maintaining in excess of 1500 function points. For poorly structured, poorly documented aging software, the assignment scope seldom rises above 500 function points. Many enterprises average around 1000 function points as their normal assignment scopes. Restructuring and geriatric care for aging software can raise the assignment scope dramatically.

The 1986 Formation of the International
Function Point Users' Group (IFPUG)

By 1986, several hundred companies, many but not all of them clients of IBM, had been using function points. The association of IBM's commercial clients, GUIDE, had established a working group on function points in 1983, but by 1986 a critical mass of function point users had occurred. It was then decided to form a new nonprofit organization devoted exclusively to the utilization of function points and the propagation of data derived from function point studies.

The new organization was named the International Function Point Users Group. Because of the length of the name, the organization is more commonly identified by the abbreviation, IFPUG, as it quickly came to be called. IFPUG has evolved from its informal beginnings into a major new association concerned with every aspect of software measurement: productivity, quality, complexity, and even sociological implications.

The IFPUG counting practices committee has become a de facto standards group for normalizing the way function points are counted, and it has done much to resolve the variations in terminology and even the misconceptions that naturally occur when a metric gains wide international use.

The 1986 Development of Feature Points for
Real-Time and Systems Software

Function points were originally invented to solve the measurement problems of classical management information systems. This MIS origin means that function points are not necessarily perceived as optimal for real-time software such as missile defense systems, systems software such as operating systems, embedded software such as radar navigation packages, communications software such as telephone switching systems, process control software such as refinery drivers, engineering applications such as CAD and CIM, discrete simulations, or mathematical software.

When function points are applied to such systems, they, of course, generate counts, but the counts perhaps appear to be misleading for software that is high in algorithmic complexity but sparse in inputs and outputs. From both a psychological and practical vantage point, the harder kinds of systems software seem to require a counting method that is equivalent to function points but is sensitive to the difficulties brought on by high algorithmic complexity. The need to support real-time and systems software can be formally stated as a tenth goal for metrics:

10. The metric should work equally well with all MIS applications, systems software, real-time software, embedded software, and all other types of software.

In 1986, Software Productivity Research developed an experimental method for applying function point logic to system software such as operating systems and telephone switching systems.[16] To avoid confusion with the IBM function point method, this experimental alternative was called *feature points*. Since the initial results of using feature points have been favorable, the method has been experimentally applied to many kinds of software: systems software, embedded software, real-time software, CAD, AI, and even MIS software.

The SPR feature point metric is a superset of the IBM function point metric. It introduces a new parameter, algorithms, in addition to the five standard function point parameters. The algorithms parameter is assigned a default weight of 3. The feature point method also reduces the empirical weights for logical data files from IBM's average value of 10 down to an average value of 7 to reflect the somewhat reduced significance of logical files for systems software vis-à-vis information systems.

As can be seen, for applications in which the number of algorithms and logical data files are the same, function points and feature points will generate the same numeric totals. But when there are many more algorithms than files, which is not uncommon with systems software, the feature points will generate a higher total than function points. Conversely, if there are only a few algorithms but many files, which is common with some information systems, feature points will generate a lower total than function points. When feature points and function points are used on classical MIS projects, the results are often almost identical. For example, one small MIS project totaled 107 function points and 107 feature points. However, when applied to the harder forms of system software, the feature point counts are significantly higher. For a PBX telephone switch, the function point total was 1845 but the feature point total was 2300 because of the high algorithmic complexity of the application.

Although both the DeMarco bang metric and feature points are aimed at systems and scientific software, feature points differ from the DeMarco bang metric in these ways:

1. Feature points are intended to be mathematically mappable to function points. The bang metric does not aim at such equivalence, although it may be possible to convert counts from a subset of the DeMarco parameters into function points.

2. Feature points are intended to preserve the essential simplicity of the SPR counting concepts; the DeMarco bang metric opts for high precision at the cost of fairly substantial counting effort.

Since feature points are driven by algorithmic complexity, a definition of "algorithm" is appropriate. An algorithm is defined as the set of rules which must be completely expressed in order to solve a significant computational problem. For example, both a square root extraction routine or a Julian date conversion routine would be considered algorithms.

The SPR feature point method is similar in concept to function points, as can be seen from Table 2.17.

The SPR feature point method and the IBM function point method are obviously similar in concept, but what about pragmatic results? As of 1990, the feature point technique is still experimental and is still undergoing field trials. Some of the results to date are as follows: When feature points and function points are used on classical MIS

TABLE 2.17 The 1986 SPR Feature Point Method

Significant parameter		Empirical weight	
Number of algorithms?	_____	× 3 =	_____
Number of inputs?	_____	× 4 =	_____
Number of outputs?	_____	× 5 =	_____
Number of inquiries?	_____	× 4 =	_____
Number of data files?	_____	× 7 =	_____
Number of interfaces?	_____	× 7 =	_____
Unadjusted total			_____
Complexity adjustment			_____
Adjusted feature point total			_____

projects, the results are often almost identical; as mentioned above one project totaled 107 function points and 107 feature points. The function point and feature point values usually converge. But when used on real-time and systems software, feature points often generate higher totals than function points. In one small real-time project, the total was 45 function points but 70 feature points.

Counting and weighting algorithms

Since the most visible difference between function points and feature points is the new parameter for "algorithms," it is worthwhile to discuss algorithmic concepts and how algorithms can be counted. An algorithm is defined in standard software engineering texts as the set of rules which must be described and encoded to solve a computational problem. Some examples of typical algorithms include calendar date routines, square root extraction routines, and overtime pay calculation routines. For feature point counting purposes, an algorithm can be defined in the following terms: "An algorithm is a bounded computational problem which is included within a specific computer program."

Algorithms obviously vary in difficulty and complexity, and the SPR treatment of algorithms assumes a range of perhaps 10 to 1 for algorithmic difficulty (the absolute range in real life is no doubt as great as 1000 to 1, but ranges of that magnitude are difficult to encompass). Algorithms requiring only basic arithmetic operations or a few simple rules would be assigned a minimum value of 1. Algorithms requiring complex equations, matrix operations, and difficult mathematical and logical processing might be assigned a weight of 10. The default weight for a normal algorithm using ordinary mathematics would be 3.

Although more than 50 software engineering books that describe and discuss algorithms are in print, it is interesting that there is no available taxonomy for classifying algorithms other than purely ad hoc methods based on what the algorithm might be used for. There is a need for a taxonomy based on complexity, and hopefully the feature point research can move toward that goal.

The basis for the provisional weights for algorithms is twofold: (1) the number of calculation steps or rules required by the algorithm and (2) the number of factors or data elements required by the algorithm. Since the feature point method is still experimental, the approach to weighting algorithms is still under evolution. For provisional purposes, Table 2.18 shows approximate equivalence between weights, rules, and factors currently being considered. Powers of 2 provide the basis of Table 2.18, as can be seen.

To illustrate the terms "rule" and "factor," consider the following

TABLE 2.18 Provisional Algorithm Weights, Rules, and Factors

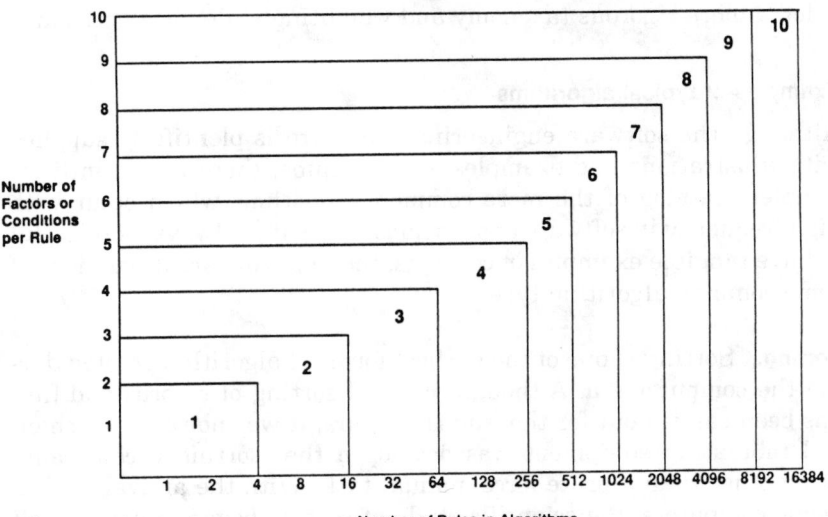

Number of Rules in Algorithms

example taken from an algorithm that selects activities in a software estimating tool: "If class is equal to 'military' and size is ⇒ 100 feature points, then independent verification and validation will be performed." The example is a single rule, and it contains two factors: class and size.

There are some supplemental rules for determining what algorithms are countable and significant:

1. The algorithm must deal with a solvable problem.
2. The algorithm must deal with a bounded problem.
3. The algorithm must deal with a definite problem.
4. The algorithm must be finite and have an end.
5. The algorithm must be precise and have no ambiguity.
6. The algorithm must have an input or starting value.
7. The algorithm must have output or produce a result.
8. The algorithm must be implementable in that each step must be capable of execution on a computer.
9. The algorithm can include or call upon subordinate algorithms.
10. The algorithm must be capable of representation via the standard structured programming concepts of sequence, if-then-else, do-while, CASE, etc.

These factors are currently being tuned and evaluated, since feature points are still experimental. However, research is underway to develop a more rigorous taxonomy and weighting scale for algorithms.

Examples of typical algorithms

Although the software engineering literature is plentifully supplied with illustrations and examples of algorithms, there is currently no complete catalog of the more common algorithms which occur with high frequency in software applications. Since it is always more useful to have tangible examples of concepts, the following are discussions of some common algorithm types:

Sorting. Sorting is one of the earliest forms of algorithm created during the computer era. Although physical sorting of records and files has been carried out for thousands of years, it was not until mechanical tabulating equipment was developed that sorting became anything other than a brute force manual task. With the arrival of electronic computers, the scientific study of sorting began. Sorting itself and the development of ever faster sorting algorithms have been among the triumphs of the software engineering community. Prior to about 1950, sorting methods were primarily simple and ad hoc. During the 1960s, 1970s, and on through to today, whole new families of sorting methods and improved algorithms were developed, including selection sorts, insertion sorts, bubble sorts, quicksort, and radix sorting.

Searching. Two of the primary functions of computers in their normal day-to-day business applications are sorting and searching. Here again, physical files have been searched for thousands of years, and techniques for facilitating the storage and retrieval of information long outdate the computer era. However, it was only after the emergence of electronic computers that the study of searching algorithms entered a rigorous and formal phase. This new research into sorting methods led to the development of binary searches, tree searches, indirect tree searches, radix searches, and many others.

Step-rate calculation functions. Under the concept of the graduated income tax, a certain level of taxable income is related to a certain tax rate. Higher incomes pay higher tax rates; lower incomes pay lower tax rates. The same logic of dealing with the dependent relations of two variables is perhaps the commonest general form of algorithm for business software. This logic, termed a "step-rate calculation function," which is used for income tax rates, can also apply to the rates for consuming public utilities such as electricity and water, for salary and performance calculations, and dividends.

Feedback loops. Feedback loops of various kinds are common algorithms in process control applications, hospital patient monitoring applications, and many forms of embedded software such as that for fuel injection, radar, and navigation. Classic feedback loops are much older than the computer era, of course, and one of the clearest examples is provided by the automatic governors on steam engines. Such governors were normally rotating metal weights whose rotation was driven by escaping steam. As the velocity of the steam increased when pressures went higher, the governors opened more widely and allowed excess steam to escape. This same concept of feedback between two variables is one of the major classes of algorithms for sensor-based applications.

Function point calculations. It is appropriate to conclude the discussion of representative algorithms with the observation that the calculation sequence for function points is itself an algorithm. Let us consider two practical examples. Suppose you were writing a computer program to calculate function points by using IBM's original 1979 methodology. The calculation sequence would be to multiply the raw data for inputs, outputs, inquiries, and master files by the empirical weights Albrecht derived, thus creating a subtotal of unadjusted function points. You would then multiply the unadjusted subtotal by a user-specified complexity factor to create the final adjusted function point total. This entire calculating sequence would comprise only one algorithm, the "function point calculation algorithm." Since the calculations consist of only five simple multiplications and two additions, the weight for this algorithm can be viewed as minimal and be assigned a weighting value of 1.

Now let us suppose you were writing a computer program to calculate function points by using IBM's methodology as it was revised in 1984 and currently exists in 1990. The calculation sequence today would be to first multiply and sum the file and data element references to determine high, low, or medium complexity of the five input parameters. You would then multiply raw data for inputs, outputs, inquiries, data files, and interfaces by the separate values for high, low, and medium complexity to quantify the unadjusted function point total.

Then the 14 influential factors would be summed and multiplied by .01 and the constant .65 would be added to create the influence multiplier weight. Finally, the unadjusted function points would be multiplied by the influence weight to yield the adjusted function point total. Calculating the function point total is still, of course, a single algorithm, but now the weight would appropriately be set at 3 to reflect the increased difficulty of the calculation sequence. Thus, the original 1979 version of IBM's function points could be programmed with a single algorithm having a total algorithmic weight of 1. The 1984 revisions of IBM's function point method now require a more normal weight of 3. As can be seen from the two examples, as the algorithmic complexity of an application moves up the difficulty scale, the feature point technique can follow closely.

Provisional Taxonomy of Algorithm Types

More than 20 software engineering books either include the word "algorithm" in the title or devote substantial sections of the text to a discussion of algorithms. Examples are *Algorithms* by Robert Sedgewick, *Algorithmics* by David Harel, and Donald Knuth's classic three-volume analysis of major algorithms. Yet in spite of the richness and volume of the literature on algorithms, a surprising gap occurs. There appears to be no overall taxonomy for classifying algorithms either by function or by difficulty or by any other regular dimension.

As part of the research associated with feature points, it has been necessary to create a provisional taxonomy of the algorithm types which are found in software programs and systems. The purposes of the taxonomy are several. The first is just to find a rational way of clumping algorithms into meaningful sets. Beyond this first purpose lie more serious ones: to establish a weighting scale of algorithmic difficulty and ultimately to develop a catalog of reusable algorithms capable of being utilized by many different applications.

The work of collecting and classifying all known algorithms will of necessity be a task of many years, and it will involve many researchers. The following is the provisional taxonomy circa 1990 developed by the author for performing initial weighting studies.

Rule-based algorithms

The rule-based algorithms share, as a generic characteristic, the fact that their operations are determined by reasonably well-defined rules that can be precisely articulated. Although some of the rule-based algorithms are extremely complex, their complexity would appear to be both finite and bounded.

Error-detection and correction algorithms

1. Signal error detection
2. Noise error detection
3. Transmission loss detection
4. Range error detection
5. Limits error detection

6. Syntactic error detection
7. Semantic error detection
8. Spelling error detection
9. Mathematical error detection
10. Data type error detection
11. Coordinates error detection
12. Factual error detection
13. Logic error detection
14. Paradox detection
15. Signal error correction
16. Noise error correction
17. Transmission loss correction
18. Range error correction
19. Limits error correction
20. Syntactic error correction
21. Semantic error correction
22. Spelling error correction
23. Mathematical error correction
24. Data type error correction
25. Coordinates error correction
26. Factual error correction
27. Logic error correction
28. Paradox correction

Data movement algorithms

1. Data compression
2. Data expansion
3. Data transmission
4. Data reception
5. Data storage
6. Data retrieval

Data selection and manipulation algorithms

1. Selection

2. Comparison

3. Sorting

4. Merging

5. Extracting

6. Substitution

7. Pattern matching

8. Replication

9. Encrypting

10. Decrypting

11. Aliasing

12. Conversion

13. Parsing

14. Augmentation

15. Tagging

16. Hashing

Data formatting and presentation algorithms

1. Formatting

2. Conversion to graphs

3. Printer drivers

4. Plotter drivers

5. Screen handling

6. Color selection

Device control algorithms

1. Interrupt sensing

2. Interrupt servicing

3. Sensor processing

4. Feedback

5. Device wake-up

6. Positioning (1 dimension)

7. Positioning (2 dimensions)

8. Positioning (3 dimensions)

9. Acceleration control

10. Velocity control

Arithmetic and logical algorithms

1. Arithmetic algorithms

2. Statistical algorithms

3. Accounting algorithms

4. Date calculation algorithms

5. Time calculation algorithms

6. Standard logic algorithms

Induction-based algorithms

The induction-based algorithms tend to operate in the reverse direction from the rule-based algorithms. They examine a large number of specific instances and then attempt to derive the rules which govern the class memberships of the instances. The overall difficulty and complexity of induction-based algorithms far exceed the values for any of the rule-based algorithms. Applications containing substantial quantities of induction-based algorithms are at the extreme limits of human endeavors.

1. Fuzzy logic

2. Pattern recognition

3. Classification

4. Rule derivation

5. Language translation

6. Prediction of future events

7. Learning

8. Diagnosis

9. Navigation

10. Viral detection

11. Viral elimination

12. Strange attractors and chaotic conditions

Additional considerations in the domain of algorithms include whether the algorithm in question lends itself to sequential or parallel processing. In addition, it is desirable to consider these aspects of algorithms:

1. Uniqueness

2. Correctness

3. Computational complexity

4. Length

5. Performance

6. Sensitivity

7. Selectivity

The research centering around the practical applications of feature points has opened up some interesting and potentially significant gaps in the software engineering literature. Notably, there seems to be no standard taxonomy for classifying algorithms, and there is no standard weighting scale for judging their difficulty or complexity.

From discussions with companies, such as DEC, Tektronix, and Motorola, that are experimenting with the feature point method, the most common question asked concerns the level of granularity of the algorithms to be counted. If the basic concept is held in mind that an "algorithm" should be bounded and complete and should perform a fairly significant business or technical function, then some practical illustrations of algorithms can be given. For example:

- In telephone switching systems, call routing is an appropriate algorithmic topic.
- In PC operating systems, floppy disk formatting is an example of an algorithm.
- In payroll programs, the calculations for hourly, exempt, managerial, and contractor pay are examples of normal algorithms.
- In process control applications, pressure monitoring and feedback are examples.

To give a somewhat more detailed example of typical algorithms and the weights assigned to them, Table 2.19 shows the major algorithms and the assigned weights in a software resource, cost, and quality estimating program as analyzed by the author.

As can be seen from Table 2.19, the level of granularity of typical algorithms is reasonably fine but not excessively so. (From examining the actual source code of the project used to provide the data of Table 2.19, the algorithms weighted 1 all took fewer than 25 statements in C to implement, the level-2 weighted algorithms usually took less than 50 C statements, the level-3 weighted algorithms usually took fewer than 100 C statements, and so on.)

Although the feature point metric is still experimental and is un-

TABLE 2.19 Examples of Algorithms in a Software Estimating Program

Algorithm	Algorithm weight
1. Defect potential prediction	3
2. Defect removal prediction	2
3. Function point calculation	2
4. Source code size prediction	2
5. Backfire function point prediction	2
6. Document size prediction	3
7. Test case and test run prediction	2
8. Reliability prediction	2
9. Paid overtime impact on project	1
10. Unpaid overtime impact on project	2
11. Development staff, effort, and schedule prediction	4
12. Activity schedule overlap prediction	3
13. Annual maintenance effort and staff prediction	3
14. Annual enhancement effort and staff prediction	3
15. Overall aggregation of project effort and costs	2
16. Overall calculation of project schedule	2
17. Effort and cost normalization	1
18. International currency conversion	1
19. Inflation rate calculation	1
20. Normalization of data to selected base metric	1

dergoing trials, it may be of interest to see some representative results. Table 2.20 gives the ranges of a dozen project types, including
sizes and overall productivity results that occur when using the feature point metric and backfiring data.

TABLE 2.20 Selected Project Results When Using the Feature Point Metric

Project type	Size range in feature points	Productivity range in feature points
1. Airline reservation	25,000–50,000	0.5–5.0
2. Billing systems	2,500–7,500	3.0–20.0
3. CAD software	600–2,500	1.0–6.5
4. Integrated CASE tools	1,000–15,000	2.5–17.5
5. Public switches	4,000–25,000	0.3–4.5
6. Compilers	600–2,000	2.5–25.0
7. Insurance claims handling	9,000–25,000	3.0–18.0
8. Operating systems	5,000–50,000	0.5–6.5
9. PBX switches	1,000–5,000	1.0–5.5
10. Project planning tools	250–1,500	3.0–12.0
11. Spreadsheet packages	1,000–3,000	2.0–10.0
12. Word processing packages	500–3,500	4.5–12.5

TABLE 2.21 Ratios of Feature Points to Function Points for Selected Application Types

Application	Function points	Feature points
Batch MIS projects	1	0.80
On-line MIS projects	1	1.00
On-line database projects	1	1.00
Switching systems projects	1	1.20
Embedded real-time projects	1	1.35
Factory automation projects	1	1.50
Diagnostic and prediction projects	1	1.75

Choosing function points or feature points

For applications in which the number of algorithms is uncertain or in which algorithmic factors are not significant, function points would be the appropriate choice for a metric. Many business applications fall within this category, perhaps accounting software, customer information systems, and marketing support systems.

For applications in which the number of algorithms is countable, and in which algorithmic factors are significant, feature points would be the appropriate choice for a metric. Many scientific, engineering, and systems applications fall within this category, perhaps telephone switching systems, process control systems, and embedded software such as fuel injection.

Although the feature point method is still experimental and comparatively sparse data is available for it, the results of some early side-by-side comparisons between function points and feature points are interesting. Table 2.21 illustrates the experimental ratios between function points and feature points for sample kinds of software.

The 1987 Merger of Function Points and Halstead Metrics

In 1987, Don Reifer published a description[17] of a metric that was based on the concept of merging the Albrecht function point technique with the older Halstead software science metric.[18] The latter is based on the work of the late Dr. Maurice Halstead of Purdue University. Like many researchers, Halstead was troubled by the ambiguity and paradoxical nature of "lines of code." His technique was an attempt to resolve the problems by looking at the specific subelements of lines of code. He divided code into two atomic units: the executable or command portion (which he termed "operators") and the data descriptive portion (which he termed "operands"). The Halstead metric centers around counts of four separate values:

1. The total number of unique operators
2. The total number of unique operands
3. The total quantity of operators in an application
4. The total quantity of operands in an application

From those four counts, a number of supporting metrics are derived including:

1. The program's vocabulary (sum of unique operators and operands)
2. The program's length (sum of total operators and total operands)

There are a number of conceptual and practical difficulties about attempting to merge function points with the Halstead software science technique. From a conceptual standpoint, function points are intended to be independent of the programming language used and capable of being applied early in a project's life cycle, as during requirements and design. Since the Halstead software science metric is basically only a more sophisticated way of counting lines of code, it appears to be a poor choice for metrics applied early in the life cycle and also to be counter to the essential philosophy of function points as being language-independent.

The practical difficulties lie in the ambiguities and uncertainties of the Halstead software science metric itself. An attempt by ITT statisticians in 1981[19] to replicate some of the published findings associated with the Halstead software science metric uncovered anomalies in the fundamental data and a number of questionable assertions. The final conclusion was that the Halstead software science metric was so intrinsically ambiguous and studies using it were so poorly constructed and controlled that the results were useless for serious economic study purposes.

There are also a few problems of an historical nature with the fundamental assertions of the software science metric. For example, the software science literature has made the correct assertion that there is a strong relation between the length and vocabulary of a program. That is, large systems will use a richer set of operator and operand constructs than small programs.

Although that observation is correct, it had actually been noted in 1935 by the linguist George Zipf for natural languages such as English and Mandarin Chinese. Indeed, Zipf's law on the relation of vocabulary and length covers the topic. As it happens, there appears to be a constant relation between length and vocabulary that would be true even if the language consisted of random characters divided into words or random lengths!

Unfortunately, few of the software science articles and reports build on those findings from conventional linguistics, and it is fair to say that the whole software science concept suffers from a tendency to be unfamiliar with conventional linguistics, even though the two domains are covering the same grounds. If the software science community had included the ideas published by linguists such as Zipf, Whorf, and Chomsky, the software science concept would not appear to be on such shaky intellectual ground.

The 1988 Publication of the British Mark II Function Point Method

In January 1988, Charles Symons, of Nolan, Norton & Company in London, published a description of his Mark II Function Point metric in the *IEEE Transactions on Software Engineering.*[20] Although Symons' work had started in the early 1980s and was announced in England in 1983, it was not well known in the United States prior to the IEEE publication in 1988.

Symons had been carrying out some function point studies at Xerox and other companies in the United Kingdom, and he had formed the opinion that the 1984 IBM method might perhaps be modified. The essence of Symons' concerns were four:

1. He wanted to reduce the subjectivity in dealing with files by measuring entities and relations among entities.

2. He wanted to modify the function point approach so that it would create the same numeric totals regardless of whether an application was implemented as a single system or as a set of related subsystems.

3. He wanted to change the fundamental rationale for function points away from value to users and switch it to the effort required to produce the functionality.

4. He felt that the 14 influential factors cited by Albrecht and IBM were insufficient, and so he added six factors.

When carried to completion, Symons' modifications of the basic function point methodology was sufficiently different from IBM's to merit the "Mark II" nomenclature. When counting the same application, the resulting function point totals differ between the IBM and Mark II by sometimes more than 30 percent, with the Mark II technique usually generating the larger totals.

Viewed objectively, Symons' four concerns are not equal in their impact, and his modifications have pros and cons. His first concern, introducing entities and relationships, does add a new dimension of rigor to function point counting, and his suggestion is starting to find widespread acceptance. His second concern, wanting total function point counts to stay constant regardless of whether an application is monolithic or distributed, is debatable and questionable. For example, in a construction project involving physical objects such as living space, there will be very significant differences in providing 1500 ft^2 of housing in the form of 10 single-family homes or in the form of 10 apartments in a single large building. It is obvious to architects and contractors that very different quantities of lumber, cement, roofing, and so on, will be required depending upon which construction choice is made.

In a parallel fashion, an application developed as an integrated, monolithic system will certainly have different needs and requirements than if the same functionality is implemented in 10 independent programs. At the very least, the interfaces will be quite different. Therefore, attempting to generate a constant function point count regardless of whether an application is monolithic or distributed seems hazardous.

Symons' third concern, wishing to change the basis of the function point method from "user value" to "development effort," appears to be a step in a retrograde direction. To continue with the parallel of the building trade, the value of a home is only partly attributable to the construction costs. The other aspects of home value deal with the architectural and design features of the home, the charm of the site, the value of surrounding homes, convenience of location, and many other topics.

In Albrecht's original concept, function points were analogous to the work of an architect in home construction: The architect works with the clients on the features and design that satisfy the clients' needs. In other words, the architect works with the client on the functionality required. In Symons' Mark II concept, function points become analogous to the work of a contractor in home construction: The contractor brings in equipment and workers and constructs the home. In other words, the contractor builds the functionality required.

Albrecht's original concept of function points appears to be preferable to the Mark II concept: Function points measure the size of the features of an application that users care about. The costs, schedules, and efficiency with which those features are built is a separate topic and should not be mixed up with the features themselves.

Symons' fourth modification, adding to IBM's 14 supplemental factors, is in keeping with his overall philosophy of switching function points from a metric dealing with value and size to a metric also including effort. The factors added by Symons are:

- Software with major systems software interfaces
- Software with very high security considerations
- Software providing direct access for third parties
- Software with special documentation requirements
- Software needing special user training
- Software needing special hardware

The additional factors considered by Symons are in real life often significant. The disadvantage in the context of function points is twofold: (1) If additional factors that influence a project are considered thoroughly, 6 is insufficient and more than 100 such factors might be added; (2) whenever such factors are added as complexity adjustments, they typically drive up the function point totals compared to the IBM standard. As more factors are added, the function point total will tend to creep up over time for reasons that appear unjustified under the assumptions of the original IBM assertions.

A practical business difficulty also stands in the way of utilizing the Mark II function point method conveniently. Unlike the IBM method, which is in the public domain, the Mark II method is a proprietary technique of the consulting group of Nolan, Norton & Company, which is a subsidiary of the larger international consulting company of Peat, Marwick, & Mitchell. Any form of automation of the Mark II method would at the moment require a licensing arrangement from the owners, which is a disadvantage in gaining widespread acceptance.

The 1989 Publication of the Dreger Function Point Tutorial

Function points were first publicly discussed in October 1979. The first college-level introductory text on function points, Dreger's *Function Point Analysis*,[21] was published in the autumn of 1989, almost exactly 10 years after the initial public presentation. Dreger's book assumes no prior knowledge of function points, and it is intended to take the reader step-by-step through the rules and regulations associated with counting function points by using the standard IBM 1984 methodology. The book succeeds quite well in accomplishing its goals, with the minor exception that Dreger tends to count slightly differently than Albrecht in a few situations. Notably, Dreger tends to accumulate slightly more kinds of things for inputs, outputs, and inquiries than would be normal when using the regular IBM method. The variations can be ignored by experienced function point users, and they are not likely to occur frequently in any case.

For first-time users of function points who would like a gentle introduction to the concept with plentiful examples and useful illustrations, the Dreger book succeeds admirably.

The 1990 IFPUG Standard Counting Practices Manual

As the number of users of function points continued to grow, more and more variations started to appear. The International Function Point Users Group (IFPUG) was created in 1986, and by 1990 it had more than 250 organizations as members. Since many of the function point users in the United States and Europe belonged to it, IFPUG became a natural focal point for function point standardization. It created several special interest groups and committees to deal with the expansion of function points into new domains. Of particular importance has been the work of the counting practices committee, which is the working group charged with creating standard guidelines and resolving inconsistencies.

The task of the counting practices committee has not been easy, since each person who created a variation in function point counting techniques naturally would want his or her particular variation endorsed by the committee. However, after several false starts and many drafts and revisions, the committee published the first version of the new counting practices manual in April 1990 at the Orlando IFPUG conference.[22]

The IFPUG counting practices generally follow the IBM 1984 standards, although a number of variations and extensions have occurred. A minor but noticeable variation concerns the nomenclature and abbreviations used by IFPUG for inputs, outputs, inquiries, and so on. Since any reasonably large case study or set of examples must repeat some of the terminology many times, the most common practice is to simply abbreviate the widely utilized terms. The following are the variations between the 1984 IBM terminology and the 1990 IFPUG terminology for the same concepts:

1984 IBM nomenclature	1990 IFPUG nomenclature
External input type (IT)	External inputs (EI)
External output type (OT)	External outputs (EO)
Logical internal file type (FT)	Internal logical files (ILF)
External interface type (EI)	External interface files (EIF)
External inquiry type (QT)	External inquiries (EQ)

At a technical level, the 1990 IFPUG counting rules both extend and somewhat modify the 1984 IBM standard. Here are brief examples of the 1990 IFPUG variations:

External inputs. The IFPUG rules count duplicate inputs twice, whereas the IBM rules count the input only once. For example, a banking system which accepts a deposit via an ATM or via manual methods would count the deposit as two inputs by using the 1990 IFPUG rules but one input by using the 1984 IBM rules.

External outputs. The IFPUG rules count duplicate outputs for each occurrence, whereas the IBM rules are not specific. For example, an output report that can either be printed on paper or sent to a disk-based print file would be counted twice under the 1990 IFPUG rules.

Internal logical files. The IFPUG rules on internal files generally agree with IBM, but they offer some extensions and additional refinements. For example, if a logical file is maintained by several applications, the 1990 IFPUG rules permit it to be counted by each application. The 1984 IBM rules do not mention this point at all and hence might be open to alternative interpretations.

External interface files. The potential variations between IBM and IFPUG are perhaps greatest in the way external interface files are counted. The 1990 IFPUG rules count external interfaces in behalf of the "receiving" application but not in behalf of the "sending" application. The 1984 IBM rules, on the other hand, credit the interface file to both the sender and the receiver. The reason for the variation is that the sending application may have no knowledge of what is happening to the interface data once it exits; it may never be received, for example. However, an application must clearly understand incoming or received interface data.

External inquiries. Inquiries have long been among the most troublesome factors when counting function points, because of the need to consider both the input and output portions. The 1990 IFPUG rules provide significantly expanded sets of examples dealing with queries. Indeed, some of the 1990 IFPUG examples are based on factors, such as context-sensitive HELP screens, which barely existed in 1984. Under the new IFPUG rules, context-sensitive HELP screens count as inquiries, as do several other forms of HELP. The 1990 IFPUG rules differ from the 1984 IBM rules in some other respects as well. For example, the new IFPUG rules state that menu screens which provide both screen and data selection should be counted as inquiries, which differs from the IBM 1984 interpretation.

Although the differences among the function point methods are noticeable, it is highly encouraging that the IFPUG counting practices committee exists at all: For almost 50 years, lines-of-code metrics have been used without the review of any standardization body of any kind. The IFPUG counting practices committee is starting to provide a true international forum for serious discussions about functional metrics, and thus will benefit the software community as a whole.

The 1990 IEEE Draft Standard on Productivity Measurement

Function points provide only part of the information needed for software productivity measurement. The other key factors include a standard set of tasks or chart of accounts and descriptions of the tools, methods, and approaches used on the projects being measured. The productivity measurement committee of the software engineering subgroup of the IEEE has been charged with drafting an international standard for software productivity measurement. The draft IEEE standard[23] existed when this book was being written, but it had not yet been voted on. Fortunately, the IEEE productivity measurement committee has been in communication with the IFPUG counting practices committee, and it appears that the function point metric will be included in the IEEE standard and endorsed by the IEEE.

The 1990 SPR Approximation Method

Function points are starting to create such an explosion of new research and new findings that it will probably be necessary to support the function point method with its own journal simply to handle the volume of new concepts that are emerging. For example, David Herron of SPR has addressed the problem of attempting to create accurate function point counts in the absence of full knowledge of an application.[24] Although at first this seems like an impossible task, Herron's method has considerable merit and appears to be leading to some powerful new capabilities.

Early in a project's requirements, it may not be possible to state with certainty the exact number of inputs, outputs, inquiries, logical files, and interfaces which will comprise the application. Prior to the Herron method, it was usually necessary to simply guess at the missing elements. Herron observed, however, that knowledge about a project is not homogeneous. Some topics are explored earlier than others. His method is based on discovering and utilizing relations between the factors that are known with some precision early and the "hidden" factors that have not yet been worked out in detail. His method is based on observable ratios of inputs, outputs, inquiries, files, and interfaces derived from various kinds of software. For example, when considering an application type such as accounting systems, Herron has observed that a pattern such as the following might occur:

Factor	Percentage of functionality
Inputs	30
Outputs	20
Inquiries	5
Logical files	40
Interfaces	5
Total	100

Herron makes the reasonable assumption that other accounting systems might well follow the pattern expressed by this one. He also makes the corollary observation that accounting systems seem to be driven by inputs and file structures, so they would probably be the first topics explored in detail. Assuming that the two assertions are correct, once a single factor (such as the inputs) has been explored in detail, it is possible to extrapolate and make reasonable assumptions about the missing or unexplored factors.

Herron's research is now moving into the task of identifying the relevant patterns associated with application classes and types such as insurance claims processing, banking transactions, process control applications, and switching systems. Preliminary results are both interesting and encouraging, and they show both the versatility of the function point method and the burst of intellectual excitement that permeates the software industry now that workable metrics exist.

The 1990 Albrecht Terminology Revision

In 1989, A. J. Albrecht retired from IBM after many years of service. His retirement did not, of course, end his interest in function points, and he put together a new and comprehensive tutorial[10] on function points which was based not only on IBM's research but also on the work of IFPUG, Software Productivity Research, and others as well. The new tutorial includes the rules for counting function points in the IBM, IFPUG, and SPR fashions, and it also encompasses the SPR feature point concept. Although the tutorial was constructed in 1989, it has been available in the U.S. only since early 1990.

The purpose of the tutorial is to broaden the appreciation of functional metrics as a general-purpose technique that can be applied to systems and scientific software as well as to classic management information systems. The tutorial has the advantage of building on the past 15 years of functional metric research, and so it is able to encompass many topics that were not previously dealt with in function point training, such as explaining the rationale behind the major function point "flavors" and dealing with the differences in productivity rates between systems software and management information systems.

The tutorial marks the first educational attempt to integrate the major forms of functional metrics and to show the similarities and differences among them. Thus, the tutorial not only includes pragmatic case studies of counting techniques but also includes comparative discussions of the entire domain of functional metric research. As part of the tutorial material, Albrecht adopted a slightly different nomenclature and a revised set of abbreviations for the five function point parameters. For comparison, here are the key terms and concepts for the four major "flavors" of function point and feature point terminologies:

1984 IBM nomenclature	1990 IFPUG nomenclature
External input type (IT)	External inputs (EI)
External output type (OT)	External outputs (EO)
Logical internal file type (FT)	Internal logical files (ILF)
External interface type (EI)	External interface files (EIF)
External inquiry type (QT)	External inquiries (EQ)

1990 Albrecht nomenclature	1986 SPR feature point nomenclature
Input type (IT)	Inputs (IT)
Output type (OT)	Outputs (OT)
Internal user data group (IU)	Logical files (FT)
External user data group (EU)	Interfaces (EI)
External inquiries (QT)	Inquiries (QT)
	Algorithms (AT)

When all of the terminologies are displayed simultaneously, it can easily be seen that they describe the same constructs. However, for users familiar with one terminology, it would be distracting to see data displayed with one of the others. One of the anticipated events of 1991 will be a standardization of terms and abbreviations for all of the various concepts associated with functional metrics.

Future Technical Developments in Functional Metrics

Functional metrics have made remarkable progress over the past 11 years. There is now a major international society of functional metric users. A working standards committee exists, and it is actively addressing both extensions to the methodology and clarification of the topics that require it. The functional metric techniques have spread from their origins in management information systems and are starting to be used for systems and scientific software as well. Exciting new developments in functional metrics are occurring on almost a daily basis. It is apparent that the following evolution of the functional metrics concepts should occur over the next few years.

Automatic derivation of function or feature points from design

Since the major factors which go into function point and feature point calculations are taken from the design of the application, it is an obvious step to forge a direct connection between design tools and a function point calculation tool. This desirable step should enable automatic and nonsubjective counts of the basic functional metric parameters. Complexity adjustments, however, may still require some form of human intervention. It is not impossible to envision that even complexity adjustments may eventually become precise and objective as a by-product of research getting under way. Software Productivity Research, for example, has begun a study of more than 150 specification and design methodologies with a view to extracting the basic function point parameters from the standard design representations or, alternatively, making minimal modifications to the standard design representations in order to facilitate direct extraction of function point or feature point parameters.

Automatic backfiring of function points and feature points from source code

Now that function points are becoming a de facto standard metric for productivity studies, there is significant interest in retrofitting function points to aging applications that might have been created even before function points were invented or, in any case, which did not use function points during their development cycles. Since backfiring of function points or converting source code size into function point totals is already possible, it is an obvious next step to automate the process. That is, it is technically possible to build a scanning tool that would analyze source code directly and create function point totals as one of its outputs.

Automatic conversion from function points to feature points, Mark II function points, DeMarco bang metrics, and other variations

One unfortunate aspect of the rapid growth of functional metrics has been the proliferation of many variations, each of which uses different

counting methods and creates different totals. It appears both technically possible and also desirable to establish conversion factors which
will allow data to be mathematically changed from method to method.
Such conversion techniques exist between the IBM function point
method and the SPR function and feature point methods, and indeed
have been done automatically by the CHECKPOINT® software tool.[13]
However, conversion factors for the DeMarco bang metric, the Reifer
merger with software science, and the British Mark II method have
not yet been published.

Extension and refinement of complexity calculations

It has been pointed out many times that the possible Achilles heel of
functional metrics in general and function points in particular is the
way complexity is treated. In the original 1979 version of function
points, complexity was purely subjective and covered a very small
range of adjustments. In the 1984 revision, the range of adjustments
was extended and the rigor of complexity analysis was improved, but
much subjectivity still remains. This assertion is also true of the other
flavors of functional metrics, such as the SPR function and feature
point techniques.

There are several objective complexity metrics, such as the McCabe
cyclomatic and essential complexity methods,[25] that appear to be
promising as possible adjuncts to functional metrics. Other researchers, such as Wayne Smith of Computer Power, have started exploring
possibilities for extending and refining business complexity concepts
for use with functional metrics. SPR has identified 20 different forms
of complexity that are possible candidates for future coupling with
functional metrics, including computational complexity, semantic
complexity, entropic complexity, and many others.[26] In any event,
complexity research in the context of functional metrics is undergoing
energetic expansion.

Publication of estimating templates based on functional metrics

From 1979 through 1990, function points had been applied to thousands
of applications. Now that so many applications have been explored, a
new form of research is starting to emerge: Patterns or "templates" of
function point totals for common application types are discovered. It
can be anticipated that the next decade will witness the publication of
standard guidelines, empirically derived, for many different kinds of
applications. These templates will allow very early estimating.

Utilization of functional metrics for studies of software consumption

During the first decade of the growth of functional metrics, almost all the studies were aimed at exploring software development or production. However, functional metrics have very powerful, and currently only partly explored, capabilities for studying software consumption as well. It can be anticipated that the next decade will see a host of new studies dealing with usage patterns and the consumption patterns of software functions.

Utilization of functional metrics for software value analysis

Assessing or predicting the value of software has been one of the most intractable measurement and estimation problems of the software era. Since the previous lines-of-code metric had essentially no commercial value and was neither the primary production unit nor the primary consumption unit of large software projects, it was essentially useless for value analysis. Although functional metrics are only just starting to be applied to value analysis, the preliminary results are encouraging enough to predict much future progress in this difficult area.

Overall prognosis for functional metrics

The software industry suffered for more than 45 years from lack of adequate measurements. Now that functional metrics have made adequate measurements technically possible, it can be anticipated that the overall rate of progress in both software productivity and software quality will improve. Measurement alone can focus attention on areas of strength and weakness, and now that software can be measured effectively, it can also be managed effectively for the first time since the software industry began!

Applying Functional Metrics to a Case Study

It is almost always easier to understand concepts from examples than from rules. Following are six examples of functional metric counting for the same application. The first example illustrates IBM's 1979 function point method, followed by IBM's 1984 function point method, then SPR's 1985 function point method, SPR's 1985 backfire method in both average and adjusted flavors, and finally SPR's 1986 feature point method.

The basic application in the example

The application to be sized in all four examples is an elementary one. The task is to write a personal computer program that automates the calculations for generating function points. The language used for the application is compiled Quick Basic™ on an IBM personal computer. The specific form of function point calculations for this application is similar to the original 1979 version of Albrecht and IBM. The sample application is only to calculate function points for new projects, not for enhancement or maintenance projects.

1. The application has one input screen through which users enter the name of the project being sized and also enter the number of inputs, outputs, data files, and inquiries and the user-specified complexity adjustment for a project for which the function points are to be calculated.

2. The application has one output screen, identical to the input screen except for the calculated outputs, that gives the results of the function point calculations.

3. The application also has the capability of printing out a one-page report showing the function point questions and the calculated results, so there are two outputs from the application. (*Note:* it is obvious that a standard print-screen function would suffice for this application, but assume that the application will develop its own print function.)

4. The application can save the inputs to a floppy disk if the user requests, so there is a single very simple data file involved with the application.

5. The application has no inquiry capabilities or any interfaces to other applications.

6. The processing logic consists of multiplying the four function point parameters by the standard weights, summing the results, and adjusting for subjective complexity. These processing steps comprise only a single algorithm of negligible complexity, and hence the algorithmic weight is 1.

7. The application is written in a compiled Microsoft Quick Basic™, and it required 600 logical source code statements, excluding remarks. Analysis of the source code revealed that 35 percent of the code was used to format and construct the input/output screens, including range and validity checking of inputs, 30 percent was used for formatting and printing the output, 25 percent was used for

disk save and retrieve operations, and only 10 percent was used for the arithmetic calculations themselves.

8. The application's input and output screens are the same; they are shown here.

FUNCTION POINT CALCULATOR

APPLICATION NAME _____

FUNCTION POINT FACTORS	RAW COUNT	EMPIRICAL WEIGHT	UNADJUSTED TOTALS
NUMBER OF INPUTS?	_____	× 4 =	_____
NUMBER OF OUTPUTS?	_____	× 5 =	_____
NUMBER OF INQUIRIES?	_____	× 4 =	_____
NUMBER OF DATA FILES?	_____	× 10 =	_____
NUMBER OF INTERFACES?	_____	× 7 =	_____
UNADJUSTED TOTAL			_____
COMPLEXITY MULTIPLIER (0.65 TO 1.35)			_____
FINAL ADJUSTED FUNCTION POINT TOTAL			_____
PRINT RESULTS (Y/N)?	_____		
SAVE FILE TO DISK (Y/N)?	_____		
RUN PROGRAM AGAIN (Y/N)?	_____		

Counting Function Points with the 1979 IBM Method

In the original 1979 version of function points, only four parameters were used. The complexity adjustment was purely subjective, and it covered a range of only ±25 percent, which is not broad enough to handle the real-life impacts of complexity on software.

Parameter	Count		Weight		Total
Number of inputs	1	×	4	=	4
Number of outputs	2	×	5	=	10
Number of inquiries	0	×	4	=	0
Number of master files	1	×	10	=	10
Unadjusted total				=	24
Complexity adjustment (± 25%)				=	−6
Adjusted total				=	18

In considering the implications of the 1979 version of function points for this very simple application, two problems are evident: (1) The empirical weight of 10 for master files seem excessive for merely storing data on a floppy disk. (2) The complexity adjustment is purely subjective and does not cover a very broad range. The −25 percent complexity weight was the maximum allowed under the 1979 conventions, and it was established by nothing more than guesswork.

Counting Function Points with IBM'S 1984 Revision

In the 1984 revision, the range of complexity adjustments was extended from a subjective ±25 percent to a more objective technique that allows adjustments spanning a range of ±125 percent. The revisions include both range adjustments in the standard empirical weights and processing adjustments based on 14 influential factors as illustrated below.

Parameter	Low complexity	Medium complexity	High complexity	Total
External inputs	1 × 3 = 3	0 × 4 = 0	0 × 6 = 0	3
External outputs	2 × 4 = 8	0 × 5 = 0	0 × 7 = 0	8
Logical files	1 × 7 = 7	0 × 10 = 0	0 × 15 = 0	7
Interfaces files	0 × 5 = 0	0 × 7 = 0	0 × 10 = 0	0
Inquiries	0 × 3 = 0	0 × 4 = 0	0 × 6 = 0	0
Unadjusted total				18

Once the basic parameters have been enumerated, multiplied by the empirical weights, and summed to create the unadjusted total, the next step is to evaluate the influence of 14 factors on the application. These factors are evaluated on a scale that runs from 0 to 5, with the following definitions:

0	The factor is not present or has no influence
1	Insignificant influence
2	Moderate influence
3	Average influence
4	Significant influence
5	Strong influence

For the simple application being used in the case study, the results of the 14 influential factors are as follows:

Data communications	0
Distributed functions	0
Heavily used configuration	0
Transaction rate	0
On-line data entry	2
End-user efficiency	3
On-line update	2
Complex processing	0
Installation ease	0
Operational ease	3
Multiple sites	0
Facilitated change	0
Total influence sum	= 10

After the 14 influential factors have been totaled, they must be converted into a complexity multiplier by using the following formula:

$$(\text{Sum}^*.01) + .65 = \text{multiplier}$$

Applying the formula yields these results

$$(10^*.01) + .65 = .75$$

As can be noted, the range of possible adjustments with the above formula is from a low of .65 (assuming all 14 factors are 0s) to a high of 1.35 (assuming all 14 factors are 5s). The final step in generating a function point total by using the revised IBM method is to multiply the unadjusted function points by the adjustment multiplier:

Unadjusted function point total	18
Processing adjustment multiplier	0.75
Adjusted function point total	13.5

Since function points are normally dealt with as integers, it would be appropriate to round the results to the nearest integer value, so the final adjusted function point total would be 14.

Counting Function Points with SPR'S 1985 Method

The SPR method of counting function points differs from the 1984 IBM method primarily in the way complexity is handled. The SPR method does not ask you to evaluate the complexity of individual inputs, outputs, inquiries, data files, and interfaces as does the IBM method, nor does it require the counting of data elements and file types. It divides the topic of complexity into three distinct questions: (1) How complex is the logic or the problems the application must deal with? (2) How complex is the code that must be written? (3) How complex is the data structure of the application? From the answers to those three questions, the SPR method develops an overall complexity weight that covers the same range as the IBM technique and returns essentially the same adjusted function point totals.

Problem complexity?   1

1. Simple algorithms and simple calculations

2. Majority of simple algorithms and calculations

3. Algorithms and calculations of average complexity

4. Some difficult or complex calculations

5. Many difficult algorithms and complex calculations

Code complexity?   3

1. Nonprocedural (generated, spreadsheet, query, etc.)

2. Well structured with reusable modules

3. Well structured (small modules and simple paths)

4. Fair structure but with some complex modules and paths

5. Poor structure with large modules and complex paths

Data complexity?   1

1. Simple data with few variables and low complexity

2. Numerous variables but simple data relationships

3. Multiple files, fields, and data interactions

4. Complex file structures and data interactions

5. Very complex file structures and data interactions

The sum of problem complexity and data complexity is used directly for function point calculations, and in this case it is a 2. The code complexity parameter is used for backfiring function points, and it is discussed in subsequent sections. By referring to the following table, it can be seen that in this instance the sum of 2 for problem complexity and data complexity will be associated with a multiplier of .6.

Sum of logic and data complexity	Complexity multiplier
2	0.6
3	0.7
4	0.8
5	0.9
6	1.0
7	1.1
8	1.2
9	1.3
10	1.4

Complexity sum = 2

Net SPR complexity multiplier = 0.6

Next, the complexity multiplier is applied to the unadjusted total, as follows:

Parameter	Raw data		Weight		Total
Number of inputs	1	×	4	=	4
Number of outputs	2	×	5	=	10
Number of inquiries	0	×	4	=	0
Number of data files	1	×	10	=	10
Number of interfaces	0	×	7	=	0
Unadjusted total					24
Complexity multiplier					0.6
Adjusted function point total					14.4
Integer value of adjusted total					14.0

Since function points are normally rounded to integer values, the final adjusted function point total with both the SPR and IBM counting methods is 14. The SPR and IBM methods use different mathematical techniques to handle complexity adjustments, but in trials of more than 100 projects the average results are within 1.5 percent of being equal. The maximum variation under controlled conditions has been only about 15 percent.

Incidentally, the code complexity question asked by the SPR method is not used for normal function point calculations and could even be omitted. Code complexity is used when retrofitting function points to existing software by using the backfire mode of calculating function points directly from source code size.

Counting with SPR'S 1985 Backfire Method

To use the 1985 SPR backfire method, it is first necessary to know both the language and the quantity of source code statements that were used to implement the application. In this case, the language was stated to be compiled Quick Basic™, which is a level-5 language and requires an average of about 64 statements per function point. Since the source code quantity was stated to be 600 statements, a first approximation by using the backfire technique can be made by simply dividing the source code count by the average ratio of statements to function points, as follows:

600 statements/64 statements per function point = 9.37 function points

With normal rounding, the backfire method would indicate a total of 9 function points. This is the fastest form of function point calculation, although it is certainly not the most precise. However, it is also possible to adjust the average backfire ratio to account for the complexity of the application. But to do that, additional information and calculations are required. First, it is necessary to sum the applications problem, code, and data complexity by using the standard five-point SPR scale.

In this example, problem complexity is a 1, code complexity is a 3, and the value of data complexity is a 1, so the sum total equals 4. By referring to Table 2.16, it can be seen that this sum is associated with an adjustment multiplier of .80. Applied to the case study at hand, the adjustment factor would be used by multiplying the average number of statements per function point for this language by the adjustment rate, as follows:

64	average statements per function point
0.80	complexity adjustment factor
51.20	statements per function points

If we now divide the 600 source code statements by the 51.2 statements per function point, the result is 11.7 function points. Using normal rounding to the next integer value, the total is 12 function points for this calculation sequence. Thus, backfiring with adjusted complexity offers the advantages of relatively high speed calculations with reasonable accuracy. Backfiring is a very useful way of applying function points to aging software when it may be too difficult or too expensive to create function point totals by normal counting methods.

Counting with SPR'S 1986 Feature Point Method

Feature points, it may be recalled, were developed to give the benefits of the function point method to real-time software, embedded software, systems software, and telecommunications software (and to other types of software with high algorithmic complexity). That is why feature points introduce the new "algorithm" parameter, which is quite significant for software outside the realm of management information systems. However, feature points can be used with MIS projects too.

The feature point method uses the SPR conventions for dealing with complexity, and it also lowers the empirical weight for data files from a 10 down to a 7 to reflect the typical situation that I/O and data file operations are not usually as significant outside the MIS world as they are within it. The following are the feature point results:

Problem complexity?   1

1. Simple algorithms and simple calculations
2. Majority of simple algorithms and calculations
3. Algorithms and calculations of average complexity
4. Some difficult or complex calculations
5. Many difficult algorithms and complex calculations

Code complexity?   3

1. Nonprocedural (generated, spreadsheet, query, etc.)
2. Well structured with reusable modules
3. Well structured (small modules and simple paths)
4. Fair structure but some complex modules and paths
5. Poor structure with large modules and complex paths

Data complexity?   1

1. Simple data with few variables and low complexity
2. Numerous variables but simple data relationships

3. Multiple files, fields, and data interactions

4. Complex file structures and data interactions

5. Very complex file structures and data interactions

Sum of logic and data complexity	Complexity multiplier
2	0.6
3	0.7
4	0.8
5	0.9
6	1.0
7	1.1
8	1.2
9	1.3
10	1.4

Sum of logic and data complexity = 2

Net SPR complexity multiplier = 0.6

Parameter	Raw data		Weight		Total
Number of algorithms	1	×	1	=	1
Number of inputs	1	×	4	=	4
Number of outputs	2	×	5	=	10
Number of inquiries	0	×	4	=	0
Number of data files	1	×	7	=	7
Number of interfaces	0	×	7	=	0
Unadjusted total					22
Complexity multiplier					0.6
Adjusted feature point total					13.2

With normal rounding to integer values, the final adjusted feature point total would be 13. Note that, since the feature point method is still experimental, the weight adjustment for algorithms has only a provisional default value of 3; it can be reset to any appropriate value over the normal range of 1 to 10. For a simple algorithm such as this example, a nominal value of 1 for the weight of the algorithm seems appropriate.

The basic rationale of the feature point method is that algorithmic complexity is an independent and significant variable. The numerical total of 13 feature points vs. the total of 14 function points is due to the simplicity of the algorithmic complexity of the application and the essentially trivial data file implications. The low feature point total may actually come closer to matching the reality of the application than function points.

Feature points are somewhat more flexible than function points, and the implementation of feature points allows for easy modification of all weighting factors. To summarize, for average applications in which algorithms and file structures are equal in number, the function point and feature point totals will be identical. For intuitively simple applications with few or very simple algorithms, feature points will generate lower counts than function points, and for intuitively complex applications with many algorithms or very complex algorithms, feature points will generate significantly higher counts than function points.

Comparison of the Case Study Results

The six versions' functional metric totals for the same application tend to illustrate the evolution of function points. Function points started as a useful but somewhat limited normalizing metric. As their value became clear, function points evolved in the direction of increasing flexibility and closer coupling to real economic productivity.

	Raw data	Adjustments	Adjusted total
1979 IBM method	24	0.75	18
1984 IBM method	18	0.75	14
1985 SPR method	24	0.60	14
1986 SPR backfire without adjustment	9	0.00	9
1986 SPR backfire with adjustment	9	1.44	13
1986 SPR feature point method	22	0.60	13

The 1979 IBM function point method is no longer in use, and it is included to provide a baseline for the newer techniques. The 1979 IBM method is easy to use, but it is limited in flexibility and is absolutely subjective in its treatment of complexity. The 1984 IBM function point method, owing to the new and more flexible way of quantifying the five basic parameters, has the lowest total of the raw data counts of any of the methods. It is probably closest to the intuitive judgment that the example is really quite simple. The IBM 1984 method of adjusting for complexity by means of 14 influential factors has the dual effect of both increasing the range of such adjustments and of adding rigor to the adjustment process.

The 1985 SPR function point method provides an adjusted count identical to that of the 1984 IBM method for this example. However, the SPR and IBM methods achieve their results somewhat differently. The SPR method has a higher raw total but a more dramatic adjustment reduction.

Both the 1984 IBM function point method and the 1985 SPR method provide much greater ranges of adjustment for complexity than did the IBM 1979 technique, and hence they yield lower adjusted function point totals. The 1985 SPR backfire method has two flavors: unadjusted averages and complexity adjusted averages. The unadjusted average method, which merely requires looking up values in Table 2.15, is plainly very quick, but it is not highly accurate. The method cannot be recommended for serious studies of function points, but it is certainly adequate for tutorial and educational purposes and for special situations in which absolute precision is not a major concern.

However, when the backfire technique is adjusted for complexity, its accuracy improves to very acceptable levels. Thus the backfire method supported by automated tools for complexity adjustment will probably find a useful niche in aiding function points to be applied historically to aging software that did not use function points when it was first being developed.

The 1986 SPR feature point method yields the lowest adjusted count for the case study, and intuitively it comes closest to matching the reality of the very simple application used. The SPR feature point method is the most flexible of any, since all of the parameters can be adjusted to two decimal places. The inclusion of the new algorithm parameter in feature points also makes the SPR feature point method suitable for real-time systems and embedded software. However, the SPR feature point method is still experimental and undergoing field trials.

The variations among the illustrated methods are significant, and care must be used when discussing productivity rates to know which method was actually used in generating the totals. (If the unillustrated British Mark II or the DeMarco bang method were used, the ranges would be even greater.) However, the ranges associated with functional metrics are trivial in comparison to the ranges of uncertainty associated with the older lines-of-code metric, whereby variations of more than 200 percent in apparent size are quite common because of the lack of standard definitions of how the code was counted.

In the future, it can be predicted the variations in counting with functional metrics will be reduced, under the influence of the IFPUG and its counting practices committee.

Selecting a Chart of Accounts for Resource and Cost Data

The function point and feature point methods are normalizing metrics whose primary purpose is to display productivity and quality data. To be meaningful, the effort and the cost data itself must be collected to a standard chart of accounts for all projects. One of the major problems with measuring software projects has been the lack of a standard chart of accounts. For example, the simplest and most primitive chart of accounts would merely be to accumulate all costs for a project without bothering to identify whether those costs were for requirements, design, coding, testing, or something else. This kind of data is essentially impossible to validate, and it is worthless for economic studies or any kind of serious exploration.

A slightly more sophisticated way to collect data would be to use a five "cost bucket" chart of accounts that segregated effort and costs among these five elements:

1. Requirements

2. Design

3. Development

4. Testing

5. Management

This technique is better than having no granularity at all, but unfortunately it is insufficient for serious economic studies. Consider, for example, the testing cost bucket. The smallest number of tests performed on a software project can be a single perfunctory unit test. Yet some large projects may carry out a 12-step series that includes unit test, function test, stress test, performance test, independent test, human factors test, integration test, regression test, system test, field test, and user acceptance test. If all testing costs are simply lumped together under a single cost bucket labeled "testing" there would be no serious way to study the economics of multistage test scenarios.

The smallest chart of accounts that has sufficient rigor to be used effectively with MIS projects, systems software, and military software contains 25 cost elements, with the total project serving as the twenty-sixth cost accumulation bucket. Software Productivity Research has produced such a uniform chart of accounts[27] suitable for all types of software and for carrying out studies of software economics.

The IBM 1984 function point chart of accounts,[9] being derived primarily from MIS projects, uses a 20-task chart of accounts that is not really suitable for military projects or systems software projects. For example, the IBM chart of accounts excludes quality assurance, independent verification and validation, independent testing, design and code inspections, and many other activities that are common outside the MIS world but not within it. The IBM chart of accounts also excludes tasks associated with really large systems, such as system architecture and project planning.

It should be clearly understood that because from 20 to 25 cost buckets are available for recording staffing, effort, schedule, and cost information, that does not imply that every project will in fact carry out all of the tasks. Indeed, MIS projects routinely perform only from 6 to 12 of the 25 tasks. Systems software projects tend to perform from 10 to 20 of the 25 tasks. Military projects tend to perform from 15 to all 25 of the tasks, which is one of the reasons for the high costs of military projects. When a project does not carry out one or more of the specific tasks in the chart of accounts, that task is simply set to contain a zero value. The following are the IBM and SPR charts of accounts for comparative purposes:

SPR chart of accounts	IBM chart of accounts
1. Requirements	1. Project management
2. Prototyping	2. Requirements
3. System architecture	3. System design
4. Project planning	4. External design
5. Initial analysis and design	5. Internal design
6. Detail design and specification	6. Program development
7. Design reviews and inspections	7. Detail design
8. Coding	8. Coding
9. Reusable code acquisition	9. Unit test
10. Purchased software acquisition	10. Program integration
11. Code reviews and inspections	11. System test
12. Independent verification and validation	12. User documentation
13. Configuration control	13. User education
14. Integration	14. File conversion
15. User documentation	15. Standard task total
16. Unit testing	16. Studies
17. Function testing	17. Package modification
18. Integration testing	18. Other
19. System testing	19. Nonstandard task total
20. Field testing	20. Development total
21. Acceptance testing	
22. Independent testing	
23. Quality assurance	
24. Installation and user training	
25. Project management	
26. Total project costs	

Note that the two charts shown above are essentially top-level charts. The SPR chart of accounts, for example, expands into a full work-breakdown structure encompassing more than 150 subordinate tasks. Use of a standard chart of accounts is of sufficient importance to merit an eleventh goal for function point metrics:

11. Hard project data (schedules, staff, effort, costs, etc.) should be collected by using a standard chart of accounts.

Because the SPR chart of accounts is a superset of IBM's, projects measured by using the SPR chart of accounts can be subset for direct comparison against projects using the IBM chart of accounts on an activity by activity basis. Note that, because of its MIS origins, the IBM chart of accounts excludes several activities that are significant and expensive for military and systems software (such as independent verification and validation). It may not be advisable to use the standard IBM chart of accounts for projects other than normal MIS applications. Be especially cautious of attempting direct comparisons of costs or productivity between MIS projects and systems or military projects comparisons.

The data collected with the standard chart of accounts is the unambiguous hard data that is not likely to be colored by subjective personal opinions:

- The size of the staff for each activity
- The total effort for each activity
- The total cost for each activity
- The schedule for each activity
- The overlap or concurrency of activity schedules
- The deliverables or work products from each activity

If, as often happens, a project did not perform every activity in the standard 25 activity chart of accounts, those cost buckets are simply filled with zero values. If, as also happens, additional activities were performed below the level of the standard 25 activity chart of accounts, subordinate cost buckets can be created. Productivity studies have sometimes been carried out by using as many as 170 cost buckets for a chart of accounts.

It is dismaying and astonishing that in almost 50 years of software history, there has never been an industry standard for the chart of accounts that should be used to collect software project resource data! Now that functional metrics are becoming the new standard, it is hoped that the importance of standardizing a chart of accounts will soon be addressed.

Summary of and Conclusions about Functional Metrics

Functional metrics in all their forms provide the best capability for measuring economic productivity in software history. Although training is necessary before starting and care must be exercised to ensure consistency, function points and feature points are worth the effort. It is appropriate to recapitulate all of the 11 essential goals of the function point and feature point concepts and to add a final twelfth goal regarding the soft information that should also be captured in order to explain variations in hard project results:

The 12 essential goals of functional metrics

1. The metric should deal with software's visible features.

2. The metric should deal with factors important to users.

3. The metric should be applicable early in the life cycle.

4. The metric should reflect real economic productivity.

5. The metric should be independent of source code.

6. The metric should be easy to apply and calculate.

7. The metric should assist in sizing all deliverables.

8. The metric should retrofit to existing software.

9. The metric should work for maintenance and enhancements.

10. The metric should work with all software types including MIS projects, systems software projects, real-time and embedded software projects, and military software projects.

11. Hard project data (schedules, staff, effort, costs, etc.) should be collected by using a standard chart of accounts.

12. Soft project data (skills, experience, methods, tools, etc.) should be collected in an unambiguous fashion that lends itself to multiple regression analysis.

Function points and feature points are new metrics, and they are still in evolution. Both methods are providing new and clear insights into software productivity and quality. They are key steps leading to the development of software engineering as a true engineering profession.

In conclusion, measurement is the key to progress in software. Without accurate measurements in the past, the software industry has managed through trial and error to make progress, but the progress has been slower than is desirable and sometimes erratic. Now that accurate measurements and metrics are available, it can be asserted that software engineering is ready to take its place beside the older engineering disciplines as a true profession, rather than an art or craft as it has been for so long.

References

1. IBM Corporation, *DP Services Size and Complexity Factor Estimator,* DP Services Technical Council, 1975.
2. Albrecht, A. J., "Measuring Application Development Productivity," *Proceedings of the Joint SHARE, GUIDE, and IBM Application Development Symposium, October 1979,* pp. 83–92.
3. Jones, C., *Programming Productivity—Issues for the Eighties* IEEE Computer Society, Catalog No. 391, 1981, Revised 2nd edition, 1986, 462 pages.
4. Jones, C., "Measuring Programming Quality and Productivity," *IBM Systems Journal,* vol. 17, no. 1, 1978, pp. 39–63. (Reprinted in Reference 3, above.)
5. Jones, C., *Programming Productivity,* McGraw-Hill, New York, 1986, 282 pages.
6. Jones, C., *A 10 Year Retrospective of Software Engineering within ITT,* Software Productivity Research, Inc., Burlington, Mass., February 1989, 25 pages.
7. Albrecht, A. J., *AD/M Productivity Measurement and Estimate Validation,* IBM Corporate Information Systems, IBM Corp., Purchase, N.Y., May 1984.
8. DeMarco, T., "Developing a Quantifiable Definition of Bang," in *Controlling Software Projects,* Yourdon Press, New York, 1982, pp. 92–110.
9. IBM Function Point Workshop Tutorial Materials, IBM Corp., available through IBM education centers in the United States, 1987.
10. Albrecht, A. J., and Herron, D., *A Functional Metric Course,* Software Productivity Research, Inc., Burlington, Mass., 1990, 400 pages.
11. *User Guide to SPQR/20,* Software Productivity Research, Inc., Burlington, Mass., October 1985, revised January 1987, 65 pages.
12. *User Guide to SPQR SIZER/FP,* Software Productivity Research, Inc., Burlington, Mass., July 1987.
13. *User Guide to CHECKPOINT®,* Software Productivity Research, Inc., Burlington, Mass., May 1989, revised April 1990, 125 pages.
14. Jones, Capers, *Preliminary Table of Languages and Levels,* Software Productivity Research, Inc., Burlington, Mass., May 1989, 18 pages.
15. Jones, Capers, *Introduction to Software Measurement and Estimation,* Software Productivity Research, Inc., Burlington, Mass., June 1988, 40 pages.
16. Jones, Capers, *A Short History of Function Points and Feature Points,* Software Productivity Research, Inc., Burlington, Mass., June 1986, 65 pages.
17. Reifer, Don, private communication and correspondence with Capers Jones, 1987.
18. Halstead, Maurice, *Elements of Software Science,* Elsevier, New York, 1977.
19. Hamer, Peter, *Analysis of Software Science Metrics,* ITT Standard Telephone Laboratories, Harlow, England, 1982, 55 pages.
20. Symons, Charles, "Function Point Analysis—Difficulties and Improvements," *IEEE Transactions on Software Engineering,* January 1988, vol. 14, no. 1, pp. 2–11.
21. Dreger, J. Brian, *Function Point Analysis,* Prentice-Hall, Englewood Cliffs, N.J., 1989, 185 pages.
22. Garmus, D. (ed.), *IFPUG Counting Practices Manual,* Release 3.0, International Function Point User's Group, Westerville, Ohio, April 1990, 73 pages.
23. IEEE Software Productivity Measurement Committee, Draft Standard; IEEE Computer Society, 1990.
24. Herron, Dave, "Proposal for Ratio-Based Function Point Calculations," unpublished communication, April 1990.
25. McCabe, Tom, "A Complexity Measure," *IEEE Transactions on Software Engineering,* SE-2,4, December 1976, pp. 308–320.
26. Jones, Capers, *Forms of Complexity that Affect Software Engineering,* Software Productivity Research, Inc., Burlington, Mass., March 1990, 5 pages.
27. Jones, Capers, *Selecting a Chart of Accounts,* Software Productivity Research, Inc., Burlington, Mass., May 1988, 5 pages.

3

United States Averages for Software Productivity and Quality

Introduction

From the 1950s through 1979 it was not possible to perform large-scale productivity or quality studies in a rational way because the standard lines-of-code metric had built-in anomalies and errors that destroyed its validity for large-scale statistical analysis. As discussed in Chap. 2, source code metrics were never standardized, and in addition they penalize high-level languages so that productivity rates move backwards for such languages even though economic productivity increases.

The advent of the function point metric by A. J. Albrecht of IBM in 1979[1] provided a mathematically consistent base for productivity studies, and it has opened up new avenues of software research.

Although attempts to deal with productivity nationally have been made without using functional metrics, such as the author's anthology of productivity reports in 1981[2] and Boehm's monumental *Software Engineering Economics* in 1982,[3] the results have been difficult to replicate and are often paradoxical because of the intrinsic errors associated with lines-of-code metrics.

It was not until 1986 that enough data had been collected by using functional metrics to attempt large-scale national studies free of the distortions associated with lines of code. The first such study known was that of the author, whose 1986 book *Programming Productivity*[4] addressed productivity nationally but made only partial use of functional metrics. This was followed by the author in 1988 with an explicit attempt to show U.S. trends[5] in the use of function points, which was the origin of the data shown here.

Other recent research in the area of large-scale national studies include Charles Symons in England, who is utilizing the Mark II function point metric to explore information systems in the United Kingdom,[6] and Chris Kemerer and R. Banker in the United States. Although Kemerer and Banker's work is weighted toward information systems, his anthology of data[7] also includes several hundred data points by other researchers which cover systems and military projects as well. The function point metric makes large-scale statistical and economic studies of software productivity and quality a rational although not necessarily easy task, whereas the older source code metrics made such studies exercises in frustration and futility.

The present report applies function point metrics to the partial historical data derived from some 4000 software projects developed between 1950 and 1990. The word "partial" is of great significance in this context: although thousands of projects have been examined, it is not the case that each project had a consistent, accurate, and fully detailed set of measurements associated with it. To date, historical software studies are uncomfortably close to the methods of an archaeological dig. One shifts and examines large heaps of rubble, and from time to time finds a significant artifact.

Since many of the projects were developed before function points were invented, much of the data has been converted retrospectively by backfiring or converting the data from the original lines-of-code metric. The backfire technique is discussed in Chap. 2. However, new project data is being added on a monthly basis by using both the IBM and the SPR methods for counting function points, as also explained in Chap. 2. Some projects also used the SPR feature point method, and the data was converted mathematically to the function point base.

Sources of Possible Errors in the Data

Readers should be aware that this study has the potential of a high error content. The raw data was partial and inconsistent in respect to the activities included, and it was often known to be incomplete or even wrong (e.g., the widespread exclusion of unpaid overtime). The projects themselves are a mixture of MIS applications, systems software, and military projects comprising both new development and enhancements. Many different companies' and some government data has been examined, and there are no current U.S. or international standards for consistent counting of software tasks and deliverables.

Since the data has such a high potential for error, it is reasonable to ask why it should be published at all. The reason for publication is the same as the reason for publishing any other scientific results based on early and provisional research. Errors in the original studies can be corrected by subsequent researchers, but if the data is not published, there is no incentive to improve it. For example, when the Danish astronomer Olaus Roemer first attempted to measure the speed of light, his results indicated only 227,000 km/s, which differs from today's accepted value of 299,792 km/s by more than 24 percent. However, prior to Roemer's publication of his research in 1676, most scientists assumed the speed of light to be infinite! Even Roemer's incorrect value started researchers along a useful path.

It is hoped that even if the data shown here is later proved to be incorrect, its publication will be at least a step toward new and correct data that will benefit the software industry. The industry cannot proceed into the twenty-first century with no quantitative data at all, which has been the case for so many years. In large-scale studies such as this, there are three major kinds of error that can distort the results:

1. Errors in determining the size of the projects
2. Errors in determining the effort or work content applied to the projects
3. Statistical or mathematical errors in aggregating and averaging the results.

Sizing errors

Since much of the size data used in this study was derived from projects originally measured in lines of code for which there has never been a national standard, the accuracy of the raw data is highly suspect. About 75 percent of the project data used here was originally recorded in lines of code for which the counting rules were incompletely expressed and in some cases were unknown. (By contrast, refer to Appendix A.) Whenever possible, size was confirmed by interviews with project personnel. Further, the backfiring process of converting lines-of-code data into function point sizes also is uncertain, as discussed and illustrated in Chap. 2.

These two sources of error mean that the actual sizes of the projects considered could vary from the provisional calculated size by unknown amounts. The best that can be asserted is that the project size data is of unknown accuracy. Hopefully, future studies using only data from projects created after 1979, in which function points were counted rather than being backfired, will correct any major errors herein. However, several hundred recent projects with validated function point counts have been plotted against the curves shown here, and the results indicate that the provisional sizing and the normative curves are at least useful for comparative purposes.

Effort and resource errors

The second source of error, dealing with mistakes in work effort, also is unfortunate, but it is a fact of life in studying software productivity in the United States. It is a regrettable fact that most corporate tracking systems for effort and costs (dollars, person-months, work-hours, etc.) tend to accidentally omit from 30 to 70 percent of the real effort applied to software projects. Thus, most companies cannot safely use their own historical data for predictive purposes. Here too, interviews with project personnel were used whenever possible to validate and correct the highly suspect tracking-system data.

The commonest omissions from historical data, ranked in order of significance, include the following:

1. Unpaid overtime by exempt staff (up to 25 percent of all effort)
2. Charging time to the wrong project (up to 20 percent of all effort)
3. User effort on projects (up to 20 percent of all effort)
4. Management effort on projects (up to 15 percent of all effort)
5. Specialist effort on projects (up to 15 percent of all effort)
   - Human factors specialists
   - Integration specialists
   - Quality assurance specialists
   - Technical writing specialists
   - Hardware engineer specialists
   - Education specialists
   - Marketing specialists
6. Effort spent prior to "turning on" the project tracking system for the project (up to 10 percent of all effort)
7. Inclusion of non-project tasks (up to 5 percent of all effort)
   - Departmental meetings
   - Courses and education
   - Travel

A more fundamental problem is that most enterprises simply do not record data for anything other than a small subset of the work that is actually performed. In carrying out interviews with project managers and project teams to validate and correct historical data, the consulting staff of SPR has observed the following patterns of incomplete and missing data by using the 25 activities of the standard SPR chart of accounts as the reference model:

Tasks performed	Completeness of historical data
1. Requirements	Missing or incomplete
2. Prototyping	Missing or incomplete
3. Architecture	Incomplete
4. Formal project plans	Incomplete
5. Initial analysis and design	Incomplete
6. Detail design	Incomplete
7. Formal design reviews	Missing or incomplete
8. Coding	Complete
9. Reusable code acquisition	Missing or incomplete
10. Purchased code acquisition	Missing or incomplete
11. Formal code inspections	Missing or incomplete
12. Independent verification and validation	Complete
13. Formal configuration management	Missing or incomplete
14. Formal integration	Missing or incomplete
15. User documentation	Missing or incomplete
16. Unit testing	Incomplete
17. Function testing	Incomplete
18. Integration testing	Incomplete
19. System testing	Incomplete
20. Field testing	Missing or incomplete
21. Acceptance testing	Missing or incomplete
22. Independent testing	Complete
23. Formal quality assurance	Missing or incomplete
24. Installation and training	Missing or incomplete
25. Project management	Missing or incomplete
26. Total project resources	Incomplete

The bulk of the secondary historical studies examined did not even define the chart of accounts used for resource data; it simply presented an overall project sum. Such gross "bottom line" data cannot readily be validated, and it is close to useless for serious economic purposes.

Given that the majority of tasks in corporate tracking systems are missing or incomplete, the question that arises is just what value tracking systems have to American businesses. When used for cost-control purposes, many tracking systems are so inaccurate that they seem to have no positive business value at all, and indeed they are the source of major cost and schedule overruns because they provide such inaccurate historical data that when project managers attempt to use the data, they place their projects in jeopardy.

Some companies, such as the IBM development laboratories and many defense contractors, tend to be more accurate in their tracking than others. For the United States as a whole, it is possible to make some general observations about the accuracy and validity of software resource tracking:

1. The MIS community is the least accurate, and the historical data for projects used internally by corporations is close to worthless for economic studies. Direct user costs are essentially never tracked;

unpaid overtime is seldom tracked; and carelessness in charging time to the correct set of project accounts is rampant in the MIS domain.

2. The defense community, because of fairly stringent accounting requirements by the Department of Defense, is the most accurate. Here too, however, such factors as unpaid overtime by exempt professionals and management tend to understate real costs. Also, time spent by military and defense department staffs in review and validation work is not always captured.

3. Computer manufacturers and commercial software producers tend to be more complete than the MIS community but less accurate than the military community. However, unpaid overtime by exempt professionals is seldom captured in this environment.

When examining the literature of other scientific disciplines, such as medicine, physics, or chemistry, about half of the page space is normally used to explain the experimental apparatus and the way measurements were taken. The remaining half of the page space discusses the conclusions and results of the study itself. The software engineering literature, unfortunately, is not so rigorous and often contains no information at all as to the origins of the data utilized.

Statistical and mathematical errors

The statistical and mathematical methods used in the current study were mixed and were not carefully controlled. Researchers attempting to replicate the curves used for averages should consider that MIS, systems, and military projects are all included. MIS projects will normally appear more productive than these curves; systems projects will appear slightly less productive; and military projects substantially will appear less productive. A rough approximation of the frequency of these various project classes for any point on a curve, for the United States as a whole, would appear to be:

$$\frac{(\text{MIS projects}*2) + \text{systems} + \text{military}}{4}$$

This reflects the fact that MIS projects appear to constitute about half of the U.S. software work and systems and military projects, taken together, the other half. Note that although the author's data collected over the years has a preponderance of systems software information, for the tables and charts reflecting U.S. averages presented in this chapter, the data was adjusted to match the approximate distribution shown above. This too is a potential source of bias.

It is quite unusual to use powers of 2 as a graph ordinate as many of these curves do. However, that particular representation tends to give a good visual approximation of the results—much more so than the more usual powers-of-10 form of representation.

Perhaps the most common form of statistical uncertainty encountered when dealing with software studies and software literature is the widespread failure by authors to state whether the "averages" cited are based on the arithmetic mean, the harmonic mean, the mode, or the median. From examination of the contents, the bulk of articles and reports on software seem to calculate mean productivity rates based on the arithmetic mean of the rates of the specific projects rather than on the harmonic mean of the weighted effort accumulated by the projects. Table 3.1 illustrates both the arithmetic and harmonic means, the mode, and the median for a hypothetical but not unusual sample of 10 projects.

When the arithmetic mean is calculated by averaging the individual productivity rates of the projects, the result is shown to be 18.0 function points per staff-month. The large number of small, high-productivity cases obviously dominate the arithmetic mean, and the impact of the single large and low-productivity example is minimized. The arithmetic mean technique is suitable if the purpose of the average is to explore the central tendencies of productivity rates. It would not be suitable, on the other hand, if the topic of interest were the resources required to build software projects.

However, if the harmonic mean (i.e., the reciprocal of the arithmetic mean of the reciprocals of the values) is calculated, quite a different

TABLE 3.1 Examples of Arithmetic and Harmonic Means, Mode, and Median Average Rates

Project	Size in function points	Function points per staff-month	Total months of effort
A	10.0	30.0	0.3
B	10.0	20.0	0.5
C	12.0	20.0	0.6
D	15.0	25.0	0.6
E	30.0	20.0	1.5
F	50.0	15.0	3.3
G	60.0	15.0	4.0
H	80.0	15.0	5.3
I	100.0	15.0	6.6
J	500.0	5.0	100.0
Totals	867.0	18.0 (arithmetic mean)	122.7
		7.0 (harmonic mean)	
		15.0 (mode)	
		20.0 (median)	

result is obtained. As can be seen by dividing the total quantity of delivered function points (867) by the total effort expended (122.7 person-months), the result is a mean value of 7.0 function points per staff-month. Obviously project J, which is simultaneously the largest and least-productive project, exerts a major impact when the harmonic mean is used. The difference between the two mean techniques is 257 percent, and it is one of the major sources of confusion when discussing overall software productivity. The harmonic mean is a better choice than the arithmetic mean when the topic of concern is the resources or total effort required to build software. In this report, the harmonic mean is used to show the information in Figs. 3.1 through 3.4 and in many of the tables, since effort is the main topic of concern.

The mode, 15.0 function points per staff-month in Table 3.1, is of interest, but modes are not often encountered in the software engineering literature. Modes are used in this report for Figs. 3.6 through 3.22, since they seem to give the best representation. The median, 20.0 function points per staff-month, is also of interest, but it too is seldom encountered in the software engineering literature. Median values are used in Table 3.3 of this report.

Software, as an industry, has not been very careful or conscientious in its choice of metrics, in validating the raw data used, or in its use of statistical methods to ascertain the results. For more than 40 years, the industry has exhibited these tendencies: (1) used a metric (lines of source code) that was never standardized and indeed violated the basic assumptions of economic productivity; (2) never reached a consensus or even a draft standard on a chart of accounts for software resource accumulation; (3) published only bottom-line data without any detail or granularity; (4) failed to validate or even assess the probable accuracy of published data; and (5) seldom bothered to even identify in print the nature of the statistical methods used to produce its reports.

Purposes of the United States Software Measurement Study

The purpose of the current study is fourfold:

1. To establish the basic set of measures, which if measured accurately, can provide useful data for software managers.

2. To explore the function point method as a consistent metric for large-scale quality and productivity rates.

3. To create an overall U.S. benchmark against which future improvements in software productivity and quality can be judged.

4. To serve as the basis for both national and international productivity and quality studies on an industry-by-industry basis to ascer-

tain why some companies and some industries are more productive than others.

The function point method does indeed provide a consistent and stable platform for exploring both productivity and quality, and on the whole it is far superior to the previous lines-of-code metric for revealing economic trends.

The United States should have a true national database of software productivity information, since software is so critical to the national economy. Unfortunately, the current study is only a small step in that direction. Given the number of companies that produce software in the United States, an effective national database would require information from perhaps 5000 companies and more than 75,000 projects, and that is more than an order of magnitude larger than the current study. (It is also larger than the sum of all of the proprietary databases known to exist in the United States including those of SEI, SPR, RADC, Kemerer, and Putnam.) The volume of soft and hard data from each project included in a national database requires more than 50 printed pages per project, so a true national database will be a major undertaking and require substantial database capabilities.

It is obviously of some importance to know national software productivity and quality levels. However, in the future it will be of much greater importance to know those levels on an industry-by-industry and company-by-company basis. In the work of assembling the data used here, both significant industry variations and even more significant company variations were noted. Since large-scale economic studies of software are only just beginning, it is not yet possible to explain with certainty why these variations occur. It is encouraging, however, to realize that both the phenomena themselves and their probable explanations are now within the scope of measurement science.

Contents of the Raw Data

The activities covered by the raw data included any or all of the 25 standard activities actually performed, including requirements, specification and design, coding, reviews and inspections, integration and test, preparation of user documentation, delivery to clients or users, and project management. (See Appendix C for an example of the activity-level measures.) In real life, of course, not all of the projects included the same set of activities, because there were local variations in recording practice and also variations in the intrinsic work content of various classes of software. Military projects perform the greatest number of activities, followed by commercial systems software, and MIS projects perform the least number of activities.

The raw data in this report comes primarily from very large enterprises: About 75 percent of the data comes from Fortune 100 corporations. This bias is due to the fact that large enterprises have been much more active in software measurements than small enterprises. The data, based on both primary and secondary sources, was collected between 1965 and 1990 as a by-product of internal and external consulting. Although the cutoff point for the data published here is late 1990, the collection of such data is a continuing task that never actually finishes.

The projects themselves in this report are biased toward systems software, which is not a perfect reflection of U.S. norms. In the United States itself, about 52 percent of all software projects appear to be of the MIS type, whereas the projects considered for this study contained over 55 percent systems projects and only about 26 percent MIS projects. This skew is caused in part by the fact that systems software is measured far more often than MIS software and in part because the author has been employed and consulted by a comparatively large number of clients who produce systems software.

Another source of bias in this report is that the included projects tended to be much larger than U.S. averages. More than 60 percent of all software projects in the United States appear to be smaller than 100 function points in size, whereas the average size (mode) of projects studied in detail by the author approaches 500 function points and the median size is over 10,000 function points! Obviously, productivity and quality consultants such as the author are seldom engaged for small projects, so data examined in the normal course of consulting business is skewed toward the large end of the spectrum. A second reason for this imbalance is that small projects in the United States are seldom measured carefully and often are not even placed in corporate tracking systems, whereas large projects have a much higher probability of being measured. It should also be noted that the function point metric itself may not be completely appropriate for either military or systems software, since it may tend to undercount software with high algorithmic complexity; at least, that is a common perception.

The author and his colleagues at Software Productivity Research have utilized SPR's standard 25-activity chart of accounts for accumulating effort and cost data. This is the smallest single-level chart of accounts than can be used interchangeably with MIS projects, systems software, and military projects.

When raw data is collected, the activities that are not performed are omitted. This allows an interesting and very useful kind of analysis to be performed in which the correlations that are made show how productivity rates vary with the number of activities actually carried out. This method also reduces error by allowing comparisons between projects to be made by activity rather than by overall totals. Table 3.2 shows the activities normally performed by MIS projects, commercial systems software, and military projects larger than 500 function points in size.

It cannot be overemphasized that serious economic analysis of software projects must be based on a standard chart of accounts. Project data based only on rough bottom-line totals without accompanying details at the chart of accounts level is worthless. Table 3.3 shows the overall ranges observed by the author for the 25 standard activities explored.

Table 3.4 shows the age distribution, in round numbers, of the projects included. Age is shown in terms of the decade in which the projects first entered production. Note that, although the author's personal research commenced in 1965, a substantial amount of historical data from older projects was then available and was explored for the purposes of historical continuity.

TABLE 3.2 Normal Software Development Activities for MIS Software, Systems Software, and Military Software Projects Larger than 500 Function Points in Size

Cost accumulators	MIS projects	Systems projects	Military projects
1. Requirements	X	X	X
2. Prototyping		X	X
3. Architecture		X	X
4. Formal project plans		X	X
5. Initial analysis and design	X	X	X
6. Detail design	X	X	X
7. Formal design reviews		X	X
8. Coding	X	X	X
9. Reusable code acquisition		X	
10. Purchased code acquisition	X		X
11. Formal code inspections		X	X
12. Independent verification and validation			X
13. Formal configuration management			X
14. Formal integration		X	X
15. User documentation	X	X	X
16. Unit testing	X	X	X
17. Function testing	X	X	X
18. Integration testing		X	X
19. System testing	X	X	X
20. Field testing		X	X
21. Acceptance testing	X		X
22. Independent testing			X
23. Formal quality assurance		X	X
24. Installation and training	X	X	X
25. Project management	X	X	X
Average number of activities	12	20	25

TABLE 3.3 **Productivity Ranges by Activity in Function Points per Staff Month**

Activity	Minimum	Median	Maximum
1. Requirements	50	175	350
2. Prototyping	75	200	500
3. Architecture	50	150	300
4. Planning	200	500	1200
5. Initial design	50	175	400
6. Detail design	25	150	300
7. Design review	75	225	400
8. Coding	3	15	50
9. Reusable code	300	400	600
10. Package acquisition	350	750	1500
11. Code inspection	75	150	300
12. IV and V	75	100	200
13. Configuration control	1000	2000	3000
14. Integration	100	250	500
15. User documentation	15	30	50
16. Unit test	100	200	400
17. Function test	25	150	300
18. Integration test	75	175	400
19. System test	100	175	400
20. Field test	75	225	500
21. Acceptance test	100	350	600
22. Independent test	100	200	300
23. Quality assurance	30	125	300
24. Installation	150	250	400
25. Management	20	75	150

Notes: 1. The arithmetic mean of the data in Table 3.3 would be quite misleading. The harmonic mean is preferred for gaining insights from this kind of information.

2. Although data is shown for all 25 activities, comparatively few projects (under 10 percent) even approach performing all 25. Therefore, it is necessary to select the activities which would be performed on a project before the data in Table 3.3 became relevant.

3. Obviously and unfortunately, very few projects can provide all data at this level of granularity. In this respect, as already mentioned, large-scale productivity studies more or less resemble archaeological digs, wherein inferences must be drawn from potsherds and rubbish.

Since the data in this report is aggregated from new projects, enhancements, and maintenance projects of a number of classes and types, Table 3.5 shows the approximate volumes of the various kinds of projects considered:

The quality data in this report is even more biased than the productivity data. About 75 percent of the total data on quality is derived from fewer than 20 large corporations, which include computer manufacturers, telecommunications manufacturers, some defense contractors, and a few leading-edge producers of MIS applications. The unfortunate reason for this bias is that more than 90 percent of U.S.

TABLE 3.4 Decade in Which Projects Entered Production

Decade	Number of projects	Percent of projects
1951–1960	150	3.6
1961–1970	500	11.9
1971–1980	1000	23.8
1981–1990	2550	60.7
Total	4200	100.0

TABLE 3.5 Distribution of Project Types Used to Determine U.S. Norms

Type	New	Enhanced	Maintained	Total	Percent
Systems	700	1500	200	2400	57
MIS	350	600	125	1075	26
Embedded	50	150	25	225	5
Military	75	100	0	175	4
Telecommunications	30	50	75	150	3
Process control	40	100	0	140	2
Scientific	50	50	0	100	2
AI	20	10	0	30	1
Totals	1315	2460	425	4200	100

enterprises do not measure quality or software defects at all. (Note: This particular statistic is derived from both the author's observations and from hand votes at a number of software conferences and seminars at which the audience was polled as to who did or did not measure defects and quality.)

The paucity of quality data in the United States, a national disgrace, explains why so many U.S. companies tend to perform poorly against international competition when quality is taken seriously. Conversely, the fact that both computer manufacturers and telecommunications companies often do measure quality appears to be one of the factors that explains why U.S. computer and telecommunications companies do better against international competition than most other segments of U.S. industry. That defense contractors tend to measure defects is in part due to military requirements and in part due to the necessities of building real-time embedded software.

The defect counts included bugs discovered in requirements, design, code, user documentation, and "bad fixes" or new bugs accidentally injected while fixing a preceding bug. The defect removal steps included both formal and informal design reviews, formal and informal code inspections, and all forms of testing. Two activities, desk checking by individuals and unit testing by individual programmers, are normally not measured (although such data is sometimes collected from volunteers).

The annual defect reports are based on the concept of "valid unique defects." That is, the bugs must be real bugs that would cause the project to stop or behave unacceptably. If more than one report for the same bug occurs, only the initial report is counted. Table 3.6 shows the average distribution of defect types used in this report.

There are significant differences in the methods used to find defects discovered before the software is delivered to its intended users. Systems software producers and military software producers use a much greater number and variety of defect removal techniques than MIS producers, and hence they have much higher average efficiencies. The average defect removal efficiency of systems and military projects appears to be higher than 90 percent, whereas for MIS projects most seem to be lower than 75 percent. That is, more than one bug out of every four will still be latent in MIS software when it is delivered. Table 3.7 shows the typical patterns of defect prevention and removal noted for projects larger than 500 function points in overall size.

The available defect removal data is actually capable of revealing the individual efficiencies of various kinds of review, inspection, and test. The results are somewhat depressing: Most forms of testing are less than 30 percent efficient, in that they will find less than one bug out of every three actually present. Formal design and code inspections tend to be the most efficient, and they alone can exceed 60 percent in defect removal efficiency.

It is also a depressing observation that design and code inspections, the two methods with the highest measured defect removal efficiencies,[8] are so infrequently utilized in the United States by software producers.

By using the Software Productivity Research backfire function

TABLE 3.6 Distribution of Defect Types Used to Determine U.S. Norms

	MIS, %	Systems, %	Military, %	Overall, %
Requirements	30	15	25	25
Design	25	30	25	27
Coding	30	40	35	35
Documents	5	10	10	7
Bad fixes	10	5	5	6
Totals	100	100	100	100

TABLE 3.7 Normal Software Defect Prevention and Removal Steps for MIS, Systems Software, and Military Software

	MIS	Systems	Military
Prevention			
Prototypes	X	X	X
JAD sessions	X		
Clean room			X
Pretest removal			
Desk checking	X	X	X
Requirements review	X		X
Design reviews		X	X
Document reviews		X	X
Code inspections		X	X
Individual verification and validation			X
Correctness proofs			X
Testing stages			
Unit test	X	X	X
Function test	X	X	X
Integration test		X	X
Regression test		X	X
System test	X	X	X
Field test		X	X
Acceptance test	X		X
Independent test			X
Average number	8	11	17
Removal efficiency	< 75%	90%	> 95%

point conversion method explained in Chap. 2, it is now possible to carry out retrospective productivity studies for historical projects developed before function points were invented simply by converting source code size data into function point form. The SPR backfire method is based on empirical observations of relations between source code size and function point totals. For example, Ada has been found to average 71 noncommentary source code statements per function point, C averages 128 statements per function point, both Cobol and Fortran average 105 statements per function point, and so forth. Although backfiring when unadjusted for complexity is not extremely accurate, there is no other convenient technique for carrying out large-scale retrospective studies.

Table 3.8 shows the approximate number of projects by language in alphabetic sequence. It should be noted that the frequency with which languages occur in this sample does not reflect overall U.S. experience, in which Cobol is far and away the most widely used language. The reason for the skew in the sample is quite straightforward: Al-

TABLE 3.8 Languages Used by Software Projects in the Sample

Language	Number of projects
Ada	70
APL	90
Assembly	900
Basic (compiled)	50
Basic (interpreted)	75
C	300
C++	25
Chill	50
Cobol	700
Forth	25
Fortran	200
Jovial	20
Lisp	35
Objective-C	75
Pascal	225
PL/I	120
PL/S	250
RPG	50
Subtotal	3260
Mixed languages: (Cobol + SQL), (C + Assembler), etc.	500
Other languages	500
Actor	
Bliss	
Coral	
CMS2	
Focus	
Gamma	
LINC	
Modula2	
Natural	
Nomad	
Pacbase	
Simscript	
SMALLTALK	
SQL	
Telon	
Total	4260

though Cobol is the most widely utilized language in the United States, it is not the language used by most projects whose productivity is measured.

By means of the backfire method, Table 3.9 shows approximate average U.S. productivity rates at 10-year intervals from 1950 to 2000. The data associated with the years 1990 and 2000 were projected using the CHECKPOINT® commercial estimating tool. The averages for each decade are based on the harmonic mean rather than the arithmetic mean.

TABLE 3.9 Average U.S. Software Productivity Rates at 10-year Intervals from 1950 to 2000 Expressed in Function Points per Person-Month

Year	Systems software	MIS software	Military software	U.S. average
1950	0.5	1.0	0.3	0.8
1960	1.0	2.0	0.5	1.5
1970	2.0	4.0	1.0	2.5
1980	3.0	6.0	2.0	3.5
1990	4.0	8.0	3.0	5.0
2000	7.0	12.0	5.0	9.0

The accuracy of the data in Table 3.9 is fairly low in terms of both the precision of the backfire function point conversion process and the validity of the resource data itself. Nevertheless, it is interesting to note the slow but steady improvements over time, with an approximate order-of-magnitude increase after 50 years. Unfortunately, the doubling of software productivity at 10-year intervals lags far behind the equivalent rates of increase in computing power and decrease in cost per MIP on the hardware side.

In performing the backfire conversion from original data expressed in lines of source code, an interesting phenomenon was observed. The early projects were, of course, written in some form of assembly language such as Autocoder or SPS, and the more recent projects were often written in higher-level languages such as Fortran, Cobol, Ada, and Objective C. The phenomenon of interest was the observation that the rate of increase in the level of languages used for software was approximately the same as the gain in overall productivity that was due to increased experience, use of structured methods, better tools, better languages, and the like.

Thus, when productivity is measured over long time spans by using lines of source code, the results tend to stay comparatively constant at about 300 to 350 statements per person-month. Indeed, between 1970 and 1980, lines-of-code metrics tend to show a decrease. What appears to occur is that the mathematical paradox defined in Chap. 2 for source code metrics has been masking true productivity gains.

The moon rotates on its axis at precisely the same rate as it revolves around the earth, so only one face of the moon is ever visible from earth. In what appears to be a similar phenomenon, the rate of increase in software productivity over time matched the increase in average language levels, so that lines-of-code metrics tend to present the same, or even declining, values over long periods. Thus, for research using lines-of-code data, it would be easy to be deceived into thinking that software productivity has not increased over the last 40 years. Indeed, some journal articles have made such an assertion. With function points, however, gains in software productivity over time can be seen to be occurring, although not as rapidly as would be desirable.

Software languages circa 1950

In 1950, all programming was done in either machine language or in very primitive assembly languages. The number of statements per function point approximated 320 and the numeric level of the languages was 1, implying the starting point of our profession.

Software languages circa 1960

In 1960, macroassembly languages had started to supplant basic assembly languages. Fortran had been available since 1957, and Cobol had been defined in 1959, although in 1960 neither Fortran nor Cobol had too many practitioners. Nonetheless, migration to higher-level languages appeared to have raised the effective level to about 1.3, which implies about 250 statements per function point.

Software languages circa 1970

By 1970, Cobol and Fortran were dominant and even more powerful languages such as APL and PL/I were starting to appear. Basic was sweeping through academic institutions after being developed at Dartmouth. Assembly languages continued to be plentiful, but the overall usage pattern was shifting. The effective level circa 1970 appears to be about 1.8, or approximately 175 statements per function point.

Software languages circa 1980

By 1980, more than 300 procedural languages had been defined and the early program and application generators such as IBM's ADF I were starting to appear. Even for systems programming, more powerful languages such as PL/S and C were supplanting assembly languages. The effective language level circa 1980 appears to be about 2.7, which implies an average of about 120 statements per function point.

Software languages circa 1990

Now, object-oriented languages such as Objective C, SMALLTALK, and C++ are on the scene, Ada is fully operational, Pascal and Modula 2 are plentiful in academia, and more than 50 commercial-grade program and application generators such as Telon, Pacbase, and

Sage are on the market. Query languages such as SQL are starting to be standard adjuncts to database applications. The effective language level circa 1991 appears to be about 4, which implies about 80 statements per function point.

Software languages circa 2000

By 2000, it can be anticipated that object-oriented languages will dominate for standard systems software and that query languages and application generators will continue to increase for MIS projects. Ada will no doubt move toward an object-oriented flavor for military projects. Cobol use will probably still be plentiful for maintenance if not for development. Hopefully, significant quantities of reusable code will be available in all of the major languages, and certainly in Ada and the object-oriented languages. Visual or icon-based programming languages will be in use too. It can be hypothesized that the probable language level circa 2000 may be about 6, which implies perhaps 50 statements per function point. The steady increase in effective language levels over time is one more strong reason for retiring lines of code as a productivity metric.

Distribution of effort related to project size

One of the most important advantages of measuring productivity at a granular level with a 25-activity chart of accounts is the ability to note variations in the distribution of effort. For example, for very small personal applications there may only be a single activity performed (coding), whereas for large applications there may sometimes be all 25. Not only are there variations in the number of activities performed, there are very marked variations in the distribution of effort among the tasks. Table 3.10 illustrates the complex changes that occur in concentration of effort between small projects and large systems.

To clarify the nature of the changes, Table 3.10 aggregates the tasks into four general categories of work: (1) management and support, (2) defect removal, (3) paperwork, and (4) coding. "Management and support" includes the work of the project management chain from first- through third-line managers plus the work of noncoding specialists who may be part of the project team. The latter can include specialists in any or all of the following: planning, estimating, measurement, configuration control, integration, hardware, human factors, and administration, as well as secretarial support.

"Defect removal" includes both public defect removal activities such as design reviews, code inspections, and formal testing plus private

TABLE 3.10 Variations in Distribution of Effort Related to Software Project Size

Size, function points	Management and support, %	Defect removal, %	Paper-work, %	Coding, %	Total, %
40,960	18	37	33	12	100
20,480	17	36	32	15	100
10,240	16	35	31	18	100
5,120	15	34	30	21	100
2,560	14	33	29	24	100
1,280	14	30	26	30	100
640	13	28	24	35	100
320	12	26	22	40	100
160	12	23	20	45	100
80	11	20	15	54	100
40	11	19	12	58	100
20	11	18	10	61	100
10	11	17	7	65	100
5	11	16	5	68	100

defect removal activities such as desk checking and unit testing by the programmers personally. "Paperwork" includes the sum of the effort devoted to production of requirements, architectural specifications, initial functional specifications, detailed design specifications, module level specifications, test plans, quality plans, publication plans, marketing plans, concepts and facilities manuals, reference manuals, user guides, tutorial materials, and marketing brochures. "Coding" includes the work normally carried out by programmers themselves: initial coding, revising code, and reusing code.

As can be seen in Table 3.10, the distribution of effort among the four categories varies significantly with the size of the applications. The implications of the variations are highly important for attempts to improve productivity.

1. Any claim that a tool or methodology will improve productivity by 10 to 1 or some other fixed amount is ipso facto fallacious. Because of the variations in effort distribution, there is no single percentage gain that can operate across all sizes of applications.

2. Tools and methods that are effective at one size may not be equally effective at other sizes. For example, coding tools will have greater impacts at the small end of the range, where the percentage of coding costs are highest. Paperwork methods will have greater impacts at the high end of the range, where paper costs are enormous.

3. It is necessary to select tools and methods to fit the size, nature, and characteristics of each project. There is no single methodology, tool set, or process that will be equally effective across all size ranges. Formal methodologies may be very useful for large paper-

intensive projects but excessive and harmful for small code-intensive projects.

4. Quality control becomes steadily more important as the size of the application goes up. It also becomes more difficult.

5. Paperwork control becomes steadily more important as the size of the application goes up. It also becomes harder.

Prior to seeing the data in graphical form, it is useful to see some of the specific data points utilized. Table 3.11 shows, for selected size ranges, five key productivity indicators: (1) the average effort expended in terms of person-months for all activities and occupational groups, (2) the average overall schedules from requirements to delivery, (3) the total staff including both technical, managerial, and administrative, (4) the "assignment scope" or quantity of function points for which one person would be responsible, (5) the "production rate" or quantity of function points which one person could produce in one U.S. standard work-month. The table includes MIS, systems, and military projects, and it also includes new, enhancement, and maintenance projects. Therefore be cautious when using Table 3.11, since the mixture of so many variables tends to produce "averages" that are often far removed from finer divisions of data.

For example, in Table 3.11 note the unexpected decline in productivity rates for smaller projects between 80 and 5 function points in size. This phenomenon is due to the fact that enhancement and main-

TABLE 3.11 Effort, Schedule, Staff, Assignment Scopes, and Production Rates for Selected Sizes of Software Projects

Size, function points	Effort, staff-months	Schedule, months	Staff	Assignment scope, function points	Production rate, function points per person-month
40,960	81,920	96	853	48	0.50
20,480	30,118	73	413	50	0.68
10,240	8,192	55	149	69	1.25
5,120	2,994	42	71	72	1.71
2,560	1,099	32	34	78	2.33
1,280	405	24	27	75	3.16
640	149	18	8	80	4.30
320	55	14	4	80	5.85
160	20	11	2	80	7.95
80	8.1	6	1.35	64	9.82
40	4.35	4.50	1.0	40	9.19
20	2.56	2.56	1.0	20	7.81
10	1.50	1.50	1.0	10	6.64
5	0.89	0.89	1.0	10	5.64

tenance projects were aggregated with new projects. The overhead effort and costs associated with recompiling and regression testing the applications which are being updated leads to the anomaly that small projects are often less productive than large when some form of modification work is carried out. If new projects alone are considered, productivity rates for the smaller projects are normally higher than for larger projects.

Averages and Ranges of U.S. Software Productivity

Figure 3.1 shows the approximate distribution of U.S. software projects into the three large, generic categories of information systems, systems software, and military software. These generic categories actually include several hundred specific classes and types, of course, but since the three generic categories share certain external aspects, it is convenient to use them for discussion purposes.

Figure 3.2 shows the approximate distribution of software projects into three other generic categories: new projects, enhancement projects, and maintenance projects (defect repairs). Here too, there are many specific subcategories below the level of these three generic categories.

In the context of Fig. 3.2, there is a great deal of apocryphal noise in the software literature to the effect that "80 percent of all software effort goes to maintenance." So far as can be determined by the author from both actual studies of clients and informal polls at software seminars and conferences (where members of the audience are asked to raise their hands in response to questions about varying levels of maintenance and enhancement effort in their companies), the data in Fig. 3.2 appears to be as realistic an approximation as could be shown without a true national census of software projects.

Figure 3.3 is a graph of the approximate average (using the har-

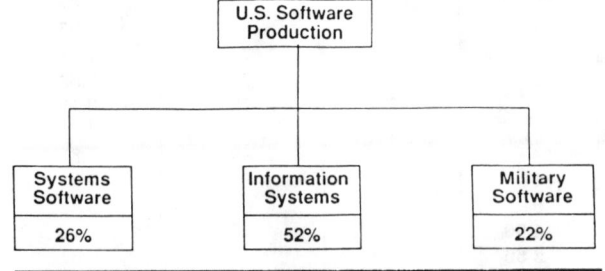

Figure 3.1 Distribution of U.S. software projects among MIS, systems, and military projects.

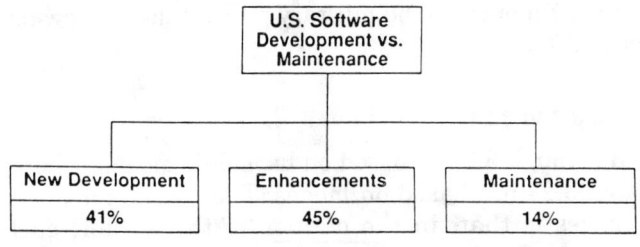

Figure 3.2 Distribution of U.S. software projects among new, enhancement, and maintenance (defect repair) projects.

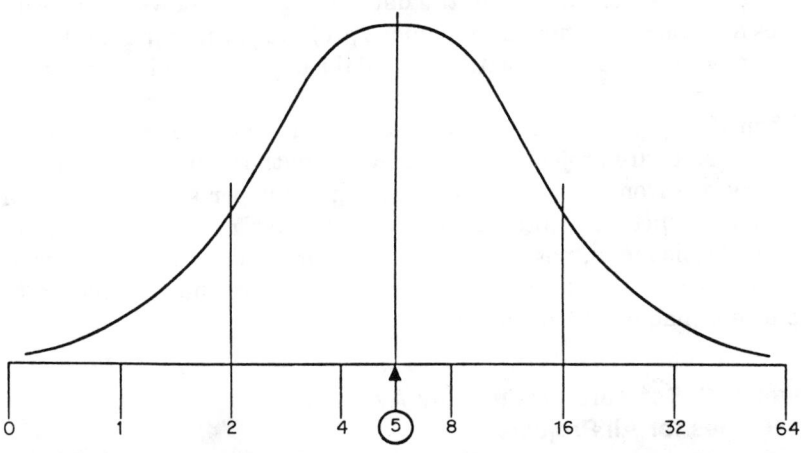

Figure 3.3 Average U.S. software productivity expressed in function points per staff-month.

monic mean) and the high and low ranges of the observed U.S. software productivity rates. Figure 3.3 includes both new projects and enhancements and combines more than 200 classes and types of software projects.

MIS projects, because of the relatively small number of tasks and the nature of the work, have the highest productivity with averages of about 8 function points per staff-month, and peak projects (i.e., small projects with stable requirements produced by expert staff using very high level languages and excellent tool sets) exceeding 140 function points per staff-month. Systems software tends to average about 4 function points per staff month and seldom exceeds a rate of 10 function points per staff-month. Some systems software projects drop below 1 function point per staff-month. Military projects tend to average about 3 function points per staff-month and seldom exceed a rate of 5 function points per staff-month. Some military projects drop below 0.5 function point per staff-month.

Use of modes in Figs. 3.7 to 3.24

Note that Figs. 3.3 through 3.7 are based on harmonic means, whereas Figs. 3.9 through 3.24 are based on modes. The reason for using two forms of averages is that, in the opinion of the author, each seems to be appropriate for the data being displayed. Since much of the data from this point on will be based on the use of modes rather than either arithmetic or harmonic means, it is useful to show why the switch to the modal form of average is advantageous and seems to give the best representation of the data. Table 3.12 shows the overall ranges and modes for new development projects of three nominal sizes as observed by the author, with the modal ranges highlighted by italic type.

When the spread or range spans more than 100 to 1 (the absolute ranges in software projects observed by the author during his consulting work are from a low of 0.31 function point per staff-month to a high of 140 function points per staff-month) then neither the median, the arithmetic mean, nor the harmonic mean tends to reveal the central tendency of the data. The mode, on the other hand, appears to give a reasonable view of the situation.

Overall U.S. Software Productivity Average and Ranges for All Projects

Figure 3.3 shows the provisional current U.S. average of about five function points per staff-month when all classes and types of new, enhancement, and maintenance projects are aggregated. The overall

TABLE 3.12 Productivity Ranges and Modes for Selected Software Project Sizes

Productivity rates in function points per staff-month	100 function points	1000 function points	10,000 function points
> 100	1.0%	0.01%	0.0%
75–100	3.0%	0.1%	0.0%
50–75	7.0%	1.0%	0.0%
25–50	15.0%	5.0%	0.1%
15–25	*40.0%**	10.0%	1.4%
5–15	25.0%	*50.0%**	13.5%
1–5	10.0%	30.0%	*70.0%**
< 1	4.0%	4.0%	15.0%

*Modes are shown in italics.

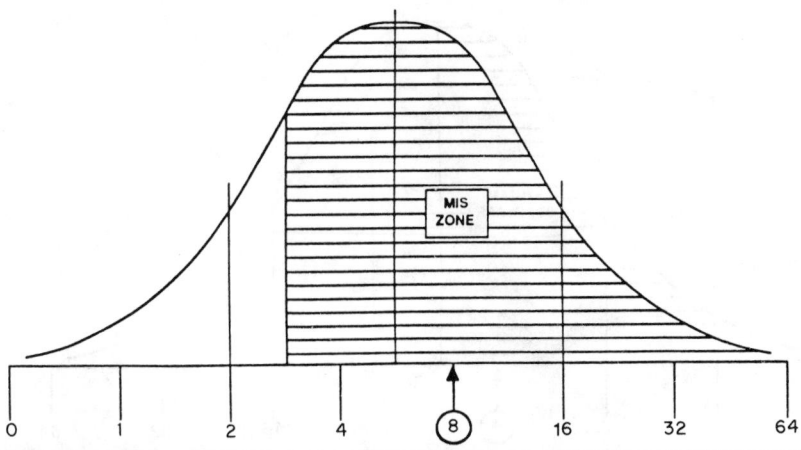

Figure 3.4 Average U.S. software productivity for MIS projects expressed in function points per staff-month.

ranges of productivity that are likely to be encountered also are shown. The absolute maximum ranges observed by the author between 1965 and 1990 are between 0.31 function points per staff-month and 140 function points per staff-month. However, about two-thirds of all projects should fall within the range of 2 to 16 function points per staff-month. The use of powers of 2 is unusual in tables of this type, but the visual representation using that form best fits the author's observations.

Zone of Management Information System Projects

Figure 3.4 shows the provisional U.S. averages and normal ranges for management information systems, or MIS projects. For the purposes of this study, MIS comprises all projects in which information is the primary target. Examples of MIS projects include both internal projects such as payroll and accounting systems and external projects that are marketed commercially, such as spreadsheets, statistical packages, and word processors. About 52 percent of all U.S. projects to date appear to be in the MIS category.

Zone of Systems Software Projects

Figure 3.5 shows the provisional U.S. average and normal ranges for systems software. For the purposes of this study, systems software comprises all projects in which the software is intended to control or

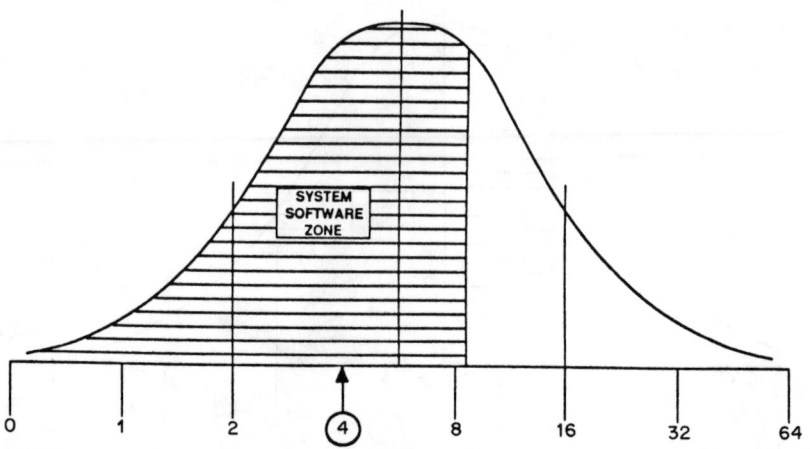

Figure 3.5 Average U.S. software productivity for systems software projects expressed in function points per staff-month.

interact with physical devices, such as computers. Examples of systems software include operating systems, process control, telephone switching systems, and embedded software within physical devices such as fuel injection, navigation software, and radar guidance software. About 26 percent of the U.S. projects to date appear to be in the generic "systems software" category.

Zone of Military Software Projects

Figure 3.6 shows the provisional U.S. average and normal ranges for military software projects. For the purpose of this study, military software comprises all projects which are constrained to follow military specifications such as 2167 and 2167A. Such projects may be exotic embedded real-time software such as that within a satellite or missile or an ordinary payroll program. The reason for this clumping of military software is that military specifications cause such an enormous quantity of paperwork to be produced that all other productivity factors tend to be comparatively insignificant.

About 22 percent of the U.S. projects to date appear to be required to follow military specifications and hence can be classified as military projects. The total of 22 percent is somewhat speculative, it should be noted. However, the United States does appear to have the highest volume of military projects in the world. (The Soviet Union may have a higher percentage of military projects than the United States, but that is due to its low volume of nonmilitary software.)

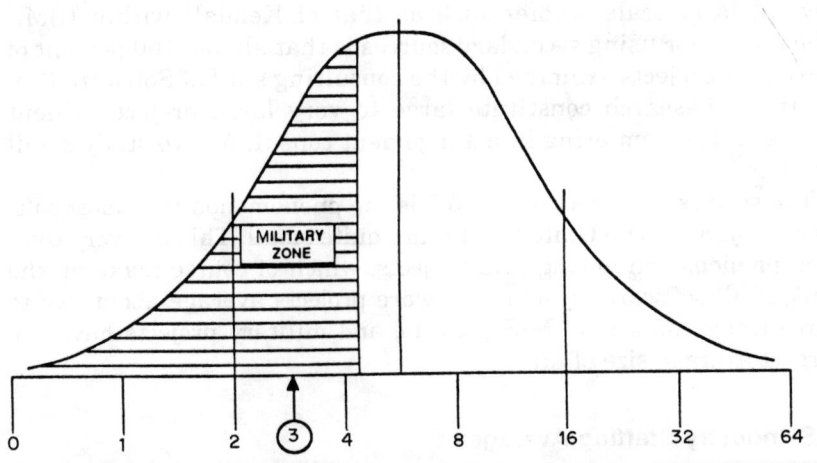

Figure 3.6 Average U.S. software productivity for military software projects expressed in function points per staff-month.

Distribution of U.S. Software Project Sizes

Figure 3.7 is a graph of the distribution of U.S. software sizes for new, enhancement, and maintenance projects. This graph, unlike the others within this report, is based on secondary data sources including

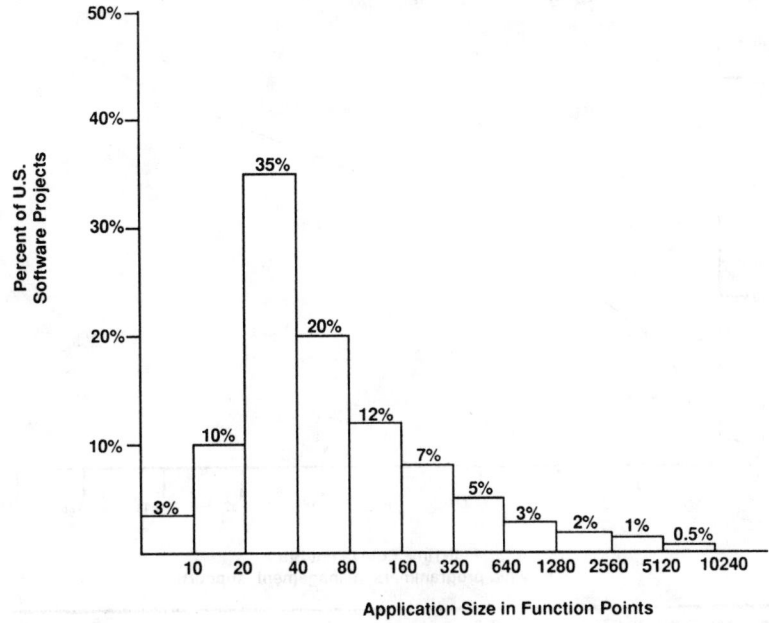

Figure 3.7 Distribution of U.S. software project sizes.

several large-scale studies such as that of Kendall within IBM.[9] The reason for using secondary sources is that almost 100 percent of the client projects examined by the consulting staff of Software Productivity Research constitute large to very large projects. Client companies seldom bring in management consultants to study small projects.

The surprising aspect of Fig. 3.7 is the phenomenon that most software projects in the United States are quite small. This is a very common phenomenon among MIS projects, which of course make up the bulk of all software. Systems software projects average about two to three times the size of MIS projects, and military projects have the largest average size of all.

U.S. Industry Staffing Averages

Figure 3.8 is a graph of the full-time direct staff associated with software projects. More than half of U.S. software production appears to be in the form of one-person projects carried out by generalists. As the overall project size goes up, both the number and diversity of project staffing increase rapidly. For very large systems of more than 5000 function points in size, coding programmers constitute only a small percent of the overall staff, and a full complement of specialists are

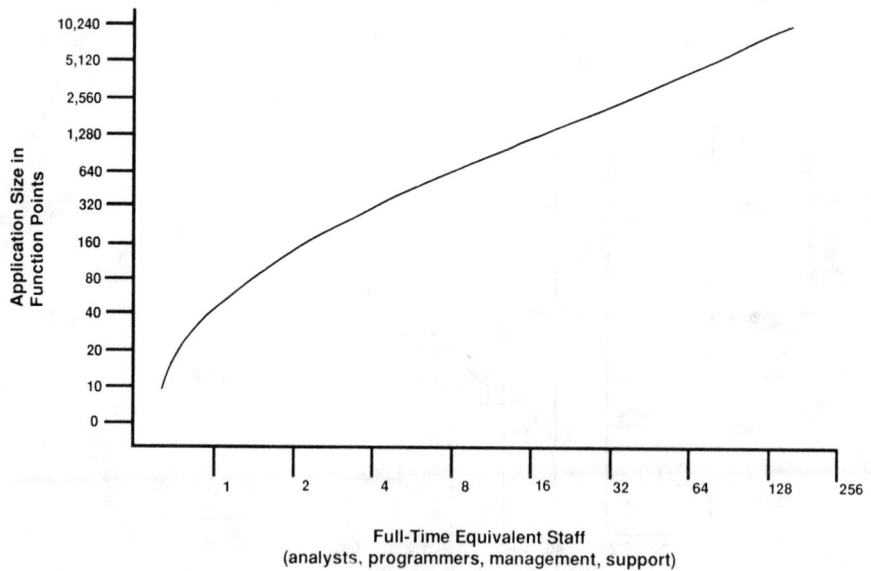

Figure 3.8 Average staffing required for software projects.

present: test specialists, technical writers, integration specialists, estimating specialists, and so on. It is unlikely that very large systems could be successfully completed by generalists alone.

As of 1990, a total of about 40 different kinds of specialists have been identified as participants on software projects. Just as medicine and law began to develop recognized specialties, it appears that software also is moving in the direction of full specialization.

U.S. Industry Schedule Averages

Figure 3.9 is a graph of the average schedules, in calendar months, from start of requirements to delivery of the software. Schedules and schedule pressure have the greatest impact on U.S. software of any known factor. Unfortunately, most U.S. projects are scheduled backwards by establishing the delivery date long before the project itself is fully specified or sized. This is why many U.S. projects miss their delivery schedules by approximately 50 percent. See Fig. 3.10 for the second major reason for missed schedules.

The heavier line in Fig. 3.9 graphs the somewhat melancholy actual delivery schedules, and the lighter line graphs the highly optimistic

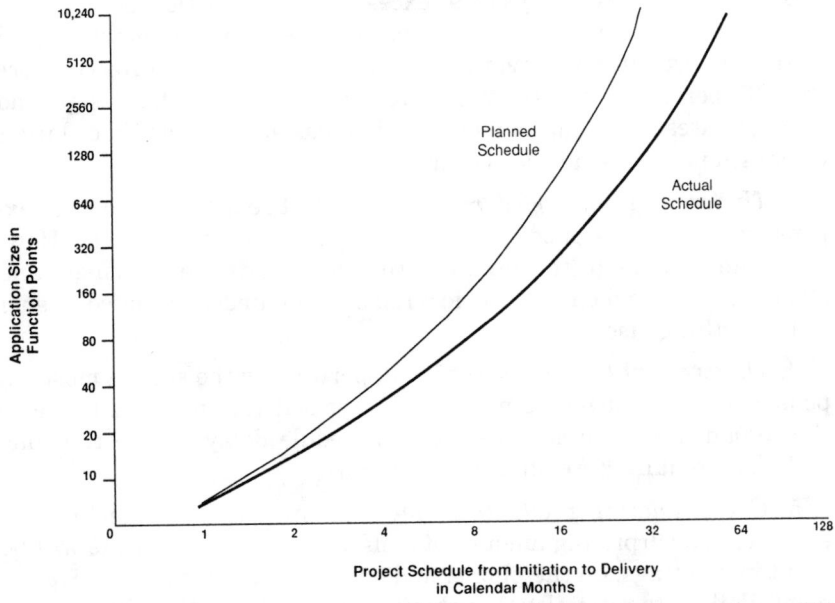

Figure 3.9 Planned vs. actual schedule duration from initiation to delivery.

initial planned schedule. It can be seen that the difference between desired schedules and actual schedules increases in direct relation to the size of the project.

This phenomenon constitutes the most visible source of dissatisfaction between software developers and their clients. Clients almost always wish to have projects finished earlier than development is capable of doing. Of all metrics, incidentally, establishing the exact starting point of a software project is the most difficult to pin down.

Since schedule delays constitute the largest complaint about software by company executives and clients, it is significant to discuss the reasons why such delays occur. Here are the major reasons for schedule delays encountered by the author and the SPR consulting staff:

1. *Irrational schedule targets:* For more than half of all projects, the desired schedule targets were established by essentially irrational means. That is, the schedules were set by decree without regard for the capabilities of the staff or the complexities of the projects.

2. *Continuous growth in functional content:* Medium-size and large software projects are seldom fully defined during the requirements phase. The late growth in functional content is proportional to the size (see Table 3.10). For projects in excess of 1000 function points more than 35 percent of the final functions delivered to users may be added to the project after the requirements phase. (For one project, more than 65 percent of the functions were added during the design and coding phases, resulting in a project that was about three times larger than estimated during the requirements).

3. *Underestimating defect removal:* Defect removal is the most expensive activity for medium-size and large software projects. However, due perhaps to the innate optimism of software managers and staffs, the time and effort for defect removal are underestimated oftener than anything else.

4. *Underestimating paperwork:* Paperwork is the second most expensive activity for medium-size and large software projects. It is also the second most common reason for schedule delays, since the time and effort required are often understated.

5. *Overestimating productive time:* In any medium-size to large enterprise, a surprising amount of staff and management time will be spent in meetings, on the phone, and on tasks outside project development. Failure to recognize this phenomenon and include it in schedule plans is a common problem.

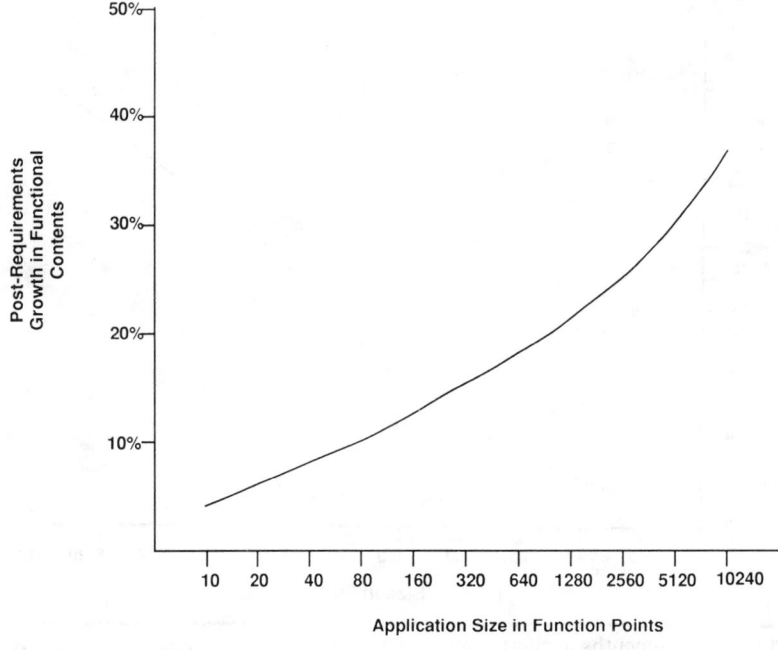

Figure 3.10   Growth in functional content after requirements have been met.

U.S. Average for Growth in Functionality after Requirements Have Been Met

Figure 3.10 is a graph of the average number of new function points added to typical software projects after the completion of the requirements phase. Figure 3.10 illustrates one of the major causative factors associated with Fig. 3.9: It is hard to achieve a fixed schedule when the functional contents of applications are not fixed. As can readily be seen, functional growth after requirements is directly related to the overall size of the application.

U.S. Industry Averages for Effort on New Projects, by Size

Figure 3.11 is a graph of the average amount of effort in person-months required to design, develop, document, and debug new software projects. The effort includes all of the direct activities from requirements to delivery and includes project management as well. The set of activities is based on the standard SPR set of up to 25 specific, measurable activities. The results may seem to include more effort

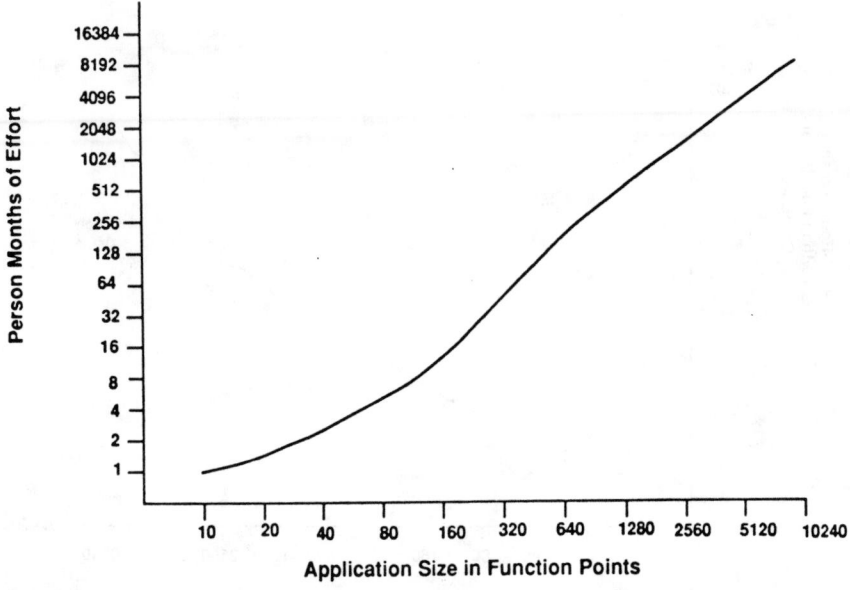

Figure 3.11   Person-months of effort required for new software projects.

than many companies view as normal. The reason is that most companies' tracking systems do not record between 30 and 70 percent of the real effort that goes into software. Much of the unpaid overtime, early requirements work, user documentation, and management effort are seldom tracked by MIS producers in the United States, although commercial software developers are not so inaccurate.

U.S. Industry Productivity Rates for New Software Projects

Figure 3.12 is a graph of net development productivity expressed in function points per staff-month. The productivity data includes all development tasks from requirements to delivery, including requirements, specification and design, coding, integration and testing, user documentation preparation, and project management. Note that, since projects do not include the same set of tasks, the range of uncertainty in Fig. 3.12 is significant. MIS projects, which perform the smallest set of tasks, will often be much higher than the curve in Fig. 3.12 suggests, and military projects will be much lower.

For enhancement projects, which follow a different curve, refer to Fig. 3.17. For maintenance projects (defect repairs), refer to Fig. 3.19.

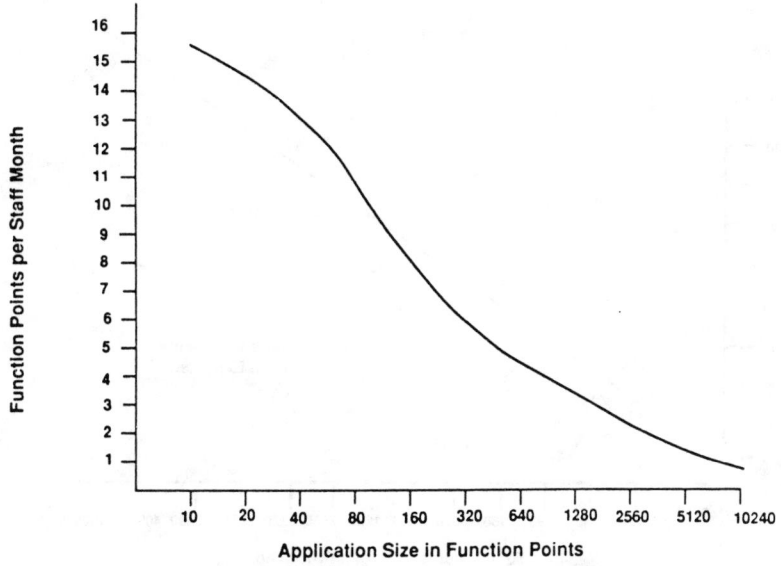

Figure 3.12 Development productivity rates for software projects.

For all three together (new, enhancement, and maintenance projects), refer to Fig. 3.20.

At a meeting in April 1990, Charles Symons of England[6] and the author discussed the productivity curves derived from their independent studies. All the data in all both studies was based on function points, although the British data was based on the Mark II function point technique which is not directly comparable to the American versions.

The Symons productivity curve from data collected in England approximated the enhancement curve shown in Figs. 3.16 and 3.20, although the slopes differed somewhat. That is, productivity was higher for midrange projects than for either very small or very large projects. This result was typical when the projects included were primarily enhancement projects, which seemed to be the case.

There is no fundamental disagreement in the data collected by Symons and the author, although it is necessary to consider the various samples used in order to explain the differences.

U.S. Averages for Volumes of Software Paperwork

Figure 3.13 is a graph of the approximate volume of paperwork contained in the sum of the requirements, specifications and design, and

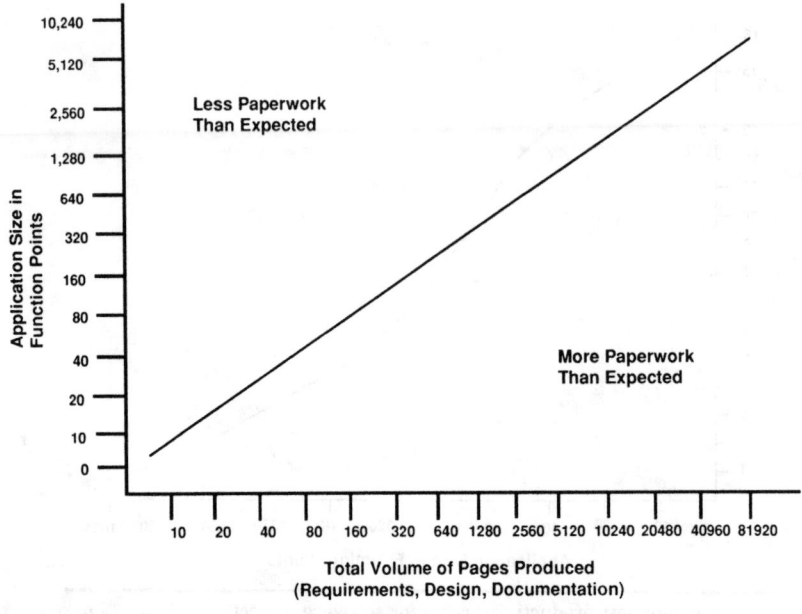

Figure 3.13   Average volumes of software paperwork.

external user, production, and maintenance documentation. This is an important productivity issue: Paperwork is the largest contributor, about 52 percent of the total, to project costs for military software, the second largest contributor to project costs for systems software, at about 35 percent, and a large contributor to the costs of MIS software, at from 15 to 30 percent of total project costs.

An internal study within IBM for systems software carried out by the author[9] found a surprising reverse correlation between the volume of specifications and the complexity of projects. The most complex projects had the smallest quantity of specifications. The reason for this surprising correlation, as it turned out, was that complex projects were assigned to experts and simple projects to novices.

Although individual company and project variations make statistical trends unreliable, there is a clear correlation between the size of software projects and the total number of discrete documents produced. Small projects will seldom be accompanied by more than a few document types such as a requirements statement, a rudimentary design document, and a small user's guide. Large projects, on the other hand, may be accompanied by more than 100 discrete document types including formal cost estimates, formal development plans, test and quality plans, marketing plans, publication plan, requirements statements, architectural specifications, hardware dependency specifications, initial and detailed functional specifications, data specifications, logic and structural specifications, and a full library of 20 or more user documents.

There is also a strong correlation between the class of software and the number of discrete document types produced. MIS projects seldom exceed 20 discrete document types. Systems software, such as operating systems and telecommunication systems, may produce more than 50 discrete documents. Military projects are the most prolix; they may exceed 100 discrete documents as well as have the highest page counts per document.

It cannot be overemphasized that paperwork is a major cost element of large software projects and that attempts to improve productivity without addressing paperwork are unlikely to succeed.

U.S. Average Risk of Project Failure and Cancellation

Figure 3.14 is a graph of the risk that projects will be canceled and not completed at all. This is an important but seldom discussed aspect of productivity. For large systems and military projects the failure rates routinely exceed 25 percent, in that 1 out of 4 projects will be termi-

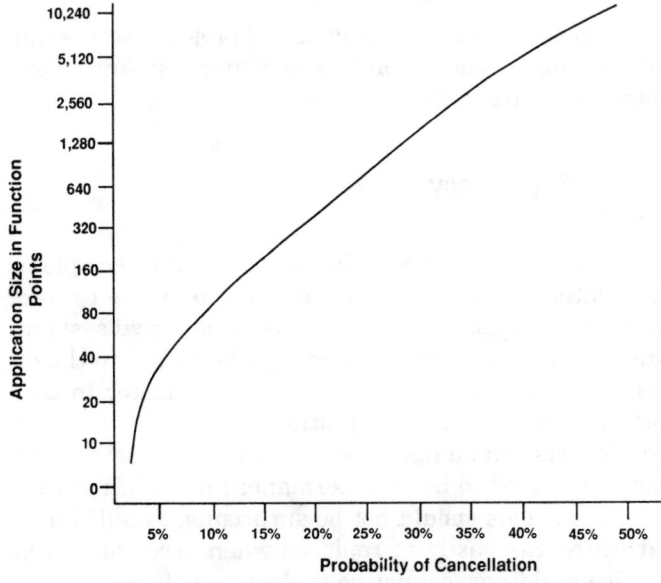

Figure 3.14 Risk of failure of cancellation of software projects.

nated. MIS failure rates are usually lower, often because MIS projects cluster in the smaller sizes, where failure rates are naturally low. Since the costs of canceled projects must be amortized across successful projects, this factor accounts for a great many otherwise inexplicable aspects of corporate and industry productivity rates.

Unfortunately, the point at which project termination occurs is distressingly late in the life cycle. In a proprietary study of large telecommunication projects carried out by the author, the termination decisions did not occur until the projects had been under development for more than 2 years and the average expenditures prior to termination had exceeded $10 million.

Projects are canceled for a variety of reasons; some of the major causes noted by the author and the SPR consulting staff include the following:

1. *Severe schedule slippages and cost overruns:*   About half of the canceled projects were already late for their planned delivery and severely over budget. The enterprises canceled the projects essentially to cut their losses.

2. *Technical infeasibility:*   About a fourth of the canceled projects turned out to be beyond the capabilities of the state of the art, or at least beyond the state of the art embodied in the staff assigned to do the work. Intractable performance problems, excessive memory utilization, or inability to meet technical constraints explained the cancellation.

3. *Change in business outlook:*   Some canceled projects were terminated because of the sale or acquisition of a subsidiary, shutdown of a plant, or some other extrinsic factor.

U.S. Average for Life Expectancy of Software Projects

Figure 3.15 is a graph of the average life expectancy of completed projects once they enter production. What appears to be the case for software is a phenomenon that is generally true in biological systems: The life expectancy of an organism is roughly proportional to the organism's volume. Average life expectancy is a major factor in both maintenance costs and value analysis equations.

Small software projects can be regarded as disposable assets. Large systems, once deployed, tend to become permanent parts of the companies which own them. This should not be surprising: Small things, such as office furniture, can easily be replaced when necessary; large things, such as office buildings, cannot be replaced easily.

Thus, once large systems go into production, the high costs of re-

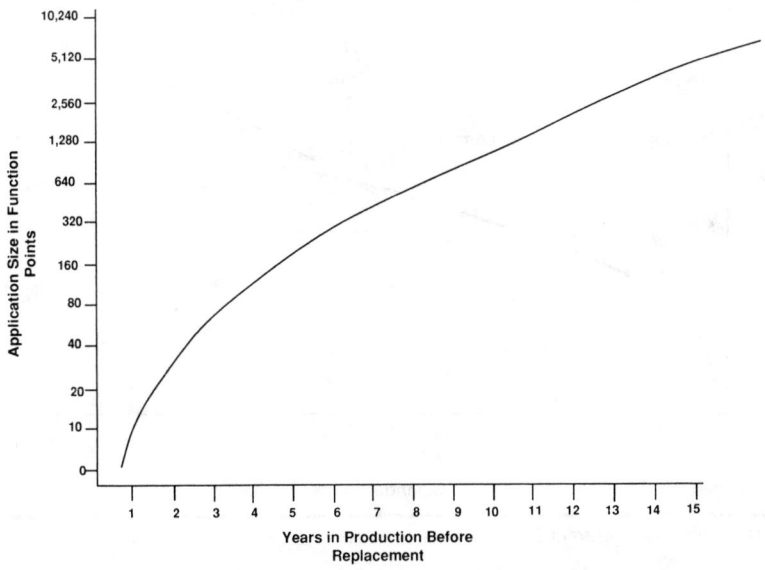

Figure 3.15   Life expectancy of software projects after delivery.

placement tend to keep them operational long past their prime. This situation contains the seeds of national disaster. Consider U.S. steel making: The high costs of replacing aging steel mills kept obsolete equipment in production long past optimal replacement periods!

Value vs. Cost for Midrange MIS Projects

This is not a U.S. average figure; it illustrates only one restricted size range of internal MIS software. Research to date indicates that, because of the enormous fluctuations in value between MIS, commercial, and military projects, value cannot be readily dealt with in terms of averages.

Figure 3.16 is a graph of the average costs per year expended for MIS software projects against the average value per year returned to the enterprise. Readers should note that value analysis is the least accurate of any metric for software projects and the most subject to dramatic deviations. Certain high-volume commercial software projects such as Lotus and Word Perfect have values that exceed their development costs by more than 1000 to 1. On the other hand, many MIS projects may have a negative value in that they never recoup their development costs but may be useful in intangible ways. The word value as used in this report reflects only tangible value such as reductions in operating costs.

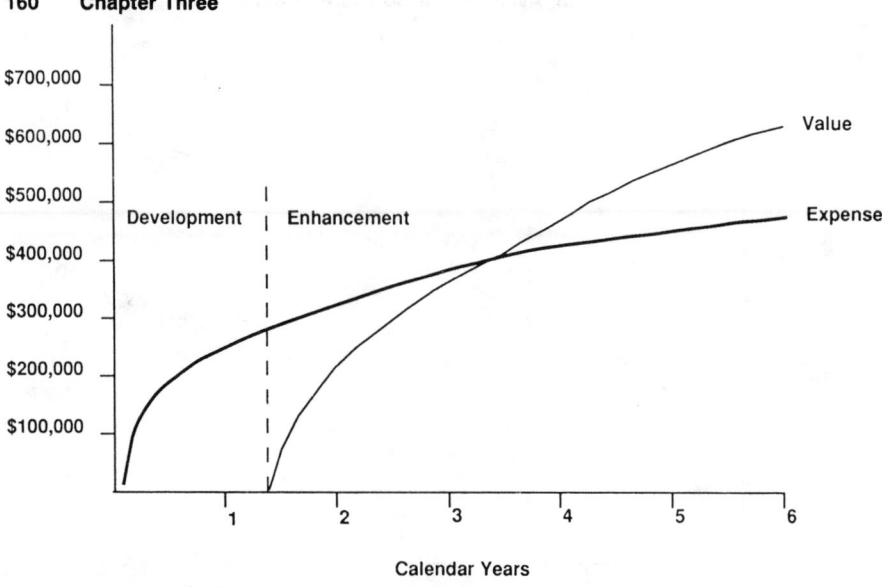

Figure 3.16   Returned value of MIS projects vs. costs.

Figure 3.16 shows only internal value for internal projects center-ing around 320 function points in size. All projects are based on a de-fault value of $5000 per fully burdened staff-month. Measuring the business value of software applications has been one of the most diffi-cult and intractable problems since the industry began, and the infor-mation in Fig. 3.14 is not very satisfying.

However, in the future the function point metric appears capable of be-ing used for more sophisticated software value studies as well as for pro-duction studies. Although the research is just beginning, it appears that function points are much more useful than lines of code for studying soft-ware usage patterns, which is one of the main factors in value analysis.

For example, retrospectively considering the 1983 software usage patterns within ITT, there were about 40,000 employees who used computers as part of their jobs. Although some employees, such as software engineers, had several thousand function points available, it appears that the average pattern for each user was about 500 function points per business day. Therefore, ITT used roughly 20 million func-tion points per day overall. Since the size of the ITT production library was about 500,000 function points, a daily use of 20 million implies that each function point, on the average, was used by 40 employees.

This method of analysis is quite new, but it appears to be very prom-ising in considering a new aspect of the business value of software projects. For example, if a planned MIS application of 500 function points will have 100 users, its first-order value might be set at 50,000 by merely multiplying users by the function point total. If the users will run the software monthly, the annual function point utilization of the application will be 600,000 function points per year. On the other hand, suppose that the 500 function point application were a high-volume commercial word processing package with 50,000 users who ran the package an average of 75 days per year. In that case the first-order value would be 25 million and the annual utilization of the application would be 1.875 billion function points per year.

Neither consumption nor use pattern is the only aspect of value that should be considered, but it is intriguing that function points may at least be of some use in dealing with the demand for as well as the production of software.

U.S. Average Volumes of Annual Enhancements to Software

Figure 3.17 is a graph of the average volume of new and changed functions added to production software in response to user requests, changes in business requirements, changes in statutes and regulations, and the like. MIS software is the most volatile and usually has the highest volume of change; it is followed by systems software, and military projects is in third place. Substantial change occurs in all classes of software except a few engineering and mathematical packages.

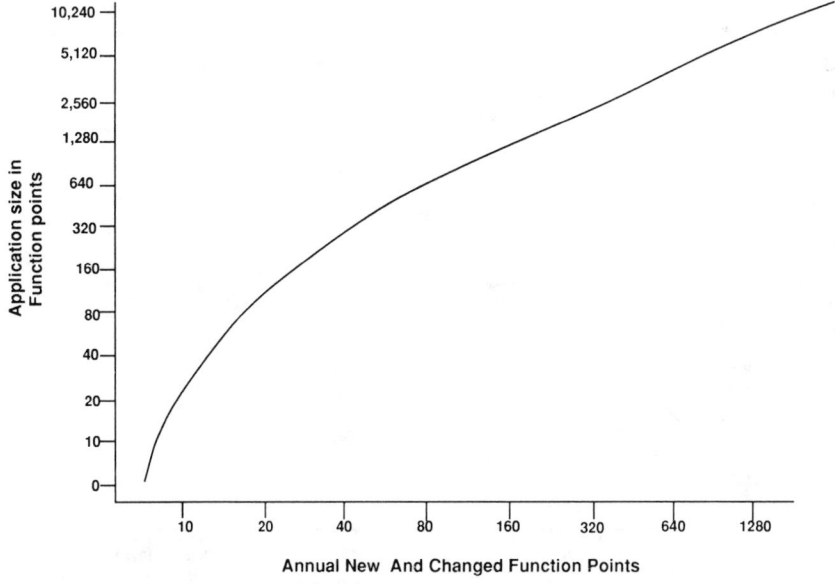

Figure 3.17   Volume of new functions added as enhancements.

Expressed simply, most applications tend to grow at a rate that approximates 5 percent new functionality each year. For MIS projects, the growth patterns of individual projects are not smooth; they tend to be characterized by abrupt jumps in functionality brought on by such external events as changes in laws. For systems software, the growth pattern is more regular and is determined by such events as new hardware devices and normal growth in functionality.

U.S. Average Productivity of Enhancement Projects

Figure 3.18 is a graph of the productivity rates associated with enhancement projects. Because enhancement productivity is not directly proportional to size in a simple fashion, this is the most complex situation yet dealt with.

Enhancement productivity peaks when the size of the enhancement is roughly 3 to 5 percent of the size of the base project being updated. Productivity declines with both smaller and larger changes. (Thus a three-dimensional graph would be required to express enhancement productivity well.) The surprising reduction in productivity for small enhancements is due to the overhead costs of analyzing, recompiling, and regression testing the base system. The productivity reduction for larger enhancements is due to the difficulty of changing the base system, plus the fact that large changes often distort the fundamental structure of the original base system.

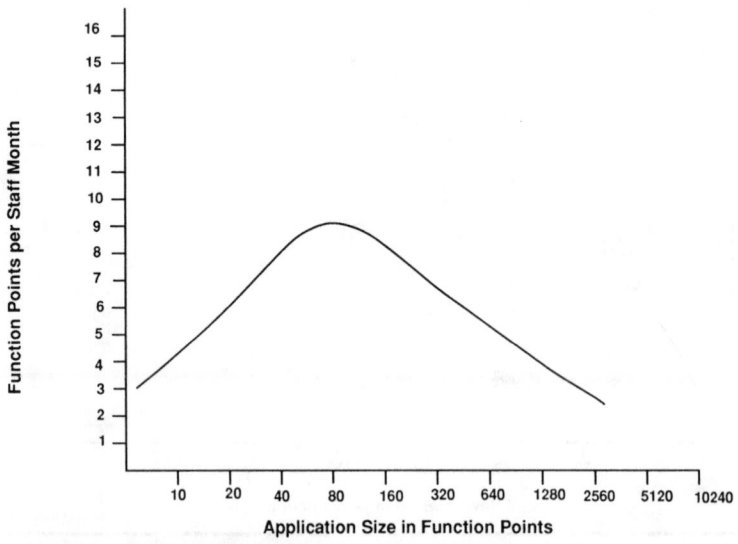

Figure 3.18   Productivity rates of enhancement projects.

As the software industry moves past age 45, more than half of all software projects are now in the maintenance and enhancement arena. That should not be a surprise: By the time the automotive industry reached the age of 45, there were more mechanics repairing automobiles than there were employees manufacturing new ones.

Enhancements will be a fact of life for software for as far into the future as can be envisioned. Entirely new subindustries are starting to emerge to provide geriatric care for aging software. Of the technologies starting to be applied to enhancement projects, several are worth noting because of their impact on productivity rates:

1. *Complexity and structural analyzers:* Enhancement productivity is based in large part on the complexity and structure of the existing software that must be updated. Therefore, it is useful to analyze the structure and complexity of the existing software and take corrective steps if needed.

2. *Restructuring tools and services:* For Cobol applications, restructuring is fast becoming a standard method. Projects that have good initial structures, or that have been restructured, tend to be substantially less costly to enhance than projects of the same size but with poor structural characteristics.

3. *Reverse and reengineering tools and services:* The data for reverse and reengineering is insufficient in 1991 to judge the efficacy of these techniques. The prognosis and fundamental concepts appear to be worthy of continued research and exploration. The essential concept is that expert systems can extract hidden design information latent in the source code of aging software and that such information can be used either to facilitate manual enhancements or, even better, to convert the application into a more modern guise.

U.S. Average Productivity of Maintenance Projects

Although it is common to lump together both enhancements and defect repairs under the term "maintenance," such an aggregation is folly from the point of view of economic understanding. Enhancements are normally funded by users and often follow rigorous development protocols. Defect repairs, on the other hand, are normally carried out on an emergency basis, sometimes late at night!

As a result of an antitrust suit in the 1970s, IBM established a rigorous distinction between enhancements and maintenance. Enhancements were projects, after the initial release, that added new functionality at the request of users. The term "maintenance" was restricted to repairs of defects. This is a reasonable and practical distinction; under it, there are no "large" maintenance projects. Many maintenance proj-

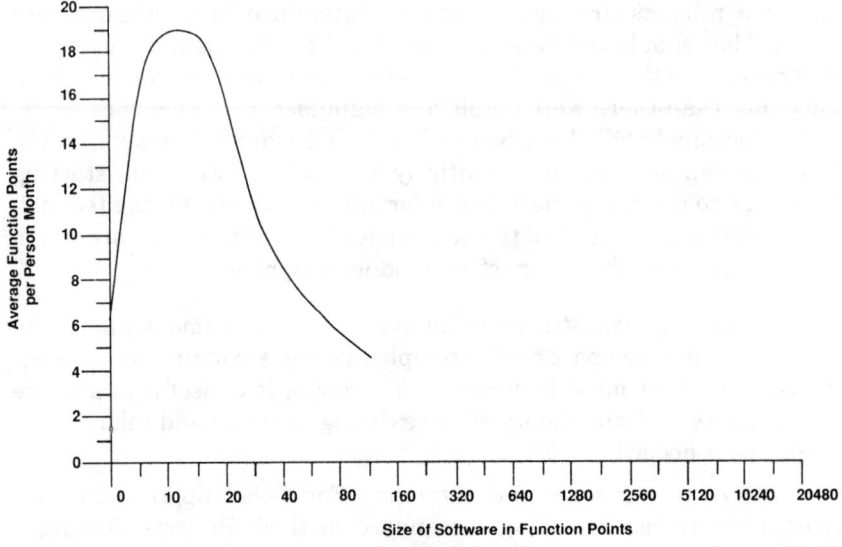

Figure 3.19 Productivity rates of maintenance projects.

ects require changing only a single line of code, and very few require more than perhaps a few hundred lines of modified or new code (Fig. 3.19). There are no new requirements, and there may not even be any externally visible changes at all. There will be substantial exploratory troubleshooting, however.

U.S. Average Productivity of New, Enhancement, and Maintenance Projects Aggregated as Single Sets

Figure 3.20 shows the approximate U.S. productivity curve when new, enhancement, and maintenance (defect repair) projects are aggregated. The obvious reason for the surprisingly low productivity for small projects is the impact of enhancements and maintenance when the projects are accompanied by the overhead of recompiling, regression testing, and redistributing the mass of the original base project. It is surprising how much the shape of the curve in Fig. 3.20 can vary in response to changes in the data used, such as dealing with new and enhancement projects separately, dealing with large and small enterprises separately, and dealing with MIS, systems software, and military projects separately. The parable of the blind men and the elephant comes readily to mind when attempting to put national trends together.

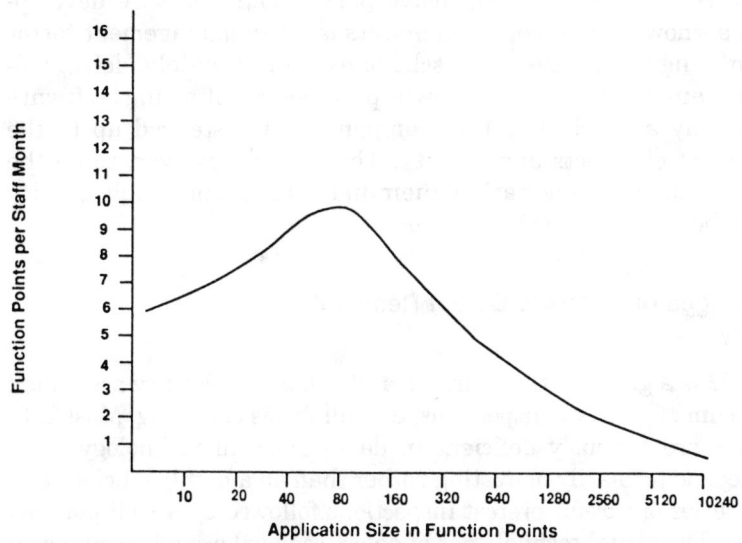

Figure 3.20 Net U.S. productivity for new projects, enhancement projects, and maintenance projects simultaneously.

U.S. Industry Averages for Software Defect Potentials

Figure 3.21 is a graph of the potential volume of defects from all major sources that will be encountered in a project: requirements bugs, design bugs, coding bugs, user documentation bugs, and bad fixes or bugs accidentally injected while repairing another defect. Defect re-

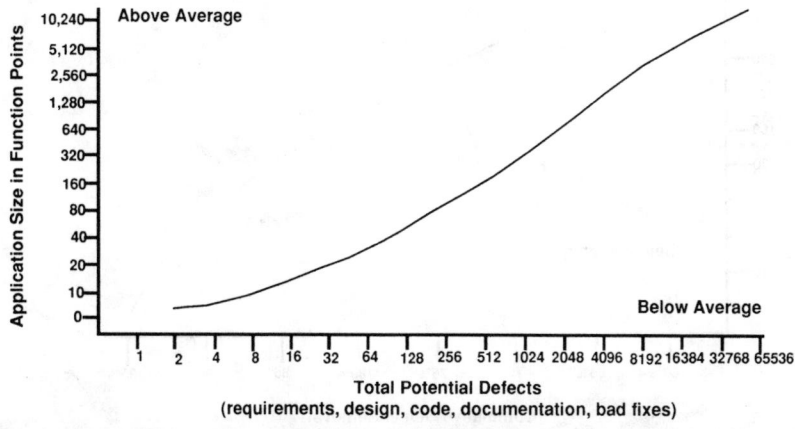

Figure 3.21   U.S. average software defect potentials.

moval is usually the most expensive part of U.S. software development, so a knowledge of potential defects is a key management factor
in determining overall costs and schedules. Unfortunately, defect volumes are among the least known parameters affecting software
projects. Only a handful of U.S. companies have stepped up to the
measurement of defects and quality. They seem, however, to be the
companies that are dominating their industries, since high quality
generally benefits high market shares.

U.S. Averages of Software Defect Removal Efficiency

Figure 3.22 is a graph of the overall defect removal efficiency associated
with the sum of reviews, inspections, and all forms of testing. Most U.S.
enterprises are seriously deficient in defect removal technology; they
tend to depend primarily on testing rather than on a highly efficient and
effective series of careful pretest inspections followed by a well-planned
test series. The actual technologies of defect removal are advancing rapidly, and leading-edge enterprises can now exceed 99 percent in cumulative defect removal efficiency. Unfortunately, the overall U.S. norms for
defect removal appear to hover around 75 percent.

Interestingly, a cumulative defect removal efficiency of 95 percent
appears to be powerful nodal point for software projects. Projects which

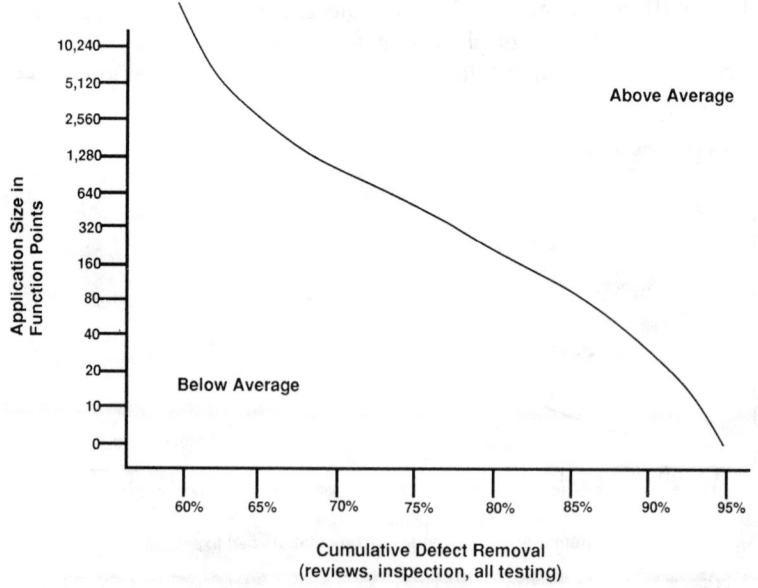

Figure 3.22   Average software defect removal efficiency.

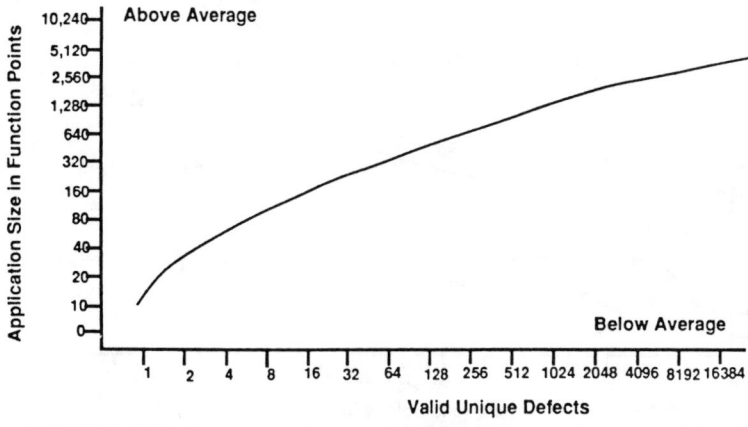

Figure 3.23   Defect volumes delivered to software users.

achieve overall removal efficiencies approximating or exceeding 95 percent tend to be optimal in three other aspects as well: (1) they have the shortest schedules for projects of their size and type; (2) they have the lowest quantity of effort in terms of person-months or person-hours; and (3) they have the highest levels of user satisfaction after release.

U.S. Averages of Defects Delivered to Users

Figure 3.23 is a graph of the quantity of latent bugs still lurking in a software product when the product starts into production. Obviously, those not removed prior to delivery of a software product will be present when the product reaches its intended users. Here too the U.S. results are not as impressive as they might be. Ordinary companies routinely deliver software with as many as 25 percent of the total defect potential still undiscovered, although leading-edge companies can reduce that volume below 5 percent.

It can be observed in passing that there is an inverse correlation between delivered defects and customer satisfaction: As the volume of delivered defects rises above 5 percent, the customer satisfaction with the project declines severely. When the volume of defects exceeds 25 percent, which implies only 75 percent cumulative removal efficiency, customer satisfaction tends to switch to customer outrage.

U.S. Averages of Defects Found by Users in the First Year of Software Use

Figure 3.24 is a graph of the annual volumes of defects reported by users of software back to the development organization. Normally,

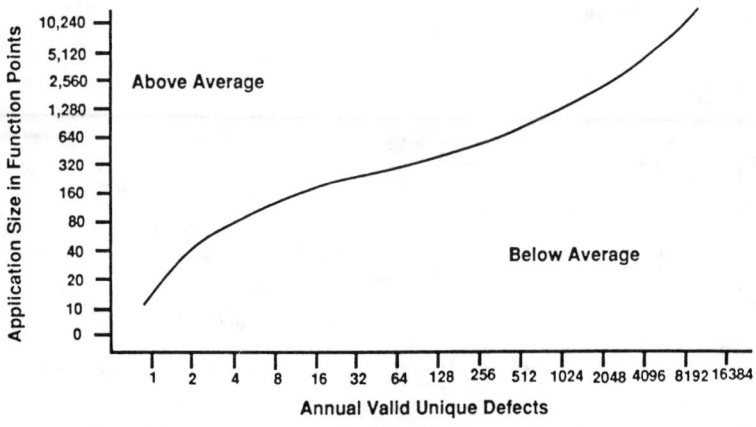

Figure 3.24   User-reported defect volumes in first year of use.

somewhere between 20 and 75 percent of the delivered bugs will be discovered in the first year of production. The actual quantity of defects found by customers will vary directly with the number of users of a product and inversely with the number of latent defects actually present. Software with a high defect load is basically unusable for the first few years, which depresses the percentage of latent defects reported. Software with a very high defect rate is a good candidate for withdrawal or cancellation, so long-term study is more difficult.

Causes for Variations in Software Productivity and Quality

There are, in general, two sets of factors that explain the variations in software productivity and quality to be considered: project factors and process factors. The first set of factors are those associated with the project itself: size, class, type, nature, and novelty. By and large, the project-related factors are outside the ability of project personnel to influence them. For example, in another domain, if your project is to climb a particular mountain, you will not be able to modify the height or steepness; you climb what is there to be climbed. The process of how you go about the climb is another matter, however.

The second set of factors is associated with the process through which the project is developed. Although the process factors are not always completely under management control, management exerts a much stronger influence here than they do on the project factors.

More than 200 process-related factors are known to exist, but some 20 of them stand out as being of truly major significance. Table 3.13

TABLE 3.13 Process Factors Causing Variations in Software Quality
and Productivity

Rank	Worst-case results	Best-case results
1	Inexperienced staff	Experienced staff
2	Irrational schedules	Realistic schedules
3	Inexperienced managers	Experienced managers
4	Unstable requirements	Stable requirements
5	Unstructured methods	Structured methods
6	No inspections	Formal inspections
7	Perfunctory testing	Planned testing
8	No measurements	Full measurements
9	Low design reuse	High design reuse
10	Low code reuse	High code reuse
11	Low-level languages	High-level languages
12	Crowded offices	Private offices
13	Poor organization	Good organization
14	Generalists only	Specialists as needed
15	Severe size constraint	No size constraint
16	Severe performance goals	No performance goals
17	Ordinary tools	Integrated CASE tools
18	Unstable hardware	Stable hardware
19	Marginal computers	Powerful computers
20	Manual planning	Automated planning

shows the best- and worst-case situations for these 20 major factors in the rank order of their impact, with the most influential factors at the top of the list.

Process improvements call for a mixture of social and technological change. By and large, the social changes are likely to be the most difficult, but sometimes they are the most effective. In any case, there is no single change that all by itself can yield enormous results. Since function points are the best metric for judging process changes, refer to *CASE Trends*[13] for the preliminary discussions of the impact.

The Ranges and Limits of Productivity and Quality

Although the averages shown in Chap. 3 are useful as provisional benchmarks, it is also desirable to consider the ranges, variations, and limits of software productivity and quality. It would be desirable to know how all of the 20 factors in Table 3.13 have been shown to influence software projects, but the permutations of so many diverse factors cannot be described succinctly (although they can be modeled via expert software applications). To illustrate the principles of changes in software technologies, here are permutations of four discrete factors shown for productivity and quality:

Productivity factors	Quality factors
Staff experience	Design inspections
Structured methods	Code inspections
CASE tools	Formal testing
High-level languages	Formal quality assurance

Note that the reason only four factors are shown is that the number of permutations rises geometrically with the number selected. The factors selected to be illustrated are the ones the author has received the most questions about in consulting and seminar engagements. They are not, of course, the only major factors that should be considered.

Ranges of Four Productivity Factors

The four productivity factors illustrated here include: (1) experience of the staff, (2) use of structured methods, (3) use of CASE tools, and (4) use of high-level languages. The following definitions are assumed.

Experienced or inexperienced staff

"Experience" is actually a multifaceted concept which includes knowledge of the application area, the language(s) used, and knowledge of various tools and methods. The phrase "experienced staff" implies good familiarity with all of those subelements; "inexperienced staff" implies poor familiarity with the application area and less than optimal familiarity with some of the technical factors such as the methods used.

Structured or unstructured methods

It is interesting that empirical studies tend to reveal a sharp distinction between the use and absence of structured methods but very little difference among the specific structured methods selected. In this case, the phrase "structured methods" defines fairly rigorous adherence to any of the well-known structured techniques, including the Yourdon method, the Warnier-Orr method, the Gane and Sarson method, Method/1, and the Martin data-analytic technique. The phrase "unstructured methods" refers to informal and ad hoc techniques that are carelessly applied.

CASE tools or ordinary tools

The phrase "CASE tools" implies any of the more powerful multifaceted tools which are commercially available, including but not limited to CADRE Teamwork, CGI Pacbase, Knowledgeware, the Texas Instruments IEF and Sage, and many others. The phrase "ordinary tools" implies a negative, or the lack of such formal CASE tools.

High- or low-level languages

Prior to the advent of function points, the concept of high- or low-level languages was very ambiguous. One of the surprising by-products of function point research is the ability to classify languages by level. Software Productivity Research has published a taxonomy of some 300 languages[14] in which the languages are ranked in terms of the number of source statements (executable plus data definitions) required to implement one function point. In this article, the phrase "low-level languages" means all languages in which more than 100 statements are required to implement a single function point. Such languages include Assembler, C, Cobol, Fortran, and many others. The phrase "high-level language" is defined as all languages requiring fewer than 50 statements to implement one function point. The set of high-level languages includes APL, Natural, object-oriented languages such as SMALLTALK and Objective C, many application and program generators, and query languages.

Sizes and classes of software projects studied

The data shown here is taken from software projects that range between 50 and 1000 function points in size (roughly equivalent to a range of from 5000 to 100,000 Cobol source statements). Very small projects tend to vary so widely that they are not always useful for technology research purposes. Very large systems, on the other hand, are so few in number that they lack day-to-day relevance.

The classes of software project include information systems, systems software, and military projects. As a general rule, the information systems are found on the high side of the productivity rate, the systems projects toward the middle, and the military projects on the low side. (Military projects which adhere to military specifications such as 2167A typically produce up to 8 times the paperwork of civilian projects of the same size.)

The activities included started with requirements and concluded with handover or installation at the customer site. The productivity rates included all direct tasks such as requirements, design, coding, reviews, testing, integration, and user documentation. The data also included managerial effort for first-line or project managers.

Although it would be better to show new projects and enhancement projects separately, both are included here. (Enhancements and new projects have notably different productivity rates for projects of less than 50 function points in size, which is why such projects were excluded here.) The 16 permutations shown here illustrate the impact of five separate plateaus of software technology change.

1. The worst-case situation with all factors at the minimum
2. The impact of changing each factor separately
3. The impact of all two-factor changes
4. The impact of all three-factor changes
5. The best-case situation with all factors at optimum

Factors	Productivity ranges in function points per staff-month		
	Lowest	Median	Highest
Single-technology changes			
1. Inexperienced staff Unstructured methods Ordinary tools Low-level languages	0.25	2.5	5.0
2. Inexperienced staff Unstructured methods *CASE tools* Low-level languages	0.3	3.5	6.0
3. Inexperienced staff *Structured methods* Ordinary tools Low-level languages	0.5	4.0	7.0
4. *Experienced staff* Unstructured methods Ordinary tools Low-level languages	0.75	4.5	8.0
5. Inexperienced staff Unstructured methods Ordinary tools *High-level languages*	1.0	5.0	9.5
Two-Technology Changes			
6. Inexperienced staff *Structured methods* *CASE tools* Low-level languages	1.5	6.0	10.0
7. Inexperienced staff Unstructured methods *CASE tools* *High-level languages*	2.0	7.0	12.0

Two-Technology Changes

8. *Experienced staff* Unstructured methods *CASE tools* Low-level languages	3.0	8.0	12.5
9. Inexperienced staff *Structured methods* Ordinary tools *High-level languages*	3.5	8.5	13.0
10. *Experienced staff* *Structured methods* Ordinary tools Low-level languages	4.0	9.0	14.0
11. *Experienced staff* Unstructured methods Ordinary tools *High-level languages*	5.0	10.0	15.0

Three-Technology Changes

12. *Experienced staff* *Structured methods* *CASE tools* Low-level languages	6.0	12.0	20.0
13. Inexperienced staff *Structured methods* *CASE tools* *High-level languages*	6.5	14.0	25.0
14. *Experienced staff* Unstructured methods *CASE tools* *High-level languages*	7.0	18.0	30.0
15. *Experienced staff* *Structured methods* Ordinary tools *High-level languages*	10.0	25.0	50.0

Four-Technology Changes

16. *Experienced staff* *Structured methods* *CASE tools* *High-level languages*	20.0	40.0	100.0

Productivity factor results and interpretation

The results are not really surprising: Changing a single factor does not generate anything like the benefits of changing two or more factors. It is also well known that changes in the experience levels or changes in the methodologies employed tend to outweigh changes in the tools. The only surprising aspect is that high-level languages tended to exert such a strong influence. In that sense, the data is somewhat distorted for the following reasons: (1) Midlevel languages such as Ada were not included and (2) very large systems in which language exerts only minor influences were excluded. For an expanded discussion of the impact of eight factors by the same author, refer to the September 1990 issue of *CASE Strategies*.[15]

The current discussion includes only 4 of the more than 200 factors which are known to influence software projects. Of course, the number of permutations of 200 factors would be impossible to demonstrate, since it is in the trillions. The purposes here are to illustrate the usefulness of function points as a standard management metric and to demonstrate that changes in a single factor are usually not enough to yield major productivity benefits.

The technique of using permutations of various factors is useful for tutorial purposes, but it is not sufficient for serious estimating or economic studies. All of the values between the extreme limits of the factors should be dealt with too. Nevertheless, studies such as this one could not have been prepared at all by using lines-of-code metrics. Here too, function points are starting to shed new light on software topics.

Ranges of Four Defect Removal and Quality Factors

The four quality factors illustrated here include: (1) the use of formal design inspections, (2) the use of formal code inspections, (3) the use of a formal and professionally staffed quality assurance group, and (4) the use of formal testing by trained specialists. The opposite, or worst case, situations include (1) no design inspections at all, (2) no code inspections at all, (3) no quality assurance program at all, and (4) ordinary testing by the development personnel, who presumably have no formal training in test methods.

It should be noted that formal design and code inspections were developed by Michael Fagan of IBM in the early 1970s, and they have been demonstrated in repeated trials to achieve generally the highest levels of defect removal efficiency of any method yet perfected.[16]

Incidentally, the best-case results assume serious attention to quality by trained professionals. In real-life terms, humans range from being very careless to very thorough, and they range from being very competent to totally inept. Within these broad boundaries, almost any results can occur. It should also be noted that the actual number of defect removal steps applied to software projects ranges from 1 (a perfunctory unit test) to more than 20. See Chap. 5 for an expanded discussion of defect removal methods and results.

Factors	Defect removal efficiency, %		
	Lowest	Median	Highest
Single-Technology Changes			
1. No design inspections No code inspections No quality assurance No formal testing	30	40	50
2. No design inspections No code inspections *Formal quality assurance* No formal testing	32	45	55
3. No design inspections No code inspections No quality assurance *Formal testing*	37	53	60
4. No design inspections *Formal code inspections* No quality assurance No formal testing	43	57	65
5. *Formal design inspections* No code inspections No quality assurance No formal testing	45	60	68
Two-Technology Changes			
6. No design inspections No code inspections *Formal quality assurance* *Formal testing*	50	65	75
7. No design inspections *Formal code inspections* *Formal quality assurance* No formal testing	53	68	78
8. No design inspections *Formal code inspections* No quality assurance *Formal testing*	55	70	80
9. *Formal design inspections* No code inspections *Formal quality assurance* No formal testing	60	75	85
10. *Formal design inspections* No code inspections No quality assurance *Formal testing*	65	80	87
11. *Formal design inspections* *Formal code inspections* No quality assurance No formal testing	70	85	90
Three-Technology Changes			
12. No design inspections	75	87	93

Continued

	Defect removal efficiency, %		
Factors	Lowest	Median	Highest
Formal code inspections			
Formal quality assurance			
Formal testing			
13. *Formal design inspections*	77	90	95
No code inspections			
Formal quality assurance			
Formal testing			
14. *Formal design inspections*	83	95	97
Formal code inspections			
Formal quality assurance			
No formal testing			
15. *Formal design inspections*	85	97	99
Formal code inspections			
No quality assurance			
Formal testing			
Four-Technology Changes			
16. *Formal design inspections*	95	99	99
Formal code inspections			
Formal quality assurance			
Formal testing			

Quality factor results and interpretation

Here too the results should not be surprising. Defect removal methods have been subject to measurement and exploration since the 1960s, and by now the removal efficiency of some 30 kinds of review, inspection, and test have been measured.

It is obvious that quality, like productivity, requires more than a change to a single factor to achieve impressive results. The leading-edge companies, such as IBM, AT&T, and Hewlett-Packard, have long known that a synergistic combination of defect removal methods will achieve the highest levels of quality and the highest levels of productivity at the same time.

Using Function Points to Establish Improvement Goals

Not only can function points be used for measurement, but they also lend themselves to the creation of improvement goals and performance targets. In other human activities, such as athletics, it is very helpful to know exactly how good your competitors are in order to judge your own performance. It is, of course, also useful to measure your own results. For example, imagine yourself as a member of a track team in training for the Olympics. What would you think if your coach discussed training in the following terms?

You're going to have to train hard to beat the competition. Of course I'm not sure how fast they actually run because I don't believe in using a stopwatch. You'll be running in events from the 100-meter dash up to 5000 meters, but I don't believe in measurements so I'm not sure exactly how long the practice track is. I want you to practice until you improve by 20 percent, but I'm not sure how fast you run today because I've never measured. It ought to be easy to do, though, because I've bought the team some new track shoes that the salesman says will improve your speed by 50 percent.

Such a conversation could never happen in real life because no track coach could succeed without measurements. Yet statements that are similar happen every day in software departments. Unfortunately, for 45 years the software profession had achieved a notorious reputation for never measuring its performance. Without a reliable metric for the output of software projects, many companies did not bother to keep accurate records of staffing, schedules, and effort expended either. In looking at the project-tracking systems used by major corporations, errors and omissions of from 30 to more than 70 percent have been the norm: unpaid overtime, user costs, project redirections, managerial effort, support costs, and overhead activities such as integration are simply not tracked by a majority of companies.

The advantage that function points brings to software projects is that they are mathematically consistent and do not behave in strange and paradoxical ways. The older lines-of-code metrics were mathematically perverse in that they sometimes moved in the direction opposite from that of real economic productivity. Function points allow software managers and executives not only to measure performance but to establish measurable goals for improvement. Function points are not the only things that should be measured or targeted, of course, but functional metrics are the heart of a modern measurement system for software.

The following goals are empirically derived from observations of what leading-edge companies are actually able to accomplish in 1991. If your company is equal to or better than these goals, then you have achieved considerable success and you can be justifiably proud of your company's performance. Although many different goals might be set, there are six key areas in which measurable goals are most important: quality, development productivity, enhancement productivity, maintenance productivity, advanced technologies, and morale and the environment.

Software quality goals

< 4   Defects per function point as the overall defect potential

< 0.025   User-reported defects per function point per year

> 90%   Annual user evaluations of "excellent" on applications

> 95%   Cumulative defect removal efficiency

0   Error-prone modules (EPM) in production systems (EPM $\geq$ 2.0 defects per function point)

Software quality is important not only because of the need for reliable systems but because defect removal is sometimes the most expensive part of building software. Therefore, quality improvement is on the critical path to productivity improvement. There are five key software quality goals, and if your enterprise exceeds them, you are doing very well indeed.

1. Achieving a defect potential of fewer than four defects per function point overall would place you in the top 10 percent of U.S. companies. (The "defect potential" is the sum of all defects: requirements, design, coding, documentation, and bad fixes.)

2. Achieving less than 0.025 user-reported defect per function point would place you in the top 5 percent of U.S. companies. A defect is a bug which causes the application to either stop or to produce incorrect results. Ordinary or trailing-edge companies have 1.0 or more user-reported defects per function point per year.

3. Not only do leading-edge enterprises carry out annual user satisfaction surveys but critical applications receive 90 percent "excellent" votes by the users polled.

4. Defect removal efficiency is defined as follows: In the course of developing software, your staff will find a certain number of bugs. In the first year of production, your users will find a certain number of bugs. When you add the two bug totals together, your staff should have found 95 percent or more of all bugs, leaving 5 percent or less for the users to find. A rate of 95 percent will place you in the top 1 percent of U.S. companies. Most MIS producers are less than 75 percent efficient, and users find 25 percent or more of all bugs.

5. Bugs are not randomly distributed through the code of large systems. They tend to clump in a very small number of places called error-prone modules. Your goal should be to eliminate all error-prone modules in your current applications and prevent them from ever occurring in the future. Fortunately, this can be done easily by means of full design and code inspections. An error-prone module is defined as one that receives more than 2.0 bugs per function point from users.

Development productivity goals

> 25   Function points per staff-month average productivity on smaller projects of from 10 to 250 function points in size

> 15   Function points per staff-month average productivity on medium projects of 250 to 1000 function points in size

> 10   Function points per staff-month on very large projects of more than 1000 function points in size

> 5   Function points per staff-month in net annual software productivity, i.e., total FP/total staff

< 5%   Canceled projects

Productivity can be measured at both the project level and at the corporate or enterprise level. Individual projects normally are much more productive than enterprise-level projects, since at the enterprise level factors such as canceled projects and indirect staff must be considered.

- Ordinary applications produced with informal normal methods and unsophisticated tools seldom achieve productivity rates greater than 5 function points per staff-month. If you are in excess of 15 function points per staff-month on major projects (projects greater than 500 function points total), then you are doing very well indeed. All the staff included in the measure should be workers on the project, i.e., analysts, programmers, technical writers, quality assurance, and first-line management.

- Each year, your organization will deliver a certain quantity of function points to your users. Large enterprises may deliver more than 10,000 function points annually. If you divide your total annual delivery by your entire staff (all direct personnel, management, and indirect staff) what is your annual rate? Typically, it will be only about one-third as high as that of individual projects because it includes time spent in training, slack time between jobs, vacations, and time spent on projects that are not delivered.

- Canceled projects are a source of negative productivity. Effort is expended, but nothing is delivered. Some companies may cancel as many as 25 percent of their major systems.

Enhancement productivity goals

> 1500   Function points per maintenance staff member as annual average assignment scope

> 20   Function points per staff-month average productivity on minor enhancements from 1 to 50 function points in size

> 15   Function points per staff-month average productivity on medium enhancements of from 50 to 250 function points in size

> 10   Function points per staff-month average productivity on major enhancements larger that 250 function points in size

100%   Use of structural analyzers on existing software

< 2.5%   Bad-fix injection rate

In 1990, already more than half of the programmers in the United States were working on maintenance and enhancement of existing applications. Therefore, enhancement goals must be of equal importance to development goals.

- If you divide the size of your production library of current applications by the size of your maintenance staff, you will create a very interesting metric called the *maintenance assignment scope:* the volume of current software that an ordinary maintenance programmer is responsible for in terms of defect repairs and minor enhancements. If you have a library of aging, unstructured applications with high complexity, the maintenance assignment scope may be fewer than 500 function points. If your maintenance assignment scope is greater than 1500 function points, the implication is that you are moving in the right direction.

- Productivity rates on enhancement projects are normally lower than rates on a same-size development project, and so a different goal is needed. Enhancement productivity is directly related to the structure and stability of existing software.

- Since it is a known fact that complex software is hard to modify, all existing projects should be subjected to formal complexity analysis, normally, using one or more of the many commercial complexity analysis tools. Overly complex portions of the software can then be slated for restructuring or some other corrective action.

- Each time an existing application is updated, there is a chance of introducing a bug. If the bug is the result of fixing a previous bug, then it is termed a "bad fix." You should target less than 2.5 percent bad-fix injection on your applications. If you are working with aging and unstructured Cobol, the bad-fix rate may exceed 15 percent.

Maintenance productivity goals

Recall that "maintenance" as used here is restricted to defect repairs, which normally are somewhat stressful and also somewhat urgent. The significant aspects of maintenance, in terms of goals, are to ensure both rapid turnaround and few bad fixes.

< 1   Minute "wait" or "hold" time when customers wish to report defects by phone or FAX.

< 24   Hour turnaround for critical defects (severity 1) from receipt of defect report until repair is available

< 5   Days turnaround for high-severity defects (severity 2) from receipt of defect report until repair is available

< 15   Days turnaround for low-severity defects (severities 3 and 4) from receipt of defect report until repair is available

< 2.5%   Bad-fix injection rate

Employee morale and environmental goals

> 10   Annual training days per staff member

> 90   Square feet per staff member of private office space

> 90%   Annual opinion survey evaluations of "good" or better

Software is a human activity, and enterprises that have the greatest respect for employees usually come out on top in terms of productivity, quality, and other tangible matters. Here are three key metrics that deal with this topic:

- Surprisingly, companies that provide 10 days of annual training per staff year seem to have higher annual rates for software productivity than companies that provide no training at all.

- In the classic study of programming productivity carried out by Tom DeMarco and Tim Lister,[11] there was a direct correlation between office space and productivity. Modern office arrangements for software professionals have also been studied by Gerald McCue, Dean of Architecture at Harvard.[12] Both studies agree: More than 90 ft^2 per professional staff member is optimal for the highest productivity rates. If your staff averages less than 45 ft^2, don't expect anything but low productivity.

- Companies that take the best care of their people have the highest productivity. How do you know if your people are being taken care of and are happy? The most effective way is to ask. Companies that have annual opinion surveys and get more than 90 percent "good" marks have higher productivity than companies than don't perform opinion surveys or that do perform them but get low marks.

Advanced technology goals

> 50%   Reusable designs, by volume of specifications

> 75%   Reusable code, by volume of specifications

100%   Use of automated planning tools

100%   Use of automated estimating tools

100%   Measurement of major software projects

—   Active research in CASE technologies

—   Active research in reengineering and reverse engineering technologies

—   Active research in repository technologies

As 1991 draws to a close, software managers and professionals should begin to think not only of next year but of the next century. It is time now to move toward the emerging domains of full design and code reusability and full automation of the more complex management tasks of planning and estimating software projects.

Summary and Conclusions

Function points do provide the ability and versatility to make uniform measures of software productivity and quality and to come to grips with the really important measurable aspects of software. The current study and the provisional establishment of U.S. norms have a high margin of error and should not be given great credibility. Even so, they provide a useful benchmark against which future studies and future improvements can be evaluated.

The set of standard metrics described in this chapter provide the basic set of measures necessary to come to grips with the numeric aspects of software productivity and quality. Obviously, the set can and should be expanded as more data becomes available. The goals or targets derived from leading-edge enterprises show both what is important in terms of the real world and also how function points can become a key business tool leading to improvements.

The data, tables, and figures included here are only provisional, and many will no doubt be proved wrong in the future. However, in spite of the high margin of error, if this preliminary data were not published, there would be no way of improving the overall accuracy of the data available to the industry. In terms of precision, it is hoped that at least the right set of curves and factors has been selected and that the general shapes and dimensions of the curves are correct. Beyond that, the comparatively small samples, the vagaries of the raw data, and the gaps and missing elements make it highly doubtful that the curves can exist without needing correction for more than a few months. Also, our industry is evolving and changing steadily, so even if the current data were highly accurate in 1990, it should be updated on an annual basis to stay current with the evolution of technologies and approaches to software engineering.

References

1. Albrecht, A. J., "Measuring Application Development Productivity," *Proceedings of the Joint SHARE, GUIDE, and IBM Application Development Symposium, October*

1979. (Reprinted in C. Jones, *Programming Productivity—Issues for the Eighties,* IEEE Press, Catalog Number EH0239-4, 1986.

2. Jones, Capers, *Programming Productivity—Issues for the Eighties,* IEEE Press, Catalog Number EHO 186-7, 1981, 448 pages.

3. Boehm, Barry, *Software Engineering Economics,* Prentice-Hall, Englewood Cliffs, N.J., 1981, 767 pages.

4. Jones, Capers, *Programming Productivity,* McGraw-Hill, New York, 1986, 280 pages.

5. Jones, Capers, *U.S. Industry Averages for Software Productivity and Quality,* Software Productivity Research, Inc., Burlington, Mass., August 1988, 23 pages.

6. Symons, Charles, "Experiences with the Mark II Function Point Method," presented at the *QAI Measurement Conference, Orlando, Florida,* April 1990, Quality Assurance Institute, Orlando, Fla.

7. Banker, R. D., and Kemerer, C. F., "Scale Economics in New Software Development," *IEEE Transactions in Software Engineering,* vol. 15, no. 10, October 1989.

8. Jones, Capers, *Software Defect Removal—A Survey of the State of the Art,* Software Productivity Research, Inc., Burlington, Mass., September 1987, 55 pages.

9. Kendall, R., and Lamb, E. C., "Management Perspectives on Programs, Programming, and Productivity," presented at *GUIDE 45, Atlanta,* reprinted in C. Jones, *Programming Productivity—Issues for the Eighties,* IEEE Press, Catalog Number EHO 186-7, 1981, pp. 201–212.

10. Jones, Capers, "A Survey of Programming Design and Specification Techniques," *Proceedings, Specifications of Reliable Software,* reprinted in C. Jones, *Programming Productivity—Issues for the Eighties,* IEEE Press, Catalog Number EHO 186-7, 1981, pp. 224–236.

11. DeMarco, T., and Lister, T., *Peopleware,* Dorset House Press, New York, 1987, 189 pages.

12. McCue, G., "IBM's Santa Teresa Laboratory—Architectural Design for Program Development," *IBM Systems Journal,* vol. 17, no. 1, 1978. Reprinted in C. Jones, *Programming Productivity—Issues for the Eighties,* IEEE Press, Catalog Number EH0239-4, 1986.

13. Jones, Capers, "Measuring Software Productivity," *CASE Trends,* vol. 2, no. 1, Jan/Feb 1990, pp. 17–24.

14. Jones, Capers, *Table of Programming Languages and Levels,* Software Productivity Research, Inc., Burlington, Mass., 1988, 35 pages.

15. "CASE and Software Productivity: A Conversation with T. Capers Jones," *CASE Strategies,* vol. II, no. 9, September 1990.

16. Fagan, M., "Design and Code Inspections to Reduce Errors in Program Development," *IBM Systems Journal,* vol. 15, no. 3, 1975, pp. 182–211.

4

The Mechanics of Measurement: Building a Baseline

Introduction

The objective of applied software measurement is insight. We don't measure software just to watch for trends; we look for ways to improve and get better. It should never be forgotten that the goal of measurement is useful information, and not just data, and that the goal of information is improvement. A medical doctor would never prescribe medicines or therapies to patients without carrying out a diagnosis first. Indeed, any doctor who behaved so foolishly could not stay licensed. Software is not yet at this level of professionalism: Consultants and vendors prescribe their tools or methods without any diagnosis at all.

A good measurement program is a diagnostic study that can identify all software problems that need therapies. The therapies themselves can often be derived from the measurements. For example, if 20 projects are measured in a company and all 20 project teams report "crowded, noisy office conditions" as an environmental factor, it is a fair conclusion that improvements in office space are needed.

Measurement can take place at the strategic or corporate level or at the project or tactical level. Both are important, but the greatest insights are normally available by careful tactical measurement on a project-by-project basis. If such a study is carried out annually, it will allow a company to create a measured baseline of where it was at a given point in time and to use that baseline to judge its rate of improvement in the future.

Once baseline measurements begin, they normally become such valuable corporate assets that they quickly become standard annual events. This implies full-time staffing and adequate support, both of which are desirable. However, the very first baseline a company carries out is a special case. It differs from a normal annual software productivity survey in several key respects:

1. The measurement team that collects the data is new, and it may be external management consultants.

2. The concept of measurement is new, and the company is uncertain of what measurement is all about.

3. The managers of the projects to be measured are probably apprehensive.

4. There is no prior model to work from, in terms of what data to include or even what the report might look like.

5. The timing and effort required for the baseline may be somewhat greater than in future baselines because of the need to climb up the learning curve.

Unless consultants are used, the first annual baseline will probably be staffed on a short-term basis by people who are fairly new to measurements and who are exploring metrics concepts. This also is a normal situation. An interesting phenomenon is that about 15 to 25 percent of the staff members who become involved with a company's initial baseline analysis become so intrigued with measurement technology that they enter new career paths and will wish to stay with measurement work permanently! That is a good sign for the software industry, since when metrics and measurements become serious enough for a career change, it indicates that a term like "software engineering" is becoming real instead of a painful misnomer.

The daily work of a physician involves diagnosis and treatment of patients. The daily work of a tactical measurement specialist involves diagnosis and treatment of projects. The project is the basic unit of study for tactical software measurement purposes. Although the term "project" is a common one, it is seldom defined. For the purposes of measurement, a project is defined as a set of coordinated tasks that are directed at producing and delivering a discrete software program, component, or system. The project team is assumed to consist of at least one manager and a varying number of technical staff members ranging from one to several hundred. The project team is also assumed to have a reasonably homogeneous set of methods and tools, which can encompass tools for requirements, design, coding, defect removal, and documentation.

Practical examples of what is meant by the term "project" include the following: an accounts payable system, an Ada compiler, a PBX switching system, a new release of a commercial software product such as WordPerfect Release 5, Lotus Release 3, or CHECKPOINT® Releases 1 and 2, an order entry system, or a personnel benefits tracking system. All of these are "projects" in the measurement sense that the components and programs were part of a single overall scheme or architecture, the staff ultimately reported to a single executive, and a homogeneous tool set was employed.

Very large systems, such as IBM's MVS operating system, would normally consist of quite a few separate projects such as the scheduler component, the supervisor component, and the access methods. The practical reason for considering these technically related components to be separate projects is that they were developed in different cities under different managers who used different methods and tool sets. For the purposes of gaining insights, it is necessary to measure the tasks of each of the groups separately if for no other reason than because some were in California and others were in New York. Obviously, the final measures can be consolidated upward, but the data itself should be derived from the specific projects within the overall system.

An annual baseline measurement study is a well-defined and thorough diagnostic technique that can be administered either by professional consultants or by the measurement team that a company creates by using its own employees. To establish a baseline initially, a reasonable sample of projects is required. Normal annual baselines include all projects above a certain size that went into production in the preceding year. Thus, a company's 1991 baseline would include all of its 1990 delivered projects.

However, the very first annual baseline is usually somewhat of an experiment, and so it may not contain 100 percent of the prior year's projects. Indeed, the very first baseline may contain projects whose completions span many years. Yet, a reasonable sample is necessary to gain insights about software issues. Normally from 10 to 30 projects will constitute the volume of an initial baseline. The projects themselves should be a mixture of new development, enhancements, and special projects (such as package acquisitions or contract projects) that reflects the kinds of software work the company actually carries out.

The baseline measurement study will examine all of the factors present in an enterprise that can affect the enterprise's software development, enhancement, and maintenance by as much as 1 percent. The baseline study can cover more than 200 soft environmental factors, and it is an attempt to bring the same level of discipline to bear on software as might be found in a thorough medical examination. As with medical examinations, a software baseline study is a diagnostic study aimed at finding problems or, in some cases, the lack of problems. After a careful diagnosis, it is possible to move toward a cure if problems are discovered. But before appropriate therapies can be prescribed, it is necessary to know the exact nature of the condition.

Why a Company Will Commission a Baseline

There are four common reasons why a company will commission a productivity analysis, and the measurement team should be very sensitive to them:

1. The company is interested in starting a software measurement program, and it wants both reliable information on current productivity and assistance in selecting and starting a software improvement program of which measurement is a key component.

2. The company wants to reduce the overall costs of software, data processing, and computing expenses with the enterprise and is looking for ways to economize.

3. The company wants to shorten software development schedules and provide needed functions to users more quickly.

4. The company has already achieved high software productivity, and it is seeking an independent validation of that fact which will be credible with enterprise management and the users of data processing.

Case 1. Measurement and improvement as the motivation

The measurement of software productivity has been a chronic weakness since the computing industry began. Based on a sample of more than 1000 software producing companies polled at various conferences, less than 10 percent of enterprises have any software measurements at all and less than 3 percent have any really useful measurements of either software productivity or software quality. (*Note:* The polling was informal: it was based on the number of hands raised in response to the questions, "How many of your companies have any software measurements?" and "How many of your companies have really useful software measurements?"

The baseline analysis will provide company executives with a first-time snapshot of productivity and quality levels in effect at the time the analysis was carried out. The results of this can be electrifying, since top management will suddenly realize how important software is and what might be done to improve its value. In this case, what will probably occur is an expansion to a full corporate measurement system including quality and user satisfaction measures, ongoing project measures, and the entire set of modern metrics.

Case 2. Cost reduction as the primary motivation

If cost reduction is the primary goal of the baseline analysis, that may imply that the company is in an economic downturn. The set of technologies and follow-on activities that can be prescribed will probably be limited to those without significant capital investment. There are methodologies, such as joint application design (JAD), structured development, the use of design and code inspections, and code restructuring that can reduce costs without incurring high levels of up-front spending and capital equipment purchases. It is usually possible to slow the rate of increase in annual software costs; it is sometimes possible to freeze spending at current levels; and it is occasionally possible to reduce spending levels slightly. However, companies should be cautioned before the baseline analysis begins that cost reduction without negative impact on operations is a difficult but not impossible goal.

Case 3. Schedule reduction as the primary motivation

If schedule reduction is the primary goal of the baseline analysis, there are powerful tools and technologies that can be prescribed: improved office environments, integrated software workstations, libraries of standard reusable code, graphics requirements and design methods, some of the better CASE tools, inspections, object-oriented languages, and many others that can collectively reduce software development times by as much as 75 percent.

However, to acquire the full set of effective schedule reduction tools may have up-front costs that reach $25,000 or even $50,000 per software engineer coupled with education and training costs that can approach $5000 per software engineer. Companies should know before the baseline analysis begins that schedule reduction technologies are powerful but not inexpensive.

Case 4. Validation of high productivity as the primary motivation

A few companies that are already at the leading edge in terms of software productivity are interested in starting a software baseline analysis because they want to have their actual productivity accomplishments validated and presented to enterprise management in a

tangible, objective way. When this situation occurs, few if any therapies may be required after the analysis is completed. The value here is
accurate quantification of productivity rates.

The ethics of measurement

Regardless of the company motivations for commissioning a baseline
analysis, the staff involved in it has an ethical obligation to make the
analysis accurate and valuable. There is no value, and there can be
considerable harm, in incomplete or inaccurate information presented
to higher management. Management has a fiduciary duty to run the
enterprise capably. The measurement team has an ethical duty to give
the executives accurate data and clear explanations of the significance
of the data.

It is important that both company management and the measurement team have a clear understanding of what results will come from
a baseline study and what will not. What will result is a very clear
picture of the software strengths and weaknesses of the enterprise
that commissioned the study. For any weaknesses that are noted, possible therapies can be prescribed. What will not result is an instanta-
neous improvement in productivity. After the analysis is over, it can
take from a month to a year to implement the therapies, and sometimes more than a year after that before tangible improvements can
begin to show up. Very large corporations with more than 1000 software professionals should extend their planning horizons out to 3
years or more.

It is unfortunate that Americans tend to like quick, simple solutions
to difficult and complicated problems. Improving software productivity and quality in a large company is a difficult and complicated problem, and an annual baseline tactical analysis is a very important part
of the entire process.

The Methodology of the Baseline Analysis

The exact methods and schedules for carrying out the baseline analysis depend upon the number of projects selected and on whether the
analysis will be performed at a single location or carried out at multiple locations and cities. Defense contractors, and other kinds of companies as well, may start their baseline work with a self-evaluation
procedure developed by the Software Engineering Institute at
Carnegie Mellon University and published by the SEI director, Watts
Humphrey.[1] This self-assessment procedure evaluates a number of
technological factors and then places the company on a "software maturity grid." The results of the self-assessment are interesting and

useful, but the SEI process is not detailed enough to serve as the basis for an accurate diagnosis of deeper conditions, nor does it tend to suggest appropriate therapies.

The normal cycle for a full annual baseline analysis runs from 2 to 3 calendar months. The methodology for the full baseline described here is based on the concepts first used at IBM and ITT and subsequently adopted by other companies such as AT&T, DEC, and Hewlett-Packard. The SPR methodology described here differs from the SEI approach in a fashion that is analogous to a full medical examination vs. a self-checking procedure to be carried out at home. The SPR methodology is intended to be administered by professional consultants assisted by statistical analysis and multiple-regression techniques. The volume of information collected by using the SPR method is more than an order of magnitude greater than the SEI method; it takes more time but leads to a fuller set of diagnoses and expanded therapies. Examples of the kinds of results that are possible are shown here in Appendices C, D, and E. Earlier results were also published in *Programming Productivity*.[2]

The very first time a full baseline is attempted, the additional start-up work can stretch out the cycle to 6 months or more. Following are the general patterns:

Executive sponsorship

As pointed out in Chap. 1, the natural initial reaction to a baseline study is apprehension and fear, with the most severe alarms being felt by the managers whose projects will be measured. Therefore, an annual baseline study will probably require an executive sponsor at the vice presidential level, or even higher, the first time it is carried out.

Selection of the measurement team

Set aside one or two months for the critical task of assembling a measurement team. No modern company would dream of turning its finances and corporate accounting over to well-intentioned amateurs without professional qualifications; yet many companies attempt to start measurement baseline programs with personnel whose only qualification is that they are between assignments and hence are available. That is not as it should be: The measurement manager selection should be based on capabilities, as should selection of the rest of the measurement team.

The first time a company performs a baseline, the managers and staff will normally be somewhat inexperienced, but the situation is quite transient. Surprisingly, measurement technology is so interesting that perhaps 15 to 25 percent of the initial staff will decide to pursue measurement as a permanent career. As of 1991, no academic courses are available to software measurement specialists, but a new career is definitely emerging.

For the initial selection of a team, the manager should have a very good grounding in software methods and tools and sufficient knowledge of statistics to know how to apply statistics to practical problems. The measurement team should include at least one person with a good background in statistics, and all of the team should be experienced in software tools and methods.

Designing the data collection instruments

The first time a company starts to create an annual baseline, it is faced with the necessity of either acquiring or constructing questionnaires or survey forms. It is also faced with the necessity of acquiring or constructing software tools that can aid in the analysis and interpretation of the collected data. A minimum of about 6 months should be allotted if the company decides to construct its own instruments and tools. About 2 to 3 months should be allotted for selecting a consulting group if the company decides on the second option.

Some of the management consulting companies offering baseline services as part of their consulting practice include (in alphabetic order) A.D. Little; Arthur Anderson; Computer Power; DMR; Index Group; Peat; Marwick & Main; Matrix; Nolan, Norton & Company; Roger Pressman Associates; Reifer Associates; Rubin Associates; and Software Productivity Research. Just as medical doctors do not diagnose patients by mail, a baseline study cannot be effectively carried out by means of mail surveys. Experienced, knowledgeable consultants must conduct face-to-face interviews with the project managers and team members to gain the really valuable insights that can occur.

Introductory session prior to commencing the annual baseline

The first public event of the baseline analysis begins with a 1- to 3-h seminar on the rationale of the baseline and what is going to be accomplished. If available, it is helpful to show what other companies in the same line of business have been learning from their baselines or what is currently known about software productivity and quality in the industry as a whole. The purposes of the introductory session are to inform all staff and management of the intent of the baseline and to gain feedback about the natural apprehensions and concerns. Although this task takes less than one day, at least a month of lead time is required to schedule the event. Also, if the session is to be given in more than one city or country (for multinationals) additional time will be required.

Preliminary discussions and project selection

Plan on at least a week, and probably 2 weeks, for project selection. After the introductory session, the next step is to select from 10 to 30 specific projects to be examined, with 12 being the average number selected. This is a delicate process in terms of corporate politics. Since the normal management reaction will be apprehension, there is sometimes a tendency to select only projects considered to be "successful." That is not as it should be. What is best is to select projects that are representative of what is really going on: good projects, bad projects, development projects, enhancement projects, completed projects, and unfinished projects are all candidates for measurement.

Scheduling the project interviews

Once the projects are selected, the first schedules will be set for the individual project analyses. A complete baseline analysis for 12 projects usually takes about 2 calendar months to complete, involves about 25 days of consulting time (15 of them on site at the project locations), and requires roughly 60 h of client staff and management time to complete the questionnaires. Each interview session of a project team will range from about 2 h to a maximum of about 4 h. The participants will include the project manager and some or all of the project team, with a limit of perhaps six people in all. The limit of six people is not absolute, but it does represent the upper bounds of meetings that can be conversational without being discursive.

Individual project analysis

Each project selected by the company should be analyzed by using a standard technique so that the data is comparable. For example, the data collection instrument used by Software Productivity Research is a tactical project evaluation questionnaire that covers a total or more than 200 factors dealing with the projects themselves, the methods and tools used, the documents produced, the languages, the specialists and the organization structure, the defect prevention and removal techniques, and so forth.

Each project analysis requires from 2 to 4 h. The participants for each analysis include the consultant, the manager of the project being analyzed, and several technical personnel: usually a design specialist, one or more programmers, and one or more technical writers if they were used for the project. If the project uses quality assurance, a quality assurance specialist should be part of the interview session. Thus, each analysis requires an investment by the project team of from 6 to perhaps 24 staff-hours.

All the participants in each analysis receive copies of the data collection questionnaire, which they are free to annotate during the analysis and to keep when the session is over. The master copy of the baseline questionnaire is kept with the actual project data by the consultant performing the analysis.

It is not uncommon for individuals on a project to have different opinions, and these ranges should be noted. Indeed, based on several hundred projects, it can be stated that managerial responses are normally about half a point more optimistic than technical staff responses when it comes to the usefulness of various methods and processes.

Although some apprehension is normal prior to the interview sessions, the apprehension vanishes almost immediately. Indeed, on the whole the managers and staff enjoy the interviews tremendously, and for perfectly valid sociological reasons:

1. They have never before had the opportunity to discuss their views of the tools, methods, and approaches in a serious and non-threatening way, and they enjoy it.

2. The interviews are a clear and definite sign that the company is starting to take software seriously. This is, of course, an encouraging fact for software professionals, who have long considered themselves to be outside the scope of their company strategy.

3. The interviews provide a rare opportunity for people working on the same project to discuss what they are doing in a well structured manner that includes, without exception, every facet that can influence the outcome of the project.

If the company is using automated tools for data collection and analysis, then before each analysis session is over, it may sometimes be possible to give the project manager a preliminary report that shows the responses for that project. Indeed, for unfinished projects it is possible to carry out a full cost estimate. However, if paper questionnaires are used, it is not convenient to provide immediate feedback.

Aggregation of data and statistical analyses

Set aside at least 10 working days for aggregation and analysis of the collected data. When all the selected projects have been individually analyzed, the combined data is aggregated and analyzed statistically. Hopefully, powerful statistical tools will be available to facilitate this aggregation. The factors that are significant include those in respect to which:

- All projects noted deficiencies or weaknesses.
- All projects noted successes or strengths.
- There were inconsistencies among projects, such as instances of some projects using formal inspections whereas similar projects did not.

Before production of the final reports, client management will be alerted to any significant findings that have emerged. The information can take the form of either an informal presentation or a draft report.

Preparation of the baseline presentation

There are two standard outputs from an annual baseline survey:

1. A presentation to executives on the findings
2. The full baseline report itself

The presentation to executives will normally be in the form of either overheads or 35-mm slides, depending upon your corporate protocols. The presentation, which may run up to 100 screens or slides, will discuss the background of the study, the weakness and strengths identified, the numerical hard data, and any possible therapies that appear to need immediate management attention. For preparation of the draft, about a week will normally be required. Production of slides and overheads may take up to 2 weeks depending upon the nature and speed of your production facilities.

For large companies, the time required to go through the presentation can range to more than half a day. The audience for the presentation will normally be senior executives, often including the CEO. The presentation will be given initially to the senior management of the company, but the normal protocols in business are such that it is highly advantageous to put on a road show and give the presentation to all company locations and managers who have any software responsibilities at all. Thus, in large corporations such as AT&T, Hewlett-Packard, ITT, and IBM, the annual baseline presentation may be given in more than 25 different cities.

Preparation of the baseline annual report

After the full analysis of the data, the final results of the baseline are prepared under the supervision of the senior baseline measurement manager. The final report, typically 70 to 100 pages in length, contains the detailed results of the productivity analysis. Appendix D discusses and gives an example of a corporate annual report.

In companies such as IBM and ITT, the annual baseline reports are prepared on the same time scale as the corporate annual reports. Indeed, the annual software report tends to be about the same size and to more or less resemble in substance a true corporate annual report. The production of a true corporate annual report for a company such as IBM, however, is about a 3-month undertaking with costs that exceed $1 million for content, layout, and production. The cost and time of a software baseline is not in that league, of course, but about 2 to 3 weeks of effort to produce the draft, followed by 1 to 2 weeks of production would be normal. The published report will differ from the slide or screen presentation in these respects:

- It will have explanatory text that discusses the significance of the findings.
- It will normally have more detail than the presentation.

The final reports vary in content with the specifics of each company, but they always include the following items:

1. An executive summary of significant diagnostic findings
2. Specific problems diagnosed in the areas of management, organization, staff specialization, policies, physical environment, methodologies, tools, the production library, and the applications backlog
3. Raw and normalized data on the projects and interpretation of the results
4. Suggested therapies that the enterprise should explore to overcome the noted problems

Overall scope and timing of the baseline

The normal scope of a baseline analysis generally runs from the initial meeting through the delivery of the final report. Although there are wide variances depending on the number of projects selected by the client, number of cities to be visited, and the like, a typical productivity analysis will take about 25 to 50 consultant days: 1 introductory day, 10 to 15 days of on-site data collection, 4 to 6 days of data analysis, 5 to 7 days of presentation creation, 4 to 7 days of written report preparation, 2 days of internal review among the measurement staff, ½ day with the senior company management for the preliminary report, 1 day for last-minute changes and corrections, and 1 full day with senior management to present the findings of the final report.

Follow-on Activities after the Baseline Is Complete

The baseline analysis will diagnose all software problems and all software strengths in an enterprise, with essentially no exceptions. As with medical diagnosis, the diagnostic stage must be followed by a therapy stage in order to cure the condition. Exactly what follow-on activities will be needed varies from client to client. There is no single pattern that always emerges, just as medical therapy varies from patient to patient and illness to illness. There are, however, five general action items which often occur as a result of a productivity analysis.

Site visits.   A very frequent adjunct to a productivity analysis are site visits by client personnel to enterprises that have already achieved high levels of productivity. There are a number of leading-edge enterprises, already well ahead of U.S. averages in terms of software productivity, that allow or encourage visitors. To cite but two, the IBM Santa Teresa Programming Center in San Jose, California, and the Hartford Insurance Company in Hartford, Connecticut, frequently receive visitors from other enterprises who are interested in seeing what has been accomplished. Site visits give client enterprises an opportunity to see real companies in action, and they are very effective in showing the pragmatics of software productivity.

Tool acquisition.   Many enterprises are found to be deficient in software tooling, such as numbers of workstations and graphics and text design packages. A very common follow-on activity is the acquisition and installation of new tools. Tool acquisition is not inexpensive, and from $3000 to more than $25,000 per software engineer may sometimes be committed.

Methodology selection.   Enterprises which lack technology exploration functions such as development centers or software research labs may be several years out of date in terms of methodology. A frequent result of a baseline analysis is the selection of and experimentation with such new methodologies as joint application design (JAD), high-speed prototyping, time-box prototyping, object-oriented languages, and inspections. Methodological changes do not require as heavy a capital investment as tool upgrades, but they do require time and educational commitments. Method upgrades can involve as much as several weeks of education time per software engineer and from $500 to $5000 per staff member in training expenses.

Policy formation.   Changes in enterprise policies and cultures are the most difficult follow-on activities after a productivity analysis. For example, implementing a dual-compensation plan, installing opinion surveys, creating an open-door policy, and changing employment contracts are major topics that involve not only the software and data processing management but also the senior management of the enterprise up to the boards of directors, together with such other functions as personnel and legal staffs.

Permanent measurement departments. The baseline analysis itself will introduce metrics such as the function point technique and the McCabe Complexity Metrics to the enterprises that commission an analysis. The analysis will also introduce the soft and hard data collection principles and many other useful metrics.

A very frequent follow-on activity to the initial baseline is the establishment by the enterprise of a permanent software measurement program, which will continue to measure software development and maintenance productivity and create annual software "state of the art" reports. This is a significant step, but it is not an inexpensive one. A permanent measurement focal point requires at least one full-time expert, and the continuing costs of a measurement function can total several person-years each calendar year.

Organizational changes. Upgrading the organization structure of an enterprise is a relatively common follow-on activity. The establishment of formal maintenance departments occurs fairly often in large enterprises after a productivity analysis. Other organizational changes may be the creation of a quality assurance function, a development center, an information center, a measurement department, and the like. Less visible changes, such as substituting hierarchical management structures for the less effective matrix structures may also occur from time to time.

Identification of Problems beyond the Current State of the Art

In the practice of medicine there are many diseases for which there is no current cure. In carrying out baseline analyses, there will be situations for which software engineering has no effective remedy. The following are examples of conditions for which no really effective therapies exist.

Irrational scheduling. Unfortunately, in the United States more than half of the large projects are scheduled in an irrational manner: A predetermined end date is selected, and it is forced on the project by arbitrary decree. If the selected date exceeds staff capabilities by more than about 25 percent, the consequences are a potential disaster. The magnitude of the disaster can include attrition of staff, whose members may leave in disgust, catastrophic cost overruns, and, of course, no reasonable hope of making the irrational schedule.

The baseline analysis will point this situation out, but once an irrational schedule has been committed to a client or, even worse, published to the outside world, there is no easy solution. There are, of course, excellent commercial estimating tools available, but less than 15 percent of U.S. companies use such tools today. Once a schedule has been committed to a client, it is embarrassing to admit that it was arbitrary. In the long run, baseline measurements will provide accurate schedule information to prevent future occurrences. However, the first creation of a baseline will probably encounter projects with the distressing problem of having irrational schedules forced upon them.

Incompetence of management and staff. As of 1991, software engineering and software management have no formal procedures for monitoring the equivalent of medical malpractice. A small but distressing number of projects will be found to be incompetently managed or developed. The situation seldom occurs in the context of baseline analyses for the pragmatic reason that companies with significant incompetence at the executive levels will probably not carry out baseline measurements at all. If the situation does occur, there is no easy therapy.

Aging non-Cobol production libraries. For aging Cobol software, restructuring and renovation services and products can extend the useful lives of aging software by automatically restructuring, redocumenting, and isolating dead code. For other languages such as Assembler, Fortran, and PL/I, there were no commercially available automatic restructuring facilities in 1990. Clients with such software either have to redevelop it, replace it, or continue to live with it. Note that automatic restructuring is theoretically possible with other languages, but the companies that provide the service have chosen not to apply their methods to non-Cobol software. That may change in the future.

Layoffs or drastic reductions in force. Enterprises that are faced with heavy competition, declining markets, or severe cash flow problems and have been forced to lay off substantial percentages of their work force may seek a baseline analysis in order to see if reduced staffing can continue to provide acceptable software functions and operations. Because so many of the powerful software technologies require upfront capital investment and substantial training expenses, clients with this situation should be warned that the set of available therapies not requiring some initial investment is neither large nor dramatically effective.

Large systems after the design phase. From time to time, clients commission a baseline analysis because they are in the middle of a major effort (more than 500 function points or 50,000 source statements) that seems to be out of control and the schedules are stretching to unacceptable lengths. Unfortunately, if the key requirements and design phases are already past, there are no technologies that can dramatically reduce the rest of the cycle. New languages usually cannot be prescribed, since their performance may not be adequate for large systems. There are techniques, such as design and code inspections that can improve quality significantly and productivity slightly, but once the design phase is passed, options become few.

Context of the Baseline and Follow-on Activities

After the final report is presented and accepted by the client, the productivity analysis is normally complete. Whether or not the analysis leads to follow-on work depends upon the nature of the diagnosis, the kinds of therapies recommended, and the capabilities of the company organization.

A baseline analysis is often followed by changes in policy, methodologies, tools, staffing patterns, measurements, expectations, or any combination of the above. To demonstrate how a productivity analysis fits in context with the other activities, Fig. 4.1 shows the normal sequences of events.

As can be seen, a baseline analysis is on the critical path to improving software productivity, but it must be followed by many other activities and events. Some of the activities, such as site visits and methodology selection, can occur fairly rapidly. Others, such as tool selection, require more extended analysis because capital investment of significant amounts may be required. The really long-term changes involve policies and organizational changes. It is seldom possible for a large company to introduce policy changes, such as dual salary plans, without many months of deliberation. Similarly, major organization

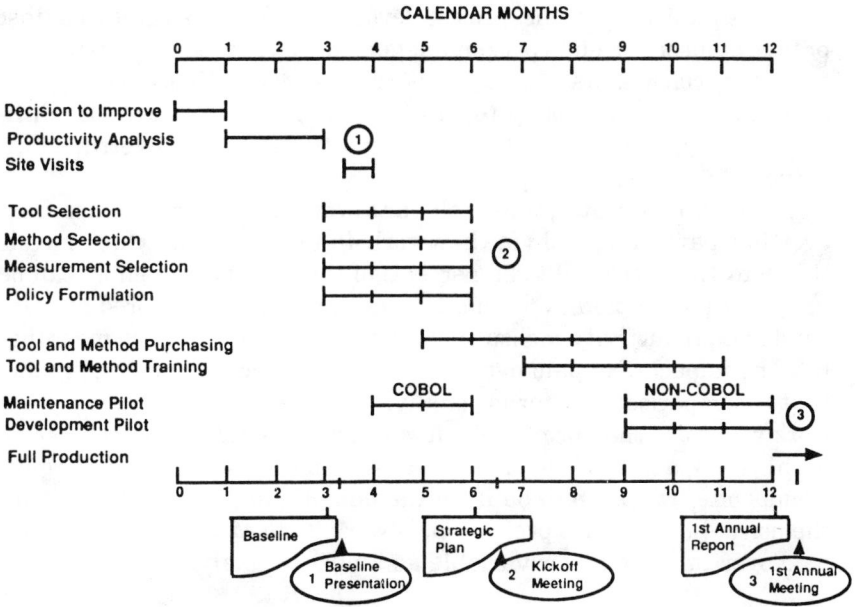

Figure 4.1   Chronological sequence of baseline analysis and follow-on improvements.

changes, such as the creation of separate test or maintenance groups, will also require substantial time for deliberation.

What a Baseline Analysis Covers

A software baseline analysis explores essentially all of the soft and hard tactical factors that impact software development and maintenance: the project itself, the tools, the methodologies, morale and policy issues, languages, customer constraints, purchased software, training, and many other things. The following is an overview of the major topics and their significance.

Project factors.   First to be covered for each project studied are the attributes of the project itself. Whether the project is a new effort or an enhancement or a modification to an existing program is a key item, since productivity rates for enhancements are dramatically lower than for new development. The scope of the project also is important; notably different results will accrue depending upon whether the project is a prototype, a stand-alone program, a component of a large system, or a large system itself.

Also significant at the project level are any constraints against project by users or enterprise management: i.e., schedule constraints, budgetary constraints, staffing constraints, and the like. Severely constrained projects are likely to run into difficulties, and are also difficult to analyze because of the large proportion of unpaid overtime that is typical on constrained projects.

In the United States, most software professionals are exempt from overtime payments, and yet they work 48 to 52 h/week, which means that 8 to 12 h/week (20 to 30 percent) of the total project effort can be in the form of unpaid overtime. Unless this factor is explored and understood, productivity measurements cannot be accurate or meaningful. The impact of unpaid overtime is also significant in doing productivity comparisons internationally. In the United States, 40-h workweeks are the norm, but software professionals often work 48 to 52 h. In Japan, 44-h workweeks are the norm, but software professionals often work up to 60 h. In Canada, 35- to 37-h workweeks are the norm, but software professionals work 35 to 42 h. In any case, unpaid overtime is a major variable and must be analyzed.

Management factors.   Achieving high productivity requires much more than just buying new tools and methods. The way employees are dealt with, the way morale issues are handled, and the way enterprises manage and organize software projects are very significant parameters. The software productivity analysis covers all of the critical managerial issues in depth. This portion of the baseline analysis may sometimes lead to the formulation of new policies and management practices.

Staff specialist factors.   More than 40 occupations and specialist types are now identified in software projects: software engineers, systems analysts, quality assurance specialists, maintenance specialists, database administrators, and so on. The baseline analysis examines which specialist types are currently available within the enterprise and which additional specialists may be needed to meet the needs of future projects.

Physical environment factors.   The availability of sufficient workspace for software development and maintenance staffs and the kinds of equipment and workstations installed are explored fully. Although few enterprises recognize the significance, the physical environment is one of the major determinants of software productivity.

Methodology factors. The word "methodology" covers a broad spectrum of methods, tools, and procedures applied to software projects. The methodology portion of the productivity analysis covers all procedures used by the enterprise for software, including the way requirements are developed, the specification and design methods used, the way documentation is handled, and all other methodological factors.

Package acquisition and modification factors. In many enterprises a significant percentage of applications is purchased from outside vendors. The baseline analysis explores enterprise methods for evaluating, acquiring, and modifying software packages. Package acquisition is often a productivity enhancement factor, but it can sometimes be a productivity reduction factor as well.

Programming language factors. With more than 500 languages available, most enterprises find it difficult to select a single language or a set of languages that is optimized for its needs. Part of the baseline analysis is to examine the future projects of the enterprise and diagnose the most effective language choices. The most appropriate languages can range across all generations. It is not accurate to prescribe fourth-generation languages exclusively, since they are not appropriate for many program and system types.

Defect removal and quality assurance factors. Eliminating bugs or defects is usually the most expensive single activity in the software world when all defect removal efforts are summed together. The baseline analysis also covers the methods and techniques used to find and remove errors: reviews, walk-throughs, inspections, all forms of testing, and proofs of correctness. For each project studied, the defect removal efficiency of the specific series of removal steps to be used is calculated. The overall effectiveness of enterprise defect removal is quantified as well. This portion of the productivity analysis often results in adoption of improved defect removal techniques.

Measurement and normalization factors. Most enterprises that commission a baseline analysis start with essentially no hard data at all on either productivity or quality. Therefore, a vital output from the analysis will be a solid benchmark of validated, hard productivity and quality data. The first baseline report will give most enterprises much better data than they have ever had or even knew was possible.

Standard design blueprints and reusable code. The baseline analysis explores whether or not standard designs, termed "blueprints," and reusable code would be appropriate technologies for the projects and enterprises studied. Reusability is one of the most effective technologies yet developed, but it is not applicable to all enterprises and project types.

Developing or Acquiring a Baseline Data Collection Instrument

Most of us have had complete physical examinations. In the course of the examination, we normally fill out a medical history form that runs to perhaps 10 pages and contains several hundred questions. A baseline measurement report is somewhat similar in logical content: It will be necessary to come to grips with several hundred factors, since software projects can be influenced by that many. This brings up an immediate need to either construct a data collection questionnaire or to acquire one from a commercial source. The questions used here to illustrate the concepts are taken from the proprietary CHECKPOINT® questionnaire developed by the author for Software Productivity Research for carrying out large-scale baseline studies.[3]

Regardless of its source, the data collection instrument must have these attributes: both hard data and soft data must be capable of statistical analysis. It is fairly straightforward to carry out statistical studies of the hard data, which is normally numeric in any case. The soft factors, on the other hand, present a special problem. Bear in mind that the soft factors are usually subjective things about which individuals may give widely differing responses. It is not sufficient to just ask for opinions, since the opinions cannot be analyzed statistically.

The approach which Software Productivity Research developed is to use multiple-choice questions built around a weighting scale, the software effectiveness level (SEL). The CHECKPOINT® questions that evaluate skill, experience, novelty, and so on, are based on the following rationale: They use a scale from 1 to 5, with 3 representing the approximate U.S. average. Numbers lower than 3 usually represent situations that are better than average; numbers higher than 3 usually represent situations that are hazardous or troublesome. The only exceptions to this rule are certain questions in which no risk or hazard at all is involved.

Note: The SEL runs in the opposite direction from the SEI maturity scale, on which 5 is the optimum level. The SEL scale is a true statistical tool, whereas the more recent SEI scale reflects only artificial and abstract levels of maturity.

Consider the following question about project novelty as it occurs in the CHECKPOINT® questionnaire:

Project novelty?   _____

1. Conversion or functional repeat of a well-known program
2. Functional repeat, but some new features
3. Even mixture of repeated and new features
4. Novel program, but with some well-understood features
5. Novel program, of a type never before attempted

It is easily seen that a 1 or 2 is less likely to be troublesome than a 4 or 5. The five possible answers somewhat resemble the Richter scale for earthquake magnitudes, in that as the numeric level of the answer goes up the potential for causing harmful situations also goes up.

The CHECKPOINT® questions are so organized that 3 represents the approximate U.S. average for the parameter in question. Thus, for the above novelty question an answer of 3, which means an even mixture of repeated and new features, is the approximate average for U.S. software. Since averages change over time, the SEL scale is recalibrated annually by Software Productivity Research.

To allow fine-tuning of client responses, the answers need not be integers, and up to two decimal places of precision can be used if desired. That is, answers such as 2.5 and 2.75 are perfectly valid and legitimate if the true situation falls between two points on the 5-point scale. Because the questionnaire is so set up that 3 represents the approximate U.S. average for most questions, it is relatively easy to evaluate projects by using the 5-point scale:

- Projects averaging less than 1.5 are generally at the very extreme leading edge of modern software methods and practices. (*Note:* This would be equivalent to a rating of 5 on the SEI maturity level scale.)

- Projects averaging between 1.5 and 2.5 are generally well ahead of norms in terms of methods and practices.

- Projects averaging between 2.5 and 3.5 are generally in the normal range in terms of methods and practices.

- Projects averaging between 3.5 and 4.5 are generally deficient in terms of methods and practices, and significant therapies may be indicated. (*Note:* This would be equivalent to a rating of 1 on the SEI maturity level scale.)

- Projects averaging more than 4.5 are generally so poorly equipped and are so backward in technology that they have a very high probability of being absolute failures that should be canceled.

TABLE 4.1 Most Common Software Weaknesses between 1987 and 1990 in the United States

1. Schedules set before project is defined
2. Excessive schedule pressure
3. Major requirements changes after the requirements phase
4. Inadequate project planning, tracking, measurement, and estimating methods
5. Inadequate pretest defect removal methods
6. Inadequate systems development methodology
7. Inadequate office space and poor environment
8. Inadequate training for management and staff
9. Inadequate support for reusable designs and code
10. Inadequate organizations and use of specialists

TABLE 4.2 Most Common Software Strengths between 1987 and 1990 in the United States

1. Staff experience in the application area
2. Staff morale and cohesiveness
3. Staff experience with programming languages
4. Staff experience with support tools
5. Staff experience with computer hardware
6. Availability of workstations or terminals
7. Availability of support tools
8. Use of adequate testing methods
9. Use of project library control methods
10. Use of structured code methods

Software Productivity Research carries out baseline studies as a standard consulting engagement, and it is interesting to see the strengths and weaknesses that occur with high frequency in the United States. Table 4.1 shows the 10 most common weaknesses and Table 4.2 the 10 most common strengths that were noted between 1987 and 1990.

A cursory examination of the commoner U.S. software weaknesses and strengths leads to the following conclusion: The problems are centered around managerial, sociological, environmental, and organizational issues. The strengths are centered around tool and technical staff skills.

There is a second form of multiple-choice question that also is useful for baseline analyses. In this second case, the 5-point rating scale is used to discover the opinions of the respondents about whether something ranges from excellent to very poor.

Figure 4.2 shows this technique for allowing managers and staff to evaluate how well they perform various kinds of defect removal operations:

Business and Legal Reviews	Excl		Avg		Poor
1 Patent or legal reviews	1	2	3	4	5
2 Import/export license reviews	1	2	3	4	5
Nontesting Defect Removal					
1 Joint application development (JAD)	1	2	3	4	5
2 Prototyping	1	2	3	4	5
3 Requirements review	1	2	3	4	5
4 Functional design review	1	2	3	4	5
5 Logic design review	1	2	3	4	5
6 Data structure design review	1	2	3	4	5
7 Module design review	1	2	3	4	5
8 User documentation review	1	2	3	4	5
9 Maintenance documentation review	1	2	3	4	5
10 Code review and inspection	1	2	3	4	5
11 Quality assurance review	1	2	3	4	5
12 Correctness proofs	1	2	3	4	5
13 Independent verification and validation	1	2	3	4	5
Testing Defect Removal					
1 Unit testing	1	2	3	4	5
2 New function testing	1	2	3	4	5
3 Regression testing					
4 Integration testing	1	2	3	4	5
5 Stress or performance testing	1	2	3	4	5
6 System testing	1	2	3	4	5
7 Field testing	1	2	3	4	5
8 User acceptance testing	1	2	3	4	5
9 Independent testing organization	1	2	3	4	5
Postrelease Defect Removal					
1 Error-prone module analysis	1	2	3	4	5
2 Automated restructuring	1	2	3	4	5
3 User satisfaction survey	1	2	3	4	5
4 Maintenance defect repair	1	2	3	4	5

Figure 4.2   Use of a 5-point scale for evaluating performance of multiple tasks.

Administering the Data Collection Questionnaire

A baseline analysis session is a sometimes intense and always candid exploration of the particular methods and tools used on a project. The participants in the session include the project manager or supervisor, one or more technical people from the project, and the consultant who is handling the analysis. From time to time, additional people may attend: quality assurance personnel, guests from other projects, and the like.

Each of the participants should have his or her own blank copy of the questionnaire, which is usually passed out about a week before the session begins but is sometimes passed out at the session itself. The participants may annotate their questionnaires if they wish. They can keep the questionnaires when the session is over, since the consultant administering the session keeps the master copy.

If, as in the case of the CHECKPOINT® questionnaire, the questions are in automated form, it is technically possible to enter the responses immediately into a computer and produce a report on the spot. Although desirable from one standpoint, the pragmatic results of having a computer in the room is not so good from a sociological standpoint. There is a tendency for the consultant who enters the data to get wrapped up in the mechanics of using the computer. There is also a certain unconscious intimidation attached to having the computer present which may discourage free conversation. On the whole, it seems preferable to use paper questionnaires for the sessions themselves and produce computerized versions later.

Some of the questions on the baseline questionnaire are general and deal with global enterprise issues, but more than two-thirds of them are quite specific and deal with individual tactical project attributes. Consultants are cautioned not to try to handle multiple projects simultaneously in workshop mode. That has occasionally been done, but the results are unsatisfactory for these reasons: (1) The large number of people in the room leads to side conversations and distractions. (2) It is difficult to keep the focus on any single project. (3) It is easy to mix up responses and make mistakes in filling out the master copy of the questionnaires.

The time allotted to a productivity analysis session is typically 3.5 h, although sessions are sometimes completed in 2 h or less and they may sometimes run as high as 6 h. If a single consultant is administering the sessions, then two sessions a day can usually be handled. The sessions are usually interesting to all concerned, and sometimes they are even enjoyable. They encourage both management and technical personnel to see that their problems and issues are being taken seriously, and the nature of the questionnaire and topics leads to very frank discussions of significant matters. Consultants and clients alike will learn a great deal from the productivity analysis sessions. The following are section-by-section discussions of a baseline questionnaire and the kinds of issues that are likely to come up during a productivity analysis session.

Recording the basic project identity

The first items to be recorded are the basic identities of the project and the participants:

- Security level

- Name and location of the company
- Name of the project
- Names, phone numbers, and locations of all of the participants in the session in case follow-ups are needed
- Date of the session
- Start date of the project (if known)
- Current status of the project (i.e., completed, canceled, or partially completed)
- Comments or free-form information

A small but important point is very significant: security level. Unless the client gives specific written permission, the data collected during a baseline analysis is normally confidential and cannot be distributed to anyone. Indeed, a nondisclosure agreement should accompany such a study if external consultants are used. For military and defense projects, even more stringent security may be required. Be sure to note the security requirements for the project being analyzed in order to protect confidentiality. For military projects, the security level should be applied to each page.

If the questionnaire is acquired from a management consulting group such as Software Productivity Research, it may ask about the optional standard industry classification or SIC code for the enterprise. This can, of course, be omitted for single-company internal studies. The U.S. Department of Commerce has developed a coding scheme for all major industries and service companies as an aid in producing statistical reports. The SIC code is included for large-scale multiclient studies to identify the industry of the clients and to aid in concealing the identity of the specific companies that participated. The remainder of the information simply serves to give a context to the study: who was present, who performed the interviews, when the interviews took place, and so forth.

Project natures, scopes, classes, and types

An annual baseline for a large company will deal with a highly heterogeneous set of projects: new projects, enhancements, prototypes, programs, systems, MIS, military, batch, on-line, and so on, are likely to be present.

It is absolutely necessary to record the specifics of the individual projects included. Software Productivity Research has developed a taxonomy for dealing with these factors which is shown in Fig. 4.3.

Project Classification

Project Nature?   _____
 1 New program development
 2 Enhancement (new functions added to existing software)
 3 Maintenance (defect repair to existing software)
 4 Conversion or adaptation (migration to new platform)

Project Scope?   _____
 1 Disposable prototype
 2 Evolutionary prototype
 3 Module or subelement of a program
 4 Reusable module or macro
 5 Complete stand-alone program
 6 Program(s) within a system
 7 Major system (multiple linked programs or components)
 8 Release (current version of an evolving system)

Release Number   _____

Project Class?   _____
 1 Personal program, for private use
 2 Personal program, to be used by others
 3 Academic program, developed in an academic environment
 4 Internal program, for use at a single location
 5 Internal program, for use at a multiple location
 6 Internal program, developed by external contractor
 7 Internal program, with functions used via time sharing
 8 Internal program, using military specifications
 9 External program, to be put in public domain
10 External program, leased to users
11 External program, bundled with hardware
12 External program, unbundled and marketed commercially
13 External program, developed under commercial contract
14 External program, developed under government contract
15 External program, developed under military contract

Project Type?   _____
 1 Nonprocedural (generated, query, spreadsheet)
 2 Batch applications program
 3 Interactive applications program
 4 Batch database applications program
 5 Interactive database applications program
 6 Scientific or mathematical program
 7 Systems or support program
 8 Communications or telecommunications program
 9 Process control program
10 Embedded or real-time program
11 Graphics, animation, or image-processing program
12 Robotics, or mechanical automation program
13 Artificial intelligence program
14 Hybrid project (multiple types)

For Hybrid Projects:
  Primary Type? _____   Secondary Type? _____

Figure 4.3 Recording project nature, scope, class, and type.

- The "nature" parameter identifies the five major flavors of software projects that are common throughout industry and which tend to have different cost and productivity profiles.

- The "scope" parameter covers the range of possibilities from disposable prototypes through major systems.

- Generally speaking, the "class" parameter is associated with the business aspects of a software project. Class determines the rigor and costs of project paperwork and the volume of paperwork can be directly correlated to class number.

- The "type" parameter is significant in determining the difficulty and complexity of the code itself.

For statistical purposes, each of the 210 possible class-type combinations will have notably different productivity, quality, and skill "signatures" associated with them. Since the form of the questionnaire puts simple project attributes at the top and complicated attributes at the bottom, it is easy to predict (and easy to validate through measurement) that projects with low class-type numbers will be much more productive than those with high class-type numbers. And, indeed, projects of the class 1, type 1 form are the most productive in the United States and elsewhere. Projects of class 15 type 14 are the least productive in both the United States and elsewhere.

Fifteen classes are identified; they range from personal software through military contract software. Classes 1 and 2 are for personal software developed informally; class 3 is for software developed in an academic environment such as a university; classes 4 through 6 are for software developed by enterprises for their own internal use; and classes 9 through 15 are for software that will be delivered to external users, such as contract software, bundled software, and licensed software. The reason for recording class is that there are dramatic differences in productivity, quality, and technologies from class to class.

Consider the documentation, for example, that might be created to support a simple Cobol application program. If the program is developed for internal use (class 4) it might require 20 different supporting documents totaling perhaps 30 English words for every line of source code. If it were developed to be leased to external users, then it would probably require more than 50 supporting documents totaling almost 80 English words for every line of source code. If the program were developed for the U.S. Department of Defense under military specifications, it would require more than 100 supporting documents totaling almost 200 English words for every line of source code. In short, class is a significant parameter to consider when it comes to prescribing therapies for software problems.

The next question, project type, has 14 possibilities. The first 13 cover standard types such as batch and interactive applications and database programs. Type 14 is reserved for hybrid projects where more than a single type will be present in the same system. When this occurs, then the primary and secondary types should be noted (and perhaps other types as well).

Project goals and constraints

When projects begin, management and staff will receive either explicit or implicit marching orders that they are asked to follow on the project. These goals and constraints should be recorded for each project included in a baseline analysis. There are many variations and flavors of goals and constraints, but the essential breakdown is simple:

1. Most projects are directed to adhere to tight schedules, and this becomes the major goal and constraint. These projects have a dreadful tendency to become disasters.

2. A few projects, such as mission-critical ones or those dealing with human life, are directed to achieve very high levels of quality and reliability.

3. Some projects are in the middle ground, and they receive no goals or constraints at all.

4. Some projects are back-burner types that are being done as fill-in between more significant projects.

Early on during the baseline analysis, the participants should discuss any goals or constraints levied against the project. This will normally generate lively discussions, and it will be the first sign that something useful is going to come out of the baseline measurement study.

Goals and constraints are critical productivity and quality issues, and consultants should be very sensitive to them. In real life, most projects start out handicapped by constraints established by client demands, managerial decrees, or some other extrinsic source. The most common, and also the most hazardous, constraints are those dealing with delivery schedules: More than 50 percent of all software projects in the United States have delivery dates established before the project requirements are fully defined!

The next most common set of constraints concerns staffing. Projects often have a locked staff and skill mix that cannot be extended but is clearly insufficient for the work at hand. A third set of constraints, to be dealt with later, concerns such technical constraints as performance, memory utilization, and disk space.

Staff availability and work-habit factors

One of the most important factors in coming to grips with productivity is that of establishing accurate corporate profiles of availability and work-hours. Staff availability questions ask whether project personnel have worked full time on the project or divided their time among multiple projects. The normal assumption is that personnel will be assigned to a project 100 percent of the time, but sometimes this assumption is not correct. If the answer is something other than 100 percent, the staff should estimate the percent of time assigned. It is also important to ascertain what percent of the project technical staff is exempt from overtime pay and will not generally be paid overtime. In the United States, most software professionals, except for junior, entry-level personnel, are exempt from overtime.

Your corporate accounting department can probably supply you with the average workday, workweek, and workyear for your company. You must be very thorough in exploring how much effort was applied to the software project being analyzed. These are important questions from a measurement view, and also from an estimating standpoint. The normal U.S. workweek is 40 h, yet software professionals frequently work in excess of 50-h weeks. Thus, 20 to 30 percent of all effort applied to a project can be in the form of unpaid overtime, a very significant factor.

It is well known from time-and-motion studies that the productive time on software projects is much lower than the normal 40-h accounting week. What is not so well known is that individual corporate cultures can make the productive week vary significantly. Therefore, capturing productive time is important. Table 4.3 shows a typical profile of work habits for knowledge workers in the United States.

Assuming that only 6 h/day is productive work and there are a practical 185 working days for actual tasks, the U.S. norm would seem to be 1110 h/year applied to knowledge work. If the 24 days of meetings are included, then another 144 h can be added to the total, bringing the total up to 1254 h of work per year. Now consider the work habits associated with critical software projects. Table 4.4 shows a software engineering workyear on a schedule-driven project.

The total number of project workdays, exclusive of meetings, is now up to 273 and includes many Saturdays, Sundays, some public holidays, and so forth. The average number of productive hours worked per day can also climb from 6 to 8, and the number of hours actually at work can climb from 8 to 10 or more. Thus, the probable number of

TABLE 4.3 Distribution of Staff Time During a Calendar Year

Time use	Average days
Normal working days	185
Weekdays (Saturdays and Sundays)	104
Meeting days	24
Vacation days	15
Public holidays	10
Slack days between tasks	7
Sick days	7
Business travel days	5
Education days	5
Conferences	3
Total	365

TABLE 4.4 Distribution of Software Staff Time During Critical Schedule-Driven Projects

Time use	Average days
Normal working days	197
Saturdays worked	40
Sundays worked	20
Nonworking weekends	44
Meeting days	24
Vacation days worked	10
Vacation days taken	5
Public holidays worked	6
Public holidays taken	4
Slack days between tasks	0
Sick days	0
Business travel days	5
Education days	0
Conferences	3
Total	365

work-hours on a critical software project can total to 2184, or to 2376 if meetings are included. This number represents more than 196 percent difference in the annual hours applied between ordinary knowledge work and critical software projects.

Obviously, this factor must be explored and studied in depth for software baselines to be accurate! Unfortunately, most corporate project-tracking systems do not record unpaid overtime. Therefore, one critical part of the baseline interview sessions is to get the software project managers and teams to reconstruct, from their memories, the real quantity of time they spent on their projects. It cannot be over-emphasized that unless it captures such factors as unpaid overtime, tracking system data is essentially worthless for serious economic studies, and it is critical for accuracy to use the memories of the project team members.

Other related issues include use of contract personnel on the project and whether or not project personnel were dividing their time among several projects or were working on the project being studied in full time mode. For contract personnel it is significant to ask what percent of the project team was comprised of contract personnel. The number can range from 0 to 100 percent. This topic is significant for both productivity and quality purposes. Generally speaking, projects developed by contract personnel are often higher in productivity and are produced with shorter schedules than similar projects developed by full-time salaried employees. However, because of contract billing rates, the projects may cost more.

Inflation rates can be significant for long-term projects that may take a number of years to develop. For example, the ITT System/12 electronic switching system started in 1976 and was not delivered until 1983, or after 7 years in development. Plainly, inflation will be significant over that span of years. For small projects that will typically take less than a year to develop, inflation rates can be omitted.

Determining the Size of the Project to Be Measured

Whether you use function points, feature points, lines of code, or something else, you will need to determine the size of an application if productivity studies are to be meaningful. There are no U.S. or world standards for counting source code, and there are very few enterprise or local standards. (Refer to Appendix A for the Software Productivity Research source- code-counting rules.) Therefore, when carrying out the first baseline analysis within a company, size information will be somewhat difficult to ascertain.

For example, on one of the first internal studies of software productivity carried out by the author at IBM in 1973, it was discovered that the major IBM divisions and labs were using six widely different conventions for counting source code size, which led to apparent differences of more than 300 percent in how large any given program or system would appear, depending on which rules were used. From that discovery, IBM standardized its source-code- counting rules and even developed an internal tool that automatically counted source lines in a consistent manner. Today, both function points and feature points provide size data independent of lines of source code. However, even though function and feature points are less variable than source code, there are still uncertainties in determining size.

More than half a dozen commercial tools that are available, such as

Battlemap, Pathview, Inspector, and ACT, which means analysis of complexity, are capable of counting source code statements. There are also several tools that can aid in the calculation of function points and feature points, but as of 1990 there are no tools that can automatically backfire function points directly from source code even though this is not an excessively difficult accomplishment.

An emerging set of new tools may soon be able to predict function point and feature point totals as a by-product of design, but such methods are still experimental. Also new are tools such as the SPR function point approximator, which enters into dialogs with a project manager about the known approximator characteristics of the project and creates a function point total as a by-product.

Even today, however, many and perhaps most companies have not yet adopted functional metrics, nor have they as yet established counting rules, nor have they acquired a counting tool. Therefore, be very careful with project sizing when carrying out your first baseline assessment.

When ITT began its first baseline assessment in 1980,[4] the ITT companies were reporting size in an astonishing variety of ways, including source lines with more than a dozen rule variations, object lines, bytes, and function points. The total range of variations, assuming one project had been counted under all possible rules, was more than an order of magnitude! It is easy to see why ITT established standard counting rules as an immediate by-product of the first baseline study.

If you use a commercial questionnaire such as CHECKPOINT®, it will contain counting rules for source code, function points, and feature points. Size determination is a major topic for productivity analysis purposes, and especially so for large-scale studies involving different labs, divisions, or companies where it is quite unlikely that the projects will obey the same conventions. It is mathematically possible to convert source code counting rules from any set of counting rules into any other arbitrary set, but you must know the rules before you can do so. You can also convert size easily between source code and functional metrics by using the backfire method explained in Chap. 2. Table 4.5 illustrates some of the possible size variations based on how lines of code might be counted in PL/I for a typical business application.

It cannot be overemphasized that in the absence of local standards, any and all variations will be used. The variations are not malicious, nor are they attempts to puff up sizes to make productivity look artificially high. It simply happens that size determination is too complicated an issue to be left to chance.

Although function points and feature points do not have the wide range of uncertainty that has always been associated with lines of

TABLE 4.5 Variations in Apparent Size of Software That Are Due to Alternative Methods for Counting Source Code

Method	Apparent size in source lines
New executable lines only	100
New executable lines + data definitions	170
New executable lines, data definitions, comments	220
New + reused executable lines	250
New + reused executable lines + data definitions	430
New + reused executable lines + data definitions + commentary lines	500

TABLE 4.6 Range of Variation Associated with Functional Metrics

Method	Automation available	Range of variation, ±%
IBM 1979	No	50
DeMarco bang metric (1982)	Yes	50
Rubin variation (1983)	Yes	50
IBM 1984	Yes	20
SPR 1985	Yes	15
SPR backfire (1986)	Yes	35
SPR feature points (1986)	Yes	25
British Mark II (1988)	No	40
Herron approximation (1989)	Yes	35
IFPUG 1990	Yes	15

code, even here there are many possible variations. So long as function point and feature point counting involves human judgment, there must necessarily be uncertainty. Table 4.6 shows the approximate ranges associated with the major flavors of function point counting. The data in Table 4.6 is based on a very small number of trials and experiments by the author as well as on second-hand reports, and must be regarded as premature for serious benchmarks. Additional projects and additional trials are needed.

Although it is hardly a valid mathematical procedure to aggregate and average the variations of unlike techniques, the average range of the entire set of methods in Table 4.6 is about 35 percent. Without multiplying examples, it can be seen that determining the size of projects for baseline purposes is not a trivial task. It requires both considerable effort and serious attempts at validation.

Standard Project Charts of Accounts

A chart of accounts is really nothing more than a convenient set of buckets into which cost and resource data can be placed. It is surprising that our industry has run for almost 50 years without any national or international standards, and very few corporate standards, on this topic. In the absence of a standard chart of accounts, many companies accumulate software project costs into a single cost bucket. Unfortunately, such an amorphous lump of data is worthless for serious economic studies because there is no way of validating it. The following sample illustrates the kinds of partial data that many companies have to utilize because they have no better:

Project	Schedule	Effort	Staff	Cost
Billing system	18 months	2000 h	3	$60,000

Note the missing elements in the above example: How much time was devoted to any particular task? What was the breakdown of the 2000-h total? Were there any missing tasks? What were the three staff members doing? There is no way to validate such amorphous data. Even worse, there is no way to gain insight from such data, which is the main purpose of measurement. The absolute minimum for a chart of accounts to have any value at all is five tasks and a total. Table 4.7 illustrates a minimal chart of accounts and the data elements to be recorded. Artificial data is inserted simply to give the chart the appearance of a completed one.

At least with a five-bucket chart of accounts, the tasks and the nature of the project begin to take on some semblance of reality. But five elements is by no means granular enough for real insight.

The CHECKPOINT® standard chart of accounts, illustrated in Chaps. 1 and 2 includes 25 development activities and a total, and it can be used for all current classes and types of software: civilian and military projects, large systems and small programs, new projects and enhancements, and so on.

That there are 25 tasks in a chart of accounts does not imply that

TABLE 4.7 Minimal Chart of Accounts for Software Projects

	Schedule, months	Effort, months	Staff	Cost
1. Requirements	1	1	1	$ 5,000
2. Design	1	1	1	5,000
3. Code development	3	3	1	15,000
4. Integration and test	2	2	1	10,000
5. Project Management	—	2	1	10,000
Project total	7	9	1.3	$45,000

TABLE 4.8 Chart of Accounts for a PBX System Software Project

	Schedule, months	Effort, Months	Staff	Cost, $
1. Requirements	2	4	2.0	20,000
2. Initial design	2	6	3.0	30,000
3. Detail design	2	10	5.0	50,000
4. Code development	4	20	5.0	100,000
5. Unit test	1	5	5.0	25,000
6. Function test	2	10	5.0	50,000
7. Integration	2	2	1.0	10,000
8. System test	3	15	5.0	75,000
9. User documentation	3	6	2.0	15,000
10. Installation	1	3	3.0	15,000
11. Project management	—	15	1.0	75,000
Total project	22	96	4.4	480,000

every project performs all tasks. The set of 25 tasks is merely the smallest set than can be applied more or less universally. A good chart of accounts is revealing not only as a data collection tool but also as identifying tasks that should have been performed for a project but were not. For example, Table 4.8 illustrates the set of tasks performed for a PBX software project by a telecommunications company. It is based on interviews with the manager and staff.

Table 4.8 may appear to be reasonably complete and, indeed, useful, but it is highly significant that the following tasks which are useful for PBX software were not performed:

Prototyping

Project planning

Reusable code acquisition

Design reviews and inspections

Code reviews and inspections

Configuration control

Quality assurance

The project in question was one that overran its budget by more than 40 percent and its schedule by more than 6 months. It quickly became obvious when looking at the tasks performed vs. what would be normal for such applications that the project had been in rush mode since it started, and the attempts to shortcut it by skipping quality control development practices led to disaster. Specifically, skimping on quality control and rushing to start coding paved the way to major delays later, when it was discovered during test that the project had so many bugs that it could not work under normal operating conditions.

Note that exploration of factors which cause success or failure is possible when a granular chart of accounts is used, but it remains outside the scope of analysis when measures are less precise.

The most useful kind of chart of accounts is one which is derived from the full work breakdown structure of the project being explored. In developing such a chart of accounts, it is significant to consider whether a single level of detail is desired or a multilevel "exploding" chart of accounts is to be used. In a single-level chart of accounts, all costs are accumulated against a small set of cost buckets. Single-level charts of accounts are easy to develop and are not burdensome to use, but they are somewhat coarse in terms of data precision. The following is an example of a single-level chart of accounts for six activities:

1. Requirements

2. Design

3. Coding

4. Documentation

5. Testing

6. Management

In multilevel charts of accounts, costs are accumulated against a variety of fairly granular "buckets" and then summarized upward to create higher levels of cost accumulation. Multilevel charts of accounts are the normal mode for accurate cost accounting, but they require more effort to establish and are somewhat more burdensome in day-to-day use. The following is an example of a multilevel chart of accounts which expands on the preceding example:

1. Requirements
    1.1. Preliminary discussion
    1.2. Joint application design
    1.3. Requirements preparation
2. Design
    2.1. Initial functional design
    2.2. Initial data flow design
    2.3. Detailed functional design
    2.4. Detailed logic design
    2.5. Design reviews
3. Coding
    3.1. New code development

3.2. Reusable code acquisition
3.3. Desk checking
3.4. Code inspections
4. Documentation
    4.1. Writing introduction
    4.2. Writing user's guide
    4.3. Writing operator's guide
    4.4. Writing maintenance manual
    4.5. Document editing
    4.6. Document printing
5. Testing
    5.1. Test planning
    5.2. Unit test
    5.3. Function test
    5.4. System test
    5.5. Acceptance test
6. Management
    6.1. Project planning and estimating
    6.2. Project milestone tracking
    6.3. Project reviews
    6.4. Project personnel management

There is no theoretical limit to the number of levels that can be used in a multilevel chart of accounts. In practice, more than 3 levels and more than about 200 subordinate tasks tend to become rather complicated. There are, of course, many commercial project management tools that can handle thousands of tasks, and large projects will normally utilize them.

It should be kept in mind that an appropriate level of granularity is one which provides meaningful information to project managers and the team itself. Data that is too coarse cannot lead to insights; data that is too granular will discourage both managers and staff alike because of the difficulty of recording the necessary information.

Identifying Occupation Groups and Staff Specialists

Now that software is becoming a full-fledged professional undertaking, many specialists are starting to become necessary for success. Just as medical practice has long been segmented into specialist areas, such as general practice, psychiatry, and neurosurgery, software is also starting to create special skill areas.

There are currently some 40 recognizable specialist skills in the area of software development and maintenance: application program-

TABLE 4.9 Software Occupation Groups Related to Software Size

Staffing profile	Small projects	Medium-size projects	Large projects
Project managers	1	2	25
Systems analysts	3	25	
Application programmers	1	5	100
System programmers	1	10	
Project librarians	1	5	
Technical writers		1	20
Database administrators		1	5
Quality assurance		1	5
Test specialists			10
Performance specialists			5
Total staff	2	15	210

mers, system programmers, database programmers, maintenance specialists, and so on. Small applications are usually done by individual programmers or software engineers; large applications not only require perhaps hundreds of workers but may also involve over dozens or even all 40 or so of the different occupation groups! Table 4.9 shows the numbers and kinds of the 10 most common software occupations typically engaged on business software applications of various sizes.

The significance of this section varies with the overall size of the enterprise being analyzed. As general rules of thumb, the following are the kinds of specialists usually found in various sizes of enterprises.

Small software staffs of fewer than 10 employees. Small shops typically run on the generalist principle, with dual-purpose programmer-analysts being the most widely encountered occupation group. When specialization does occur, it usually consists of segmenting the analysis work from the programming work and sometimes segmenting applications programming from systems programming.

Medium software staffs with 10 to 100 employees. When enterprises grow from small to medium, an increase in specialists is usually noted: Database programmers, sometimes network or communication programmers, and a definite split between system and application programming are frequent attributes.

Large software staffs with 100 to 1000 employees. Large enterprises enjoy the luxury of many specialists that smaller enterprises can seldom afford: professional writers for documentation, test specialists, maintenance specialists, tool and support specialists and the like. From a productivity analysis point of view, large enterprises that do *not* have full specialization are candidates for staff structure improvements.

Very large software staffs with more than 1000 employees. Very large enterprises usually have all 40 of the major specialist types and sometimes other types unique to their own businesses as well. Very large organizations that do not have maintenance specialists, test specialists, documentation specialists, and so on, are candidates for staffing upgrades.

Superlarge software staffs with more than 10,000 employees. At the extreme end of the scale will be found enterprises such as AT&T, IBM, the Department of Defense, and a few other organizations with more than 10,000 software employees overall. The norm here is for not only full specialization, but for planned organizations built around the needs of the specialists. The adoption of full specialization and the supporting apparatus for them is one way to explain the phenomenon that productivity rates may be higher at the extremely large end than in the middle, in terms of staff sizes.

The hazards of generalists in specialist situations. In all human situations, so far as can be determined, specialists tend to outperform generalists. It is certainly true that in knowledge work the advance from amateur to professional status is marked by such an enormous increase in the knowledge content that one person can no longer absorb all of it, and so specialization is a necessary adjunct to the growth of a profession. Consider the number of medical and legal specialties, for example.

As for software, this phenomenon has only started to be explored and measured. Figure 4.4 gives the results to date. As can be seen, enterprise software productivity rates sag notably as the number of members on a professional staff begins to climb. In really large companies, however, the rate starts to climb again. One of the main reasons for that climb is that really large companies, such as IBM, Hewlett-Packard, and ITT, have gone beyond generalists and have moved toward full specialization and the organizations needed to support specialists.

Staff Skill and Personnel Variables

Psychologists who have studied software success patterns, such as Curtis,[5] Schneiderman,[6] and Weinberg,[7] agree that experience is

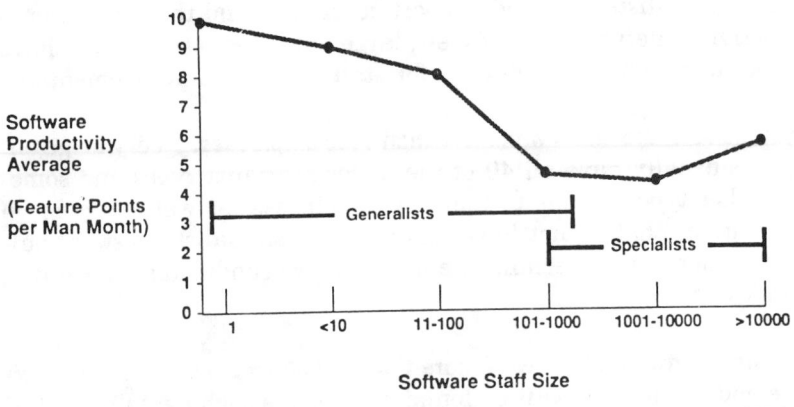

Figure 4.4   U.S. software productivity and total staff size.

correlated with both productivity and quality. Breadth of experience is more important than length of time, incidentally.

Of all the variables known to affect software, "individual human variation" has the greatest known impact. In controlled studies, in which eight programmers were asked to develop identical applications, the participants varied by more than 20 to 1 in productivity and by more than 10 to 1 in errors.

Yet this variable is difficult to capture and evaluate, and it is one of the most subjective of all soft factors. Not only is the factor subjective, but it must be measured carefully to avoid injustice to the people themselves. One of the chronic problems of personnel management is a phenomenon termed "appraisal skew," which means that managers tend to habitually appraise staff in accordance with their personal patterns rather than objective facts. Some managers consistently appraise high; others consistently appraise low. (As a young programmer, one of the first serious programming tasks performed by the author was a project to measure appraisal skew of a large government agency.) Multinational companies must use extreme caution in measuring this parameter, since it is illegal in parts of Europe to record information about a worker's performance in a computerized database.

For the purposes of a baseline analysis, staff experience should be noted. There are eight major breakdowns of staff experience that are significant:

1. Experience in the application area

2. Experience with tools

3. Experience with methods

4. Experience with analysis and design

5. Experience with languages

6. Experience with reviews and inspections

7. Experience with testing techniques

8. Experience with the development hardware

Not only is staff experience significant, but, surprisingly, user experience and user cooperation provide two of the stronger positive correlations with productivity. There are three major user experience topics that should be recorded:

1. User experience with software in general

2. User experience with automation in his or her job area

3. User experience as a participant in software projects

Management Project and Personnel Variables

Management topics are among the most sensitive and important sets of questions in the entire baseline analysis. The questions in this section should explore the fundamental policy and morale issues of the enterprise as well as the specific management environment for the project being analyzed. Most enterprises are highly political internally. Managerial power struggles, disputes, and dislikes can be very significant productivity parameters. Major projects are sometimes canceled or significantly thrown off track because key managers are fighting about goals, methods, or status.

From a productivity improvement standpoint, the problems and issues which the managerial section can highlight are very difficult to treat or cure. Making changes in personnel and morale policies is outside the scope of authority of most software and data processing managers. Nonetheless, the managerial section is a critical one which will give both clients and consultants significant insights into enterprise cultural attributes.

Some of the topics to be explored in dealing with management issues include:

1. Management agreement or disagreement on project goals

2. Management authority to acquire tools or change methods

3. Management planning and estimating capabilities

4. Management commitment to quality or schedule constraints

5. The impact of corporate politics on the project

Of all of the factors which management can influence, and which management tends to be influenced by, schedule pressures stand out as the most significant. Some schedule pressure can actually benefit morale, but excessive or irrational schedules are probably the single most destructive influence in all of software. Not only do irrational schedules tend to kill the projects, but they cause extraordinarily high voluntary turnover among staff members. Even worse, the turnover tends to be greatest among the most capable personnel with the highest appraisals. Figure 4.5 illustrates the results of schedule pressure on staff morale.

It should be noted in conclusion that management has a much greater impact on both companies and projects than almost any other measured phenomenon. The leading-edge companies that know this, such as IBM, tend to go to extraordinary lengths to select managers carefully and to provide them with adequate training and support once they have been selected. Such companies are also careful to monitor manager performance and to find other work should a manager lack all of the attributes of successful management. Indeed, reverse appraisals in which staff members assess managers as well as management appraising staff members are utilized by leading-edge enter-

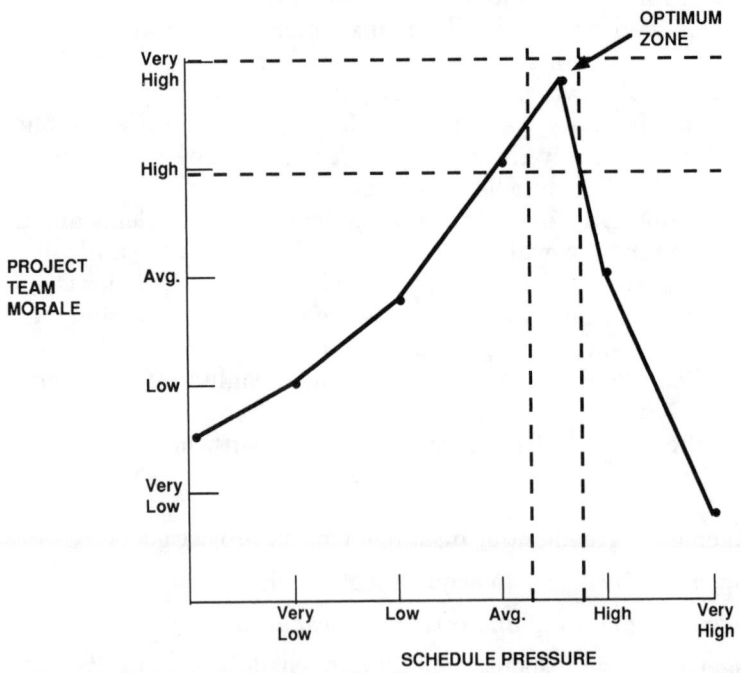

Figure 4.5   The impact of schedule pressure on staff morale.

prises as part of their programs to ensure high management capabilities. A baseline study is not a direct tool for studying management capabilities, but those who have carried out baseline studies realize that it will point out strengths and weaknesses in this area.

Project Attribute Variables

The term "attribute" includes the impact of the physical office space for the software team and also the impacts of the workstations, tools, and methodologies in current use. Most of the attribute questions are reasonably self-explanatory, but the significance of the answers varies considerably. The most obvious kinds of attribute topics are concerned with the available tools and methods which the project team can use:

1. Requirements methods

2. Design methods and tools

3. Formal or informal system development methodologies

4. Formal or informal standards

5. Integration methods (discrete, continuous, etc.)

In recent studies such as those of Tom DeMarco and Tim Lister,[8] some unexpected findings and conclusions regarding the physical environment itself have turned up.

In a large-scale study involving more than 300 programmers, the DeMarco-Lister research noted the surprising finding that the programmers in the high quartile for productivity had office space that was approximately double the space available for programmers in the low quartile (more than 78 vs. 44 ft^2). In an older but even larger study by Gerald McCue[9] that was commissioned by IBM and involved more than 1000 programmers at the Santa Teresa Programming Center, the physical environment with all programmers having 10-by-10-ft private offices resulted in productivity rates some 11 percent higher than the same personnel had achieved in their previous office buildings, which had 8-by-10-ft cubicles shared by two programmers.

These are significant and even poignant findings: Because of the rapid growth of numbers of computer professionals in most enterprises, lack of space is a national problem. Most companies allot scarcely more than 50 ft^2 of noisy space to their software professionals, with very unsatisfactory results. Unfortunately, physical space is one of the most expensive and difficult problems to solve. Poor available space is not quite an incurable problem, but it is among the most difficult problems in the industry.

Another aspect of environment is that of available computer resources and the impact of computer response time on development productivity. Thadani of IBM[10] explored this, and he concluded that slow response times (> 1 s) exerted a disproportionate loss in productivity because programmers tended to lose concentration and drift off for several additional seconds before recovering their train of thought. All physical, social, and technological aspects of the environment should be explored as part of the baseline analysis. If a commercial-grade questionnaire is used, such as the CHECKPOINT® questionnaire, more than 50 environmental factors will be included.

From studying the environments of several hundred companies and government agencies in the United States, Canada, England, Australia, Europe, and Asia, quite a large number of chronic environmental and methodological problems have been noted. They appear to be endemic around the world.

- Requirements methodologies are deficient in more than 75 percent of all enterprises.

- Use of prototyping is starting to increase, but more than 85 percent of enterprises do not use prototype methods.

- Software design automation is almost totally lacking in more than 50 percent of all enterprises, and it is inadequate in more than 75 percent of all enterprises.

- Software documentation methods are inadequate in more than 85 percent of all enterprises.

- Office space and physical environment are inadequate in more than 80 percent of all enterprises.

- Management tools (estimating, tracking, planning) are inadequate in more than 60 percent of all enterprises.

- Software measurements are inadequate in more than 90 percent of all enterprises.

- Software defect removal methods are inadequate in more than 80 percent of all enterprises.

Consultants and clients should keep in mind that a baseline analysis is a diagnostic technique which will find environmental problems but will not cure them. The cures will come from upgrading the environmental deficiencies.

Yet another aspect of the environment to be considered is the sociological aspect. In this case, topics to be explored are whether the organization reacts positively or negatively to change and how long it might take to carry out some of the following changes®:

- Introduce a new methodology such as inspections or JAD sessions
- Acquire new tools such as workstations
- Create a new department such as a quality assurance group, a measurement group, or a development center
- React to competitive situations

Surprising contradictions sometimes occur when sociological issues are explored. For example, in the early 1980s the stated goal of the ITT chairman was to improve software productivity rapidly. However, the executive charged with that task discovered that the purchase of a new tool required an average of eight approval signatures and more than 6 months of calendar time! Before it was possible to make rapid progress in software technologies, it was necessary to examine and streamline the purchasing process.

The topics of both bureaucratic friction and of change facilitation are normal parts of a baseline analysis. These topics are also supported by a substantial body of literature that deals not only with software but with other areas of human endeavor. Since the natural human response to new ideas is to reject them until someone else has proved that they work, this topic is quite significant.

Contract Project Variables (Optional)

In a baseline analysis, contract projects should be included if the company or agency utilizes contract personnel in any significant quantity. The questions that might be asked about contract projects are optional, and they are used only when the baseline analysis is actually studying a project which is being developed by a contracting organization. Contract software generally encompasses five different contractual arrangements:

1. Contracts with private individuals on a work-for-hire basis.
2. Contracts with consulting organizations for staff and services on site at the client locations.
3. Contracts with software houses or consulting organizations for custom packages: The work is performed at the contractor's location.
4. Contracts with civilian government agencies at local, state, or national levels.
5. Contracts with military services or the Department of Defense.

Each of these has different pros and cons, legal obligations, and the like.

Contract work can be surprisingly effective. A proprietary study of

New England banking applications carried out by the author noted that contract projects averaged about twice the productivity, in function points per staff-month, of projects the same size and class developed by employees of the banks. There were four reasons for this phenomenon: (1) The banks were more careful in defining requirements with contractors than with their own staff; (2) the contractors were fairly experienced in the applications; (3) the contractors had access to reusable code from similar applications; and (4) the contractors worked substantial amounts of overtime that was not billed back to the clients.

Software Package Acquisition (Optional)

Software packages and acquired software are definitely mainstream topics for a baseline analysis. When ITT carried out its initial baseline in the early 1980s,[4] the team was surprised to discover that out of some 65,000 source code statements (equivalent to about 520,000 function points) some 26 percent of the total software owned by ITT had been acquired from vendors rather than developed by ITT personnel.

The questions about packages are optional, and they are used only when the baseline analysis is studying a project that included or was based on a purchased package. In real life, purchasing packages is often a cost-effective way to get functions into production rapidly. Indeed, in terms of function points delivered per unit of effort, packages exceed all other forms in overall productivity. Depending upon the size and evaluation concerned, productivity rates in excess of 1000 function points per staff-month are possible for packages. Cost per function point, on the other hand, may or may not be as favorable.

One major caution regarding packages should never be ignored: Package modification is a high-risk activity with a significant chance of failure and disaster. Not only is productivity normally low for modifying purchased packages, but if the vendors are reluctant to provide support, modification can easily be more expensive than custom development. As a rule of thumb, package modification is feasible only if the vendor is cooperative and supportive and if the package is well structured and well documented. Even then, changes that equal more than about 15 percent of the volume of the original software should be avoided. For older packages, poorly structured packages, and those for which vendor cooperation is minimal or even hostile, changes of more than 5 percent should be avoided. Indeed, searching for a second vendor or a more modern package should be considered.

Software Defect Removal Methods

Since software defect removal methods were inadequate in about 80 percent of all enterprises in 1990, a baseline analysis nearly always results in recommendations to upgrade defect removal methods via inspections, increased quality assurance funding, modernizing, testing, and the like.

A baseline analysis is not the only method for actually measuring quality, since it can take more than a year to accumulate enough quality data to calibrate defect removal efficiency. (Chapter 5 discusses the techniques for quality and user satisfaction measurement.) However, baseline analysis can and should provide context and background information on these topics:

1. Does the company really care about quality?

2. Are defect prevention methods adequate?

3. Are defect removal methods adequate?

4. Is a formal quality assurance organization in existence?

5. Is the quality assurance organization properly staffed and missioned?

6. Does the company measure quality numerically?

7. Are there any numeric quality targets for executives?

There are very significant differences in the kinds of defect removal activities practiced by companies on internal software, by vendors of commercial software, and by companies that work with the Department of Defense under military specifications. Defect removal for internal software is almost universally inadequate. Typically, enterprises use only perfunctory design reviews, no code inspections at all, no quality assurance, and a minimal test series that includes unit test, function test, and customer acceptance test. The cumulative defect removal efficiency of the whole series seldom goes above 80 percent, which is why it takes a long time for most internal production software to stabilize: 20 percent of the bugs are still in it.

Defect removal for commercial software, at least that sold by major vendors such as IBM, is significantly more thorough than for internal software. Vendors usually have a formal quality assurance review, design and code inspections, and in many cases a separate test department. The test series for commercial software starts with unit testing and includes regression testing, system testing, and field testing with early customers. Typical defect removal efficiencies for commercial software run from 90 to 96 percent.

Defect removal for Department of Defense (DOD) software under military specifications is similar to that for commercial software, but it includes several activities unique to the DOD environment: independent validation and verification by an outside source, and independent testing by an outside source. Although DOD and military specification requirements add significantly to costs, there is no hard evidence that DOD software has either higher overall defect removal efficiencies or higher reliability than commercial software. Neither the DOD itself nor most contractors measure defect removal efficiency as a general rule, but the few that do seem to be about the same or slightly higher in efficiency than commercial houses: perhaps 90 to 97 percent cumulative efficiency. The baseline analysis methodology concentrates very heavily on defect prevention and removal methods for very pragmatic reasons:

1. Defect removal is often the most expensive single software activity.

2. It is not possible to make significant improvements in software productivity without first improving software quality.

An internal study within IBM in 1975 noted the impact of quality on productivity for marketed commercial software products. The study revealed that the products with the highest quality after delivery had also achieved the highest development productivity. This study was surprising at the time, but when the economics of the situation were explored, the results were easily predictable. Projects that paid attention to quality did not get hung up during integration and test, nor did they receive negative evaluations from the IBM quality assurance organizations. Such findings are in the public domain today, but in spite of that fact, very few companies really understand the linkage between quality and productivity.

Software Documentation Variables

There are 10 general classes of documentation that should be studied as part of a baseline analysis, and more than 100 different kinds of documents can be produced in support of software. Software is astonishingly paper-intensive: For software projects developed under military specifications and a DOD contract, paperwork will be the most expensive part of the project. DOD contract projects often generate more than 200 English words for every line of source code, and paperwork production can hit peaks of 60 percent of the entire project costs.

For commercial software produced by major vendors such as IBM, DEC, Hewlett-Packard, Burroughs, CDC, and Honeywell, paperwork will usually be the second most expensive activity ranking just after defect removal. Here too, however, the costs are a significant proportion of overall expenses. Commercial software will typically generate around 75 English words for every line of source code, and paperwork costs can amount to 40 percent of the total project.

For internal software and information systems, paperwork can be significant, but nothing nearly as dramatic as the two preceding cases. Typically, in-house information systems will generate about 30 English words for every line of source code, and perhaps 25 to 30 percent of the total project costs will be devoted to paperwork.

Although paperwork costs are always in the top three expense categories for software, and often are number 1, most companies are totally unaware of the significance of this cost element. Baseline analyses carried out in computer companies and defense contractor environments almost always shock the managers and executives when they discover that 30 to 60 percent of their total software costs go to paperwork and less than 15 percent goes to coding. The 10 major classes of paperwork to be included in a baseline analysis include:

1. Planning documents
   - Development plans
   - Business plans

2. Business and financial documents
   - Requests for proposals (RFPs)
   - Cost estimates
   - Budgets
   - Capital expenditure requests

3. Control documents
   - Milestone reports
   - Monthly progress reports
   - Budget variance reports

4. Technical documents
   - Requirements
   - Initial functional specifications
   - Final functional specifications
   - Module design specifications

5. On-line documents
   - Help screens
   - Readme files
   - Hypertext links

6. User-oriented documents

- Reference manuals
- User's guides
- Systems programmer's guides
- Maintenance manuals

7. Tutorial documents
   - Introductions
   - Course materials

8. Marketing documents
   - Sales brochures
   - Advertisements

9. Quality and defect removal documents
   - Inspection reports
   - Quality assurance reports
   - Audit reports
   - Test reports
   - User bug reports

10. Correspondence and miscellaneous documents
    - Letters
    - Staff resumes
    - 35-mm slides
    - Overheads

One of the newer and very promising applications of the function point technique is the ability to predict and measure the volume of software paperwork: a task obviously beyond the capabilities of lines of code. Table 4.10 shows the use of function points for quantifying the

TABLE 4.10 Normalized Volumes of Paperwork for a Commercial Software Package

Documents	Pages per function point	Pages per function point	Words per function point
Planning	0.275	0.188	113
Business	0.138	0.000	38
Control	0.188	0.000	80
Technical	7.125	1.250	2,250
On-line	1.500	0.750	125
User-oriented	6.250	1.875	2,188
Tutorial	1.250	1.250	625
Marketing	0.063	0.123	63
Quality control	15.000	0.313	3,750
Correspondence	2.500	0.625	1,250
Totals	34.300	6.375	10,450

volume of documents measured for a large commercial database product produced by a major computer company.

Maintenance and Enhancement Project Variables

The word "maintenance" is ambiguous in the software industry as of 1991, and it can mean either defect repairs of or the addition of new functions and enhancements to a software product. Not only that, but for commercial software producers such as IBM, DEC, and Hewlett-Packard, "maintenance" can include delivery support, field service, hot-line support, and several other activities not usually found associated with internal software.

A baseline analysis will have quite a wide variance in scope for the maintenance area, depending on whether the client enterprise has commissioned the study for internal software, for commercial software, or for military software. In a baseline analysis, enhancements are generally treated as equivalent to new development and are studied as such, although their "hard" data should be broken out and shown separately because productivity rates for enhancements are quite different from new development. Specific maintenance questions should be included to cover defect repairs and the special considerations for commercial software, such as customer support and field service.

It is interesting that enhancement productivity follows a curve totally different from that for new projects. Enhancement productivity peaks, for example, when the size of the change is roughly 3 to 5 percent of the size of the system being modified. Smaller changes have high overhead costs associated with recompiling and regression testing, so productivity is low. Larger changes normally tend to damage the structure of the original system, so again productivity is low. Both enhancement and maintenance productivity are very sensitive to the structure of the base code being updated: Modifying well-structured code is more than twice as productive as modifying older unstructured software.

For maintenance or defect repairs of commercial software, totally new factors appear. Examples are "invalid" defect reports in which users report faults that in fact are caused by something other than the software itself, "duplicates" whereby several users report the same bug, and "abeyancies" whereby a problem found by a user cannot be replicated at the system repair center. The baseline analysis methodology should cover all of those aspects, but it varies significantly with the kind of software and client enterprise being analyzed.

A critical phenomenon often occurs when an industry approaches 50

TABLE 4.11 Population of Development, Enhancement, and Maintenance Programmers at 10-year Intervals

Year	Programmers, new projects	Programmers, enhancement	Programmers, repairs	Total
1950	90	3	7	100
1960	8,500	500	1,000	10,000
1970	65,000	15,000	20,000	100,000
1980	1,200,000	600,000	200,000	2,000,000
1990	3,000,000	3,000,000	1,000,000	7,000,000
2000	4,000,000	4,500,000	1,500,000	10,000,000
2010	5,000,000	7,000,000	2,000,000	14,000,000
2020	7,000,000	11,000,000	3,000,000	21,000,000

years of age: It takes more workers to perform maintenance than it does to build new products. For example, by the time automotive production was 50 years of age, there were many more mechanics in the United States repairing automobiles than there were workers in Detroit and elsewhere building new cars.

Software will soon be 50 years of age, and we appear to be following a similar trend. Table 4.11 shows the approximate numbers of world programmers working on development, enhancements, and maintenance from 1950 through 1990, with projections forward to 2000. The data is partly empirical and partly extrapolation from client studies. The message of Table 4.11 is probably valid, but the reliability of the data itself is low.

Project Risk and Value Factors

A very important aspect of a baseline analysis is to try to come to grips with the value and also the risks of the projects that are included. Value and risks are opposite sides of a coin, so they should be studied simultaneously. The value factors to be explored include:

1. Tangible value (cost reduction primarily)
2. Direct revenues (marketed software only)
3. Indirect revenues (hardware drag along)
4. Intangible value (enhanced capabilities, morale, etc.)
5. Competitive value

The risk factors to be explored include:

1. Risk of absolute failure or cancellation
2. Risk of excessive schedule pressure

3. Risk of unstable requirements

4. Risk of poor quality

5. Risk of inadequate staff or inadequate skills

Risk and value analyses are in rapid transition that should continue through the 1990s. The early forms of value analysis dealt only with tangible cost savings associated with software projects. It was realized during the 1980s that the strategic value of software was often greater than that of any other aspect, but the measurement of strategic value is a complex task. The most recent approach to measuring the value of software is to use function points and feature points to explore consumption patterns of software once the software is deployed. Risk analysis too is evolving, and we should see substantial progress. The Department of Defense is extremely interested in it, and so it will continue to be researched.

Complexity and Source Code Factors

Every project studied in a baseline analysis should be evaluated for complexity in at least three different forms: (1) the complexity of the underlying problem and algorithms, (2) the complexity of the source code, and (3) the complexity of the data and data structures. Although the questions that might be asked about complexity are usually self-explanatory, the implications of the answers are not. Software complexity analysis in 1990 is not an exact science. There are techniques, such as the McCabe cyclomatic complexity metric,[11] with which source code structural complexity can be measured.

The McCabe technique yields very useful insights and provides a good quantification of practical software complexity. Small well-structured programs with straight-line logic will have a "cyclomatic complexity" of 1; that is, they have no branching logic. Empirical studies reveal that programs with cyclomatic complexities of less than 5 are generally considered simple and easy to understand. Cyclomatic complexities of 10 or less are considered not too difficult. When the cyclomatic complexity is more than 20, the complexity is perceived as high. When the McCabe number exceeds 50, the software for practical purposes becomes untestable.

There are no measures at all of problem or algorithmic complexity, and empirical studies suggest that much of the observed complexity actually seen with source code is accidental or is caused by poorly trained programmers rather than by the problem itself. Data complexity is also generally unmeasured, although counting the entity types referenced by the program or system holds significant promise. (Entities are persons or objects whose attributes comprise the data the program is manipulating.)

One other gap in complexity theory also is notable: All of the complexity research on software to date has been based on new programs. There are no pragmatic studies on complexity when updating an existing system, although empirical evidence reveals that updates have perhaps 3 times the error potential of new code for equal volumes and that errors correlate with structure. When the major forms of complexity that affect software projects are considered, there are at least 20 of them. As of 1991, only a few of them have been measured objectively and numerically; the rest still await exploration. The 20 varieties of complexity include the following:

1. *Algorithmic complexity*   (deals with spatial complexity and algorithmic volumes). This form of complexity is one of the classic topics of software engineering. The basic concept is the length and structure of algorithms intended to solve various computable problems. Some algorithms are quite simple, such as one that finds the circumference of a circle, C = pi $*$ diameter. Other problems, such as those involving random or nonlinear phenomena, may require extremely long algorithms. Problems with high complexity tend to be perceived as difficult by the humans engaged in trying to solve them. Examples of problems with high algorithmic complexity include radar tracking and target acquisition.

2. *Computational complexity*   (deals with chronological complexity and run time lengths). This form of complexity also is a classic topic of software engineering. The basic concern is the amount of computer time or the number of iterations required to solve a computational problem or execute an algorithm. Some forms of algorithms, such as those involving random or nonlinear phenomena, may require enormous amounts of computer time for solution. Examples of problems with high computational complexity include long-range weather prediction and cryptographic analysis.

3. *Informational complexity*   (deals with entities and relationships). This form of complexity has become significant with the rise of large database applications. The basic concern is with the kinds of entities about which information must be stored and with the relations among those entities. Examples of problems with high informational complexity include airline reservation systems, integrated manufacturing systems, and large inventory management systems.

4. *Data complexity*   (deals with numbers of entity attributes and relationships). This form of complexity, similar in concept to informational complexity, deals with the number of attributes that a single entity might have. For example, some of the attributes that might be

used to describe a human being include sex, weight, height, date of birth, occupation, and marital status.

5. *Structural complexity* (deals with patterns and connections). This form of complexity deals with the overall nature of structures. Highly ordered structures, such as crystals, are often low in complexity. Other forms of structure include networks, lists, fluids, relational data structures, planetary orbits, and atomic structures.

6. *Logical complexity* (deals with combinations of AND/OR/NOR/NAND logic). This form of complexity deals with the kinds of logical operations that comprise syllogisms, statements, and assertions. It is much older than software engineering, but it has become relevant to software because there is a need for precise specification of software functions.

7. *Combinatorial complexity* (deals with permutations and combinations). This form of complexity deals with the numbers of subsets and sets that can be assembled out of component parts. In any large software project, there are usually many different programs and components that require integration to complete the tasks of the application.

8. *Cyclomatic complexity* (deals with nodes and edges of graphs). This form of complexity has been popularized by Tom McCabe. Its basic concern is with the graph formed by the control flow of an application. Unlike some of the other forms of complexity, this one can be quantified precisely. It is defined as the number of edges of a graph, minus the number of nodes, plus 2. Pragmatically, this is a significant metric for software, since modules or programs with high cyclomatic complexity are often difficult to maintain and tend to become error-prone.

9. *Essential complexity* (deals with nodes and edges of reduced graphs). This form of complexity is similar in concept to cyclomatic complexity, but it deals with a graph after the graph has been simplified by the removal of redundant paths. Essential complexity has been popularized by Tom McCabe.

10. *Topologic complexity* (deals with rotations and folding patterns). This form of complexity is explored widely by mathematicians but seldom by software engineers. It deals with the various forms of rotation and folding that are permissible in a basic structure. The idea is relevant to software, since it can be applied to one of the intractable problems of software engineering: attempting to find the optimal structure for a large system.

11. *Harmonic complexity* (deals with waveforms and Fourier transformations). This form of complexity is concerned with the vari-

ous waveforms that together create an integrated wave pattern. The topic is very important in physics and engineering, but it is only just being explored by software engineers.

12. *Syntactic complexity* (deals with grammatical structures of descriptions). This form of complexity deals with the structure and grammar of text passages. Although the field is more than 100 years old and is quite useful for software, it has seldom been utilized by software engineers. Its primary utility would be in looking at the observed complexity of specifications with a view to simplifying them for easier comprehension. It has a number of fairly precise quantifications, such as the FOG index and the Fleish index.

13. *Semantic complexity* (deals with ambiguities and definitions of terms). This form of complexity is often a companion to syntactic complexity. It deals with the definitions of terms and the meaning of words and phrases. Unlike syntactic complexity, it is rather amorphous in its results.

14. *Mnemonic complexity* (deals with factors affecting memorization). This form of complexity deals with the factors that cause topics to be easy or difficult to memorize. It is widely known that human memories have both a temporary and a permanent component. Memorization of text, verbal data, mathematics, and symbols normally involves temporary memory, which is quite limited in capacity. (A famous assertion holds that temporary memory can absorb only seven chunks of information at a time, plus or minus two.) Permanent memory is not fully understood, but it may involve some form of holographic distribution of engrams over the neural net of the brain. Visual data such as peoples' faces bypass temporary memory and are entered directly into permanent memory, which explains why it is easy to remember faces but not names.

15. *Perceptional complexity* (deals with surfaces and edges). This form of complexity deals with the visual appearance of artifacts and whether they appear complex or simple to the human perceiver. Regular patterns, for example, tend to appear simpler than random configurations with the same number of elements.

16. *Flow complexity* (deals with channels and fluid dynamics of processes). This form of complexity concerns fluid dynamics, and it is a major topic of physics, medicine, and hydrology. Since software systems also are dynamic and since information flow is a major aspect of design, this topic has a great relevance to software engineering. Within the past few years, a great deal of exciting research has taken place in the area of flow dynamics, and particularly in the area of turbulence. An entirely new subdiscipline of mathematical physics

termed "chaos" has started to emerge, and it seems to have many interactions with software engineering.

17. *Entropic complexity* (deals with decay and disorder rates). All known systems have a tendency to move toward disorder over time, which is equivalent to saying that things decay. Software, it has been discovered, also decays with the passage of time even though it is not a physical system. Each time a change is made, the structure of a software system tends to degrade slightly. With the passage of enough time, the disorder accumulates sufficiently to make the system unmaintainable. This form of complexity is very significant in physics and astronomy and is starting to be explored in software engineering.

18. *Functional complexity* (deals with patterns and sequences of user tasks). When users of a software system call the system "complex," what exactly do they mean? This form of complexity concerns the user perception of the way functions within a software system are located, turned on, utilized for some purpose, modified if necessary, and turned off again.

19. *Organizational complexity* (deals with hierarchies and matrices of groups). This form of complexity deals not with a software project directly, but with the organizational structures of the staff that will design and develop it. It has been studied by management scientists and psychologists for more than 100 years, but only recently has it been discovered to be relevant to software projects. A surprising finding has been that large systems tend to be decomposed into components that match the organizational structures of the developing enterprise rather than components that match the needs of the software itself.

20. *Diagnostic complexity* (deals with factors affecting identification of malfunctions). When a medical doctor is diagnosing a patient, certain combinations of temperature, blood pressure, pulse rates, and other signs are the clues needed to diagnose specific illnesses. Similarly, when software malfunctions, certain combinations of symptoms can be used to identify the underlying cause. This form of complexity analysis is just starting to be significant for software projects.

Measuring the Hard Data for Software Projects

Each major task in a software project will produce some kind of a deliverable, and the volume of the deliverables should be measured as part of a baseline analysis. The normal kinds of deliverables for software projects can be divided into two sets: natural and synthetic. The natural deliverables of a software project are the tangible outputs of many tasks, and they include:

1. Pages of paper documents

2. Source code

3. Test cases

The synthetic deliverables of a software project are the volumes of abstract constructs, and they include:

1. Function points (in all variations)

2. Feature points

Although the synthetic functional deliverables are superior to the natural deliverables for economic studies, it is also useful to record the volumes of natural deliverables as well. Table 4.12 shows a typical set of hard data measurements using natural deliverables.

There are several equations developed by the author for software measurement that can be used interchangeably with both natural and synthetic deliverables. The equations are concerned with relationships between assignment scopes and production rates for software deliverables. An assignment scope is the amount of a deliverable for which one person is normally responsible. A "production rate" is the amount of a deliverable which one person can normally produce in an hour, day, week, or month.

The equations have several interesting attributes: (1) they allow software projects to be measured with reasonably low error; (2) they work equally well with function points, pages of documentation, and lines of source code; (3) they can be used with any source language; (4) they can be used for estimating as well as measurement; (5) they can be used for individual activities, complete programs, large systems, or entire enterprises; (6) they establish regular and predictable relationships among the major attributes of software projects: staff sizes, human effort, schedules, and costs. There are three fundamental equa-

TABLE 4.12 Measurement of Hard Data for Project Deliverables

Activity	Deliverable	Size	Assignment scope	Production rate per month
Requirements	Pages	100	50	25
Design	Pages	250	150	25
Coding	Statements	25,000	7,500	1,250
User documents	Pages	300	200	50
Unit test	Test cases	2,500	500	250
Function test	Test cases	750	250	125

tions and three supplemental equations in the set. The fundamental equations are:

1. Staff size = product size/assignment scope
2. Effort = product size/production rate
3. Schedule = effort/staff size

Although simple in concept and use, the fundamental equations are surprising. They allow any real software project to be matched with very low error for the attributes of staff size, effort, and schedules.

The three supplemental equations are:

4. Cost = (effort*salary) + other costs
5. Assignment scope = product size/staff size
6. Production rate = product size/effort

It is surprising how useful equations as simple as these can be. Let us consider each one in turn. The first equation solves the troublesome question of how large staff sizes are likely to be for any given project. To repeat, the assignment scope is the average quantity of work for which an average staff employee is responsible on any given project. For example, on small to medium-size software projects, an average programmer might be responsible for completing 5000 lines of Cobol source code. Expressed in function points, the same assignment scope would be 47 function points.

Once an enterprise begins to think in terms of and measure assignment scopes, a great many troublesome points can be resolved. For example, in dealing with a natural deliverable such as lines of source code, once an enterprise knows that its average coding assignment scope is 3000, 4000, or 5000 lines (assignment scopes range up to 20,000 lines) then optimal staff sizes for new projects can easily be calculated. Assume an enterprise is planning a new 50,000-source-line Cobol system and its average coding assignment scope has been 5000 lines. Dividing product size (50,000 lines) by assignment scope (5000 lines) indicates that a staff of 10 programmers would be needed.

Assignment scopes can also be used with synthetic deliverables such as function points. For example, a typical maintenance assignment scope for a programmer who performs defect repairs and minor updates would be about 500 function points in size. In real life, assignment scopes vary in response to skill levels, source languages, product sizes, and environmental factors. But the assignment scope concept is worth understanding and using.

It is immediately apparent that the terms of the equation can be reversed. For example, to ascertain a typical coding assignment scope for historical projects that are completed, it is only necessary to divide product size (50,000 statements, for example) by the number of programmers (10, for example) to find the average assignment scope: 5000 in this example.

The second fundamental equation solves the problem of how much human effort will be required for a software project. In this equation, product size is once again used (and either lines of source code or function points will work). Product size is divided by production rate to find out how much human effort will be required. For example, in the 50,000 Cobol source-line system used in the previous example, a typical pure code production rate might be 2000 lines of source code per month. Dividing product size (50,000 Cobol statements) by production rate (2000 lines of source code per month) yields 250 person-months of effort to code the system.

Here too it is apparent that the terms of the equation can be reversed: To find the productivity rate for any completed project; merely dividing product size by actual effort will give the productivity rate. The equation also works with function points or any other deliverable object such as documentation pages, test cases, or even bug reports.

Although the assignment scope parameter and the equations that use it are comparatively new to software engineering, the production rate factor has been in existence for many years.

The third fundamental equation solves the problem of development schedules. Effort (as calculated by the second equation) is divided by staff size (as calculated by the first equation) to yield the calendar time needed to develop the program. In the example already used, effort was calculated at 100 person-months and staff size was calculated at 10, so the schedule would be 10 calendar months.

The fourth equation, for cost, is not fundamental, but it is useful. Project cost is calculated by simply multiplying effort by average burdened salary. Assuming for the example discussed thus far that the average burdened salary rate per month is $5000, the basic product cost can be calculated by multiplying the 100 months of effort by $5000 to yield a basic product cost of $500,000.

Although this is a simplistic way to deal with costs, it is reasonably satisfactory. The remaining term of the fourth equation ("other costs") is to be used for cost items outside the scope of normal burdened salaries—heavy capital equipment investments, moving and living costs, real estate, and the like.

Of the six equations, only the first one, which introduces the assignment scope variable, is comparatively new to software engineering, having been used for project estimating since about 1984. However, since assignment scope allows the problem of staff size prediction to be handled relatively unambiguously, it is the keystone of the equation set.

Measuring Project, Activity, and Task Schedules

Among the most difficult and taxing forms of hard data measurement is that of project and task schedules. The initial difficulty with schedule measurement is a basic one: identifying the starting point of any given project! Very seldom are projects started so crisply and precisely that a manager or user can assert "Project XYZ began on April 25, 1990." Usually there is a great deal of exploratory discussion and informal work, which can sometimes span a year or more, before an actual project finally coalesces.

Once an approximate start date for a project is identified, the next set of difficulties involves overlaps among tasks. The original waterfall model concept contained the naive assumption that a task would not begin until its predecessor ended, as shown in Figure 4.6. It quickly became evident to all who worked on real projects that the assumption of waiting until a task ended before the next task began was unrealistic. Given normal schedule pressures and software work habits, it is quite common to start the next task in sequence long before a predecessor task is over. Indeed, from analysis of several hundred projects since 1985 it can be asserted that the approximate average overlap is 25 percent; that is, about one-fourth of any given task will remain unfinished at the time the next task in sequence is begun. That average is often exceeded, and overlaps of 50 or even 100 percent (which implies true concurrency) are frequently encountered.

Figure 4.7 shows how the waterfall model tended to be implemented in real-life terms. Although overlap is simple and easy to understand

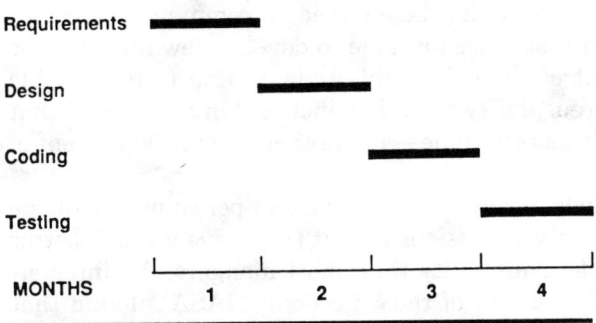

Figure 4.6   Original assumption of zero overlap with the waterfall model.

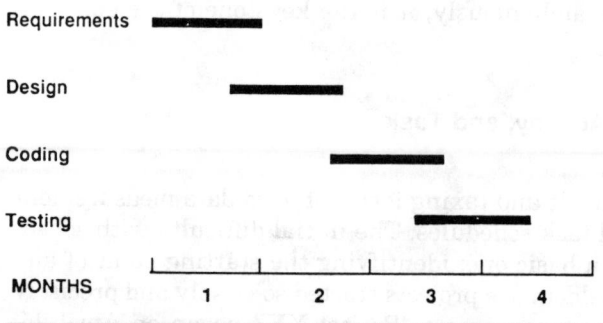

Figure 4.7   Revised assumption of 25 percent overlap with the waterfall model.

in principle, it is quite difficult to measure in real life. The problems are not insoluble, however. If a formal project planning system is used, it will show not only the overlaps but the actual calendar dates as well.

If formal project planning systems are not used, it is seldom possible to reconstruct the actual dates from memory. A useful approximation, however, is to ask the project managers and staff to express overlap in percentage terms; i.e., "coding overlapped design by 50 percent." Unless overlaps are measured and included in historical data, it will be very difficult to use such data for predicting future projects. The gross schedule from the beginning to the end of a project is insufficient for accurate estimation.

Reusable Design and Code Factors (Optional)

Reusable designs are less common than reusable code, although they are no less important. Reusable code is one of the most powerful productivity techniques available. Leading-edge companies such as Toshiba and Hartford Insurance are able to develop new applications with up to 85 percent of the deliverable code coming from reusable sources. The topic of reusability should be included in all projects that actually make use of this technique—and in theory some 90 percent of all project could.

One of the reasons why design and development personnel should be part of the baseline analysis sessions is that they have a much better idea about reused code availability than most mangers. An interesting study by Barry Silverman of reused code at NASA[12] found that managers thought that the reused code volumes in the projects studied totaled to less than 5 percent, whereas the programmers on the projects said that the volume approached 60 percent.

Whenever really high productivity rates occur (i.e., more than 5000 source code statements or 50 function points per person-month) there is a very strong probability that at least half of the code in question was reused. Prescribing reusability as a therapy will occur in quite a large number of enterprises. Consultants should definitely consider reusability when doing productivity analyses within all large enterprises with more than 200 programmers and analysts. Certain industry types are especially good candidates for reusability: aerospace, banking, computers, electronics, communications, insurance, public utilities, and telephone operating companies, for example. These enterprises do large numbers of very similar applications, and that is exactly the domain where reusability is most effective.

Base Code Factors for Maintenance and Enhancement Projects

For projects that either enhance existing software or perform major defect repairs, an exploration of base code is quite important. For new programs and systems the section should be omitted completely.

The long-range growth of software over time, and also the growth in entropy or complexity, can be modeled with high precision. Such modeling can lead to decisions on what interventions or therapies may be needed to slow down or reverse the decay normally associated with aging software. The 10-year evolution of software projects was described by the author in the *Journal of Software Maintenance Practice and Experience.*[13]

The costs, schedules, risks, and defect potentials of enhancing or modifying an existing system are dramatically different from those typical of entirely new software. Adding 1000 Cobol source lines to an aging, poorly structured, and partially undocumented system can easily be 3 times as expensive and take more than twice as long as writing a new program of 1000 Cobol statements. Moreover, because of the difficulty of updating aging software safely, the potential defects when updating old software can be 3 times higher than for new software, and the average defect removal efficiency is 5 to 10 percent lower for enhancement work than for new software.

It very often happens during a baseline analysis that clients want explicit advice and counsel on therapies that can improve aging software. Starting in 1980 a new software subindustry began to emerge that by 1990 appears to be generating some millions of dollars in annual revenues. It consists of the companies that provide "geriatric care" for aging software—automated restructuring services or products, and the even newer reverse engineering and reengineering products. By the end of the 1990s, this subindustry is likely to have 15 or 20 companies engaged with accumulated annual revenues exceeding $100 million.

The more sophisticated restructuring algorithms, such as those developed by Eric Bush of Language Technology or Chris Miller of Catalyst (now Peat, Marwick) are derived from graph theory and work surprisingly well. With few exceptions, interviews with more than a dozen users of the major restructuring tools indicate very high satisfaction levels for all Cobol systems restructured.

Not only is the code itself restructured well enough that the cyclomatic complexity number often drops to 1, but the code is also redocumented, dead code is identified, and various other minor improvements are made.

In 1986, the companies offering geriatric care (such as Language Technology, Systems and Programming Resources, and Peat, Marwick) were primarily supporting only Cobol software. That was for reason of business and not technology limitations: The fundamental mathematics of restructuring could also be applied to PL/I, Fortran, and other languages if the volume of business made the investment attractive.

The costs of restructuring range from perhaps 2 cents to more than $1 per source line depending on the volume of code, the service selected, and whether or not any manual intervention is required to perform such tasks as remodulatization that are normally performed by the restructuring tools. Most of the companies in the restructuring business have some kind of free trial arrangement under which up to 5000 source lines can be tried for nothing. If the baseline analysis turns up significant quantities of aging Cobol, restructuring is a recommended therapy. Unfortunately, many companies have aging libraries of programs in other languages that cannot be automatically restructured: Assembler, Fortran, PL/I, PLS, RPG, APL, and the like.

Two newer technologies, reverse engineering and reengineering, have recently joined the restructuring concept in providing geriatric care. Reverse engineering uses expert system techniques to extract the hidden design elements from the source code itself, with a view to performing either manual or automatic conversion once the design (long lost from human view) is recovered. Reengineering is concerned with the automatic migration of aging software to new platforms, new languages, or more robust forms. Both reverse engineering and reengineering are so new as this book is written that empirical evidence about them is scarce, although the technologies appear to be well formed and may be effective.

The set of therapies for non-Cobol source code is both limited in effectiveness and expensive to apply. Pragmatically, the most effective therapy yet observed for other languages is the manual removal of error-prone modules.

Internal studies by IBM in the 1970s indicated that software errors are not smoothly or randomly distributed throughout the modules of large software systems. The errors tend to clump in a very small number of very buggy modules. In the case of one of IBM's commercial software products, the IMS Data Base, 57 percent of all errors were found in only 5 percent of the modules. More than 60 percent of the modules had no errors at all. Other companies studying software errors have made similar findings.

It is possible to analyze production software manually, isolate the error-prone modules, and either redevelop the modules or upgrade them substantially. That is not a particularly easy task, and it requires highly skilled professional programmers who may be occupied for very long periods of time—a year or more—while the work is going on.

Some other therapies in the maintenance and enhancement area are also worth noting. As of 1990, most companies with fewer than about 200 total software professionals usually handle maintenance on an informal basis whereby development personnel fix bugs as the need arises. Companies with more than 200 software personnel often have separate maintenance departments staffed by professionals who concentrate on defect repairs and small enhancements.

Quite a few companies that had more than 200 professionals in 1990 only a few years before had 50 or fewer. Since organization structures typically change more slowly than staffs grow in size, it is often useful to consider the establishment of professional software maintenance units if the enterprise is of the right size and does substantial amounts of maintenance. These specialist groups are usually more productive than ad hoc maintenance by developers, and the separation of tasks allows both development and maintenance professionals to concentrate their skills.

Delta Code Factors for Maintenance and Enhancement Projects

The delta code examination is used only to cover the structure and complexity of enhancements of or modifications to existing systems. The distinction between delta code and new code is minor but significant: The delta code will be added to the existing system as discrete blocks or modules, will require internal changes to the existing source code inside the current program, or will be both added and changed simultaneously. Productivity rates, risks, potential bad fixes, costs, and schedules are significantly worse when the delta changes require updating existing code than they are when the delta code is merely added on top of the original program.

When delta code is added to an existing system, the new code will either utilize or modify the existing data structures of the original program. Since modifying an existing data structure is sometimes very intricate, it is significant to note this factor if it occurs. The phrase "bad fix" refers to an error accidentally inserted into a program or system while trying to fix a previous error. This is a surprisingly common occurrence, and an internal study within IBM revealed that a full 20 percent of the customer-reported bugs against the MVS operating system were bad fixes.

The probability of making bad fixes is directly proportional to the structure of the original code: For cyclomatic complexity numbers of less than 10, the probability is about 1 bad fix per 20 changes (i.e., a 5 percent bad fix probability). For cyclomatic complexity number of 20 to 30, the bad fix probability rises to about 20 percent, and for McCabe complexity numbers greater than 50, the bad fix probability is approximately 40 percent. In extreme cases, when the McCabe number approaches 100, bad fixes can hit 60 percent.

The therapies that minimize bad fix potentials include automatic restructuring (available for Cobol only), code inspections, and testing of all modifications before releasing the change. This last step, although intuitively obvious, is often not performed because of schedule pressures.

Descriptive Materials and Comments

The last set of topics of a baseline analysis is intended to explore specific information about the project that may require text and comments: the computers, operating systems, and tools used on the project, database packages if any, and the like. A section is also reserved for comments by the clients or consultants of any unusual aspects of the project being analyzed. Unusual aspects that can impact productivity and quality include, but are not limited to, the following:

- Transfer of the project from one city to another
- Physical movement of the project team from one location to another
- Significant expansion of requirements or project scope during mid-development
- Significant technical redirections or restarts
- Staff attrition rates higher than 20 percent per year

- Use of a new programming language or major new tool for the very first time

- Change in hardware or software environment after the project started

- Disasters, such as the California earthquake, fires in a data center or office building, and so on

When the last comments are recorded, the analysis of the project is completed. The consultant administering the questionnaire should use the comments section for recording the start and stop times of session, as a planning aid for future sessions. Finally, the consultant should close by asking the participants if there are any factors or issues that have not yet been covered.

Since a full baseline analysis will include from 5 to 20 projects, the consultant might tell the participants how many other projects are being analyzed and what the approximate schedules are for the aggregation and statistical analysis of the entire set.

Analysis and Aggregation of the Baseline Data

Since Appendix C illustrates the kind of output that results from a baseline analysis, it is sufficient here to discuss the overall results from a human factors standpoint. The interview sessions themselves, and the kinds of information collected, are quickly perceived by all participants as benign and even helpful. This situation is natural and beneficial. Indeed, the results are favorable enough that spontaneous requests for additional interviews occur frequently.

The technology developed for carrying out software baseline analyses is thorough and accurate. Most enterprises have never before experienced such a detailed examination of their software policies, methods, tools, metrics, and environment. Although the practical results of a baseline analysis depend upon the specific diagnoses that are made, they often include the following improvements in client software environments:

- Establishment of a software metrics program and the adoption of leading-edge measurement techniques

- Enhanced credibility with users and enterprise management in terms of schedule and resource commitments

- Changes in the training and education made available to management and technical personnel

- Establishment of new policies dealing with morale and human relations issues

- Adoption of leading-edge software requirements and design techniques

- Adoption of leading-edge defect removal and quality assurance techniques

- Adoption of new technologies for restoration of aging software systems

- Changes in the physical environment, the supporting tools, and the workstations available for software professionals

- Measurable and validated increases in productivity and quality simultaneously

The overall goal of the baseline analysis technology is to inform all participants of the exact strengths and weaknesses that were discovered during the diagnosis. Only from the basis of firm diagnostic knowledge is it possible to plan effective therapies.

The specific therapies prescribed can encompass tools, policy changes, methodological changes, organizations changes, staffing level changes, or all of the above simultaneously. The baseline analysis will diagnose all known problems affecting software, but therapy selection requires skilled and knowledgeable consultants and clients.

References

1. Humphrey, Watts, *Measuring the Software Process*, Addison-Wesley, Reading, Mass., 1989, 489 pp.
2. Jones, Capers, *Programming Productivity*, McGraw-Hill, New York, 1986, 279 pp.
3. SPR, CHECKPOINT®, "Data Collection Questionnaire," Software Productivity Research, Inc., Burlington, Mass., 1990, 35 pp.
4. Jones, Capers, "A 10 Year Retrospective of Software Engineering within ITT," Software Productivity Research, Inc., Burlington, Mass., 1989, 35 pp.
5. Curtis, B., *Human Factors in Software Development*, IEEE catalog number EHO229-5, 2d ed., IEEE Press, Washington, D.C., 1986, 730 pp.
6. Schneiderman, B., *Software Psychology—Human Factors in Computer and Information Systems*, Winthrop, Cambridge, Mass., 1980, 320 pp.
7. Weinberg, G., *The Psychology of Computer Programming*, Reinhold, New York, 1971, 288 pp.
8. DeMarco, T., and T. Lister, *Peopleware*, Dorset House, New York, 1987, 188 pp.
9. McCue, G., "IBM's Santa Teresa Laboratory—Architectural Design for Program Development," *IBM Systems Journal*, vol. 17, no. 1, 1978. Reprinted in C. Jones, *Programming Productivity—Issues for the Eighties*, IEEE catalog number EHO239-4, 2d ed., IEEE Press, Washington, D.C., 1986, 462 pp.
10. Thadani, A. J., "Factors Affecting Programmer Productivity During Development," *IBM Systems Journal*, vol. 23, no. 1, 1984, pp. 19–35.
11. McCabe, T., "A Software Complexity Measure," *IEEE Transactions on Software Engineering*, vol. 2, December 1976, pp. 308–320.
12. Silverman, B., "Software Cost and Productivity Improvements: An Analogical View," *Computer*, May 1985, pp. 86–96. Reprinted in C. Jones, *Programming Productivity—Issues for the Eighties*, IEEE catalog number EHO239-4, 2d ed., IEEE Press, Washington, D.C., 1986, 462 pp.
13. Jones, Capers, "Long-Range Enhancement Modelling," *Journal of Software Maintenance—Practice and Experience*, vol. 1, no. 2, 1990.

Measuring Software Quality and User Satisfaction

Quality Control and International Competition

There are four critical business factors which tend to determine successful competition in global markets:

1. Cost of production

2. Time to market

3. Quality and reliability

4. User satisfaction

All four are important, and all four depend upon careful measurement for a company to make tangible improvements. Cost of production has been a major factor for hundreds of years, and it has proved its importance in both natural products (agriculture, minerals, metals, and so on) and manufactured durable goods, as well as services. Indeed, cost of production was the first business factor to be measured and explored in depth.

Time to market has become progressively important in recent years as new manufacturing technologies and rapid communication make international competition more speed-intensive than the former durable goods economy. Time to market has been particularly important in the twentieth century; it is a key consideration for consumer goods and such personal electronics as Walkman-class radios, cassette players, and compact disk players. It is also a major factor for industrial and commercial products.

Only since the 1950s have quality, reliability, and user satisfaction been recognized as the major driving force for high-technology products and hence a key ingredient in long-range national and industrial success. Quality, reliability, and user satisfaction are turning out to be the driving force of competition for high-technology products, including automobiles, computers, telecommunications equipment, and many modern consumer products such as kitchen appliances and power tools.

It is primarily quality control, rather than cost of production or time to market, that explains the unprecedented success of Japan in modern high-technology competition. Indeed, the pioneering work of Deming[1] on quality measurement and statistical quality control that was widely adopted by Japanese industry has perhaps been the single most important factor in Japan's favorable balance of trade vis-à-vis the United States.

Further, in the specific case of software, quality control is on the critical path for reducing cost of production and shortening time to market. It is also important in determining user satisfaction. The importance of quality control cannot be overstressed: software producers who do not control quality risk being driven from their markets and perhaps out of business by competitors who do control quality! Before dealing with the measurement of quality, it is useful to consider the significance of this factor on high-technology products in general and on software in particular.

Since the reemergence of Japanese industry after World War II, Japan has followed one of the most successful industrial strategies in all human history. The basic strategy has two aspects:

1. Concentrate on high-technology products, since the value per shipped ton is greater than for any other kinds of product.

2. Compete by achieving quality levels at least 25 percent higher than those of U.S. and European companies while holding prices to within ±10 percent of U.S. and European levels.

In research of the factors that contribute to market share of high-technology products, the customer perception of quality has turned out to be the dominant factor for large market shares. For high-technology products, quality and user satisfaction even outweigh time to market and cost of production in terms of overall market share and competitive significance.

A question that arises is why the widely publicized Japanese strategy has been so successful against U.S. and European companies when those companies can easily follow the same strategy themselves? The answer is that U.S. and European business strategies evolved more than 100 years ago during an earlier industrial era when factors such as least-cost production were dominant in creating market shares and quality was often a secondary issue. Many U.S. and European executives either ignored quality or perceived it to be an optional item that was of secondary importance. That was a mistake, and the United States and Europe are now paying the price for it.

The whole postwar generation of U.S. and European executives were playing by the rules of a 100-year old game while Japanese executives were playing a modern high-technology game. The following is a list of 10 high-technology products the quality of which is the dominant factor leading to market shares:

1. Automobiles
2. Cameras
3. Compact disk players
4. Computers
5. Machine tools
6. Medical instruments
7. Stereo receivers
8. Telephone handsets
9. Television sets
10. Watches

Japan has become the world's largest producer of 5 of the 10 products and is a major producer of all of the others. The United States has steadily lost global market share in all of the areas except computers.

Another significant aspect of industry as the twentieth century draws to a close is that microcomputers and software are embedded in all 10 of the product types listed above. The 1990 model year automobiles, for example, included cars with as many as 12 separate on-board computers governing fuel injection, cooling and heating, audio equipment, odometers and tachometers, and other instruments!

As computers and software continue to expand into consumer product areas, companies must recognize that success in software is on the critical path to corporate survival. The future success of the United States against global competition requires that the CEO's of U.S. industries understand the true factors of global competition in the twenty-first century:

1. High-technology products are critical to U.S. success.
2. Quality is the dominant marketing factor for high-technology products.

3. High-technology products depend upon computing and software.

4. Quality is the key to success in computing and software.

5. Quality must start at the top and become part of the U.S. corporate culture.

By the end of the twentieth century, it can be seen that two new business laws may become operational and drive successful businesses and industries into the twenty-first century:

Law 1. Enterprises that master computers and software will succeed; enterprises that fall behind in computing and software will fail.

Law 2. Quality control is the key to mastering computing and software; enterprises that control software quality will also control schedules and productivity. Enterprises that do not control quality will fail.

Defining Quality for Measurement and Estimation

Readers with a philosophical turn of mind may have noticed a curious anomaly in this chapter so far. The term "quality" has been used many times on every page but has not yet been defined. This anomaly is a symptom of a classic industrial paradox which deserves discussion. Quality and quality control are agreed by all observers to be major international business factors, yet the terms are extraordinarily difficult to define precisely. This phenomenon permeates one of the finest although unusual books on quality ever written: *Zen and the Art of Motorcycle Maintenance,* by Robert Pirsig.[2] In his book, Pirsig ruminates that quality is easy to see and is immediately apparent when encountered. But when you try to pin it down or define what it is, you find the concept is elusive and slips away. It is not the complexity, but the utter simplicity of quality that defies explanation.

In the writings of software quality specialists, and in informal discussions with most of them, there are a variety of concepts centering around software quality. Here are the concepts expressed by several software specialists, in alphabetical order:

- Dr. Barry Boehm, formerly of TRW and now with DARPA, tends to think of quality as "Achieving high levels of user satisfaction, portability, maintainability, robustness, and fitness for use."

- Phil Crosby, the former ITT vice president of quality, has created the definition with the widest currency because of its publication in his famous book *Quality Is Free.*[3] Phil states that quality means "conformance to user requirements."

- W. Edwards Deming, in his lectures and writings, considers quality to be "striving for excellence in reliability and functions by continuous improvement in the process of development, supported by statistical analysis of the causes of failure."

- Watts Humphrey, of the Software Engineering Institute, tends to speak of quality as "achieving excellent levels of fitness for use, conformance to requirements, reliability, and maintainability."

- The author defines software quality as "the absence of defects that would make software either stop completely or produce unacceptable results. Defects can be traced to requirements, to design, to code, to documentation, or to bad fixes of previous defects. Defects can range in severity from minor to major."

- James Martin, in his public lectures, has asserted that software quality means being on time, within budget, and meeting user needs.

- Tom McCabe, the complexity specialist, tends to define quality in his lectures as "high levels of user satisfaction and low defect levels, often associated with low complexity."

- John Musa of Bell Laboratories, the well-known reliability modeler, states that quality means a combination of "low defect levels, adherence of software functions to user needs, and high reliability."[4]

- Bill Perry, head of the Quality Assurance Institute, has defined quality in his speeches as "high levels of user satisfaction and adherence to requirements."

Considered individually, each of the definitions has merit and raises valid points. Taken collectively, the situation resembles the ancient Buddhist parable of the blind men and the elephant: The elephant was described as being like a rope, a wall, or a snake depending upon whether the blind man touched the tail, the side, or the trunk. For practical day-to-day purposes, a working definition of quality must meet two criteria:

1. Quality must be measurable when it occurs.

2. Quality should be predictable before it occurs.

Table 5.1 lists the elements of the major definitions quoted above and indicates which elements meet both criteria.

Although Table 5.1 does not contain many surprises, it is important to understand the limitations for measurement purposes of two important concepts: conformance to requirements and user satisfaction. For software, Phil Crosby's widely quoted definition of quality as "conformance to requirements" suffers from two serious limitations:

TABLE 5.1 **Predictability and Measurability of Quality Factors**

Quality factor	Predictable	Measurable
Defect levels	Yes	Yes
Defect origins	Yes	Yes
Defect severity	Yes	Yes
Defect removal efficiency	Yes	Yes
Product complexity	Yes	Yes
Project reliability	Yes	Yes
Project maintainability	Yes	Yes
Project schedules	Yes	Yes
Project budgets	Yes	Yes
Portability	Yes	Yes
Conformance to requirements	No	Yes
User satisfaction	No	Yes
Fitness for use	No	Yes
Robustness	No	No

1. Although this can be measured after the fact, there are no a priori estimating techniques that can predict the phenomenon ahead of time.

2. When software defect origins are measured, "requirements" is one of the chief sources of error. To define quality as conformance to a major source of error leads to problems of circular reasoning, and prevents either measurement or estimation with accuracy.

User satisfaction with software is certainly capable of being measured with high precision after the fact. But there are currently no effective estimating techniques that can directly predict the presence or absence of this phenomenon far enough ahead of time to take effective action. There are, however, very strong correlations between user satisfaction and factors that can be estimated. For example, there is a very strong inverse correlation between software defect levels and user satisfaction. So far as can be determined, there has never been a software product with high defect levels that was satisfactory to its users. The opposite situation, however, does not correlate so well: There are software products with low defect levels that are not satisfactory to users.

Another aspect of user satisfaction is an obvious one: Since this factor depends on users, it is hard to carry out early measurements. In the case of defects, for example, measurements can start as early as the requirements phase. As for user satisfaction, it is hard to begin until there is something to use. These considerations mean that, in a practical day-to-day measurement system, user satisfaction is a special case that should be dealt with on its own terms, and it should be decoupled from ordinary defect and removal metrics. The bulk of the other metrics in Table 5.1 meet the two criteria of being both predictable and measurable. Therefore, any or all of them can be used effectively for quality control purposes.

Five Steps to Software Quality Control

These five steps to software quality control have been observed in the course of software management consulting in leading corporations:

Step 1   Establish a software quality metrics program

Software achieved a notorious reputation during the first 45 years of its history as the high-technology occupation with the worst track record in terms of measurements. Over the last 10 years, improvements in measurement technology have enabled leading-edge companies to measure both software quality and productivity with high precision. If your company has not yet adopted leading-edge quality metrics for key products, you are headed for a disturbing future as your more advanced competitors pull ahead.

The significance of this step cannot be overstated: If you look inside the leading companies within an industry you will find full-scale measurements programs and hence executive abilities to receive early warnings and cure problems. For example, IBM and AT&T have had quality measurements since before World War II and software quality measurements since the 1960s. Quality measurement is a critical factor in high-technology products, and all the companies which have tended to become household words have quality measurement programs: DEC, Hewlett-Packard, IBM, and many others. The lagging enterprises which have no software measures also have virtually no ability to apply executive control to the software process.

Step 2   Establish tangible executive software performance goals

Does your enterprise have any meaningful software quality or productivity goals operational? The answer for many U.S. companies would be no, but for leading-edge companies such as IBM and Hewlett-Packard it will be yes. Now that software can be measured, it is possible to establish tangible, pragmatic performance goals for both software quality and productivity. Since the two key aspects of software quality are defect removal efficiency and customer satisfaction, reasonable executive targets would be to achieve higher than 95 percent efficiency in finding software bugs and higher than 90 percent "good" or "excellent" customer satisfaction ratings.

Step 3   Establish meaningful software quality assurance

One of the most significant differences between leading and lagging U.S. enterprises is the attention paid to software quality. It can be strongly asserted that the U.S. companies that concentrate on software quality have higher productivity, shorter development schedules, and higher levels of customer satisfaction than companies that ignore quality. Since the steps needed to achieve high quality include both defect prevention and defect removal, a permanent quality assurance organization can facilitate the move toward quality control.

It is possible, in theory, to achieve high quality without a formal quality assurance organization. Unfortunately, the American psychology often tends to need the external prompting which a formal quality assurance organization provides. An effective, active quality assurance team can provide a continuous boost in the quality arena.

Step 4   Develop a leading-edge corporate culture

Business activities have a cultural component as well as a technological component. The companies that tend to excel in both market leadership and software engineering technologies are those whose corporate cultures reflect the ideals of excellence and fair play. If your corporate culture stresses quality, service to clients, innovation, and fairness to employees, there is a good chance that your enterprise is an industry leader. If your corporate culture primarily stresses only schedule adherence or cost control, as important as those topics are, you may not ultimately succeed. An interesting correlation can be noted between corporate culture and quality control. Of the companies that produce software listed in *The 100 Best Companies to Work for in America*[5] most have formal software quality programs.

There is no external source of corporate culture. The board of directors, the CEO, and the senior executives are the only people who can forge a corporate culture, and it is their responsibility to do it well. As Tom Peters has pointed out in his landmark book, *In Search of Excellence*,[6] the truly excellent enterprises are excellent from top to bottom. If the top is not interested in industry leadership or doesn't know how to achieve it, the entire enterprise will pay the penalty.

Step 5 Determine your software strengths and weaknesses

More than 200 different factors can affect software productivity and quality; they include the available tools and workstations, the physical environment, staff training and education, and even your compensation plans. In order to find out how your enterprise ranks against U.S. or industry norms and whether you have the appropriate set of tools and methods in place, it is usually necessary to bring in one of the handful of U.S. management consulting organizations that specializes in such knowledge.

This step is logically equivalent to a complete medical examination in a major medical institution. No physician would ever prescribe therapies without a thorough examination and diagnosis of the patient. The same situation should hold true for software: Do not jump into therapy acquisition without knowing what is right and wrong in all aspects of your software practice.

Software Quality Control in the United States

Computing and software have become dominant issues for corporate success and even corporate survival. As the twentieth century draws to a close, the enterprises that can master computing and software will probably be the key enterprises of the next century. The enterprises that do not master computing and software may not survive to see the next century!

Quality control is the key to mastering computing and software, and the enterprises that succeed in quality control will succeed in optimizing productivity, schedules, and customer satisfaction also. Following are short discussions of some of the quality control methods used in the United States.

Quality assurance organizations

Most United States commercial, military, and systems software producers have found it useful to establish formal quality assurance (QA) organizations. These QA organizations vary significantly in their roles, authorities, and responsibilities. The most successful of the QA organizations, which are typical of large computer manufacturers and major software vendors, are capable of serving as general models.

Quality assurance organization types.   There are two common forms of QA organization; they might be termed "active" and "passive." Of these, the active QA organization is usually more successful, although more expensive as well.

Active quality assurance.   The phrase "active quality assurance" means a formal quality assurance organization that plays an active part in software projects. This is the form of quality assurance most often practiced by leading-edge computer manufacturers, defense contractors, and other high-technology enterprises. This form is recommended above the passive form. Typical roles encompassed by active QA organizations include:

1. Moderating design and code inspections

2. Collecting and analyzing defect data

3. Developing and running test scenarios

4. Estimating defect potentials

5. Recommending corrective actions for quality problems

6. Teaching courses on quality-related topics

Active quality assurance groups normally start work on projects during or shortly after the requirements phase and are continuously engaged throughout a project's development cycle.

Because of the scope and amount of work carried out by active quality assurance groups, the staffing requirements are not insignificant: Most active QA organizations are in the range of 3 to 5 percent of the size of the software development organizations they support. Some, such as the IBM QA organization supporting commercial and systems software, approach 10 percent of the entire software staff. Active QA organizations normally are managerially independent of development, which is a pragmatic necessity to guarantee independence and avoid coercion by development project management.

Passive quality assurance.   The phrase "passive quality assurance" refers to a group whose primary task is observation to ensure that the relevant quality standards and guidelines are in fact adhered to by development personnel. The passive QA organizations can, of course, be much smaller than the active ones, and typically they are in the range of 1 to 2 percent of the size of the development groups they support. However, the effectiveness of passive QA is necessarily less than that of the active form. Some of the roles performed by the passive QA organizations include:

1. Observing a sample of design and code inspections

2. Analyzing defect data collected by development personnel

3. Recommending corrective actions for quality problems

Passive QA organizations, like the active forms, are normally managerially independent of development, which is a pragmatic necessity to guarantee independence and to avoid coercion by development project management.

Reviews, walk-throughs, and inspections

Informal reviews have been held spontaneously since the earliest days of software, and the first such reviews may even have taken place prior to 1950. However, in the burst of really large system projects starting in the 1960s and 1970s, it became obvious that testing was too late in the development cycle, too inefficient, and not fully effective.

Several IBM researchers turned their attention to the review process, and three alternative approaches surfaced more or less at the same time: Design reviews and code reviews originated at the IBM San Jose laboratories in the early 1970s. Structured walk-throughs originated concurrently at the IBM Poughkeepsie laboratory. Formal design and code inspections originated slightly after walk-throughs; they were created at the IBM Kingston laboratory and were based on the analysis of Michael Fagan.

After considerable debate and trial, the formal inspection process tended to come out ahead in terms of overall rigor and efficiency and gradually moved toward becoming a standard technique within IBM. Indeed, inspections appear to be the most efficient form of defect removal yet developed, and only formal inspections tend to consistently exceed 60 percent in defect removal efficiency. External publication of the method in 1976 by Fagan[7] brought the inspection technique into more widespread use. IBM began to offer external training in inspections by 1979, and other companies such as ITT and AT&T adopted the method as an internal standard. By 1990, a dozen or more computer, consulting, and educational companies including SPR were teaching inspections, and the method continues to expand.

Formal inspections differ from reviews and walk-throughs primarily in the rigor of the preparation, the formal roles assigned, and the post-inspection follow-up. To be deemed an "inspection" it is necessary to obey the following protocols:

1. The participants must receive training prior to taking part in their first inspection.

2. There will be sufficient time available for preparation before the inspection sessions take place.
3. In the inspection sessions, there will be at least the following staff present:
   - A moderator (to keep the discussions within bounds)
   - A reader (to paraphrase the work being inspected)
   - A recorder (to keep records of all defects)
   - An inspector (to identify any problems)
   - An author (whose work is being inspected)

All five (or more) may be present for large projects. For small projects dual roles can be assigned, so that the minimum number for a true inspection is three: moderator, author, and one other person.

4. The inspection sessions will follow normal protocols in terms of timing, recording defects, and polling participants.
5. There will be follow-up after the inspection process to ensure the identified defects are repaired.
6. The defect data will not be used for appraisal or punitive purposes.

The purpose of inspections is simply to find, early in the process, problems which if not eliminated could cause trouble later. It should be emphatically stated that the purpose of inspections is not to humiliate the authors, nor is it to fix the problems. Defect repairs take place later. The purpose, once again, is simply to find problems.

Inspections are not inexpensive, but they are highly efficient. Prior to first utilizing this method, there will be a natural reluctance on the part of programmers and analysts to submit to what may seem an unwarranted intrusion into their professional competence. However, this apprehension immediately disappears after the first inspections, and the methodology is surprisingly popular after the start-up phase.

Any deliverable can be inspected, and the method has been used successfully on the following:

- Requirements
- Initial and detailed specifications
- Development plans
- Test plans
- Test cases
- Source code
- User documentation

TABLE 5.2 Typical Inspection Preparation and Execution Times

Deliverable	Preparation	Meeting
Requirements	25 pages/h	12 pages/h
Functional specification	45 pages/h	15 pages/h
Logic specification	50 pages/h	20 pages/h
Source code	150 LOC/h	75 LOC/h
User documents	35 pages/h	20 pages/h

- Training materials
- Screen displays

For initial planning purposes, Table 5.2 shows the normal times required to prepare for and carry out inspections for typical deliverables. Table 5.2 is taken from the SPR inspection training materials[8] as updated for 1991. Note that the variations for both preparation and meeting effort can exceed ±50 percent of the figures in Table 5.2, based upon individual human factors, interruptions, and the numbers of problems encountered. Normal single-column pages in a 10-pitch type with a normal volume of graphics are assumed: roughly 500 words per text page and about 150 words per page containing charts, diagrams, or illustrations. For source code, normal formatting of about 50 statements per page of listing and a single statement per physical line is the assumption.

The business advantages of inspections can be illustrated by two simple figures. Figure 5.1 shows the distressing gaps in the timing between defect introduction and defect discovery in situations where testing alone is used. Figure 5.2 shows the comparatively short intervals between defect creation and defect discovery that is associated with inspections.

Inspections tend to benefit project schedules and effort as well as quality. They are extremely efficient in finding interface problems between components and in using the human capacity for inductive reasoning to find subtle errors that testing will miss. They are not very effective, of course, in finding performance-related problems.

Quality circles

The technique of quality circles[9] became enormously popular in Japan, where many thousands of quality circles have been registered. The concept is that ordinary workers, given the opportunity and some basic training in cause-effect analysis, can provide a powerful quality assurance and productivity boost for their employers. Quality circles have demonstrated their value in manufactured goods, electronics, au-

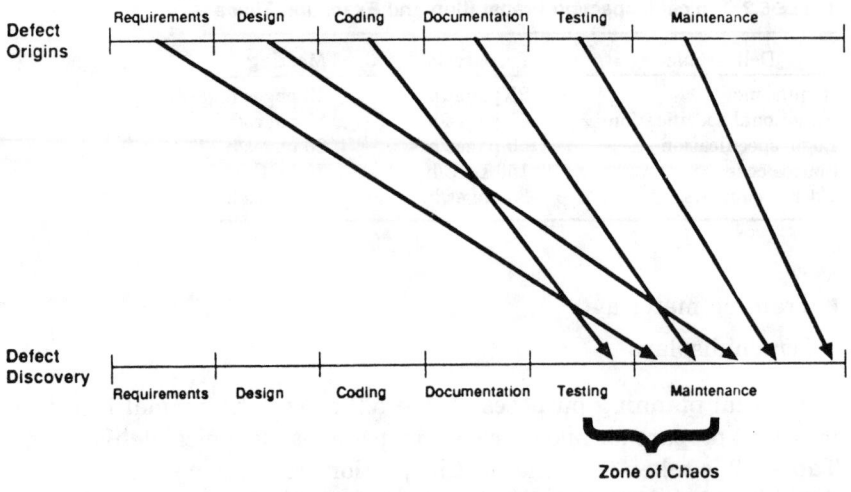

Figure 5.1 Delays between defect creation and discovery when testing is the primary removal method.

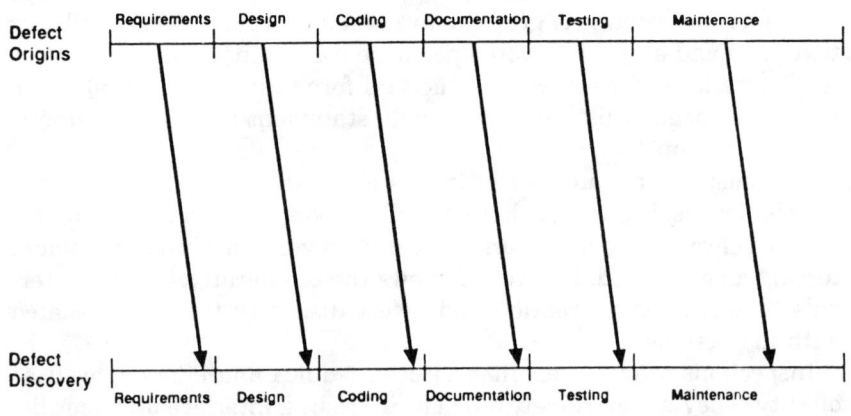

Figure 5.2 Reduced delays between defect creation and discovery associated with formal inspections.

tomotive production, and aircraft production. In Japan, at least, the technique has also worked well for software. Here in the United States, the approach has not been widely utilized for software, nor is there enough empirical data reported in the literature to even judge the effectiveness for U.S. software.

Zero-defect programs

The concepts of zero defects originated in aviation and defense companies in the late 1950s. Halpin wrote an excellent tutorial on the method in the mid-1960s.[10] The approach, valid from a psychological viewpoint, is that if each worker and manager individually strives for excellence and zero defects, the final product has a good chance of achieving zero defects. The concept is normally supported by substantial public relations work in companies which adopt the philosophy. Interestingly, some zero-defect software applications of comparatively small size have been developed. Unfortunately, however, most software practitioners who live with software daily tend to doubt that the method can actually work for large or complex systems. There is certainly no empirical evidence that zero-defect large systems have yet been built.

Proofs of correctness

The concepts of correctness proofs originated in the domain of systems software, and they have been made well known by such authors as Mills[11] and Martin.[12] Unfortunately, there is no empirical data that demonstrates that software proved correct has a lower defect rate under field conditions than software not proved correct. Anecdotal evidence indicates that proofs are fairly hard to create, and indeed there may be errors in a substantial number of the proofs themselves. Also, proofs are very time consuming. On the whole, this technology lacks empirical validation.

Independent verification and validation

Military projects following military specifications such as 2167A are constrained to use outside specialists for reviewing major deliverables, and indeed for independent testing as well.[13] Independent verification and validation is normally termed "IV&V," since the whole name is too long for convenience. Although the concept seems sound enough, there is insufficient empirical evidence that military projects have significantly higher quality or reliability than ordinary systems software projects of the same size and complexity, which do not use IV&V. Mission-critical military projects seem to have reasonably high levels of quality and reliability, however.

There are also commercial IV&V companies which offer testing and verification services to their clients. Since testing is a technical specialty, these commercial testing houses often do a better job than the informal, "amateur" testing carried out by ordinary programmers who lack training in test methods.

Professionally staffed testing departments

In almost every human activity, specialists tend to outperform generalists. That is decidedly true of software testing, which is a highly sophisticated technical specialty if it is to be performed well. As a rule of thumb, companies that have testing departments staffed by trained specialists will average about 10 to 15 percent higher in cumulative testing efficiency than companies which attempt testing by using their ordinary programming staffs. Normal unit testing by programmers is seldom more than 25 percent efficient, in that only about 1 bug in 4 will be found, and most other forms of testing are usually less than 30 percent efficient when carried out by untrained generalists. A series of well-planned tests by a professionally staffed testing group can exceed 35 percent per stage, and 80 percent in overall cumulative testing efficiency.

Clean-room development

The concept of clean-room development as described by Dr. Harlan Mills and his colleagues at IBM is based on the physically clean rooms used to construct sensitive electronic devices, where any impurity can damage the process. For software, clean-room development implies careful control of all deliverables prior to turning the deliverable over to any downstream worker. The clean-room method also envisions the usage of formal specification methods, formal structural methods, and also proofs of correctness applied to critical algorithms. The clean-room concept is new, and it is intuitively appealing. However, empirical evidence is scarce, and no large-scale successes have yet been reported. The federal and military support groups of the IBM corporation have been the most active U.S. adherents to the clean-room concept.

Prototyping

Prototyping is more of a defect prevention than a defect removal technique, although the impact on a certain class of defects is very high. Projects which use prototypes tend to reach functional stability earlier than those which do not. Therefore, prototyped projects usually add only 10 percent or less of their functions after the requirements phase, whereas unprototyped projects tend to add 30 percent or more of their functions after the requirements phase. Since the defect rates associated with late, rushed functions are more than twice as high as normal averages, it can be stated that prototyping is a very effective defect prevention method. It is most successful for mid-size projects—between about 100 and 1000 function points. For very small projects, the project itself serves the same purpose as the prototype. For very large projects, it is not usually possible for the prototype to reflect all of the functionality.

Joint application design

The joint application design (JAD) methodology originated in Canada at the IBM Toronto programming laboratory, and it has now spread throughout the world. More than a dozen companies now teach JAD-like techniques and offer consulting services to facilitate JAD sessions. Like prototyping, the JAD technique is more of a defect prevention method than a defect removal method. It is an improved method of deriving the requirements for a software project by means of structured, joint sessions of user representatives and the software design team. The sessions follow a structured format, and they are facilitated by a trained moderator. As with prototypes, projects using the JAD approach reach functional stability earlier, and they usually add less than 10 percent of their final functionality as afterthoughts. It should be noted that the JAD method is synergistic with prototyping, and the two techniques together seem to be a very effective combination.

The JAD method originated in the domain of management information systems, and assumes that there will be an available set of users who can participate. Thus, for projects for which users are either not available or there may be thousands of them (as with spreadsheets or word processing software), the JAD method may not be useful.

Software complexity analysis

There is a strong and direct correlation between code complexity and software defect rates. Since code complexity can be directly measured by means of a dozen or so commercially available tools, a useful first step in improving quality is to analyze the complexity of existing software. The programs or components of systems that have dangerously high complexity levels can then be isolated and corrected.

Error-prone module removal

In all of the large software systems that have yet been studied by major corporations, including IBM, DEC, Wang, AT&T, and Hewlett-Packard, the bugs or defects have not been randomly distributed through the systems. Instead, they have clumped in surprisingly localized sections termed "error-prone modules." As a rule of thumb, about 5 percent of the modules in a large system may receive almost 50 percent of the total defect reports. Once such modules have been identified, the problems can often be corrected. Although high complexity and poor coding practices are often associated with error-prone modules, there are other factors too. Often error-prone modules are those added to the system late, after requirements and design were nominally finished. In many cases, the late arrival of the code led to the embarrassing situation of having no test cases created for it, since the test and quality assurance groups did not know the code had been added!

Restructuring, reverse engineering, and reengineering

In 1985, a new subindustry started to form; it comprised companies that offered various geriatric services for aging software. The first such services to be offered were automatic or semi-automatic restructuring of Cobol source code. The general results were favorable, in that the restructured code was easier to modify and maintain than the previous unstructured versions. However, restructuring did not change the size of the modules, so manual remodularization was often used as an adjunct to reduce the sizes of the modules down to manageable levels (fewer than 500 source code statements). Here too, the results have generally been favorable. Some companies, indeed, have experimented with using the restructuring techniques on new applications, since the standardized results make it easier for programmers to maintain applications other than those they wrote themselves. Here too, the results are favorable.

The impact of restructuring and remodularization on software quality is significant, but it is largely indirect. Restructuring and remodularization will find some bugs and dead code, of course, but the primary benefit is a reduction in the effort associated with defect repairs and enhancements once the transformation is finished. More recently, such companies as Bachman Associates, CGI, CADRE Technologies, and Language Technology have announced capabilities of expert systems which can analyze existing source code and create a synthetic specification from latent information present in the code itself. This process, termed "reverse engineering," is based on the thesis that the original specifications have long since fallen into decay, leaving the enterprise with nothing but aging source code and human knowledge to work from when updating applications. Obviously, aging source code is not a good starting point for major enhancements or updates of the application.

The next step beyond reverse engineering is reengineering, or semi-automatic conversion of an aging application into a modern one, perhaps by using different languages and running on a different platform. The concepts of reverse engineering and reengineering are appealing, but not enough empirical data exists at present to state whether they will be truly successful.

Total quality management programs

The newest quality control concept, which started to become popular only in 1989, is an approach called total quality management (TQM) or sometimes total quality control (TQC). This concept, derived from Deming, assumes that all aspects of both a product and its supporting processes must be geared to achieve quality. TQM programs encompass not only standard reviews and inspections but also deliberate improvements in methods and processes, quality standards for purchased or incoming subcomponents, and quality at all levels of the organization from executive ranks downward. Although the concepts of total quality management programs are intuitively appealing, there is as yet little or no hard data to determine whether the approach will actually work or merely become a passing idea such as the zero-defect programs of the 1950s.

The Malcolm Baldridge awards

One does not ordinarily associate governments with quality, yet the government-sponsored Baldridge awards for quality have become a major factor in U.S. business and hopefully will remain so in the future. To win a Baldridge award, it is necessary to not only achieve high quality in real-life but also to measure the results in a statistically valid way. Associated with the Baldridge concept is the famous six-sigma metric, or achieving no more than about three defects per million parts. Thus far, the Baldridge awards have stirred up more action in the engineering world than in the software world, but several leading software producers are actually attempting a run at one of these prestigious awards. All of us in the software industry should wish them luck, since winning the award would benefit the entire industry. For the Baldridge awards to stay effective, great care must be exercised in whom they are given to. Nothing can damage the impact of such an award more quickly than giving to an enterprise that does not truly deserve it!

Measuring Software Defect Removal

The word "quality" has so many possible definitions for software that it has tended to become an intangible term. As already discussed, it can mean user satisfaction, conformance to requirements, or any combination of a host of concepts that end with "ility" such as reliability, maintainability, and portability. These abstract definitions can be measured subjectively, but the measurements are often vague and unsatisfying.

There is one major aspect of quality that can be measured in a tangible and convincing way. The hard, tangible aspect of quality is the measurement of defect removal. Not only can defect removal be measured with high precision, but this metric is one of the fundamental parameters that should be included in all corporate software measurement programs.

Projects that perform well in terms of defect removal often perform well with such other aspects of quality as conformance to requirements and user satisfaction. On the other hand, projects with inadequate defect removal are seldom successful in the other aspects of quality either.

Reporting frequency for defect measurements

The natural frequency for defect measurement is monthly. That is, every month a standard report that shows all of the defects found in the course of the prior month should be produced. The monthly report should contain at least the following sections:

1. Defects found by reviews and inspections

2. Defects found by testing

3. Defects found and reported by users

More sophisticated defect reports, such as those produced by large commercial software producers like IBM, are capable of showing this additional information:

4. Defects found by product and product line

5. Defects found by geographic region (country, city, state, etc.)

6. Defects found by customer

7. Defect found by industry (banking, insurance, etc.)

All of this data can be condensed and summarized on an annual basis, but the fundamental reporting frequency should be monthly.

Turning on the defect count "clock"

Productivity data can be reconstructed from the memories of the project teams. Indeed, such reconstructed data is sometimes better than the data that comes out of a tracking system because it lacks the errors of the typical tracking system.

Quality data, on the other hand, cannot be reconstructed. It must be measured, and it must be accumulated for quite some time before enough of it is available to be useful. If you start counting today, it can be more than a year before you accumulate enough data to really understand your company's quality levels. However, if you do not start today, or at least fairly soon, you may never understand your company's quality levels. Indeed, if your competitors measure quality and your company does not, they may very well put your company out of business before you can even know why! There are three natural starting places for beginning to count defect levels:

1. As early as possible, such as during requirements
2. When testing begins
3. When customers begin to use the software

From consulting engagements with several hundred clients in large corporations, the norm (among those who measure defects at all) is, unfortunately, number 3. That is not as it should be. The true starting place, in order to gain insights that can make major improvements, is to start as early as possible. IBM, for example, starts its defect "clock" during the requirements phase and keeps it running through the entire life cycle. This kind of data is invaluable for insights and subsequent defect prevention.

Late starts with defect counting tends to obscure problems with requirements and design, which typically comprise the bulk of all problems for major systems. The earlier the counting begins, the better the insights that can be gained. Early starting, of course, involves cultural changes within a company and some careful preparation in order to make defect measures a useful corporate tool.

Definition of a software defect

A software defect is simply a bug which if not removed would cause a program or system to fail or to produce incorrect results. *Note:* The very common idea that a defect is a failure to adhere to some user requirement is unsatisfactory because it offers no way to measure requirements defects themselves, which constitute one of the larger categories of software error.

Defects can have five different origins in a software project, and it is normal to assign an origin code to each discovered defect. Examples of the five defect origins include requirements errors, such as accidentally leaving out a necessary input screen; design defects, such as a mistake in an algorithm; coding defects, such as branching to a wrong location; documentation defects, such as giving the incorrect command for starting a program; and bad fixes, such as making a fresh mistake while fixing a previous bug.

When measuring defect removal, it is normal to assign the responsibility for determining whether or not a given problem is a defect to the quality assurance manager. If the project does not have a quality assurance manager assigned, the project manager or supervisor should assign the origin code after the defect has been technically analyzed.

Some defects will be reported more than once, especially when the software has many users. Although duplicate reports of the same bug are recorded, the normal defect removal metric is based on a "valid unique defect," or the first report of any given bug. From time to time, defect reports that are submitted turn out, upon examination, to be either user errors or problems that are external to the software itself. These are termed "invalid defect reports," and they are excluded from the software defect measures. They are, however, recorded for historical and statistical purposes. There are also various plateaus of defect severity. The four-point severity scale used by IBM for software looks like this:

Severity 1   System or program inoperable
Severity 2   Major functions disabled or incorrect
Severity 3   Minor functions disabled or incorrect
Severity 4   Superficial error

An initial defect severity code is often assigned by the client or user of the software such as a tester. However, since users have a natural tendency to code most defects severity 1 or severity 2, the final severity level is usually determined by a quality assurance manager or an objective source. In summary, defects are counted as totals and then sorted into subcategories as follows:

Unique defect reports versus duplicate defect reports
Valid defect reports versus invalid defect reports

Defect reports by origin:

1. Requirements defects

2. Design defects

3. Coding defects

4. Documentation defects

5. Bad fixes

Defect reports by severity:

1. Severity 1 defects

2. Severity 2 defects

3. Severity 3 defects

4. Severity 4 defects

TABLE 5.3 Distribution of Software Defect Origins and Severities

Defect origin	1, %	2, %	3, %	4, %	Total, %
		Severity level			
Requirements	5.0	5.0	3.0	2.0	15.0
Design	3.0	22.0	10.0	5.0	40.0
Coding	2.0	10.0	10.0	8.0	30.0
Documentation	0.0	1.0	2.0	2.0	5.0
Bad fixes	0.0	2.0	5.0	3.0	10.0
Total defects	10.0	40.0	30.0	20.0	100.0

If you measure software defects by using these concepts, a typical distribution of valid unique defects for a medium to large system might look like the data shown in Table 5.3.

Note the interesting skew in the distribution in Table 5.3: For critical severity-1 defects, requirements errors are dominant; for severity-2 defects, design errors are dominant. Coding errors are in second place overall, but they do not comprise the largest source of error except for the comparatively unimportant severity-4 category. Of course, the table reflects the results of medium-size to large systems of 50,000 Cobol statements and larger. For small programs of 5000 Cobol statements or less, coding errors would comprise more than 50 percent of the total error density. In addition to the valid unique defects which the table reflects, you can expect an invalid defect for each valid defect. If you have multiple users of or clients for your software, you can expect one duplicate defect report for every five users.

Measuring Defect Removal Efficiency

Once a satisfactory encoding scheme for your basic defect counts has been adopted, the next stage is to measure the defects found by each removal activity. Typical MIS projects go through pretest requirements and design reviews, partial code walk-throughs, and from two to five testing steps depending on the size and nature of the project. A typical MIS defect removal series might look like this:

1. Requirements review

2. Design review

3. Desk checking by individual programmers (not measured)

4. Code walk-through

5. Unit testing by individual programmers (not measured)

6. Integration testing of entire program or system

7. Acceptance testing by users

At this point it should be noted that tasks 3 and 5 (desk checking and unit testing) are often not measured, since they are carried out by the individual programmers themselves. (However, some programmers have volunteered to record defects found during these activities, simply to complete the data necessary to evaluate a full defect removal series.) Assuming that you will measure only the public defect removal activities and not the private ones, your data might look like the information in Table 5.4 for a 50,000-source-statement Cobol application that also contained some 500 function points. Note that Table 5.4 makes the simplifying assumption that it takes 100 Cobol statements to implement one function point. The average value is actually 105 statements per function point, but for tutorial purposes an even amount was selected.

At this point, you will not yet be able to complete the final set of quality measures. That requires collecting defect data reported by actual users of the project. You will normally collect data from users for as long as the project is in use, but after one year of production, and then annually for each additional year of use, you will be able to complete a very significant analysis of the defect removal efficiencies of your review, inspection, and test series. Assume that the first year of production by your users generated the number of defects shown in Table 5.5. You will now be able to calculate one of the most important and meaningful metrics in all software: your defect removal efficiency.

The general formula for defect removal efficiency is quite simple: It is the ratio of bugs found prior to delivery by your staff to the total number of bugs. The total number of bugs is found by summing bugs you discovered with the bugs your clients discovered in a predetermined time period. In this example, the bugs that your staff removed before delivery totaled 1125. The bugs found by your users in the first year totaled 400. If you add those two values together, the sum is

TABLE 5.4 **Software Defect Distributions by Removal Step**

Removal activity	Defects found	Defects per KLOC	Defects per function point
Requirements review	125	2.5	0.25
Design review	250	5.0	0.50
Code inspection	500	10.0	1.00
Integration test	150	3.0	0.30
Acceptance test	100	2.0	0.20
Total defects	1125	22.5	2.25

TABLE 5.5 User-Reported Defects from One Year of Production Runs

Activity	Defects found	Defects per KLOC	Defects per function point
First-year user defect reports	400	8.0	0.8

1525. That is equal to 30.5 bugs per KLOC, or 3.05 bugs per function point, which are middle-range values for Cobol applications of this size. (Leading-edge applications will total fewer than 15 bugs per KLOC, whereas the real disasters may go above 75 bugs per KLOC.)

Cumulative defect removal efficiency is defined as the percentage of bugs found by the development team before a software product is delivered to its users. Efficiency cannot be measured until after a predetermined time period has gone by, and the first year of use is a convenient interval for the first calculation. Of course, not all bugs will be found after only one year, so recalculation after 2 or even 3 years would also be useful.

In this example, finding 1125 bugs out of 1525 amounts to only 73.8 percent, which is a typical but mediocre result. The normal defect removal efficiency for MIS projects is somewhere between 50 and 75 percent when measured. Leading-edge MIS companies will find more than 90 percent of the bugs, while leading-edge commercial and military software producers will find more than 95 percent of the bugs.

Defect removal efficiency is a very important metric, because raising efficiency above 90 percent can improve quality, productivity, and user satisfaction at the same time. Indeed, a cumulative total of 95 percent appears to be one of the most powerful node points in all of software engineering, since schedules, quality, effort, and user satisfaction all tend to approach optimum levels when this target is achieved.

Not only can the cumulative defect removal efficiency of a series of removal steps be measured; it is also possible to measure the individual net efficiency of each step. In real life, each defect removal step will have a differential efficiency against each source of defect. Table 5.6 shows typical efficiencies against four defect origins for a variety of reviews, inspections, and tests. The efficiencies in Table 5.6 were calculated from empirical studies, although significant variations can and do occur.

The table of defect removal efficiencies actually matches real-life re-

TABLE 5.6 Defect Removal Efficiencies by Defect Origin

Removal step	Defects by origin, %			
	Requirements	Design	Coding	Documentation
JAD	50	25	10	15
Prototyping	40	35	35	15
Requirements review	40	15	0	5
Design review	15	55	0	15
Code inspection	20	40	65	25
Subtotal	75	85	73	50
Unit test	1	5	20	0
Function test	10	15	30	5
System test	10	15	35	20
Field test	20	20	25	25
Subtotal	35	45	75	43
Cumulative	87	92	94	72

sults fairly closely. Coding defects are the easiest to remove, and hence they have the highest overall efficiencies against them. Requirements defects are the most troublesome, and normally they have the lowest efficiencies. Although documentation defects are not intrinsically difficult to remove (journals such as *Scientific American* exceed 99.5 percent in net efficiency), most software projects simply do not use high-efficiency techniques such as copy editing by professional editors or proofreading by pairs of readers.

In terms of the removal methods themselves, detailed code inspections are the most efficient form of defect removal yet measured, whereas most testing steps are less than 35 percent efficient. That is, most forms of testing find less than one bug out of every three bugs that actually exist. Once you have measured a reasonably large sample of projects (more than 50), you will be able to use the data you've collected to make very accurate quality and reliability estimates.

Some of the implications of Table 5.6 deserve discussion. First, given the low efficiencies of testing, it is obviously impossible to achieve high levels of cumulative efficiency without up-front activities such as prototyping, reviews, or inspections. To be blunt, companies that only perform testing will never go much beyond 75 percent in cumulative defect removal efficiency; that is, they will deliver at least one out of every four bugs to their clients.

Second, testing ranges from moderate to useless in its ability to come to grips with front-end defects such as requirements and design. Indeed, it is surprising that testing can find requirements defects at all. Therefore, it is imperative to utilize the high-efficiency pretest activities in order to control these major sources of system problems.

Given the magnitude of defects associated with requirements and design, it is obvious that these important defect sources must be included in quality control planning. Even a cursory inspection of removal efficiencies demonstrates that JADs, prototyping, and up-front inspections are logically necessary to control front-end bugs.

Third, there are some special calculations needed to include bad fixes, or bugs accidentally introduced as by-products of fixing previous bugs. The total quantity of bad fixes averages about 5 to 10 percent, and it will be directly related to the complexity of the work product being repaired.

Fourth, given the low average efficiencies of most removal steps, it is obvious that to achieve a high cumulate efficiency, it will be necessary to use many steps. Commercial and military software producers, for example, may include as many as 20 to 25 discrete removal activities. This is one of the key differences between systems software and MIS projects. MIS projects normally utilize only five to seven different kinds of removal, and they seldom utilize the rigorous inspection process.

Fifth, serious quality control requires a synergistic combination of multiple techniques, with each removal step aimed at the class of defects for which its efficiency is highest. Figure 5.3 illustrates a typical synergy among defect removal methods. The moral of the figure is quite simple: Choose the combination of defect removal steps that will achieve the highest overall efficiency for the lowest actual costs.

Here is a final point on defect measurement and defect removal in general. Finding and fixing bugs has been among the most expensive, if not the most expensive, activity for software since the industry be-

	Requirements Defects	Design Defects	Code Defects	Document Defects
Reviews/ Inspections	Fair	Excellent	Excellent	Good
Prototypes	Good	Fair	Fair	Not Applicable
Testing (all forms)	Poor	Poor	Good	Fair
Correctness Proofs	Poor	Poor	Fair	Fair

Figure 5.3 Synergy among defect removal techniques.

gan. Companies that do measure quality and defect removal have a tremendous competitive advantage against those who do not. Historically, certain industries such as computers and telecommunications paid serious attention to both hardware quality and software quality and introduced quality measurement programs, in some cases, more than 30 years ago. These industries have been capable of withstanding overseas competition much better than such industries as automotive construction, which learned about quality control far too late. Quality control is the key to corporate survival in the twenty-first century, and measurement is the key to quality control. Now is the time to start!

Finding and Eliminating Error-Prone Modules

In the late 1960s Gary Okimoto, a researcher at the IBM Endicott laboratory, carried out a study in which he looked at the distribution of defects within the OS/360 operating system. To his surprise, and to the surprise of everyone else who knew of the study, the defects were not smoothly or randomly distributed throughout the modules of the system. Instead, they clumped in a small number of very buggy modules. Some 4 percent of the modules contained 38 percent of the errors in the entire operating system. This study is perhaps the original discovery of the error-prone module concept. In any case, it is the first such study known to the author.

The study was replicated against other IBM software products, and it invariably produced striking results. For example, when west coast researchers at IBM's Palo Alto laboratory carried out a similar study on the IMS database product, some 57 percent of the errors were concentrated in only 31 modules, which constituted about 7 percent of the modules of the product and about 12 percent of the code.

Other companies, including AT&T, ITT, Wang, and Hewlett-Packard, have come to regard error-prone module analysis as a normal aspect of quality control. So far as can be determined from all of the studies yet carried out, error-prone modules are a very common phenomenon and will occur in all large systems unless deliberate corrective steps are taken. Fortunately, a number of corrective steps that can eliminate error-prone modules from software products are available. The most basic step is to measure defects down to the level of modules in inspections, testing, and maintenance. Any module with more than about ten defects per KLOC is a candidate for a full review to explore its status. From the error-prone modules that have been explored in depth, a number of causative factors have been identified. The most significant among them are:

1. Excessive schedule pressure applied to the developers
2. Excessive complexity that is due to either:

   - Failure to use proper structured techniques
   - Intrinsic nature of the problem to be encoded

3. Excessive size of individual modules (>500 statements)
4. Failure to test the module after code was complete

The first three factors are intuitive and even self-explanatory, but the fourth factor is something of a surprise. Even more surprising is the high frequency with which this phenomenon occurs. Normally, error-prone modules that have not been tested are those which were created very late in a product's development cycle, often while testing was nearing completion. These modules were rushed into production without bothering to update the specifications or the test case libraries! The solution to this problem is a rigorous module promotion process, which includes "locked" master copies of a software product with no way to add modules unless careful quality control procedures are followed.

Using Metrics to Evaluate Test-Case Coverage

As of 1990, there are perhaps 15 to 20 commercially available tools that can be used to assist in measuring test-case coverage. These tools normally trace the execution sequence of code when it is executing, and they can isolate and identify sequences that are not executed while testing. Although such tools are very useful, it should be clearly realized that there is a striking discontinuity between test coverage and testing efficiency. Even though a particular test step, such as function testing, for example, causes the execution of more than 90 percent of the instructions in a program, that does not imply that 90 percent of the bugs will be found. Indeed, normally less than 30 percent of the bugs will be found by function testing. The reason for the discontinuity is fairly straightforward: Just because instructions have been executed does not guarantee that they are doing what was actually intended.

It should also be noted that there is no guarantee that the test cases themselves are correct. Indeed, a study at IBM's Kingston laboratory in the middle 1970s found that test cases often had a higher error content than the products for which the test cases were constructed! Another surprising finding was that about one-third of the test cases appeared to be duplicates, which added nothing to testing rigor but quite a bit to testing costs.

TABLE 5.7 Relation between Defect Levels and Reliability

Defect levels in defects per KLOC	Approximate mean time to failure (MTTF)
More than 30	Less than 2 min
20–30	4–15 min
10–20	5–60 min
5–10	1–4 h
2–5	4–24 h
1–2	24–160 h
Less than 1	Indefinite

Using Metrics for Reliability Prediction

Quality and reliability are logically related topics. Surprisingly, they are often decoupled in the software engineering literature. Many articles on quality do not mention reliability, and many articles on reliability do not mention quality.

The reliability domain has built up a large body of both theoretical and empirical models and a number of supporting metrics such as mean time to failure (MTTF) and mean time between failures (MTBF). A good overview of the reliability domain is provided by Musa, Iannino, and Okumoto.[4]

Because the topics of quality and reliability are so often separated, it is useful to show at least the crude correlations between them. Table 5.7 is derived from empirical data collected by the author at IBM in the 1970s for systems software written in Assembler. The data was collected from unit, function, component, and system test runs.

Measuring the Costs of Defect Removal

Since the computing and software era began, the largest single identifiable cost element has been that of finding and fixing bugs. It is astonishing, therefore, that so few companies have measured this cost with accuracy. It is also embarrassing that attempts to measure defect removal have so often been paradoxical in economic terms.

The paradox of "cost per defect"

For at perhaps 10 years, the commonest unit of measure for assessing defect removal has been "cost per defect." At least 50 referenced journal articles and perhaps half a dozen software management books have contained the statement, "It costs 100 times as much to fix a bug in production as it does during design." The concept of cost per defect is to accumulate the total costs associated with defect removal for a particular activity class such as testing and then divide the cost by number of defects found. Thus, if a particular test step found 100 defects and cost $2500 to carry out, the cost per defect would be $25.

Unfortunately, as it is commonly calculated, cost per defect is one of the worst and most foolish metrics ever devised. It contains a built-in mathematical paradox that causes it to penalize high quality and to do so in direct proportion to the level of quality achieved. The best programs and systems with the fewest defects will look the worst and the most decrepit and bug-ridden applications will look the best!

To understand the nature of the problems with cost per defect, it is necessary to look at the detailed economic picture of removing defects in software. Every software defect removal activity, regardless of whether it is a review, an inspection, a test, or maintenance, will have three basic cost elements associated with it:

1. Preparation costs
2. Execution costs
3. Repair costs

Preparation costs consist of the things which must be performed prior to carrying out a specific form of defect removal. For example, prior to testing a program, it is necessary to create test cases. Prior to carrying out a design review, it is necessary to read the specifications. Preparation costs are essentially fixed; they will remain comparatively constant regardless of how many bugs are present. Thus, even for zero-defect software it will still be necessary to write test cases and read the descriptive materials. Execution costs are associated with the actual events of the defect removal activity. For testing, execution consists of running the application against the set of prepared test cases. For reviews and inspections, execution is the cost of actually holding the review and inspection sessions. Execution costs are not fixed costs, but they are somewhat inelastic. That is, the cost of executing a review or test only partly associated with the number of defects present. The bulk of the costs is associated with the mere mechanics of going through the exercise. Thus, even zero-defect applications will accumulate some costs for carrying out reviews and inspections and running test cases, and even zero-defect applications can have maintenance costs. That is surprising but true, since user errors and invalid defects will probably be reported against the product.

Defect repair costs are those associated with actually fixing any bugs or defects that were identified. Defect repairs are true variable

TABLE 5.8 The Paradox of Cost per Defect for Quality Measures

	Low-quality Ada application	High-quality Ada application
Size in KLOC	10	10
Size in function points	150	150
Defects found	500	5
Preparation costs	$ 5,000	$ 5,000
Execution costs	$25,000	$ 2,500
Defect repairs	$25,000	$ 2,500
Total removal cost	$35,000	$10,000
Cost per defect	$ 70	$ 2,000
Cost per function point	$ 233.33	$ 66.66

costs, and they are the only cost elements that will drop to zero if zero bugs are present in a program or system. When quality improves, the cost per defect will tend to get higher rather than lower, since the fixed and inelastic preparation and execution costs will become progressively more important. Table 5.8 illustrates the paradox of cost per defect in the case of high quality for two applications in Ada, both of which were 150 function points, or 10,000 source statements, in size. Assume $5000 per person-month as the normal labor rate.

Consider the economic fallacy of cost per defect. The true costs of defect removal declined from $35,000 to only $10,000, or better than 70 percent. The costs of the critical defect repair component declined by a full 10 to 1 between the low-quality and high-quality examples. Yet while the real economics of defect removal improved tremendously, the "cost per defect" skyrocketed from $70 to $2000! It is obvious that if the high-quality product had achieved zero-defect status, there still would have been expenses for preparation and execution. In this case, the cost per defect would have been infinity, since there would be tangible costs divided by zero defects!

Plainly, cost per defect is not a suitable metric for economic studies associated with software quality. Here too, function points are much better for economic purposes. Since both versions of the application contained 150 function points, it can be seen that the metric defect removal costs per function point matches economic assumptions perfectly. For the low-quality version, $233.33 per function point was spent for defect removal; for the high-quality version, only $66.66 was spent.

Collecting defect removal data

Although cost per defect is not valid in the way it is normally used—with preparation and execution simply clumped with repairs, the metric can be explored by time-and-motion studies and utilized in conjunction with functional metrics. Table 5.9 shows the effort associated with common forms of defect removal in terms of preparation, execution, and defect repairs. Preparation and execution are measured in work-hours per function point and repair (and only repair) is measured in hours per defect repaired. The final total of effort is normalized to person-hours per function point.

For economic study purposes, it is necessary to convert all of the final effort data into a per function-point basis. For example, assume that you are carrying out a design inspection with five participants on a project that totals 100 function points and in the course of the inspection you find 50 bugs that need repairs. From the data in Table 5.9, the preparation effort would amount to 25 h and the inspection sessions would amount to 50 work-hours (but only 10 clock hours). The 50 bugs would require 75 h. Thus the entire process totaled as follows:

Preparation		Execution		Repair		
25 h	+	50 h	+	75 h	=	150 h

The overall inspection, including preparation, execution, and repair netted out to 1.5 work-hours per function point. In this example, the effort per bug would be 3.0 h per bug for the sum of preparation, execution, and repair. Consider the same basic example, only this time assume that only 10 bugs were found:

Preparation		Execution		Repair		
25 h	+	50 h	+	15 h	=	90 h

In this second situation, the overall inspection process amounted to only 0.9 h per function point, which is substantially below the previous rate of 1.5 h per function point. However, the "effort per bug" has now tripled and is up to 9.0 h per bug! As can easily be seen, the fixed

TABLE 5.9 Preparation, Execution, and Defect Repair Effort

Removal step	Preparation, hours per function point	Execution, hours per function point	Repairs, hours per defect
JAD	0.15	0.25	1.00
Prototyping	0.25	1.00	1.00
Requirements review	0.15	0.25	1.00
Design inspection	0.15	0.50	1.50
Code inspection	0.25	0.75	1.50
Unit test	0.50	0.25	2.50
Function test	0.75	0.50	5.00
System test	1.00	0.50	10.00
Field test	0.50	0.50	10.00

and inelastic costs of preparation and execution tend to distort the per-bug metric so that it becomes paradoxically more expensive as quality improves. A metric that penalizes the very goal you are seeking is hardly suitable for serious economic studies.

The Cost-of-Quality Concept

Phil Crosby's famous book, *Quality Is Free*,[3] made popular a cost collection method termed "cost of quality." Although this concept originated in the domain of manufactured products, it has been applied to software projects as well. It is fairly thorough in its approach, and it captures costs associated with rework, scrap, warranty repairs, complaint handling, inspections, and testing. There are three large cost buckets associated with the concept:

1. Prevention costs
2. Appraisal costs
3. Failure costs

Crosby's descriptions of these costs are based on manufactured products, and they are somewhat orthogonal to software. For software purposes, prevention would encompass methods that simplified complexity and reduced the human tendency to make errors. Examples of prevention costs include the costs of training staff in structured design and coding techniques. Joint application design (JAD) also comes under the heading of prevention, since it is one of the key by-products of the approach.

Appraisal costs for software include inspections and all forms of testing. For military projects, appraisal costs also include independent verification and validation, or IV&V as it is called. In one sense, fixing bugs found by testing might be thought of as failure costs, but it seems more appropriate to count the costs as appraisal elements, since they normally occur prior to delivery of the software to its final customers. Failure costs of software are the costs associated with post-release bug repairs: field service, maintenance, warranty repairs, and in some cases liability damages and litigation expenses.

Evaluating Defect Prevention Methods

Defect removal deals with tangible things such as bug reports that can be counted fairly easily. Defect prevention, on the other hand, is much harder to come to grips with. This phenomenon is true of other human activities as well. For example, the cost and efficacy of preven-

	Requirements Defects	Design Defects	Code Defects	Document Defects
JAD's	Excellent	Good	Not Applicable	Fair
Prototypes	Excellent	Excellent	Fair	Not Applicable
Structured Methods	Fair	Good	Excellent	Fair
CASE Tools	Fair	Good	Fair	Fair
Blueprints & Reusable Code	Excellent	Excellent	Excellent	Excellent

Figure 5.4   Synergy among defect prevention techniques.

tive medicine is much more uncertain than the cost and efficacy of treating conditions once they occur. The term "defect prevention" means the overall set of technologies that simplify complexity and minimize a natural human tendency to make errors while performing complex tasks. Examples of defect prevention technologies include prototypes, JAD sessions, graphic design methods, formal architectures, structured techniques, and high-level languages. Indeed, some defect removal methods, such as inspections, are also effective in terms of defect prevention because participants will spontaneously avoid making mistakes which they observe during the inspection sessions. Figure 5.4 illustrates some of the synergies among defect prevention methods.

Long-range monitoring of defect prevention and defect removal

After quality measurement programs get underway, they can be used to monitor long-term effects over a period of many years. For example, Table 5.10 illustrates a 5-year trend by a major computer manufacturer for both applications and systems software. The original data has been simplified and rounded to demonstrate the trends.

TABLE 5.10 Long-Range Improvements in Defect Prevention and Defect Removal

	1985	1986	1987	1988	1990
Potential defects per function point	5.0	4.5	4.0	3.5	3.0
Removal efficiency	70%	80%	85%	90%	95%
Delivered defects per function point	1.5	0.9	0.6	0.35	0.15

The overall combination of defect prevention and defect removal improvements led to a full order of magnitude improvement in defects as received by clients. It cannot be overemphasized that both defect prevention and defect removal need to be part of an effective quality program: Neither is sufficient alone; together, they are synergistic. Finally, it cannot be overemphasized that without measurements carefully carried out over many years, none of the improvements would be either possible or visible.

Measuring Customer-Reported Defects

For many years, relations between defects actually delivered to customers and the number of defects found and reported back by customers has been known only to perhaps three or four major computer and telecommunication manufacturers. The relations are not intrinsically mysterious, but only a few companies had measurement systems that were sophisticated enough to study them. The fundamental problem posed by the situation is this: If you deliver a software product to a certain number of customers and it has 100 latent defects still present at the time of delivery, how many of those defects will be found and reported back by the customers in the first year? How many in the second year? The answers obey two general rules:

1. The number of defects found correlates directly with the number of users; the more users, the greater the number of defects found.

2. The number of defects found correlates inversely with the number of defects that are present; the more defects, the fewer the defects found.

The first rule is intuitive and easy to understand; the second is counterintuitive and, at first glance, very hard to understand. It would seem that the more bugs present in software, the greater the number that would be found and reported, but that is not the case. As it happens, rule 2 tends to be in direct conflict with rule 1 for the following reason: Very buggy software cannot or will not be used. Therefore, if your company ships software with more than a certain quantity of bugs latent within it, those bugs will prevent the utilization of the software, will slow down sales, and will in general stretch out the time before the bugs are found and fixed.

Tables 5.11 and 5.12 illustrate these phenomena. They show the impacts of changing numbers of users and then the impact of changing numbers of latent defects with a specific number of users.

Table 5.11 illustrates the phenomenon that somewhere between about 20 percent of the bugs and 95 percent of the bugs will normally be found in the first year of production, based on the number of users of the software. Since only high-volume production by large numbers

TABLE 5.11 Relations between Users and First-Year Defect Reports

	Case 1	Case 2	Case 3	Case 4
Number of users	1	10	100	1000
Defects present	100	100	100	100
Number of defects found in year 1	20	40	75	95
Percent of defects found in year 1	20%	40%	75%	95%
Number of defects remaining in year 2	80	60	25	5
Number of years to remove all defects	5	3	2.5	2

TABLE 5.12 Relations between Defect Quantities and First-Year Defect Reports

	Case 1	Case 2	Case 3	Case 4
Number of users	100	100	100	100
Number of delivered defects	100	200	300	400
Number of defects found in year 1	60	80	100	100
Percent of defects found in year 1	60%	40%	33%	25%
Number of defects after year 1	40	120	200	300
Number of years to the removal of all defects	2	4	5	7

of users can approach 100 percent in overall removal efficiency, it can clearly be seen that the greater the number of users, the higher the percentage of first-year bug removal.

Table 5.12 illustrates the counterintuitive phenomenon that the number of bugs found by users is inversely related to the number of bugs present. The unfortunate truth is that buggy software will not (and sometimes can not) be put into high-volume production. The initial users of the software will generally have such a bad experience with buggy software that references are impossible. Indeed, if the software package and the vendor are of sufficient magnitude that user groups exist, word of the poor quality will spread like wildfire and will slow down subsequent sales.

The findings in Table 5.12 are counterintuitive, but they are derived from empirical studies with actual projects. The distressingly low rate of only 25 percent in the high-defect case 4 is due, in such situations, to the fact that users do not trust the products and will not use them except in the most timid and careful fashion. Only software with a low level of initial defects will go into fully productive use fast enough to flush out the latent defects in a short time.

The data in Tables 5.11 and 5.12 implies that a calculation of defect

TABLE 5.13 Severity Levels of Customer-Reported Defects

Severity level	Percent of defect reports	Probable distribution, %
Severity 1 (system unusable)	3	3
Severity 2 (major function disabled)	47	15
Severity 3 (minor function disabled)	35	60
Severity 4 (no functions disabled: superficial problem)	15	22
Total	100	100

removal efficiency after one year of service will probably be artificially high, since not all of the bugs will have been found in only one year. That is true, and it explains why companies such as IBM will recalculate defect removal efficiency after two or more years.

One other aspect of customer reported bugs also is counterintuitive, and that is the severity levels reported by users. In this case, the reason is that the reported data is simply wrong, because of business factors. Table 5.13 shows the numbers of customer-reported bugs for commercial grade software received by a major computer company.

What is counterintuitive about the table is the astonishing 47 percent shown in the left column for severity-2 levels. At first glance, it would seem that the manufacturer was seriously amiss in quality control. In this case, however, appearances are deceiving. What was happening is that the vendor tried to fix severity-1 bugs within a week and severity-2 bugs within 2 weeks. Severity-3 bugs were fixed within about a month, and severity-4 bugs were not fixed until the next normal release. Obviously, every customer wanted his or her bug report processed promptly, so this tended to create an artificial bulge of severity-2 defects. The probable number of real severity-2 bugs was something approaching 15 percent, as shown in the second column.

Measuring Invalid Defects, Duplicate Defects, and Special Cases

Companies that produce commercial software are aware that they not only must deal with real bugs but must also deal with enormous quantities of bugs that are not really the fault of the software against which the bug was reported. For example, in a modern multivendor environment utilizing commercial operating systems, databases, query languages, and user applications, it is quite easy to mistake the origin of a defect. Thus, a customer can send in a bug report for a seeming error in a query language when it might actually be against the user application, the operating system, or something else. As a rule of thumb, software vendors will receive two invalid defect reports for every valid report of an actual bug.

An even more common problem is duplicate reports of the same bug. For example, when WordPerfect release 5.0 was first issued, a fairly simple bug in the installation procedure generated more than 10,000 telephone calls from users on the same day to report the same bug, temporarily shutting down phone service into Utah! The costs and effort to service the duplicate calls far exceeded the costs of actually fixing the bug itself. As a rule of thumb, about 70 percent of all commercial software bugs will be found by more than one user. About 15 percent will be found by many users.

A third problem that should be measured is that of "abeyant defects." This term is used for a bug such that the system repair center cannot recreate it or make the failure happen. Obviously, some special combination of circumstances at the user location is causing the bug, but finding out exactly what it is may require on-site assistance and considerable expense! As a rule of thumb, about 20 percent of commercial software bugs will require additional information because the bugs will not occur at the repair location. The collected costs of processing invalid bug reports, duplicates, and abeyant bug reports can exceed 25 percent of the total cost of fixing real bugs. That is too big an amount to ignore, and certainly too big to leave out of quality and maintenance plans.

Finally, the most expensive single aspect of mainframe commercial software has been field service. Companies, such as IBM, DEC, and Hewlett-Packard, that send service representatives on-site to customer locations to aid in defect identification and repair can for some products spend more effort and costs on field service than on the entire total of software development and internal maintenance!

Measuring User Satisfaction

Measurement of user satisfaction differs from measurement of software defects in a number of important respects:

1. User satisfaction measures are normally annual events; defect measures are normally monthly events.

2. User satisfaction data requires active effort in order to collect it; defect reports may arrive in an unsolicited manner.

3. The staff that measures user satisfaction is normally not the staff that measured defects.

4. The changes required to improve user satisfaction may go far beyond the product itself and may encompass changes in customer support, service policies, and corporate goals.

For commercial software, user satisfaction surveys are normally carried out by the vendor's sales force on an annual basis. The sales personnel will interview their clients and will then report the findings back to the sales organization, which in turn will pass them on to the development groups. It should be noted that many commercial software products have large user associations. In that case, the user satisfaction studies may even be carried out by the user's association itself. It should also be noted that for the most successful and widely used commercial software packages, user satisfaction surveys will probably be carried out by one or more of the major industry journals such as *Datamation, ComputerWorld,* and *Software.* These studies tend to include multiple vendors and multiple products at the same time, and they are exceptionally good sources of comparative information. For internal software such as MIS projects, user satisfaction surveys can be carried out by quality assurance personnel (assuming the company has any) or by designated staff assigned by software management.

Contents and topics of user satisfaction surveys

Because of the multiple kinds of information normally included on user satisfaction surveys, it is appropriate to give an actual example of some of the topics discussed. Following are actual excerpts from a user satisfaction survey[14] developed by Software Productivity Research. The survey questions included stress the major topics of the survey, but in order to concentrate on essential factors, they omit basic boilerplate information such as the name of the product and the name of the company.

Excerpts from the SPR User Satisfaction Questionnaire

Nature of product usage?   _____

1. Job-related or business usage only

2. Mixture of job-related and personal usage

3. Personal usage only

Frequency of product usage?   _____

1. Product is used continuously around the clock
2. Product is used continuously during business hours
3. Product is used as needed on a daily basis
4. Product is used daily on a regular basis
5. Product is used weekly on a regular basis
6. Product is used monthly on a regular basis
7. Product is used annually on a regular basis
8. Product is used intermittently (several times a year)
9. Product is used infrequently (less than once a year)

Importance of product to your job functions?   _____

1. Product is mandatory for your job functions
2. Product is of major importance to your job
3. Product is of some importance to your job
4. Product is of minor importance to your job
5. Product is of no importance to your job

How product functions were performed previously?   _____

1. Functions could not be performed previously
2. Functions were performed manually
3. Functions were performed mechanically
4. Functions were performed electronically
5. Functions were performed by other software

Primary benefits from use of current product?   _____

1. Product performs tasks beyond normal human abilities
2. Product simplifies complex decisions
3. Product simplifies tedious calculations
4. Product shortens critical timing situations
5. Product reduces manual effort

6. Other: _____

7. Hybrid: product has multiple benefits

Primary benefit? _____

Secondary benefit? _____

Product user evaluation

Ease of learning to use product initially?   _____

1. Very easy to learn
2. Fairly easy to learn
3. Moderately easy to learn, with some difficult topics
4. Difficult to learn
5. Very difficult to learn

Ease of installing product initially?   _____

1. Little or no effort to install
2. Fairly easy to install
3. Moderately easy to install, with some difficult spots
4. Difficult to install
5. Very difficult to install

Ease of customizing to local requirements?   _____

1. Little or no customization needed
2. Fairly easy to customize
3. Moderately easy to customize, with some difficult spots
4. Difficult to customize
5. Very difficult to customize

Ease of logging on and starting product?   _____

1. Very easy to start
2. Fairly easy to start
3. Moderately easy to start, with some difficult spots
4. Difficult to start
5. Very difficult to start

Ease of product use for normal tasks? _____

1. Very easy to use
2. Fairly easy to use
3. Moderately easy to use, with some difficult spots
4. Difficult to use
5. Very difficult to use

Ease of product use for unusual or infrequent tasks? _____

1. Very easy to use
2. Fairly easy to use
3. Moderately easy to use, with some difficult spots
4. Difficult to use
5. Very difficult to use

Ease of logging off and exiting product? _____

1. Very easy to exit
2. Fairly easy to exit
3. Moderately easy to exit, with some difficult spots
4. Difficult to exit
5. Very difficult to exit

Product handling of user errors? _____

1. Very natural and safe error handling
2. Fairly good error handling
3. Moderately good error handling, but some caution needed
4. User errors can sometimes hang up system
5. User errors often hang up system or stop product

Product speed or performance in use? _____

1. Very good performance
2. Fairly good performance
3. Moderately good normal performance but some delays

4. Performance is sometimes deficient

5. Performance is unacceptably slow or poor

Product memory utilization when in use? _____

1. No memory utilization problems with this product

2. Minimal memory utilization problems with this product

3. Moderate use of memory by this product

4. Significant memory required to use this product

5. Product memory use is excessive and unwarranted

Product compatibility with other software products? _____

1. Very good compatibility with other products

2. Fairly good compatibility with other products

3. Moderately good compatibility with other products

4. Significant compatibility problems

5. Product is highly incompatible with other software

Product quality and defect levels? _____

1. Excellent quality with few defects

2. Good quality, with some defects

3. Average quality, with normal defect levels

4. Worse than average quality, with high defect levels

5. Poor quality with excessive defect levels

Product reliability and failure intervals? _____

1. Product has never failed or almost never fails

2. Product fails less than once a year

3. Product fails or crashes a few times a year

4. Product fails fairly often and lacks reliability

5. Product fails often and is highly unreliable

Quality of training and tutorial materials? _____

1. Excellent training and tutorial materials

2. Good training and tutorial materials

3. Average training and tutorial materials

4. Worse than average training and tutorial materials

5. Poor or unacceptable training and tutorial materials

Quality of user reference manuals?   _____

1. Excellent user reference manuals

2. Good user reference manuals

3. Average user reference manuals

4. Worse than average user reference manuals

5. Poor or unacceptable user reference manuals

Quality of on-screen prompts and help messages?   _____

1. Excellent and lucid prompts and help messages

2. Good prompts and help messages

3. Average prompts and help messages

4. Worse than average prompts and help messages

5. Poor or unacceptable prompts and help messages

Quality of output created by product?   _____

1. Excellent and easy to use product outputs

2. Good product outputs, fairly easy to use

3. Average product outputs, normal ease of use

4. Worse than average product outputs

5. Poor or unacceptable product outputs

Functionality of product?   _____

1. Excellent—product meets all functional needs

2. Good—product meets most functional needs

3. Average—product meets many functional needs

4. Deficient—product meets few functional needs

5. Unacceptable—product meets no functional needs

Vendor support of product?   _____

1. Excellent—product support is outstanding
2. Good—product support is better than many
3. Average—product support is acceptable
4. Deficient—product has limited support
5. Unacceptable—little or no product support

Status of product versus major competitive products?   _____

1. Clearly superior to competitors in all respects
2. Superior to competitors in many respects
3. Equal to competitors, with some superior features
4. Behind competitors in some respects
5. Clearly inferior to competitors in all respects

Value of product to you personally?   _____

1. Excellent—product is highly valuable
2. Good—product is quite valuable
3. Average—product has acceptable value
4. Deficient—product is not valuable
5. Unacceptable—product is a loss

List the five best features of the product:

1. _____
2. _____
3. _____
4. _____
5. _____

List the five worst features of the product:

1. _____
2. _____

3. _____
4. _____
5. _____

List five improvements you would like to see in the product:

1. _____
2. _____
3. _____
4. _____
5. _____

As can be seen, a full user satisfaction survey covers a wide variety of topics. This brings up a significant decision for software vendors:

1. Should user surveys be carried out by live interviews?
2. Should user surveys be carried out by mail survey?
3. Should user surveys include both live interviews and mail surveys?

The pragmatic answer to these options depends upon the number of users, the available staff, and the geographic scatter of the users themselves. Normally, for major mission-critical systems and large mainframe packages, it is desirable to carry out the survey in the form of live interviews. Mail surveys are appropriate under the following conditions:

1. The product has more than 1000 users. (That is the minimum number for which mail surveys will typically generate an adequate volume of responses.)
2. The product is distributed through secondary channels, such as distributors or by mail itself.
3. The customers are widely dispersed geographically.

A hybrid methodology that utilizes both mail questionnaires and live surveys is a technique frequently employed by computer manufacturers and large software houses. The mail surveys, normally somewhat simplified, will be widely distributed to several thousand customers. Sales personnel will then carry out in-depth user satisfaction surveys with perhaps a 5 percent sample of customers or with customers that meet certain prerequisites. Typical prerequisites might include number of copies of the product acquired by the customer, size of the customer's company, or other salient factors.

Combining User Satisfaction and Defect Data

Although user satisfaction data and defect data are collected at different intervals, by different staff, and for different purposes, it is an extremely useful undertaking to combine these two measurements at least once a year. A very useful technique for combining the two kinds of information is a simple scatter graph which shows user satisfaction on one axis and user-reported defect levels on the other axis. Figure 5.5 illustrates such a combination graph. Obviously, the four different conditions shown by the figure can lead to four different business responses.

1 High levels of user satisfaction and low levels of defects. This situation implies an excellent product, and it is the desirable goal of all software. Companies that measure both user satisfaction and numeric defect levels quickly realize the strong correlation between the two phenomena. Software products with high defect levels never generate satisfactory levels of user satisfaction. Leading software vendors and computer manufacturers can achieve more than 90 percent of all products within this quadrant.

2 Low levels of user satisfaction and low levels of defects. Products falling within this quadrant have obviously missed the mark in some attribute other than pure defect levels. The most common factors identified for products in this quadrant are insufficient functionality, cumbersome human interfaces, and inadequate training or documentation.

USER SATISFACTION

	HIGH	LOW
HIGH DEFECT LEVELS	ZONE OF URGENT REPAIRS	ZONE OF URGENT REPLACEMENT
LOW DEFECT LEVELS	ZONE OF EXCELLENT APPLICATONS	ZONE OF FUNCTIONAL ENHANCEMENT

Figure 5.5 Scatter graph of user satisfaction and defect data.

3 High levels of user satisfaction and high levels of defects. This particular quadrant is included primarily for consistency, and it will normally have very few if any projects falling within it. Any software product that does fall here is a candidate for full inspections and quality upgrading. Typically, the only projects within this quadrant will be initial releases with fairly important new functionality.

4 Low levels of user satisfaction and high levels of defects. Products falling within this quadrant are candidates for emergency handling and perhaps replacement. The steps that can be handled on an emergency basis include searching for and eliminating error-prone modules, full inspections, and perhaps retesting. The longer-range solutions may include restructuring the product, rewriting the documentation, and including additional functions.

Since this quadrant represents project failure in its most embarrassing form, it is significant to note that a majority of products falling here were rushed during their development. Excessive schedule pressures coupled with inadequate defect prevention and removal technologies are the factors most often associated with projects in this quadrant.

Summary and Conclusions

The measurement of quality, reliability, and user satisfaction are factors that separate the leading-edge companies from the laggards. On a global basis, high quality is the main driving force for high-technology products. The companies that recognize this basic fact are poised for success in the twenty-first century; the companies that do not recognize it may not last to see the twenty-first century!

Suggested Readings

Because quality control and user satisfaction are such major topics, it is desirable to conclude with a short reading list of some of the more notable books that expand upon the topics discussed herein.

Japanese competitive methods

Walton, Mary, *The Deming Management Method,* Putnam, New York, 1986; 262 pages. No single individual in all history has had more impact on the global economic balance than W. Edwards Deming. Deming moved to Japan after World War II, and he was the primary source of Japan's manufacturing quality control methods. He has now returned to the United States, and he is belatedly being listened to by U.S. companies that refused his advice for more than 30 years.

Noda, Nabuo, *How Japan Absorbed American Management Methods,* Asian Productivity Organization Press, Tokyo, 1981, 37 pages. The Asian Productivity organization is sponsored by the national governments of Japan, Korea, Thailand, the Republic of China, and several other countries. This short pamphlet is an interesting chronology of the absorption of statistics-based quality control and psychology-based management practices in Japan.

Matsumoto, Koji, *Organizing for Higher Productivity: An Analysis of Japanese Systems and Practices,* Asian Productivity Organization Press, Tokyo, 1982, 75 pages. This is yet another of the interesting studies of Japanese methods and techniques. The author is an official of the Ministry of International Trade and Industry (MITI), and he is in a good position to speak about Japanese industrial and management practices.

Ohmae, Kenichi, *The Mind of the Strategist: The Art of Japanese Business,* McGraw-Hill, New York, 1982, 283 pages. Kenichi Ohmae is a director of the prestigious McKinsey & Company management consulting organization. This book gives his observations as a leading business consultant to major Japanese corporations. Since strategic planning in Japan is often more sophisticated than in the United States, this book is quite valuable to U.S. readers.

Crocker, Olga, C. Charney, and J. S. L. Chiu, *Quality Circles,* Mentor, New York, 1984, 361 pages. Quality circles are derived from the work of the American W. Edwards Deming, but they are much more popular in Japan, where more than 7000 of them are registered with the Japanese national registry of quality control. The appealing concept of quality circles is that, given the chance and training, employees want to improve quality and help their employers. The quality circle methodology formalizes that concept, and this book shows managers and executives what they can do to tap this valuable resource.

Pascale, Richard Tanner, and A. G. Athos, *The Art of Japanese Management,* Warner, New York, 1982, 363 pages. This interesting book contrasts Matsushita from Japan and ITT from the United States. Both enterprises had charismatic senior executives and were introducing novel and exciting management principles, but each reflected the paradigm of the nation in which the enterprise developed.

Feigenbaum, Edward, and Pamela McCorduck, *The Fifth Generation,* Addison-Wesley, Reading, Mass., 1983, 275 pages. Edward Feigenbaum is an eminent computer scientist and scholar, and this book explores the concepts of the major Japanese attempt to wrest the lead in computing technology from the United States. The "fifth generation" idea is to leapfrog the United States in both computer architecture and software methodologies, since computing and software technologies are so important that the world leader in these technologies will be the world leader in many derivative industries as well.

Morita, Akio, E. M. Reingold, and M. Shimomura, *Made in Japan,* Penguin, New York, 1986, 343 pages. This is an autobiography of Akio Morita, the founder of Sony corporation. The book is interesting because it reveals not only the details of Sony's industrial growth but also the personality of its founder. Sony shared the typical high quality of other Japanese companies in product manufacture, but it also had an unusually perceptive sense of market trends.

Random, Michel, *Japan: The Strategy of the Unseen,* Aquarian, Wellingborough, England, 1987, 205 pages. This book, translated from the original French, is a tutorial for European, British, and American business travelers visiting Japan. It discusses the historical and philosophical background of Bushido, the code of the Samurai in medieval Japan. This is a major part of modern Japanese business practice, and Westerners who have no knowledge of Samurai history will be at a disadvantage.

Masuda, Yoneji, *The Information Society,* World Future Society, Bethesda, Md., 1981, 170 pages. This book is now somewhat dated, but in one sense that may add to its importance. It discusses some of the large-scale experiments carried out in Japan to explore the concepts of full computerization and communication capabilities in ordinary households. Entire villages were equipped with terminals and communication networks that allowed such functions as remote purchasing from stores, remote emergency medical advice, and even some direct participation in town government functions. Similar large-scale experiments have taken place in other countries such as Sweden, France, and Canada, but the Japanese experiments are perhaps the largest yet carried out.

Halberstam, David, *The Reckoning,* Avon, New York, 1987, 786 pages. This book is a massive history of the automotive industry that concentrates on Ford and Toyota, and it deals with both the companies and the executives who founded them. The major point of the book is that, through a combination of arrogance and ignorance, the mightiest industry in America was struck a damaging blow by Japanese competition. U.S. automotive executives ignored quality and disregarded its importance until it was almost too late to recover. They also were guilty of ethnocentrism and the naive assumption that U.S. technology would permanently dominate the postwar world.

Quality control and corporate excellence

Crosby, Philip B., *Quality Is Free,* Mentor, 1980, 270 pages. Phil Crosby was the ITT Vice President of Quality, and he was the person who introduced modern quality control practices into the ITT system. His famous book, long a best-seller, derives its title from the empirical observation that the economic advantages of quality control far overshadow the costs. Phil Crosby and W. Edwards Deming were two of the pioneers in this field of study.

Geneen, Harold, and A. Moscow, *Managing,* Avon, New York, 1984, 305 pages. Harold Geneen was the Chairman and CEO that took ITT from a medium-size telecommunications company to the most diverse and largest conglomerate in U.S. history. His style was unique, but his observations on running very large enterprises are worthy of note. It is interesting that Phil Crosby dedicated his *Quality Is Free* to Harold Geneen, since Harold's support was vital to establishing statistical quality methods within ITT.

Peters, Tom, *In Search of Excellence,* Random House, 1985, 389 pages. This is one of the most widely discussed books of the 1980s. In it, Peters discusses the characteristics which tend to separate leading enterprises from laggards. Excellence in all its forms, human, cultural, and business, is part of the pattern of success.

Levering, Robert, M. Moskowitz, and M. Katz, *The 100 Best Companies to Work for in America,* New American Library, New York, 1985, 396 pages. Although intended as an aid for job hunters, this book reveals interesting aspects of U.S. corporate culture. It is a useful book for executives, whom it enables to get a glimpse of what some of the most successful U.S. enterprises are doing to ensure corporate excellence.

Pirsig, Robert, *Zen and the Art of Motorcycle Maintenance,* In spite of the unusual title and the fact that it is a novel rather than a technical book, Pirsig's book is in fact a book on quality that is good enough to have been used by IBM as part of its quality assurance training. The book deals with a cross-country motorcycle trip taken by Pirsig and his son. In the course of the trip, the author discusses the meaning of quality and the difficulty of coming to grips with this elusive concept. The fundamental points are that doing things well provides great satisfaction to the doer as well as to the beneficiary, and that quality is easy to experience but difficult to define.

Software engineering and software quality control

Jones, Capers, *Programming Productivity,* McGraw-Hill, New York, 1986, 278 pages. This book explores the technologies that affect software productivity and concludes that since defect removal is the most expensive aspect of software, quality control is on the critical path to success. The book also discusses the impact of staff skills, the physical environment, tools, languages, and other factors of significance. The impact of quality on software productivity discussed in this book was in part observed during Jones' tenure at IBM and ITT; he served 12 years at IBM and four years at ITT.

Freedman, D., and G. M. Weinberg, *A Handbook of Walkthroughs, Inspections, and Technical Reviews*, Little, Brown, Boston, 1982, 450 pages. Daniel Freedman and Jerry Weinberg are two well-known consultants to the software industry. This book provides an excellent introduction to the various forms of review and inspection that have proved to be so effective for software projects. The book is in question-and-answer form, and it covers all of the topics that naturally occur to first-time participants of reviews and inspections.

DeMarco, Tom, and Tim Lister, *Peopleware,* Dorset House, New York, 1987, 188 pages. This book deals with the human side of software; it discusses the concept that so long as software is a human occupation, optimizing the treatment and conditions of software staff will be beneficial. The book goes beyond merely stating a point, however, and discusses large-scale empirical studies that buttress some of its conclusions. Among the most surprising observations was the discovery that the physical office environment had a direct correlation with software productivity: programmers in the high quartile had more than 78 ft^2 of office space, and those in the low quartile had either open offices or less than 44 ft^2. DeMarco was the recipient of the 1987 Warnier prize for outstanding contributions to computer and information science.

DeMarco, Tom, *Controlling Software Projects,* Yourdon Press, New York, 1982, 284 pages. This book gives the advice of one of the industry leaders in keeping software projects under control in terms of a variety of dimensions: quality, schedule, costs, and others. The book also introduced DeMarco's bang functional metric.

Boehm, Barry, *Software Engineering Economics,* Prentice-Hall, Englewood Cliffs, N.J., 1981, 767 pages. This book is perhaps the largest ever written on the costs associated with software projects. It certainly has one of the largest and most complete sets of references to the relevant literature. The book contains the original equations for the COCOMO estimating model, and it presents one of the few nonproprietary descriptions of how a software cost-estimating model might work. It h s been a best-seller since it originally appeared.

Humph ey, Watts, *Managing the Software Process,* Addison-Wesley, Reading, Mass., 1989, 489 pages. Humphrey, formerly at IBM, was head of the prestigious Software Engineering Institute (SEI) associated with Carnegie Mellon University. This book contains both his observations on the software process and also his method for evaluating the five stages of maturing of software development organizations.

Biggerstaff, T., and A. Perlis, *Software Reusability,* Vols. 1 and 2, Addison-Wesley, Reading, Mass., 1989, Vol. 1, 424 pages; Vol. 2, 386 pages. Dr. Biggerstaff was part of the ITT Programming Technology Center. Together with Dr. Perlis of Yale, he was cochairman of the famous 1983 ITT conference on software reusability. This two-volume set builds upon a kernel of papers that were presented at that conference, but it brings the entire subject up to date. Biggerstaff heads the reusability project at the Microcomputer and Electronics Corporation (MCC).

Glass, Robert L., *Modern Programming Practices: A Report From Industry,* Prentice-Hall, Englewood Cliffs, N.J., 1982, 311 pages. Books on software engineering theory outnumber books on software engineering practices by at least 20 to 1. This one is based on interviews and empirical observations carried out within large companies—Martin Marietta, TRW, CSC, and others. Although somewhat dated, it is an interesting attempt to describe what goes on day-to-day when large companies build software.

Dunn, Robert, and Richard Ullman, *Quality Assurance for Computer Software,* McGraw-Hill, New York, 1982, 349 pages. This book is yet another that originated with research carried out within ITT. Dunn and Ullman were quality assurance specialists for one of ITT's divisions and later for the corporate offices. It summarizes, broadly, all of the major tasks and issues regarding setting up a quality assurance organization for modern software engineering projects.

Dunn, Robert, *Software Defect Removal,* McGraw-Hill, New York, 1984, 331 pages. Bob Dunn continues his explication of software quality methods with a broad-based survey of all of the major forms of defect removal. As with the preceding title, this book comprises part of the set of methods for quality assurance used within the ITT system.

Chow, Tsun S., *Software Quality Assurance,* IEEE Press, Catalog Number EH0223-8, 1984, 500 pages. Tsun Chow's tutorial volume is part of the IEEE series on software engineering. It contains some 50 articles by various authors covering all of the major software QA topics.

Myers, Glenford, *The Art of Software Testing,* Wiley, New York, 1978, 177 pages. Although this book is now 10 years old, it is still regarded as a classic text on software testing and is still a textbook in many university and graduate school curricula. Myers is a multifaceted researcher who was also one of the originators of structured design and a contributor to computer architecture as well. He was the 1988 recipient of the Warnier prize for outstanding contributions to computer and information science.

Brooks, Fred, *The Mythical Man-Month,* Addison-Wesley, Reading, Mass., 1982, 195 pages. This book has sold more copies than any other book on a software topic since the industry began. Brooks was the IBM director who first developed the operating system software for the IBM System/360 computer line, which was one of IBM's first major efforts to run far beyond planned budgets and schedules. His report is a classic account of why even large and well-managed enterprises such as IBM run into trouble when building large software systems. The cover art of the book captures the problems exactly: giant prehistoric ground sloths struggling to free themselves from the La Brea tar pits! The message is that, once the problems of large systems get started, no amount of money or extra staff can easily recover the situation.

Pressman, Roger, *Software Engineering: A Practitioner's Approach,* McGraw-Hill, New York, 1982, 352 pages. This book, widely used as a college text, is an excellent introduction to all of the major topics of concern to both software engineers and to software managers as well. It is organized chronologically and is based on the phases of a software lifecycle. It is much broader in scope than many other software engineering texts in that it includes management topics such as planning, estimating, and measurement. It also covers requirements, design, coding, testing and defect removal, and maintenance. It would be difficult to find a more suitable introduction to all of the critical topics than is contained in this book.

References

1. Walton, Mary, *The Deming Management Method,* Perigree, New York, 1986, 262 pp.
2. Pirsig, R., *Zen and the Art of Motorcycle Maintenance,*
3. Crosby, Phil, *Quality Is Free: The Art of Making Quality Certain,* McGraw-Hill, New York, 1979.
4. Musa, J., A. Iannino, and K. Okumoto, *Software Reliability: Measurement, Prediction, Application,* McGraw-Hill, New York, 1987, 619 pp.
5. Levering, R., M. Moskowitz, and M. Katz, *The 100 Best Companies to Work for in America,* Addison-Wesley, New York, 1985, 396 pp.
6. Peters, Tom, *In Search of Excellence,* Random House, New York, 1985, 385 pp.
7. Fagan, M., "Design and Code Inspections to Reduce Errors in Program Development," *IBM Systems Journal,* vol. 15, no. 3, 1976, pp. 182–211.
8. SPR, "Software Design Inspections," Software Productivity Research, Burlington, Mass., 1990, 35 pp.
9. Crocker, O. L. S. Charney, and J. S. L. Chieu, *Quality Circles,* Mentor, New York, 1984, 361 pp.
10. Halpin, J. F., *Zero Defects—A New Dimension in Quality Assurance,* McGraw-Hill, New York, 1966, 228 pp.
11. Mills, H., "The New Math of Computer Programming," *CACM,* vol. 18, January 1975, pp. 43–48.
12. Martin, J., *System Design That Is Provably Bug Free,* Prentice-Hall, Englewood Cliffs, N.J., 1985.
13. Deutsch, M., *Software Verification and Validation: Realistic Project Approaches,* Prentice-Hall, Englewood Cliffs, N.J., 1982.
14. SPR, "User Satisfaction Survey Questionnaire," Software Productivity Research, Burlington, Mass., 1989.

Rules for Counting
Procedural Source Code

Introduction

It is quite astonishing that in 45 years of software engineering and programming history, there has never been a true international standard that defined exactly what is meant by "a line of source code." The following rules for counting source code were created by Software Productivity Research. They are intended to provide at least minimal consistency with clients when discussing productivity issues in terms of "lines of source code."

Indeed, the rules have been embodied in a size conversion tool that can convert apparent size by using any arbitrary combination of rules into the equivalent size when some other combination is used. Such a tool is more or less necessary when an attempt is made to compare productivity between companies, departments, and even projects by using lines of source code.

The general principle of the following rules can be stated briefly: "Count as you think." Counting should come as close as possible to being intuitive and natural, and it should avoid being artificial and stilted. In the rules, the SPR standard is indicated by an asterisk, i.e., * The SPR standard is not necessarily the optimum choice, but in general it seems to be pragmatic and make sense.

Project Source Code Counting Rules

Multiple-language counting _____

*1. Each language is counted separately

2. All languages are lumped and counted together

---

* = SPR standard counting technique

Source code termination   _____

    *1. Delimiters
    2. Physical lines

Source code counting   _____

    1. Executable statements only
    *2. Executable statements + data definitions
    3. Executable statements + data definitions + comments

Macro instruction and expansion counting   _____

    0. Project does not have macro instructions or expansions
    1. Macro instructions and expansions are not counted
    2. Macro instructions are counted, but not expansions
    *3. Macro instructions and unique expansions are counted
    4. Macro instructions and all expansions counted separately
    5. Macro instructions and all expansions lumped with product

Reusable code counting   _____

    0. Project does not have reusable code
    1. Reusable modules are not counted
    *2. Unique reusable modules are counted separately
    3. All uses of reusable modules are counted separately
    4. Reused modules are lumped and counted with product code

Program and application generator counting   _____

    0. Project does not have generator statements
    1. Generator statements are not counted
    2. Generator input statements are counted
    *3. Generator inputs and outputs are counted separately
    4. Generator inputs and outputs are lumped together

Job control language counting   _____

   0. Project does not have job control language

   1. Job control language is not counted

  *2. Job control language is counted separately

   3. Job control language is lumped and counted with product

Changed code counting   _____

   0. Project does not have changed code

   1. Changed code is not counted

  *2. Changed code is counted separately from new code

   3. Changed code is lumped and counted with new code

Base code counting   _____

   0. Product does not have base code

   1. Base code is not counted

  *2. Base code is counted separately

   3. Base code is lumped and counted with new and changed code

Deleted code counting   _____

   0. Project does not have deleted code

   1. Deleted code is not counted

  *2. Deleted code is counted separately

   3. Deleted code is lumped with new and changed code

Scaffold code counting   _____

   0. Project does not have scaffold code

   1. Scaffold code is not counted

  *2. Scaffold code is counted separately from product code

   3. Scaffold code is lumped and counted with product code

Support code counting   _____

    0. Project does not have support code

    1. Support code is not counted

  *2. Support code is counted separately from product code

    3. Support code is lumped and counted with product code

Test case code counting   _____

    0. Project does not have test case code

    1. Test case code is not counted

  *2. Test case code is counted separately from product code

    3. Test case code is lumped and counted with product code

General Rules for Counting Code within Applications

- Do not count commentary lines or information appended to executable lines for informational purposes.
- Count verbs or action statements, such as assignments, print commands, conditionals, and loops.
- Count equations and mathematical expressions.
- Count data definitions, including both variables and constants, and also type definitions.
- Count initialization of data definitions.
- Count procedure definitions.
- Count each formal parameter within a procedure.
- Count procedure labels.
- Count unexpanded macro calls if you are interested in development size.
- Count expanded macro instructions if you are interested in delivered size.
- Clearly identify and explain the specific counting rules you have selected.
- Be aware that individual human variation can and will cause notable differences in the sizes of programs that are logically identical. In a controlled study, eight programmers varied by 5 to 1 in

the number of statements they used to implement the same algorithm.

Examples of the SPR Source Code
Counting Rules

- Do not count commentary lines or statements that are used purely for information purposes; i.e., the following statement would not be counted:
```
REM THIS ROUTINE CALCULATES GROSS PAY
```

- For strongly typed languages, count data definitions statements as 1 statement; i.e., the following example counts as 1 statement:
```
WEEKDAY = (MONDAY, TUESDAY, WEDNESDAY, THURSDAY, FRIDAY,
    SATURDAY, SUNDAY)
```

- For weakly typed languages, count data definitions statements as 1 statement; i.e., the following example counts as 1 statement:
```
DATA = MONDAY, TUESDAY, WEDNESDAY, THURSDAY, FRIDAY,
    SATURDAY, SUNDAY
```

- Count assignment statements as 1 statement; i.e.,
```
A = B + C
```

- Count equations as you would treat them in mathematics; i.e., as a single unit or line. The following expression counts as 1 statement:
```
A = ((B * C) / (D - E)) + ((F + G + H) * I))
```

- For languages that allow multiple logical statements per physical line, count the logical statements. (This is the same as counting delimiters.) The following example counts as 3 statements:
```
BASE = 0: BASE = HOURS * RATE: PRINT BASE
```

  Note: The two colons and the carriage return at the end of the line are the 3 delimiters.

- Count procedure or function calls as 1 statement; i.e.,
```
CALL PRINTDRV
```

- Count IF's and THEN's as separate statements; i.e., the following example would count as 2 statements:
```
IF A OCCURS
THEN UPDATE B
```

- Count IF's followed by GOTO's as separate statements; i.e., the following example would count as 2 statements:
```
IF A OCCURS THEN GOTO NEWSTART
```

- Count IF's, THEN's, and ELSE's as separate statements; i.e., the following example would count as 3 statements:

```
  IF A OCCURS
THEN UPDATE B
  ELSE UPDATE C
```

- Count CASE statements as separate statements; i.e., the following example would count as 5 statements:

```
SELECT CASE NUMBER$
  CASE ''ONE'': PRINT ''1''
  CASE ''TWO'': PRINT ''2''
  CASE ''THREE'': PRINT ''3''
  CASE ''FOUR'': PRINT ''4''
END SELECT
```

- Count DO-WHILE constructions as 1 statement; i.e., the following example would count as 4 statements:

```
WHILE J>10 DO
  PRINT HEADER
  PRINT LINENUM
  PRINT MESSAGE
```

- Count FOR-NEXT constructions as 1 statement; i.e., the following example would count as 4 statements:

```
FOR J=1 TO 10
  PRINT HEADER
  PRINT LINENUM
  PRINT MESSAGE
NEXT J
```

- Count REPEAT-UNTIL constructions as 1 statement; i.e., the following example would count as 4 statements:

```
REPEAT
  PRINT HEADER
  PRINT LINENUM
  PRINT MESSAGE
UNTIL INDEX >10
```

- Count nested constructions in accordance with the individual element rules; i.e., the following example would count as 8 statements:

```
FOR J=1 TO 10
  PRINT HEADER
    FOR K=1 TO 3
      PRINT NUMBER
      PRINT STREET
      PRINT CITY
    NEXT K
  PRINT LINENUM
  PRINT MESSAGE
NEXT J
```

Software Productivity Research
Cobol-Counting Rules

Although Cobol is the most widely used language in the world and approximately 50 percent of all software is written in it, there are currently no national or international standards that actually define exactly what is meant by "a line of Cobol source code" for the purposes of measuring productivity.

The most basic problem with Cobol counting is the fundamental decision whether to count physical lines or logical lines. Among SPR clients, about 75 percent count physical lines, which is definitely the most convenient method since many library tools and Cobol compilers themselves can provide such data.

However, since the actual work required to produce an application correlates rather poorly with physical lines, it is often more useful for productivity studies to count logical lines. Because Cobol tends to have conditional statements that span several physical lines, a count of logical lines can reduce the apparent size of the application by more than 2 to 1. For productivity purposes, this is very troublesome—especially in light of the fact that few productivity authors actually state which rules they used for line counting!

If you do wish to count logical lines, you face two problems: (1) What are the exact rules that define logical lines? (2) How can logical lines be counted other than by a laborious manual analysis? It is remarkable that, after so many years of Cobol's history, these problems remain. The answer to both questions is the same: It is necessary to build or acquire a line-counting tool that embodies your corporate standards (since there are no global standards). Several Cobol-line-counting tools are commercially available, and they can be set to match your corporate rules.

The following rules by Software Productivity Research are a surrogate for a true standard, and they should be used with caution. *Note:* The Cobol rules are based on the general rules for procedural languages given in the preceding section.

As stated before, try to count as you think: If a statement represents a unit of thought, it should also represent a unit of work and hence deserves to be counted.

1. Statements within the IDENTIFICATION DIVISION are not counted by SPR, since they are essentially comments. If you choose to count them, suggested rules are as follows:

   - PROGRAM ID and the ID itself count as 1 line.
   - AUTHOR and the author's name count as 1 line.
   - INSTALLATION and following text count as 1 line.
   - DATE WRITTEN and following text count as 1 line.

- DATE COMPILED and following text count as 1 line.
- SECURITY and following text count as 1 line.
- COMMENTS and following text do not count, since commentary lines are normally excluded.

2. Statements within the ENVIRONMENT DIVISION are similar to comments in some ways, but because they are volatile and change when applications migrate, it is appropriate to count the FILE CONTROL SELECT statements.

3. Count statements within the DATA DIVISION in accordance with these rules:

- Each statement in the FILE section counts as 1 line, e.g., BLOCK, RECORD, and VALUE OF.
- COPY statements themselves count as 1 line each. The code that is actually copied from a source statement library is reused code and should be counted as such. If you are interested in development productivity, it can be ignored. If you are interested in delivery productivity, it should be counted.
- Each numbered FIELD or SUBFIELD statement (01, 02, 66, etc.) including the PICTURE clause counts as 1 line.
- Statements in the WORKING STORAGE section follow the same rules as for the FILE section.

4. Count statements within the PROCEDURE DIVISION in accordance with these rules:

- Count procedure labels as 1 line; i.e., MAIN-ROUTINE of END-OF-JOB routine would count as 1 line each.
- Count verbal expressions as 1 line; i.e., OPEN, WRITE, CLOSE, MOVE, ADD, etc. count as 1 line each.
- Count CALL statements as 1 line; i.e., CALL 'GRCALC' by USING CR-HOURS, CR-RATE, WS-GROSS counts as 1 line.
- Count PERFORM statements as 1 line; i.e., PERFORM RATE-LOOKUP THROUGH RATE-EXIT counts as 1 line.
- Count IF logic as separate statements; i.e., the following expression counts as 3 lines:
```
IF HOURS IS GREATER THAN 40
    SUBTRACT 40 FROM HOURS GIVING OVERTIME
    MULTIPLY OVERTIME BY 1.5 GIVING PREMIUM
```
- Count IF-ELSE-GO TO logic as separate statements; i.e, the following expression counts as 3 lines:
```
IF LINE-COUNT = 50 OR LINE-COUNT >50 GOTO PRINT-
HEADINGS
    ELSE GO TO PRINT-HEADINGS-EXIT
```

Rules for Counting Function Points and Feature Points

This appendix provides a set of quick reference rules and counting recommendations for both function points and feature points. The rules were prepared by A. J. Albrecht and David Herron, and they are current through the end of 1990. Rules such as those are revised from time to time in accordance with revisions by the IFPUG Counting Practices Committee (for function points) and the Software Productivity Research corporation (for feature points).

This set of rules is in the concise format suitable for a folding, pocket-size card. This format is very common, and it provides a convenient tool for staff and management personnel who are engaged in counting function or feature points at a number of diverse locations.

SPR METRIC ANALYSIS

REFERENCE CARD

**Counting Rules for
Function Points
Feature Points**

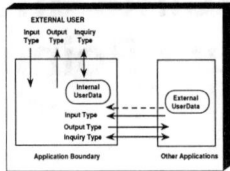

Software Productivity Research, Inc.

77 South Bedford Street
Burlington, MA 01803
(617) 273-0140

INTERNAL USER DATA GROUP (IU)

Count each major logical group of user data or control information in the application as an internal user data group. Include each logical file, or within a database, each logical group of data from the viewpoint of the user that is generated, used, and maintained by the application. Count each logical group of data as viewed by the user and as defined in the external design or data analysis rather than on the physical implementation.

COUNTING RECOMMENDATIONS

Do not include logical internal files that are not accessible to the user through external input, output or inquiry types.

Description	Count
• Logical entity of data from user viewpoint	1 IU
• Logical internal files generated or maintained by the application	1 IU
• User maintained table or file	1 IU
• Files accessible to the user through keyword(s) or parameter(s)	1 IU
• File used for data or control by sequential (batch) application	1 IU
• Each hierarchical path (leg) through a database, derived from user requirements (include paths formed by secondary indices and logical relationships)	1 IU
• Intermediate or sort work file	0 IU
• File created by technology used (e.g., index file)	0 IU
• A "master file" only read by application	0 IU

EXTERNAL USER DATA GROUP (EU)

Count each major logical group of user data or control information used by the application (but maintained by another application) which crosses the application boundary. Include each logical file, or logical group of data from the viewpoint of the user, that is used by the application.

COUNTING RECOMMENDATIONS

Count each major logical group of user data or control information that enters the application from another application as an external user data group.

Description	Count
• File of records from another application	1 EU
• Database shared from other applications	1 EU
• Logical internal file from another application used as a transaction	0 EU, 1 IT
• Each hierarchical path (leg) through a database, from another application derived from user requirements (include paths formed by secondary indices and logical relationships)	1 EU

INPUT TYPE (IT)

Count each unique user data or user control input type that enters the external boundary of the application being measured, and adds, changes, or deletes data in an internal user data group. An external input type should be considered unique if it has a different format, or if the external logical design requires a processing logic different from other external input types of the same format.

COUNTING RECOMMENDATIONS

The recommendation most closely describing each input type should be used in counting each input type.

Description	Count
• Data screen	1 IT
• Multiple screens accumulated and processed as one transaction	1 IT
• Two data screens with the same format and processing logic	1 IT
• Two data screens with the same format and different processing logic	2 IT
• Data screen that is both input and output	1 IT, 1 OT
• Selection menu with save capability	1 IT
• Data screen with multiple functions	1 IT/Funct.
• Automatic data or transactions from other applications	1 IT
• User application control input	1 IT
• Input forms (OCR)	1 IT
• An update function following a query	1 IT
• Individual selections on menu screen	0 IT
• User maintained table or file	1 IT
• PF Key duplicate of a screen already counted as input	0 IT
• Light pen duplicate of a screen already counted as input	0 IT
• External input types introduced only because of the technology used	0 IT

OUTPUT TYPE (OT)

Count each unique user data or control output type that leaves the external boundary of the application being measured. An external output type should be considered unique if it has a different format, or if the external design requires a processing logic different from other external output types of the same format. External output types usually consist of reports or messages to the user.

COUNTING RECOMMENDATIONS

The recommendations most closely describing each output type should be used in counting each output type.

Description	Count
• Data screen output	1 OT
• Batch report	1 OT
• Screen error message format associated with input type	1 OT

Continued...

Figure B.1   SPR metric analysis reference card. Sheet 1.

COUNTING RECOMMENDATIONS (Cont)

• Data screen output	1 OT
• Start screen display or end screen display	1 OT
• Transaction file crossing the application boundary	(at least) 1 OT
• Automatic data or transactions to other applications	1 OT
• Single error message on a screen	0 OT
• Error message sent to an operator as a result of an input transaction	1 OT
• Backup files (only if requested by the user)	0 OT
• Selection menu screen with save capability	1 OT
• Output to screen and to printer	2 OT
• Output files created for technical reasons	0 OT
• User maintained table or file	(at least) 1 OT

EXTERNAL INQUIRIES (QT)

Count each unique input/output combination, where an input causes and generates an immediate output, as an external inquiry type. An external inquiry type should be considered unique if it has a format different from other external inquiry types in either its input or output parts, or if the external design requires a processing logic different from other external inquiry types of the same format.

COUNTING RECOMMENDATIONS

The recommendation most closely describing each inquiry type should be used in counting each inquiry type.

Description	Count
• Online input and online output with no update of data in files	1 QT
• Inquiry followed by an update input	1 QT, 1 IT
• Help screen input and output	1 QT
• Selection menu screen input and output	1 QT
• ADF Key Selection screen input and output	1 QT
• ADF Master Rules screen input and output	1 QT

Note: A major query facility or language should be decomposed into its hierarchical structure of IT(s), OT(s), and QT(s) using the existing definitions and current practices.

"BACKFIRE" METHOD

The "backfire" method for estimating Function Points is based on empirical relationships discovered to exist between source code and Function Points in all known languages. This method is based on tables of average values. It is useful for doing retrospective studies of projects completed long ago, and for easing the transition to Function Point metrics for people who are familiar with lines-of-code metrics.

Assembler	320*	DB Languages	40
C	128	Object Oriented	29
COBOL	107	Query Languages	25
Ada	71	Generators	16

*Statements per Function Point

FUNCTION POINT METHODOLOGY

The primary difference between the IBM and SPR Function Point methodologies is in the way they deal with complexity. The IBM techniques for assessing complexity are based on weighing 14 influence factors and evaluating the numbers of field and file references.

The SPR technique for dealing with complexity separates the overall topic of "complexity" into two distinct questions that can be dealt with intuitively: 1) How complex are the algorithms or equations or problems in the software?; 2) How complex is the data structure of the application?

With the SPR Function Point method, it is not necessary to count the number of data element types, file types referenced, or record types. Neither is it necessary to assign low, average, or high values to each specific input, output, inquiry, data file, or interface.

The SPR complexity questions can be answered quickly by anyone familiar with an application, and they deal with the entire application, rather than with its elements.

FEATURE POINT METHODOLOGY

The SPR Feature Point metric is a superset of the IBM Function Point metric and introduces a new element (algorithms) in addition to the five standard Function Point parameters. The Feature Point method also reduces the Internal User Data Group weight from IBM's average value of 10 to an average value of 7.

Since Feature Points include algorithmic complexity, a definition of "algorithm" is appropriate. An algorithm is defined as the set of user required rules which must be completely expressed in order to solve a significant computational problem. For example, a square root extraction routine, a Julian date conversion routine, or an overtime pay calculation routine are all considered algorithms.

COMPLEXITY FACTOR

The complexity factor and multiplier is used to compute the Function Point Count measure. SPR uses a "quick-fire" method which can adjust the function point count by ±40%.

IBM and SPR use the same principles to identify the five elements (six with Feature Points) of counting. IBM then applies a weighting factor of high, low or average, depending on the number of data elements, file types referenced and record types invoked. SPR's quick-fire method assumes average weight in its methodology.

To adjust the raw FP count, IBM looks at 14 variables of complexity that will adjust the count by ±35%. SPR simply requires answers to two questions which summarize the intent of IBM's 14 complexity factors.

By answering 1 through 5 on both questions and adding the two values together, a complexity multiplier is then obtained using the simple chart provided.

Function Point Counting

Element	Count		Weight		Total
Input		x 4		=	_____
Output		x 5		=	_____
Inquiry		x 4		=	_____
Internal User Data Group		x 10		=	_____
External User Data Group		x 7		=	_____
				TOTAL	_____

· OR ·

Feature Point Counting

Element	Count		Weight		Total
Input		x 4		=	_____
Output		x 5		=	_____
Inquiry		x 4		=	_____
Internal User Data Group		x 7		=	_____
External User Data Group		x 7		=	_____
Algorithm		x 3		=	_____
				TOTAL	_____

Function/Feature Count (FC)

Total Unadjusted Function/Feature Points   _____

Complexity Factor and Multiplier

Problem Complexity?
1) Simple algorithms and simple calculations
2) Majority of simple algorithms and calculations
3) Algorithms and calculations of average complexity
4) Some difficult or complex algorithms
5) Many difficult algorithms and complex calculations

Data Complexity?
1) Simple data with few variables
2) Numerous variables, but simple data relationships
3) Multiple files, fields, and data intersections
4) Complex file structures and data intersections
5) Very complex file structures and data intersections

Sum of Problem and Data Complexity	2	3	4	5	6	7	8	9	10
Complexity Multiplier	.6	.7	.8	.9	1.0	1.1	1.2	1.3	1.4

FP Count Measure:
FC X Complexity Multiplier   =   _____

Figure B.2   SPR metric analysis reference card. Sheet 2.

Example of a Fully Measured Software Project

Introduction

The volume of useful information that can be collected about a software project is roughly in the same league with the volume of information collected about a patient who is undergoing a thorough medical examination. In the course of the latter, the patient will provide some of the information, such as a medical history; various diagnostic laboratories and equipment will provide some of the information, such as the results of blood tests; and the examining physicians will provide some of the information. The total volume of information in a full medical examination can exceed 200 pages.

In software projects, the term "full measurement" also includes multiple sources of information. The project manager provides some of the information; the project staff provides some; tracking tools and accounting systems provide some; quality assurance provides some; and the users themselves provide some. Here too the full volume of information can exceed 200 pages. However, that much data is difficult to utilize conveniently, so it is normal to both condense it and to select key highlights, such as factors by which the project was either well ahead in terms of technology, or perhaps somewhat behind. The purpose of measuring a software project in considerable detail is twofold, and it is very similar to the purpose of medical records:

1. Accurate measurements can be used as early warnings to head off problems.

2. Accurate measurement can be turned into powerful "templates" for estimating future projects.

Three kinds of information must be recorded if software project measurements are to actually be useful:

1. Hard data
2. Soft data
3. Normalized data

The hard data consists of the quantified facts about a project that can be measured with high precision and low ambiguity. Examples of hard data include the schedules of each task performed, the staffing required, the effort expended, the money expended, and the sizes of key deliverables such as specifications, source code, and test cases. The soft data consists of the facts about a project or its staff wherein subjective human opinions come into play. For examples of soft data, consider the clarity or ambiguity of the requirements, the usefulness of the tools and methods, the skills of the staff, the cooperation of the users, and the adequacy of the office space. The normalized data consists of selected hard-data elements converted into a standard metric for comparative purposes. For examples of normalized data, consider "cost per function point," "function points per staff-hour," and "cost per KLOC."

The following sample report of a fully measured project includes all three kinds of data. The data itself is taken from several actual projects, but it is melded together and rounded to ensure confidentiality of the sources of the information. Although the volume of data is large, the effort to fully measure a software project is not excessive. In round numbers, about 25 staff-hours is required. This is not a significant amount in a project such as the example, which totaled over 110 person-months of effort and more than 15 calendar months of time. Indeed, the effort devoted to this project's measurement is only slightly more than 0.1 percent.

Context and Background of the Example

The sample project is hypothetical, but it is based on a classic MIS application: a payroll program for exempt and hourly workers. The example application is written in Cobol on an IBM AS/400. The size of the application is about 35,000 new Cobol statements and 5000 reused ones for common processing functions, bringing the total size to 40,000 statements in all. In terms of function points, the overall size is 319.

The project is new rather than an enhancement. The scope of the project is that of a small system consisting of several linked components. The class is that of an internal project for use at a single location. The type is hybrid, being partly a batch application and partly an on-line database application using CICS.

The experience level of the staff for this kind of application is fairly high, and the staff is very experienced in the Cobol language, the hardware environment, and the software environment. The users themselves are also fairly experienced, and they are active participants during early JAD sessions as well as later. User time as well as development time should be recorded for completeness.

It might be of interest to illustrate two salient features of this measured project, since such information is seldom available: (1) the overall distribution of effort among the key tasks of the project when it is first developed and (2) the lifetime distribution of effort for both the initial release and 10 years of maintenance and enhancement. Table C.1 shows the distribution of normal paid project effort among the key tasks.

Table C.1 shows a fairly average distribution for MIS projects of this size. Note that the paperwork cost actually exceeds the cost of any other element. However, paperwork, coding, and testing are all significant in their contribution to the project totals.

Table C.2 shows information that is even rarer: the lifetime total effort for a project including the initial release, 10 years of maintenance (defect repairs), and 10 years of enhancements (adding new features). In this case, the postrelease maintenance and enhancement costs are estimated and included to show the overall relative proportions. These proportions, however, are about average for MIS projects such as the example.

TABLE C.1 Distribution of Project Effort among Key Tasks

Major task groups	Person-months of effort	Proportion, %
Paperwork-related effort (specification, user documents, etc.)	39	35
Code-related effort (coding, desk checking)	28	25
Testing-related effort (all test steps from unit to system test)	27	24
Management-related effort (first-line management only)	14	12
Miscellaneous activities meetings, presentations, etc.)	5	4
Total	113	100

TABLE C.2 Lifetime Distribution of Effort for Initial Development and
10 Years of Maintenance and Project Enhancement

Lifetime activity	Person-months of effort	Proportion, %
Initial development	113.0	25.5
User involvement	19.0	4.3
10 years of maintenance	65.0	14.7
10 years of enhancement	245.5	55.5
Total	442.5	100.0

Measurement Tool Used

The data was collected by using Release 1.1.C of the commercial
CHECKPOINT® integrated measurement and estimation tool developed by Software Productivity Research. The tool operates in both
measurement and estimation mode, and both modes were used to
produce the following reports. The measurement mode was used for
development data and the recording of project soft factors, and the estimating mode was used to predict the 10-year maintenance and enhancement data.

Contents of the Measurement Example

The example is divided into two main sections: (1) the input data provided by the project manager and staff and (2) the output reports and
normalized data produced by the measurement tool.

One of the conveniences offered by such tools is the automatic conversion and normalization of hard data into useful metrics. For example, for a given task such as requirements it is only necessary for the
user to enter raw data on the staff, effort, schedule, and deliverable
outputs. The tool itself will add the requirements data to the overall
project totals and convert the data into normalized results such as requirements pages per function point and requirements cost per function point.

The input section of the measured
project report

The input section shows the actual kinds of information supplied by
the project managers and staff, and it includes these major topics:

1. Basic identity and security levels of the project.

2. Nature, scope, class, and type information for the project (i.e., is

the project new or an enhancement, a small program or a large system, internal or external, batch or on-line, and so forth).

3. Goals or constraints levied against the project by higher management or user demands.

4. Work-hour and staff availability profiles.

5. Occupation groups and specialists needed.

6. Answers to any of the multiple-choice questions that define the tools, methods, experience, and environment for the project. (Not every question need be answered, but the more that are answered the more complete the historical data for future reference.)

7. Size information in the form preferred by the project manager or by company policy. Size can be expressed in function points, feature points, or lines of source code and in any language or combination of languages.

8. Information on the specific computers, operating systems, and support software used; also information on specific tools and methods used such as "Yourdon design method" or "Method/1."

9. Free-form commentary text in the form of notes attached to any input item to provide additional information over and above that provided by the multiple-choice questions.

10. Additional remarks on any special events or unique factors that might have impacted the project outcome, such as "the development laboratory was relocated due to earthquake damage."

**The output sections of the measured
project report**

For this book, only the major output reports have been selected in order to conserve space and highlight the major results of the project. The output reports include:

1. A summary total for the project that includes development of the initial release, user effort, maintenance (defect repairs) for 10 years, and enhancements (adding features) for 10 years.

2. Detailed task-by-task information showing the resources and schedule for each task performed, which in this case consisted of 13 tasks out of the set of 25 possible tasks that could be measured by the tool utilized.

3. Normalized data for each task showing task performance in terms of both function points and source lines. (The sample project had a

net development productivity rate of 2.82 function points, or 337.52 source lines, per staff-month.)

4. Defect and quality data which is shown here in summary form to conserve space. (The project had a total defect quantity of 1400 bugs of all levels of severity. A total of 943, or 59.43 percent, was removed prior to delivery, although there were 111 bad fixes or fresh bugs added back in. The total quantity of bugs found by users was 568.)

5. Detailed task-by-task information showing the user resources and schedule for each task performed, which in this case consisted of three tasks out of the set of five common user tasks.

6. Maintenance effort and costs for up to 10 years after the initial release of the project. (*Note:* This is estimated data, since the project is new.)

7. Enhancement effort and costs, plus the growth in size of the project, for up to 10 years after the initial release. (*Note:* this is estimated data, since the project is new.)

8. The identified strengths and weaknesses that impacted costs, effort, quality, and productivity. A "strength" is defined as a factor in respect to which the project performed better than U.S. averages based on the SPR 5-point rating scale. A "weakness" is defined as a factor in respect to which the project performed worse than U.S. averages based on the same 5-point rating scale.

9. Printed notes, which were recorded during the measurement process. (When the tool is actually used with a computer, the notes are associated with specific factors they comment on and are displayed as optional windows.)

10. The page counts for the documents actually produced out of the total of 56 different possible documents which the tool can record.

Outputs excluded from the example.   In order to conserve space and concentrate on normal project measurements, a variety of additional factors which might be recorded or estimated were deliberately omitted from this example. Some of the omitted outputs include:

1. Project assessment against U.S. norms for similar projects.

2. Specific defect removal efficiencies for each review, inspection, and test actually utilized. (Summary information was provided to conserve space.)

3. Alternative scenarios of what the project might have been like had different languages or technologies been utilized.

Summary of and Conclusions about Software Project Measurement

The volume of data that can and should be recorded on software projects is roughly equivalent to the volume of medical information that can and should be recorded about patients undergoing full physical examinations. In both cases, the information can be used to avoid serious problems by identifying them before they become serious. The data can also be used for future estimates and long-range diagnostic studies.

This kind of information about all or a significant sample of projects within an enterprise makes it possible to carry out a new and powerful kind of analysis. When large collections of soft and hard data are analyzed statistically, it becomes possible to identify strengths and weaknesses that affect not only individual projects but also departments, laboratories, divisions, companies, and eventually entire industries.

Measurement Input Section

The data in the following section is typical of the kinds of information provided by the project manager and the technical staff of the project.

Project identity.   The basic identity of the project is established by recording both the project name and also a set of standard facts about the project. In this case, the project has these attributes:

- Its "nature" is that of a new project, rather than an enhancement.
- Its "scope" is that of a system comprised of several programs, rather than a single program.
- Its "class" is internal, and the project was intended for use at a single location rather than as a distributed application.
- Its "type" is hybrid; it consists of both on-line and batch components.
- Its "goal" as assigned by senior management was "to complete the project in the shortest possible time."

Project occupation groups

With about 40 different kinds of specialists to choose from, it is significant to record the kinds of staff that worked on the project. This is different from simply recording hours, since the goal is to identify any special skills that might have been utilized. For the project included here, a comparatively ordinary MIS project, the kinds of occupation groups used for development included:

Project management

Systems analysts

Application programmers

Database administrators

Tool specialists

Management consultant

The kinds of occupation groups identified for maintenance included:

Project management

Maintenance programmers

Customer support specialists

Staff availability and work patterns

It is very important to record whether or not the staff members on a project could devote their full time to the project, or were dividing their time among several projects. It is also very important to record the basic work-hour pattern that was applied. For the project shown here, the accounting day was the normal U.S. 8-h day. Only an average of 6 h/day was applied to the project, but there was an average of 1 h/day of unpaid overtime by the project staff. Unpaid overtime is a weak link in most project-tracking systems, and this kind of data requires actual interviews with the staff to explore how much unpaid time was really applied.

Complexity, functionality, and reusability

Several topics are closely interrelated and should be considered together: The overall complexity of the problems, code, and data structure for the project should be recorded. The function point totals should be recorded, assuming that the project uses function points. Finally, and perhaps the most difficult, the amount of reusable code should be noted.

For the project shown here, some 4850 Cobol statements were estimated to be reused by the project team, and that amounted to about 48 function points. The pattern for the reused code also should be noted. In this case, the purposes of the reused code included, among others:

Date and calendar management

Report formatting

Printer control

Screen formats

Skill and environmental factors— The soft data

It is very important to record data on the skills, tools, methods, and environment that affected the project in a way that lends itself to statistical analysis. This requirement rules out straight text, and it implies some kind of a coding scheme. Since this project was measured by using the CHECKPOINT® tool, it should be recalled that its encoding scheme is a 5-point scale set up in general as follows:

1   Much better than U.S. norms
2   Better than U.S. norms
3   Approximately at the U.S. average level
4   Worse than U.S. norms
5   Much worse than U.S. norms

There are more than two hundred soft questions that can be answered by using the 5-point scale. That allows a number of interesting conclusions to be drawn via multiple-regression techniques. The sets of major soft-data factors that should be measured include:

Staff experience with tools and methods

User experience and participation during the project

Usefulness of tools and methods

Stability of requirements

Convenience or inconvenience of the physical office arrangement

Organization structures used on the project

Descriptive materials and remarks

It is not possible to record all significant information by using only multiple-choice questions. Therefore, project measurement and management tools should also include the ability to accept textual information in several forms:

- Names of specific vendors, tools, and people associated with the project
- Notes on random but important topics, e.g., the disruption caused by a physical event such as the California earthquake

Measurement Output Section

The inputs to a project measurement system are organized for convenience in collecting the data. The outputs, on the other hand, should be organized to make the insights and information from measurement clear and easy to grasp. The outputs shown here begin with the hard numerical information about the project and then give the supporting information derived from the soft factors in later sections.

Summary of total project effort, staffing, schedules, and costs

Since the first thing that senior management often asks for is the "bottom line" of a project, the first item reported is the overall cost, effort, and staffing for these major elements:

Development

User involvement

Maintenance (defect repairs)

Enhancements

This summary information is followed by other quick looks at important factors, such as quality and defect removal, all intended to give an overall view of the project from a high-level vantage point.

Detailed breakdowns of effort, staffing, schedules, and costs by activity

Although the summary presentation condenses information for executive purposes, the follow-on data should be quite granular. The schedule, effort, staff, and cost information should be recorded by activity. In the project shown here that means that 13 out of the 25 possible activities were performed and so had data collected for them.

When the data is recorded by using a software tool, derivative forms of information can be provided automatically. For example, the percentages of project effort and percentages of project schedule which each activity required can be automatically calculated.

Templates for using historical data in estimating. One of the most important of all applications for measured historical data is using the information to estimate future projects. In spite of the widespread desirability of this function, exactly what information should be used has been uncertain. The essence of converting historical data into estimating templates requires knowledge of four things:

1. The nature of the primary deliverable from each activity or task

2. The sizes of the deliverables in terms of "natural" units such as the page counts of specifications and the number of test cases

3. The "assignment scopes," or the amounts of each deliverable which on the average is assigned to one staff member

4. The "production rates," or the amounts of each deliverable which one person actually produced in an hour, day, week, month, or year

With automatic measurement tools such as CHECKPOINT®, templates are a standard output.

Normalized data in function point, feature point, or lines of code

For purposes of comparison with other projects or with industry norms, it is necessary to convert the raw data into a standard metric. Although function points have started to replace lines of code for this purpose, both forms are widely utilized. With a software measurement tool, it is easy to have the data converted into either metric or, as shown here, into both metrics in a side-by-side form.

Defect and quality data

Since one of the most expensive tasks in all of software engineering history is the cost of finding and fixing bugs, it is quite desirable to record the number, origins, and severities of the bugs and the amount of effort required to find and fix them.

Documentation data

Since paperwork in all its forms (plans, requirements, specifications, user documents, and so on) is often much more expensive than coding, it is desirable to measure the sets of actual documents produced, their sizes, and the effort associated with their production. When computerized measurement software is used, some additional calculations that can be performed are interesting. For example, since ordinary typed pages contain an average of perhaps 500 words, it is easily possible to calculate the number of words produced in support of a software project.

User effort data

In MIS projects such as the example shown here, the users of the projects are often active participants. Users are almost always participants during requirements and frequently during prototyping. They take part in reviews, and in many cases users or staff personnel in the user organization will produce the final user documentation. They can have heavy involvement in acceptance testing, and in some cases they also participate in project management. Since they are not part of the development organization, the time and effort they devote to projects is seldom recorded. However, that is not as it should be. For purposes of both historical accuracy and economic validity, user cost should be recorded. With computerized measurement software, it is possible to record user effort separately and then add that effort to the overall project.

Maintenance and enhancement data

Project measurements should not, of course, stop with the first release of a new software project. It is desirable to continue the project cost accounting on a month-by-month or year-by-year basis for as long as the software is in production. The example shown here includes 10 years of maintenance and enhancements costs. Since the project used was new, the costs were estimated rather than measured, but as time passed, the estimated values would gradually be replaced by historical data.

It is significant for companies that do business with the Department of Defense that, as of 1990, estimating tools are being asked to produce 20-year estimates of maintenance and enhancements. No one, least of all developers of estimating tools, actually believes that 20-year predictions will be accurate. Nonetheless, this kind of long-range information can certainly be produced.

It should be noted that "maintenance" as used here means defect repairs. Adding new features and meeting new requirements is defined as "enhancements." The dichotomy is more accurate from an accounting standpoint and also makes it easier to separate the widely differing productivity rates.

It should be noted again that software projects, like all physical systems, are subject to entropy. Entropy is, of course, a gradual increase in disorder over time. For software, each change made to the existing system will slightly degrade its original structure. Over long periods of time, these slight degradations in structure tend to accumulate until the system can ultimately become unmaintainable. Corrective actions, such as restructuring and reengineering are possible. However, unless deliberate action is taken, the long-term growth in system complexity will go up, and that will reduce both the assignment scopes and production rates of future updates. Thus, if a given update required 1 person-month in 1990, by 1995 the complexity of the system might have increased so much that the same update would take 5 person-weeks. By 2000, the same update might require 2 person-months. One of the most useful by-products of long-range historical measurements, as an aid in planning corrective actions, is the ability to calculate the rates at which systems decay.

Project strengths and weaknesses

One of the convenient features of computerized measurement tools is the ability to carry out complex tasks that make it easy to gain insights into why projects are better or worse than expected. Since the soft environmental factors were recorded by using a 5-point scale with 1 and 2 being better and 4 and 5 being worse than U.S. averages, it is easy to separate a project's strengths from its weaknesses. In the example given here, strengths are defined as factors averaging 2.5 or less and weaknesses as factors averaging 3.5 or higher. The zone from 2.5 to 3.5 is the approximate U.S. average, and it can be presumed to not have a significant outcome on the project in question.

Not every environmental factor influences every aspect of a project. With expert systems, it is easy to pick out the soft environmental factors that influence project characteristics significant to managers.

There is a rough equivalence between the SPR strength and weakness averages and the SEI maturity levels, as shown in the following table.

SPR average	Rating	SEI maturity level	
1.00 to 1.99	Excellent	5	Optimizing
2.00 to 2.49	Good	4	Managed
2.50 to 3.49	Average	3	Defined
3.50 to 3.99	Below average	2	Repeatable
4.00 to 5.00	Deficient	1	Initial

Notes and comments

Obviously, not every point of significance can be reduced to a multiple-choice question and a 5-point scale. Computerized measurement systems also provide the ability to record miscellaneous comments about whatever seems important to the staff or management.

Paperwork volumes

Not all projects produce the same set of written materials. It is desirable to record which specific documents were actually produced and compare that to an overall list of document types. In the example given here, 24 discrete kinds of documents were produced out of the set of 56 total possible kinds of documents.

Security Level: NONE   Date: 5/15/90
                                                            Time: 7:50:27

Project: DEMO2   Scenario: MEASURED MIS SAMPLE
Location: BOSTON, MASSACHUSETTS

CHECKPOINT(tm) REPORT

```
┌─────────────────────────────────────────────┐
│                                             │
│          MIS EXAMPLE                        │
│                                             │
└─────────────────────────────────────────────┘
```

Contents: Input Summary

Security Level: NONE   Page 1

Project: DEMO2   Scenario: MEASURED MIS SAMPLE
Location: BOSTON, MASSACHUSETTS

Security Level: NONE

Organization: ABC CORPORATION

SIC Code: 123

Location: BOSTON, MASSACHUSETTS

Project: DEMO2

Scenario: MEASURED MIS SAMPLE

Manager: J. DOE

Estimator: CAPERS JONES

Consultant: CAPERS JONES

Current Date: 05/15/90

Project Start: 05/15/90

Project Delivery: 10/06/91

Project: DEMO2   Scenario: MEASURED MIS SAMPLE
Location: BOSTON, MASSACHUSETTS

PROJECT TYPE AND PROJECT CLASSIFICATION

    Project Nature: 1
       New program development

    Project Scope : 7
       System: Multiple linked programs or components

    Project Class : 4
       Internal program, for use at a single location

    Project Type : 14
       Hybrid project: Multiple types

          Primary Type : 5
             Interactive data base applications program
          Secondary Type: 4
             Batch data base applications program
          Hybrid Type   : 5.25

    Current project phase: 1
       Planning or proposal

PROJECT GOALS AND CONSTRAINTS

    Project goals: 2
       Find the shortest development schedule with extra staff

PROJECT OCCUPATION GROUP CONSTRAINTS

Development Staff Salaries

	Average Salary	Average Staff	Maximum Staff
Project managers	5,500	1.00	1.00
Systems analysis	5,200	5.00	7.00
Applications programmers	5,000	8.00	9.00
Database administrators	5,000	1.00	1.00
Overall Development Staff	5,100	15.00	18.00

Project: DEMO2   Scenario: MEASURED MIS SAMPLE
Location: BOSTON, MASSACHUSETTS

Maintenance Staff

	Average Salary	Average Staff	Maximum Staff
Project managers	5,500	1.00	1.00
Customer support specialists	4,500	1.00	1.00
Maintenance programmers	5,000	1.00	1.00
Overall Maintenance Staff	5,000	3.00	3.00

Specialist Staff

	Average Salary	Average Staff	Maximum Staff
Tool/Support specialists	5,200	1.00	1.00
Overall Specialists Staff	5,200	1.00	1.00

External Consultant Staff

	Average Salary	Average Staff	Maximum Staff
Management consultants	8,000	1.00	1.00
Overall Ext. Consultant Staff	8,000	1.00	1.00

PROJECT STAFF AVAILABILITY

    Development contract personnel: --%

    Maintenance contract personnel: --%

    Development staff availability: 100%

    Maintenance staff availability: 100%

    Overtime premium rate: 150%

    Average annual inflation rate: 10%

Project: DEMO2   Scenario: MEASURED MIS SAMPLE
Location: BOSTON, MASSACHUSETTS

	Hours per day	Hours per week	Days per year
Accounting	8.00	40.00	220.00
Productive Work	6.00	30.00	210.00
Overtime (all)	1.00	5.00	10.00

Unpaid Overtime

    Development: 100%
    Maintenance: 100%

ADDITIONAL PROJECT COSTS

    Project Capital Equipment Costs: $ 25,000

    Travel Costs: $ 10,000

    Other Project Costs: $ 5,000

PROGRAM COMPLEXITY VARIABLES

    Problem Complexity

       New Code: 4.00
          Some difficult or complex calculations.

    Code Complexity

       New Code: 3.50
          Well structured (small modules and simple paths).
          Fair structure, but some complex paths or modules.

    Data Complexity

       New Code: 3.50
          Multiple files, switches, and data interactions.
          Complex data elements and complex data interactions.

    Complexity

       New Code: 32.0

Project: DEMO2   Scenario: MEASURED MIS SAMPLE
Location: BOSTON, MASSACHUSETTS

SOURCE CODE LANGUAGES

New Code Langauge   COBOL   Level   3.00

Reusable Code Language   COBOL   Level   3.00

FUNCTION POINT ANALYSIS

New and reused code

Inputs	8 X	4 =	32
Outputs	12 X	5 =	60
Inquiries	15 X	4 =	60
Data files	10 X	10 =	100
Interfaces	2 X	7 =	14

                        Raw Total :   266

                        Adjustment :   1.20

                        Net Total :   319

        Percentage Reused :   15.00 %

SOURCE CODE SIZE

	Estimated KLOC	Projected KLOC	Function Points
New Code	33.28	33.28	271.32
Reused code	4.85	4.85	47.88
	38.13	38.13	319.20

Project: DEMO2   Scenario: MEASURED MIS SAMPLE
Location: BOSTON, MASSACHUSETTS

REUSABLE CODE PURPOSES

    Values range from 1 (All reused code) to 5 (no reused code)

Date and calender management	1.00
Mathematical formulae or equations	4.00
Error checking	3.00
Data and file management	1.00
General screen management	2.00
Print and output formatting	1.00
Printer and device drivers	1.00
Communications protocols	2.00

STAFF AND USER PERSONNEL EXPERIENCE

Development personnel application experience	2.50
Majority of experts, but some new hires or novices.	
Even mixture of experts, new hires, and novices.	
Development personnel tool and method experience	2.00
Majority of experts in the tools and methods.	
Development personnel analysis and design experience	3.00
Even mixture of experts, new hires, and novices.	
Development personnel programming language experience	1.00
All experts in the language(s) used for the project.	
Development hardware experience	1.00
All experts in the hardware used for the project.	
Pre-test defect removal experience	3.50
Even mixture of experienced and inexperienced personnel.	
Most personnel inexperienced in Reviews/Inspections.	
Testing defect removal experience	3.00
Even mixture of experienced and inexperienced personnel.	
User personnel experience with software projects	2.00
All or a majority of users have software experience.	
User personnel experience with application type	2.00
All or a strong majority of users are experts.	
User involvement during requirements	2.00
Users are heavily involved during requirements/design.	

MANAGEMENT AND PROJECT PERSONNEL VARIABLES

Legal and statutory impacts	1.00
No known legal or statutory constraints.	
Project organization structure	3.00
Conventional departments, with hierarchical organization.	
Project team morale	3.00
Normal project morale and enthusiasm.	

Project: DEMO2   Scenario: MEASURED MIS SAMPLE
Location: BOSTON, MASSACHUSETTS

Project managerial and technical cohesiveness   3.00
    Some disagreement on project goals, schedules, methods.
System development methodology   3.50
    Manual and effective system development methodology.
    Manual and cumbersome system development methodology.
Productivity measurements   4.00
    Manual and partial lifecycle productivity measures.
Tools, Equipment, and Supplies   3.00
    Tools and equipment for project already in use.

MAINTENANCE PROJECT AND PERSONNEL VARIABLES

Software warranty coverage   1.00
    No explicit or implicit warranties on software.
Customer support   3.00
    Informal telephone support; normal write-in support.
Delivery support   3.00
    On-site support for early customers.
Central maintenance   3.00
    Informal defect repairs and update distribution.
Field maintenance   1.00
    No field maintenance for project.
Maintenance personnel staffing   4.00
    Most maintenance done by development personnel.
Maintenance personnel class   3.00
    Even mixture of experts, new hires, and novices.
Maintenance personnel education   5.00
    Little or no training in projects or tools.
Maintenance computing support   3.00
    Computer support is usually adequate and effective.
Replacement and restructure planning   2.00
    Automated code analysis and restructuring tools.
Long range program stability   3.00
    New functions, data types, and hardware may occur.
Program execution frequency   2.00
    Monthly or weekly runs.
Installation and production geography   1.00
    Single production site, in a single city.

Restructure interval (years)   --
Annual new and changed code percent   10.00
Annual deleted code percent   2.50

Number of system installation sites   1
Annual growth rate of installation sites   --
Number of system maintenance sites   1
Anticipated years of system useful life   10

Project: DEMO2   Scenario: MEASURED MIS SAMPLE
Location: BOSTON, MASSACHUSETTS

ENVIRONMENTAL VARIABLES AND CASE TOOLS

```
Individual office environment                                4.00
   Less than 60 square feet of enclosed space per worker.
Office noise and interruption environment                    4.00
   Some background noise and frequent interruptions.
Workstation environment                                      2.00
   Shared workstations (Two employees per workstation).
Requirements environment                                     2.00
   JAD methodology or very clear user requirements.
Protyping environment                                        5.00
   No prototyping at all.
Analysis environment                                         3.00
   Informal or partial data and function analysis.
Design automation environment                                4.00
   Semi-formal design with text automation only.
Project novelty                                              3.00
   Even mixture of repeated and new features.
Hardware novelty                                             1.00
   All hardware is familiar and well understood by staff.
Support software novelty                                     2.00
   Most support software is familiar and well understood.
Support software effectiveness environment                   2.00
   Most support tools and software are effective.
Development computing support environment                    3.00
   Computer support is usually adequate and effective.
Hardware stability environment                               2.00
   Single vendor hardware with moderate compatibility.
Response time environment                                    3.00
   One to five second response time is the norm.
Data administration environment                              4.00
   Partial data dictionary available.
Project Library environment,                                 4.00
   Manual source code and documentation control.
User and external document production environment            4.00
   Text automation; manual graphics support.
Product performance or execution speed environment           2.00
   Minor performance or execution speed restrictions.
Product memory utilization environment                       1.00
   No memory utilization restrictions.
Reusability environment                                      3.00
   Moderate usage of reusable code.    [> 25%]
Development geography                                        2.00
   Multiple development departments within same site.
```

Number of development locations: 1.00

Project: DEMO2   Scenario: MEASURED MIS SAMPLE
Location: BOSTON, MASSACHUSETTS

DEFECT REMOVAL TOOLS AND FUNCTIONS

Pre-test defect removal support	4.00
Limited training for reviews and inspections.	
Pre-test defect removal scheduling	3.00
Satisfactory time for preparation and sessions.	
Pre-test defect removal facilities	4.00
Very limited availability of facilities for reviews	
Program debugging tools	1.00
Full screen editor, traces, cross-references, etc.	
Testing function	3.00
Formal testing with results compared to known criteria.	
Quality assurance function	5.00
No QA function exists for the project.	
Quality measurement database	5.00
No defect tracking.	

DEFECT REMOVAL ACTIVITIES

Values range from 1 (Excellent) to 5 (Poor)

Pre-Test Defect Removal
Joint application and design	2.00
Prototyping	3.00
Data structures and design review	3.00

Testing
Unit testing	3.00
New function testing	2.00
Regression testing	3.00
System testing	3.00
User acceptance testing	2.00

Post-Release Defect Removal
Automated restructuring	3.00

PROJECT DOCUMENTATION CONVENTIONS

Normal documentation preparation	2.00
End users of the software	
Normal documentation page format	1.00
Single column.	
Normal documentation type size	3.00
Ten point. [Equivalent to PICA type]	
Normal graphics production	3.00
Partially automated.	

Project: DEMO2   Scenario: MEASURED MIS SAMPLE
Location: BOSTON, MASSACHUSETTS

    Normal documentation output devices   3.00
      Text laser printing.
    Normal documentation preparation and updating   3.00
      Microcomputer word processing.
    Normal documentation distribution to team members   3.00
      Hard copy distribution to individual team members.
    Overall satisfaction with documentation methods   3.00
      Average documentation methods.

PROJECT VALUE ANALYSIS INPUTS

    Values range from 1 (very high impact) to 5 (low impact)

    Value to morale and human relations   2.00
    Value to enterprise prestige   2.00
    Value to enterprise operating costs   2.00
    Value to enterprise operating speed   2.00
    Impact on future or related projects   3.00

PROJECT RISKS ANALYSIS INPUTS

    Risks range from 1 (very low risk) to 5 (high risk)

    Risk of high project novelty   3.00
    Risk of unstable user requirements   3.00
    Risk of change in project architecture   3.00
    Risk of change in development hardware   2.00
    Risk of inadequate speed or memory compacity 1.00
    Risk of inadequate functionality   3.00
    Risk of poor quality and reliability   4.00
    Risk of significant usability problems   4.00
    Risk of significant schedule overruns   4.00
    Risk of significant cost overruns   4.00
    Risk of insufficient project staffing   2.00
    Risk of insufficient project skill levels   3.00
    Risk of excessive schedule pressure   4.00
    Risk of high staff turnover and attrition   3.00
    Risk of major management disagreements   2.00

Project: DEMO2   Scenario: MEASURED MIS SAMPLE
Location: BOSTON, MASSACHUSETTS

NET VALUE FACTORS OVER 10 YEARS (IN THOUSANDS OF DOLLARS)

```
        Year  1:        $ 25
        Year  2:          50
        Year  3:         100
        Year  4:         150
        Year  5:         250
        Year  6:         300
        Year  7:         350
        Year  8:         300
        Year  9:         200
        Year 10:         100
```

        Cost of capital: 10.00 %

ANTICIPATED DOLLAR VALUES FROM FIVE YEARS OF PRODUCTION

        Five-year operating costs reduction $ 575,000

        Five-year total anticipated value $ 575,000

DESCRIPTIVE MATERIALS AND COMMENTS

        Development computer(s): IBM AS 400

        Production computer(s): IBM AS 400

        Development operating system(s): IBM DOS

        Production operating system(s): IBM DOS

        Data base: IBM CICS

        Data dictionary: IBM DATA DICTIONARY

        Data communication: IBM DC

        Management methods/tools: SPQR/20, CHECKPOINT, PROJ MGT WORKBENCH

        Requirements methods/tools: JAD

        Design methods/tools: NO FORMAL TOOLS

        Coding methods/tools: STRUCTURED COBOL

Project: DEMO2   Scenario: MEASURED MIS SAMPLE
Location: BOSTON, MASSACHUSETTS

Test/debugging methods/tools: EXPEDITER

Documentation methods/tools: NORMAL WORD PROCESSING

Maintenance methods/tools: NO FORMAL TOOLS

Unusual events:
Water pipe in building burst during winter freeze and damaged
development AS 400. Repairs and replacement took 10 days.

Comments and additional explanations:
Normal project: two months late; 20% over budget.

SOURCE CODE COUNTING RULES

Multiple language counting	1.00
Each language is counted separately.*	
Source code termination	1.00
Delimiters.*	
Source code counting	2.00
Executable statements + data definitions.*	
Macro instruction and expansion counting	3.00
Macro instructions and unique expansions are counted.*	
Reusable code counting	2.00
Unique reusable modules are counted separately.*	
Program and application generator counting	3.00
Generator inputs and outputs are counted separately.*	
Job control language counting	1.00
Job control language is not counted.	
Changed code counting	2.00
Changed code is counted separately from new code.*	
Deleted code counting	1.00
Deleted code is not counted.	
Scaffold code counting	1.00
Scaffold code is not counted.	
Support code counting	1.00
Support code is not counted.	
Test code counting	1.00
Test case code is not counted.	

* Software Productivity Research Counting Rules

Security Level: NONE

Date: 5/14/90
Time: 4:12:43

Project: DEMO   Scenario: MEASURED MIS SAMPLE
Location: BOSTON, MASSACHUSETTS

CHECKPOINT(tm) REPORT

```
┌─────────────────────────────────────────┐
│                                         │
│    MIS EXAMPLE                          │
│                                         │
└─────────────────────────────────────────┘
```

Output Reports

Contents: Summary Totals
                 Development Totals
                 User Involvement Totals
                 Maintenance Totals
                 Enhancement Totals
                 Strength/weaknesses Analysis
                 Note Pads
                 Documentation Analysis
                 Risk/Value Analysis

Security Level: NONE   Page 1

Project: DEMO   Scenario: MEASURED MIS SAMPLE
Location: BOSTON, MASSACHUSETTS

Security Level: NONE

Organization: ABC CORPORATION

SIC Code: 123

Location: BOSTON, MASSACHUSETTS

Project: DEMO

Scenario: MEASURED MIS SAMPLE

Manager: J. DOE

Estimator: CAPERS JONES

Consultant: CAPERS JONES

Current Date: 05/15/90

Project Start: 05/15/90

Project Delivery: 10/06/91

Project: DEMO   Scenario: MEASURED MIS SAMPLE
Location: BOSTON, MASSACHUSETTS

TOTAL PROJECT COSTS

Development	$ 589.1
User Involvement	63.8
Maintenance	1,036.2
Enhancement	2,472.6∎
Subtotal	$ 4,161.7∎
Project Hiring and Relocation Costs	$ 0.0
Project Capital Equipment Costs	25.0
Project Travel Costs	10.0
Other Project Costs; Fees, Services	5.0
Total Project Cost in Thousands	$ 4,201.7∎

TOTAL PROJECT STAFFING AND EFFORT

	Staffing Headcount	Effort Months
Development	7.3	113.0
User Involvement	1.2	19.0
Maintenance	1.9	65.0
Enhancement	1.9∎	245.5∎
Total Project	3.1∎	442.4∎

Project: DEMO   Scenario: MEASURED MIS SAMPLE
Location: BOSTON, MASSACHUSETTS

PROJECT QUALITY AND RELIABILITY

    Quality

        Defect potentials   1,400

        - Defects removed   943■

        + Bad fixes   111■

                                 _____

        Delivered defects   568■

    Reliability

        Months to stabilization   7.5■ Months

        Mean hours to failure

            At delivery   4.0■ Hours

            At stabilization   67.5■ Hours

PROJECT PRODUCTIVITY

        Ratio   Dollars
                            _____

        Total Cost/F.P. $ 13,171.50■

        Total Cost/KLOC $ 110,194.26■

        Total Cost/defect $ 7,397.37■

        Ratio   Effort Months
                            _____

        Total Effort/F.P.   1.39■

        Total Effort/KLOC   11.60■

        Total Effort/defect   0.78■

Project: DEMO   Scenario: MEASURED MIS SAMPLE
Location: BOSTON, MASSACHUSETTS

PROJECT SCHEDULE

Development   15.42   Months

User Involvement   15.42   Months

Project: DEMO   Scenario: MEASURED MIS SAMPLE
Location: BOSTON, MASSACHUSETTS

DEVELOPMENT CHART OF ACCOUNTS

     13 Included

          1 Requirements
          5 Initial analysis and design
          6 Detail design and specifications
          8 Coding
          9 Reusable code acquisition
         14 Integration
         15 User documentation
         16 Unit testing
         17 Function testing
         19 Systems testing
         21 Acceptance testing
         24 Installation
         25 Development management

     12 Excluded

          2 Prototyping
          3 System architecture
          4 Project planning
          7 Design review and inspections
         10 Purchased application acquisition
         11 Code review and inspections
         12 Independent verification and validation
         13 Configuration control
         18 Integration testing
         20 Field testing
         22 Independent testing
         23 Quality assurance

Project: DEMO   Scenario: MEASURED MIS SAMPLE
Location: BOSTON, MASSACHUSETTS

DEVELOPMENT SCHEDULE, EFFORT, STAFF, COST

No	Activity	Schedule Months	Effort Months	Staff Size	Costs in $Thousands
1	Requirements	2.5	3.8	1.5	$ 18.3
5	Init analysis/design	1.9	3.8	2.0	18.6
6	Detail design/specs	4.0	24.0	6.0	122.4
8	Coding	4.5	31.5	7.0	160.6
9	Reusable code acquis.	1.0	0.2	0.2	1.0
14	Integration	6.0	3.0	0.5	15.3
15	User documentation	3.5	7.0	2.0	39.3
16	Unit testing	0.9	6.7	7.0	37.3
17	Function testing	3.0	9.0	3.0	50.5
19	Systems testing	2.0	6.0	3.0	33.7
21	Acceptance testing	1.5	4.5	3.0	24.1
24	Installation	1.0	1.0	1.0	5.4
25	Development management	15.4	12.6	0.8	62.6

		Schedule	Effort	Staff	Costs
	Total Development	31.9	113.0	7.3	$ 589.1
	Overlapped	15.4			
	Unpaid Effort		15.1		

GANTT CHART: DEVELOPMENT

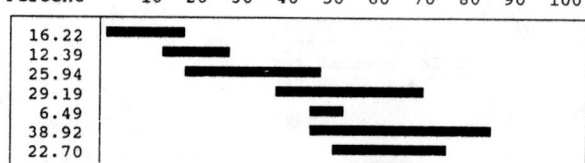

Activity	Percent	May15 90 ... Aug27 91
Requirements	16.22
Init analysis/design	12.39
Detail design/specs	25.94
Coding	29.19
Reusable code acquis.	6.49
Integration	38.92
User documentation	22.70
Unit testing	6.16
Function testing	19.46
Systems testing	12.97
Acceptance testing	9.73
Installation	6.49
Development management	100.00

Project: DEMO   Scenario: MEASURED MIS SAMPLE
Location: BOSTON, MASSACHUSETTS

DEVELOPMENT UNPAID OVERTIME

No	Activity	Paid Effort Months	Unpaid Effort Months	Total Effort Months
1	Requirements	3.6	0.2	3.8
5	Init analysis/design	3.7	0.2	3.8
6	Detail design/specs	20.4	3.6	24.0
8	Coding	26.8	4.7	31.5
9	Reusable code acquis.	0.2	0.0	0.2
14	Integration	2.7	0.3	3.0
15	User documentation	5.6	1.4	7.0
16	Unit testing	5.7	1.0	6.7
17	Function testing	7.2	1.8	9.0
19	Systems testing	4.8	1.2	6.0
21	Acceptance testing	4.3	0.2	4.5
24	Installation	1.0	0.0	1.0
25	Development management	12.1	0.5	12.6
	Total Development	97.9	15.1	113.0

DEVELOPMENT DELIVERABLES, SIZES, SCOPES AND PRODUCTION RATES

No	Activity	Primary Deliverable	Size of Deliverable	Assignment Scope	Production per Months
1	Requirements	Pages	100	66.67	26.67
5	Init analysis/design	Pages	100	50.00	26.18
6	Detail design/specs	Pages	250	41.67	10.42
8	Coding	Code Lines	35,000	5,000.00	1,111.11
9	Reusable code acquis.	Code Lines	5,000	25,000.00	25,000.00
14	Integration	Code Lines	45,000	90,000.00	15,000.00
15	User documentation	Pages	250	125.00	35.71
16	Unit testing	Test Cases	750	107.14	112.78
17	Function testing	Test Cases	300	100.00	33.33
19	Systems testing	Test Cases	300	100.00	50.00
21	Acceptance testing	Test Cases	50	16.67	11.11
24	Installation	Code Lines	45,000	45,000.00	45,000.00
25	Development management	Employees	7	8.00	0.52

Project: DEMO   Scenario: MEASURED MIS SAMPLE
Location: BOSTON, MASSACHUSETTS

DEVELOPMENT EFFORT AND SCHEDULE PERCENTAGES

No	Activity	Percent of Effort	Percent of Schedule
1	Requirements	3.32 %	16.22 %
5	Init analysis/design	3.38	12.39
6	Detail design/specs	21.24	25.94
8	Coding	27.88	29.19
9	Reusable code acquis.	0.18	6.49
14	Integration	2.66	38.92
15	User documentation	6.20	22.70
16	Unit testing	5.89	6.16
17	Function testing	7.97	19.46
19	Systems testing	5.31	12.97
21	Acceptance testing	3.98	9.73
24	Installation	0.89	6.49
25	Development management	11.11	100.00
	Total	100.00 %	306.65 %

Project: DEMO   Scenario: MEASURED MIS SAMPLE
Location: BOSTON, MASSACHUSETTS

DEVELOPMENT EFFORT PERCENTAGES GRAPH

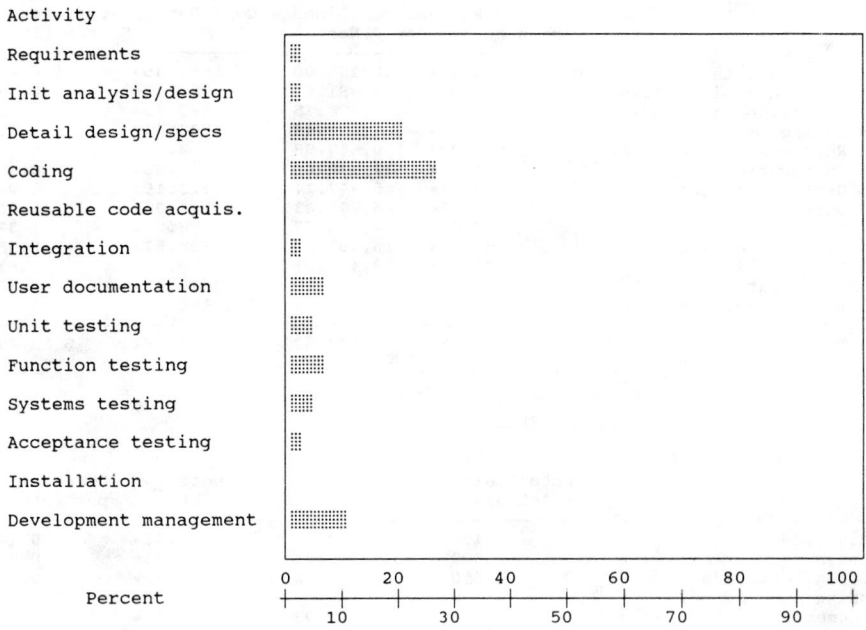

Activity
Requirements
Init analysis/design
Detail design/specs
Coding
Reusable code acquis.
Integration
User documentation
Unit testing
Function testing
Systems testing
Acceptance testing
Installation
Development management

```
            0       20       40       60       80      100
Percent     +---+----+----+----+----+----+----+----+----+
               10       30       50       70       90
```

Project: DEMO   Scenario: MEASURED MIS SAMPLE
Location: BOSTON, MASSACHUSETTS

DEVELOPMENT COST/EFFORT RATIOS

No	Activity	F. Pts Per Person Months	Source Lines Per P.Months	Cost Per F. Pt.	Cost Per Source Line
1	Requirements	85.07∎	10,168.00	$ 57.35∎	$ 0.48
5	Init analysis/design	83.51∎	9,981.67	58.42∎	0.49
6	Detail design/specs	13.29∎	1,588.75	383.70∎	3.21
8	Coding	10.13∎	1,210.48	503.61∎	4.21
9	Reusable code acquis.	1,595.00∎	190,649.98	3.06∎	0.03
14	Integration	106.33∎	12,710.00	47.96∎	0.40
15	User documentation	45.57∎	5,447.14	123.10∎	1.03
16	Unit testing	47.97∎	5,733.83	116.95∎	0.98
17	Function testing	35.44∎	4,236.67	158.28∎	1.32
19	Systems testing	53.17∎	6,355.00	105.52∎	0.88
21	Acceptance testing	70.89∎	8,473.33	75.70∎	0.63
24	Installation	319.00∎	38,130.00	16.82∎	0.14
25	Development management	25.41∎	3,037.64	196.21∎	1.64
	Total	2.82∎	337.52	$ 1,846.66∎	$ 15.45

DEVELOPMENT POTENTIAL/ACTUAL DEFECTS

Defect Origins	Potentials/ Actuals	Defects per KLOC	Defects per F.P.	Defects per Page
Requirements	100	2.62	0.31∎	0.14
Design	600	15.74	1.88∎	0.86
Coding: New code	550	14.42	1.72∎	0.79
Coding: Reused code	0	0.00	0.00∎	0.00
Documentation	150	3.93	0.47∎	0.21
Development totals	1,400	36.72	4.39∎	2.00

Project: DEMO   Scenario: MEASURED MIS SAMPLE
Location: BOSTON, MASSACHUSETTS

DEVELOPMENT DEFECT SEVERITIES

Severity: Effect	Number	Percent
1: System inoperable	126∎	9.0∎%
2: Major functions disabled or incorrect	350∎	25.0∎
3: Minor functions disabled or incorrect	630∎	45.0∎
4: Superficial error	294∎	21.0∎
Total Development	1,400	100.0∎%

DEVELOPMENT DEFECT REMOVAL EFFICIENCIES

	Require. Defects	Design Defects	Coding Defects	Document Defects	Total Defects
Defect Potential	100∎	600	550	150	1,400
- Removed	63∎	326∎	475∎	79∎	943∎
+ Bad fixes	3∎	38∎	57∎	13∎	111∎
Delivered defects	40∎	312∎	132∎	84∎	568∎
Removal efficiencies	60.00∎	48.00∎	76.00∎	44.00∎	59.43∎
Removed per KLOC	1.57∎	7.55∎	10.96∎	1.73∎	21.82∎
Removed per F.P.	0.19∎	0.90∎	1.31∎	0.21∎	2.61∎

Project: DEMO   Scenario: MEASURED MIS SAMPLE
Location: BOSTON, MASSACHUSETTS

DEVELOPMENT DEFECT REMOVAL EFFORT/COSTS

	Effort in Person Months	Cost in $Thousands
Preparation	4.01▪	45.5▪
Execution	9.67▪	78.4▪
Defect repairs	24.22▪	95.6▪
Total	37.90▪	219.4▪
per F.P.	0.12▪	0.69▪
per KLOC	0.99▪	5.75▪
per defect	0.04▪	0.23▪

DELIVERED DEFECT SEVERITIES

Severity: Effect	Number	Percent
1: System inoperable	44▪	7.7▪%
2: Major functions disabled or incorrect	132▪	23.2▪
3: Minor functions disabled or incorrect	274▪	48.3▪
4: Superficial error	118▪	20.9▪
Total Delivered	568▪	100.0▪%

Project: DEMO   Scenario: MEASURED MIS SAMPLE
Location: BOSTON, MASSACHUSETTS

DEVELOPMENT TESTING SUMMARY

Development Test Activity	Test Cases Count	Test Cases per F.P.	Test Cases per KLOC
Unit Testing	750	2.35■	19.67
Function Testing	300	0.94■	7.87
Integration Testing	0	0.00■	0.00
System Testing	300	0.94■	7.87
Field Testing	0	0.00■	0.00
Acceptance Testing	50	0.16■	1.31
Independent Testing	0	0.00■	0.00
Total Testing	1,400	4.39■	36.72

Percent of Development Costs for Testing: 24.72 %

DEVELOPMENT DOCUMENTATION

Document Types	Pages Per F.P.	Pages Per KLOC	Words Per F.P.	Words Per KLOC
Requirements	0.31■	2.62	172.41■	1,442.43■
Architecture	0.00■	0.00	0.00■	0.00■
Plans	0.00■	0.00	0.00■	0.00■
Design	1.10■	9.18	548.59■	4,589.56■
User Documents	0.78■	6.56	431.03■	3,606.08■
Total	2.19■	18.36	1,152.04■	9,638.08■

Diagrams	155■
Total Pages	700
Total Words	367,500■
Diagrams per 1000 Words	0.42■
Words per Page	525.00■
Total Words per Source Line	9.64■

Percent of Development Costs for Paperwork: 33.71 %

Project: DEMO   Scenario: MEASURED MIS SAMPLE
Location: BOSTON, MASSACHUSETTS

DEVELOPMENT STAFFING BY MONTH FOR UP TO TEN YEARS

Yr	Jan	Feb	Mar	Apr	May	Jun	Jul	Aug	Sep	Oct	Nov	Dec
90	0	0	0	0	1	3	4	7	8	7	12	11
91	11	15	17	6	6	5	6	5	0	0	0	0

PERCENT OF DEVELOPMENT COST

Percent of Development costs for Paperwork	33.71
Percent of Development costs for Quality Assurance	0.00
Percent of Development costs for Reviews/Inspections	0.00
Percent of Development costs for Testing	24.72
Percent of Development costs for Coding	27.44
Percent of Development costs for Management	10.63
Percent of Development costs for other activities	3.51
	100.00 %

OUTPUT RATIOS

Development Activities	Source Lines per Month		F.Pts. per Month	
	w/o Reused	with Reused	w/o Reused	with Reused
Excluding Upaid OT				
All Development	339.88	389.41	2.77▪	3.26▪
Coding	1,242.95	1,424.09	10.13▪	11.91▪
Including Unpaid OT				
All Development	294.58	337.52	2.40▪	2.82▪
Coding	1,056.51	1,210.48	8.61▪	10.13▪

Pages produced per calendar month	2.48
Average staff per calendar month	7.33
Money spent per calendar month	$ 38.21

Project: DEMO   Scenario: MEASURED MIS SAMPLE
Location: BOSTON, MASSACHUSETTS

HEADCOUNT RATIOS

Activities	per Employee	per Programmer
New Function Pts.	37.00■	38.74■
Reused Function Pts.	6.53■	6.84■
New Source code	4,541.76	4,754.29
Reused Source code	661.89	692.86
Document pages	95.53	100.00
Potential defects	191.06	200.00
Test cases	191.06	200.00

Project: DEMO   Scenario: MEASURED MIS SAMPLE
Location: BOSTON, MASSACHUSETTS

USER INVOLVEMENT CHART OF ACCOUNTS

        3 Included

            1 User Requirements
            4 User Documentation
            5 User Acceptance Testing

        2 Excluded

            2 User Prototyping
            3 User Design/Reviews and Inspections

USER INVOLVEMENT SCHEDULE, EFFORT, STAFF, COST

No	Activity	Schedule Months	Effort Months	Staff Size	Costs in $Thousands
1	User Requirements	1.0	2.0	2.0	$ 9.8
4	User Documentation	4.0	8.0	2.0	42.9
5	User Acceptance Test.	0.6	9.0	3.0	11.1
	Total User	5.6	19.0	1.2	$ 63.8
	Overlapped	15.4			
	Unpaid Effort		1.3		

Project: DEMO   Scenario: MEASURED MIS SAMPLE
Location: BOSTON, MASSACHUSETTS

GANTT CHART: DEVELOPMENT AND USER INVOLVEMENT

```
                            ┌May15 90                    Aug27 91┐
  Activity          Percent    10   20   30   40   50   60   70   80   90   100

  Requirements       16.22  ████▌
  User requirements   6.49  ██▌
  Init analysis/design 12.39    ███▌
  Detail design/specs 25.94       ███████▌
  Coding             29.19            ████████▌
  Reusable code acquis. 6.49             ██▌
  Integration        38.92                  ███████████▌
  User documentation 22.70                     ██████▌
  User inv. documentation 25.94                   ███████▌
  Unit testing        6.16                         ██▌
  Function testing   19.46                         █████▌
  Systems testing    12.97                                 ███▌
  Acceptance testing  9.73                                    ██▌
  User acceptance testing 3.89                                  █▌
  Installation        6.49                                      █▌
  Development management 100.00  ████████████████████████████████████
```


USER INVOLVEMENT UNPAID OVERTIME

No	Activity	Paid Effort Months	Unpaid Effort Months	Total Effort Months
1	User Requirements	1.9	0.1	2.0
4	User Documentation	7.7	0.3	8.0
5	User Acceptance Test.	8.1	0.9	9.0
	Total Project	17.7	1.3	19.0

USER INVOLVEMENT DELIVERABLES, SIZES, SCOPES AND PRODUCTION RATES

No	Activity	Primary Deliverable	Size of Deliverable	Assignment Scope	Production per Month
1	User Requirements	Pages	100	50.00	50.00
4	User Documentation	Pages	250	125.00	31.25
5	User Acceptance Test.	Test Cases	100	33.33	11.11

Project: DEMO   Scenario: MEASURED MIS SAMPLE
Location: BOSTON, MASSACHUSETTS

USER INVOLVEMENT EFFORT AND SCHEDULE PERCENTAGES

No	Activity	Percent of Effort	Percent of Schedule
1	User Requirements	10.53 %	6.49 %
4	User Documentation	42.11	25.94
5	User Acceptance Test.	47.37	3.89
	Total	100.00 %	36.32 %

USER INVOLVEMENT EFFORT PERCENTAGES GRAPH

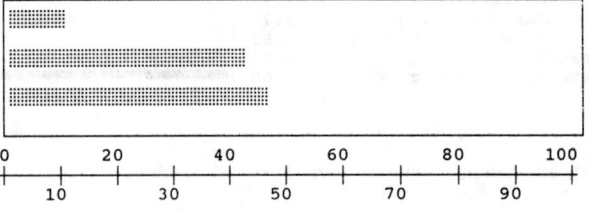

Activity	
User Requirements	
User Documentation	
User Acceptance Test.	

```
              0      20      40      60      80     100
   Percent    +---+---+---+---+---+---+---+---+---+---+
                 10      30      50      70      90
```


USER INVOLVEMENT RATIOS

No	Activity	F. Pts Per Person Months	Source Lines Per P.Months	Cost Per F. Pt.	Cost Per Source Line
1	User Requirements	159.50∎	19,065.00	$ 30.58∎	$ 0.26
4	User Documentation	39.88∎	4,766.25	134.57∎	1.13
5	User Acceptance Test.	35.44∎	4,236.67	34.82∎	0.29
		16.79∎	2,006.84	$ 199.98∎	$ 1.67

Project: DEMO   Scenario: MEASURED MIS SAMPLE
Location: BOSTON, MASSACHUSETTS

MAINTENANCE CHART OF ACCOUNTS

        3 Included

            1 Central Maintenance
            3 Customer Support
            4 Maintenance Management

        1 Excluded

            2 Field Service

MAINTENANCE STAFF EFFORT, COSTS

Year	Staff	Effort Months	Costs in Thousands
1	3.00	17.00	$ 214.6
2	2.00	18.00	158.0
3	2.00	10.00	173.8
4	1.70	12.00	162.2
5	1.50	5.00	154.8
6	1.50	3.00	172.8
7	0.00	0.00	0.0
8	0.00	0.00	0.0
9	0.00	0.00	0.0
10	0.00	0.00	0.0
	1.95	65.00	$ 1,036.2

Project: DEMO   Scenario: MEASURED MIS SAMPLE
Location: BOSTON, MASSACHUSETTS

MAINTENANCE COSTS DETAIL

Year	Central Maintenance	Field Maintenance	Customer Support	Maintenance Management	Total Costs*
1	$ 108.90	$ 0.00	$ 69.44	$ 36.30	$ 214.64
2	79.86	0.00	38.19	39.93	157.98
3	87.85	0.00	42.01	43.92	173.78
4	67.64	0.00	46.21	48.32	162.17
5	53.15	0.00	50.84	50.84	154.82
6	58.46	0.00	55.92	58.46	172.84
7	0.00	0.00	0.00	0.00	0.00
8	0.00	0.00	0.00	0.00	0.00
9	0.00	0.00	0.00	0.00	0.00
10	0.00	0.00	0.00	0.00	0.00
	$ 455.86	$ 0.00	$ 302.62	$ 277.77	$ 1,036.24

* Costs in Thousands

MAINTENANCE EFFORT DETAIL

Year	Central Maintenance	Field Maintenance	Customer Support	Maintenance Management	Total Effort*
1	12.00	0.00	2.00	3.00	17.00
2	12.00	0.00	3.00	3.00	18.00
3	6.00	0.00	1.00	3.00	10.00
4	8.00	0.00	1.00	3.00	12.00
5	3.00	0.00	1.00	1.00	5.00
6	1.50	0.00	0.50	1.00	3.00
7	0.00	0.00	0.00	0.00	0.00
8	0.00	0.00	0.00	0.00	0.00
9	0.00	0.00	0.00	0.00	0.00
10	0.00	0.00	0.00	0.00	0.00
	42.50	0.00	8.50	14.00	65.00

* Effort in Months

Project: DEMO   Scenario: MEASURED MIS SAMPLE
Location: BOSTON, MASSACHUSETTS

MAINTENANCE STAFFING DETAIL

Year	Central Maintenance	Field Maintenance	Customer Support	Maintenance Management	Total Staffing
1	1.50	0.00	1.00	0.50	3.00
2	1.00	0.00	0.50	0.50	2.00
3	1.00	0.00	0.50	0.50	2.00
4	0.70	0.00	0.50	0.50	1.70
5	0.50	0.00	0.50	0.50	1.50
6	0.50	0.00	0.50	0.50	1.50
7	0.00	0.00	0.00	0.00	0.00
8	0.00	0.00	0.00	0.00	0.00
9	0.00	0.00	0.00	0.00	0.00
10	0.00	0.00	0.00	0.00	0.00
	0.87	0.00	0.58	0.50	1.95

MAINTENANCE DEFECT REPAIRS

Year	Valid Defects	Duplicate Defects	Invalid Defects
1	140	5	15
2	70	3	10
3	40	3	5
4	25	1	5
5	10	0	1
6	7	0	1
7	5	0	0
8	3	0	0
9	0	0	0
10	0	0	0
	300	12	37

Project: DEMO   Scenario: MEASURED MIS SAMPLE
Location: BOSTON, MASSACHUSETTS

MAINTENANCE QUALITY AND PRODUCTIVITY RATIOS

        Total Effort Per KLOC: 1.70 Months
        Total Effort Per F.P.:   0.20■ Months
        Total Effort Per Defect: 0.11■ Months

        Total Cost Per KLOC: $ 27,176.58 Dollars
        Total Cost Per F.P.: $ 3,248.41■ Dollars
        Total Cost Per Defect: $ 1,824.37■ Dollars

        Valid defects Per KLOC: 7.87
        Valid defects Per F.P.:   0.94■

Project: DEMO   Scenario: MEASURED MIS SAMPLE
Location: BOSTON, MASSACHUSETTS

ENHANCEMENTS: CODE SIZING (FROM Sep 1991)

Year	Code Added	Code Deleted	Current Size	Average Complexity	
1	3,328■	832■	35,776■	35■	
2	3,578■	894■	38,459■	37■	
3	3,846■	961■	41,344■	40■	
4	4,134■	1,034■	44,444■	44■	
5	4,444■	1,111■	47,778■	47■	
6	4,778■	1,194■	51,361■	51■	UNTESTABLE
7	5,136■	1,284■	55,213■	55■	UNTESTABLE
8	5,521■	1,380■	59,354■	59■	UNTESTABLE
9	5,935■	1,484■	63,806■	64■	UNTESTABLE
10	6,381■	1,595■	68,591■	69■	UNTESTABLE
	47,082■	11,770■			

ENHANCEMENTS: F. POINTS SIZING (FROM Sep 1991)

Year	F. Pts. Added	F. Pts. Deleted	Current F. Pts.	Average Complexity	
1	27■	7■	291■	35■	
2	29■	7■	313■	37■	
3	31■	8■	337■	40■	
4	34■	8■	362■	44■	
5	36■	9■	389■	47■	
6	39■	10■	418■	51■	UNTESTABLE
7	42■	10■	450■	55■	UNTESTABLE
8	45■	11■	484■	59■	UNTESTABLE
9	48■	12■	520■	64■	UNTESTABLE
10	52■	13■	559■	69■	UNTESTABLE
	384■	96■			

Project: DEMO   Scenario: MEASURED MIS SAMPLE
Location: BOSTON, MASSACHUSETTS

ENHANCEMENTS: STAFF, EFFORT AND COSTS (FROM Sep 1991)

Year	Staff	Effort Months	Costs Thousands	Average Complexity	
1	1.1■	14.4■	$ 83.8■	35■	
2	1.3■	16.0■	102.1■	37■	
3	1.4■	17.7■	124.5■	40■	
4	1.5■	19.6■	151.7■	44■	
5	1.7■	21.9■	186.8■	47■	
6	1.9■	24.3■	227.6■	51■	UNTESTABLE
7	2.1■	27.2■	280.2■	55■	UNTESTABLE
8	2.4■	30.7■	348.4■	59■	UNTESTABLE
9	2.7■	34.4■	428.9■	64■	UNTESTABLE
10	3.1■	39.3■	538.7■	69■	UNTESTABLE
	1.9■	245.5■	2,472.6■		

ENHANCEMENTS: PRODUCTIVITY (FROM Sep 1991)

Year	Code A. Scope	Code Prod. Rate	F. Pts. A. Scope	F. Pts. Prod. Rate	Avg Cmplx	
1	29,403■	288.72■	240■	2.35■	35■	
2	28,530■	280.15■	232■	2.28■	37■	
3	27,682■	271.83■	226■	2.21■	40■	
4	26,860■	263.75■	219■	2.15■	44■	
5	25,802■	253.36■	210■	2.06■	47■	
6	25,035■	245.84■	204■	2.00■	51■	UNTESTABLE
7	24,049■	236.15■	196■	1.92■	55■	UNTESTABLE
8	22,870■	224.57■	186■	1.83■	59■	UNTESTABLE
9	21,969■	215.73■	179■	1.76■	64■	UNTESTABLE
10	20,683■	203.10■	169■	1.65■	69■	UNTESTABLE

Project: DEMO   Scenario: MEASURED MIS SAMPLE
Location: BOSTON, MASSACHUSETTS

COST STRENGTHS

```
        Workstation environment                               2.00
            Shared workstations (Two employees per workstation).
        Requirements environment                              2.00
            JAD methodology or very clear user requirements.
        Support software effectiveness environment            2.00
            Most support tools and software are effective.
        Hardware stability environment                        2.00
            Single vendor hardware with moderate compatibility.
        Product performance or execution speed environment    2.00
            Minor performance or execution speed restrictions.
        Product memory utilization environment                1.00
            No memory utilization restrictions.
        Development geography                                  2.00
            Multiple development departments within same site.
        Software warranty coverage                            1.00
            No explicit or implicit warranties on software.
        Field maintenance                                     1.00
            No field maintenance for project.
```


COST WEAKNESSES

```
        Individual office environment                         4.00
            Less than 60 square feet of enclosed space per worker.
        Office noise and interruption environment             4.00
            Some background noise and frequent interruptions.
        Prototyping environment                               5.00
            No prototyping at all.
        Design automation environment                         4.00
            Semi-formal design with text automation only.
        User and external document production environment     4.00
            Text automation; manual graphics support.
        New code problem complexity                           4.00
            Some difficult or complex calculations.
```


EFFORT STRENGTHS

```
        Workstation environment                               2.00
            Shared workstations (Two employees per workstation).
```

Project: DEMO   Scenario: MEASURED MIS SAMPLE
Location: BOSTON, MASSACHUSETTS

Requirements environment	2.00
JAD methodology or very clear user requirements.	
Support software effectiveness environment	2.00
Most support tools and software are effective.	
Product performance or execution speed environment	2.00
Minor performance or execution speed restrictions.	
Product memory utilization environment	1.00
No memory utilization restrictions.	
Field maintenance	1.00
No field maintenance for project.	

EFFORT WEAKNESSES

Individual office environment	4.00
Less than 60 square feet of enclosed space per worker.	
Office noise and interruption environment	4.00
Some background noise and frequent interruptions.	
Design automation environment	4.00
Semi-formal design with text automation only.	
User and external document production environment	4.00
Text automation; manual graphics support.	
New code problem complexity	4.00
Some difficult or complex calculations.	

QUALITY STRENGTHS

Development personnel tool and method experience	2.00
Majority of experts in the tools and methods.	
Development personnel programming language experience	1.00
All experts in the language(s) used for the project.	
User involvement during requirements	2.00
Users are heavily involved during requirements/design.	
Support software effectiveness environment	2.00
Most support tools and software are effective.	
Program debugging tools	1.00
Full screen editor, traces, cross-references, etc.	
Joint application design	2.00
Good	
New function testing	2.00
Good	
User acceptance testing	2.00
Good	
Software warranty coverage	1.00
No explicit or implicit warranties on software.	

Project: DEMO   Scenario: MEASURED MIS SAMPLE
Location: BOSTON, MASSACHUSETTS

        Replacement and restructure planning   2.00
            Automated code analysis and restructuring tools.

QUALITY WEAKNESSES

        Prototyping environment   5.00
            No prototyping at all.
        Design automation environment   4.00
            Semi-formal design with text automation only.
        Project library environment   4.00
            Manual source code and documentation control.
        Pre-test defect removal support   4.00
            Limited training for reviews and inspections.
        Pre-test defect removal facilities   4.00
            Very limited availability of facilities for reviews
        Quality assurance function   5.00
            No QA function exists for the project.
        Quality measurement database   5.00
            No defect tracking.
        Maintenance personnel education   5.00
            Little or no training in projects or tools.
        New code problem complexity   4.00
            Some difficult or complex calculations.

PRODUCTIVITY STRENGTHS

        Development personnel tool and method experience   2.00
            Majority of experts in the tools and methods.
        Development personnel programming language experience 1.00
            All experts in the language(s) used for the project.
        Development hardware experience   1.00
            All experts in the hardware used for the project.
        User personnel experience with software projects   2.00
            All or a majority of users have software experience.
        User personnel experience with application type   2.00
            All or a strong majority of users are experts.
        User involvement during requirements   2.00
            Users are heavily involved during requirements/design.
        Workstation environment   2.00
            Shared workstations (Two employees per workstation).
        Support software effectiveness environment   2.00
            Most support tools and software are effective.
        Hardware stability environment   2.00
            Single vendor hardware with moderate compatibility.

Project: DEMO   Scenario: MEASURED MIS SAMPLE
Location: BOSTON, MASSACHUSETTS

         Development geography   2.00
            Multiple development departments within same site.

PRODUCTIVITY WEAKNESSES

         Individual office environment   4.00
            Less than 60 square feet of enclosed space per worker.
         Office noise and interruption environment   4.00
            Some background noise and frequent interruptions.
         Prototyping environment   5.00
            No prototyping at all.
         Design automation environment   4.00
            Semi-formal design with text automation only.
         User and external document production environment   4.00
            Text automation; manual graphics support.
         New code problem complexity   4.00
            Some difficult or complex calculations.

SCHEDULE STRENGTHS

         User personnel experience with software projects   2.00
            All or a majority of users have software experience.
         User personnel experience with application type   2.00
            All or a strong majority of users are experts.
         User involvement during requirements   2.00
            Users are heavily involved during requirements/design.
         Workstation environment   2.00
            Shared workstations (Two employees per workstation).
         Requirements environment   2.00
            JAD methodology or very clear user requirements.
         Hardware novelty   1.00
            All hardware is familiar and well understood by staff.
         Support software novelty   2.00
            Most support software is familiar and well understood.
         Hardware stability environment   2.00
            Single vendor hardware with moderate compatibility.

SCHEDULE WEAKNESSES

         Individual office environment   4.00
            Less than 60 square feet of enclosed space per worker.

Project: DEMO   Scenario: MEASURED MIS SAMPLE
Location: BOSTON, MASSACHUSETTS

        Office noise and interruption environment   4.00
           Some background noise and frequent interruptions.
        Design automation environment   4.00
           Semi-formal design with text automation only.
        Maintenance personnel staffing   4.00
           Most maintenance done by development personnel.

PERSONNEL RESOURCE STRENGTHS

        Development personnel tool and method experience   2.00
           Majority of experts in the tools and methods.
        Development personnel programming language experience   1.00
           All experts in the language(s) used for the project.
        Development hardware experience   1.00
           All experts in the hardware used for the project.
        User personnel experience with software projects   2.00
           All or a majority of users have software experience.
        User personnel experience with application type   2.00
           All or a strong majority of users are experts.
        User involvement during requirements   2.00
           Users are heavily involved during requirements/design.
        Legal and statutory impacts   1.00
           No known legal or statutory constraints.

PERSONNEL RESOURCE WEAKNESSES

        Productivity measurements   4.00
           Manual and partial lifecycle productivity measures.

ENVIRONMENTAL STRENGTHS

        Workstation environment   2.00
           Shared workstations (Two employees per workstation).
        Requirements environment   2.00
           JAD methodology or very clear user requirements.
        Hardware novelty   1.00
           All hardware is familiar and well understood by staff.
        Support software novelty   2.00
           Most support software is familiar and well understood.

Project: DEMO   Scenario: MEASURED MIS SAMPLE
Location: BOSTON, MASSACHUSETTS

Support software effectiveness environment	2.00
Most support tools and software are effective.	
Hardware stability environment	2.00
Single vendor hardware with moderate compatibility.	
Product performance or execution speed environment	2.00
Minor performance or execution speed restrictions.	
Product memory utilization environment	1.00
No memory utilization restrictions.	
Development geography	2.00
Multiple development departments within same site.	
Program debugging tools	1.00
Full screen editor, traces, cross-references, etc.	
Joint application design	2.00
Good	
New function testing	2.00
Good	
User acceptance testing	2.00
Good	
Software warranty coverage	1.00
No explicit or implicit warranties on software.	
Field maintenance	1.00
No field maintenance for project.	
Replacement and restructure planning	2.00
Automated code analysis and restructuring tools.	
Program execution frequency	2.00
Monthly or weekly runs.	
Installation and production geography	1.00
Single production site, in a single city.	

ENVIRONMENTAL WEAKNESSES

Individual office environment	4.00
Less than 60 square feet of enclosed space per worker.	
Office noise and interruption environment	4.00
Some background noise and frequent interruptions.	
Prototyping environment	5.00
No prototyping at all.	
Design automation environment	4.00
Semi-formal design with text automation only.	
Data administration environment	4.00
Partial data dictionary available.	
Project library environment	4.00
Manual source code and documentation control.	
User and external document production environment	4.00
Text automation; manual graphics support.	
Pre-test defect removal support	4.00
Limited training for reviews and inspections.	

Project: DEMO   Scenario: MEASURED MIS SAMPLE
Location: BOSTON, MASSACHUSETTS

        Pre-test defect removal facilities   4.00
            Very limited availability of facilities for reviews
        Quality assurance function   5.00
            No QA function exists for the project.
        Quality measurement database   5.00
            No defect tracking.
        Maintenance personnel staffing   4.00
            Most maintenance done by development personnel.
        Maintenance personnel education   5.00
            Little or no training in projects or tools.

Project: DEMO   Scenario: MEASURED MIS SAMPLE
Location: BOSTON, MASSACHUSETTS

PROJECT INFORMATION

Scenario
This is a composite project derived
from several actual MIS examples.
The data shows typical environment
and methodologies that produce
typical productivity and quality.

PROJECT TYPE AND CLASSIFICATION

Project class
This project represents a normal
MIS project being built for the
internal use of a company, where
only one location in one state is
involved.

Project type
Hybrid projects that are made up
of several types are the most
common in the United States.

PROJECT GOALS AND CONSTRAINTS

Project goals
This goal, of "do the project as
quickly as possible" is the most
common, but is not usually very
successful. Striving for quality
yields better results.

OCCUPATION GROUP CONSTRAINTS: DEVELOPMENT

Average Salary

Project managers average salary
MIS projects are normally developed
by generalists, and so few of the
many specialist groups are found
here.

Project: DEMO   Scenario: MEASURED MIS SAMPLE
Location: BOSTON, MASSACHUSETTS

SOURCE CODE LANGUAGES

New code language
COBOL remains far and away the most
common language for MIS projects.

STAFF AND USER PERSONNEL EXPERIENCE

Pre-test defect removal experience
Most MIS projects are weak in
reviews and inspections. Indeed,
many MIS developers do not even
know how to carry out such tasks!

MANAGEMENT PROJECT AND PERSONNEL VARIABLES

System development methodology
Many MIS projects lack formal or
even rudimentary system development
methodologies.

MAINTENANCE PROJECT AND PERSONNEL VARIABLES

Maintenance personnel staffing
MIS projects, unlike systems and
military projects, usually have the
maintenance performed by developers
on as "as needed" basis. This is
not very efficient or productive.

Restructure interval (years)
Users of Checkpoint should try out
making the restructure interval at
1, 3, and 5 year periods and note
the results. In real life, COBOL
benefits from restructuring.

Number of system installation sites
Single-site installation is the
most common for MIS projects.

Project: DEMO   Scenario: MEASURED MIS SAMPLE
Location: BOSTON, MASSACHUSETTS

Anticipated years of systems useful life
The life expectancy of software is
surprising: large systems last for
many years, but small applications
quickly disappear.

ENVIRONMENTAL VARIABLES AND CASE TOOLS

Individual office environment
Overcrowded offices are sadly the
norm in the United States, which
lowers software productivity by a
surprising amount: more than 10%.

PROJECT VALUE AND RISK ANALYSIS

Risk Analysis

Risk of excessive schedule pressure
Excessive schedule pressure by
users, management, or users is one
of the major causes of project
failures and disasters.

Project: DEMO   Scenario: MEASURED MIS SAMPLE
Location: BOSTON, MASSACHUSETTS

PROJECT SOFTWARE DOCUMENTATION PRODUCTION

Planning documents

	Pages
Proposal	0
Development plan	0
Marketing plan	0
Review and inspection plan	0
Test plan	30
Quality assurance plan	0
Documentation plan	0
Maintenance and customer support plan	0
Training plan	0
Sub Total	30

Tracking and Control Documents

	Pages
Budget variance reports	50
Progress and milestone reports	15
Review/inspection status reports	0
Test status reports	5
Sales reports	0
Sub Total	70

Quality and Defect Removal Documents

	Pages
Pre-delivery defect reports	300
Post-delivery defect reports	300
Quality assurance reports	0
Acceptance test reports	20
Project-post mortems	0
Sub Total	620

Project: DEMO   Scenario: MEASURED MIS SAMPLE
Location: BOSTON, MASSACHUSETTS

Financial Documents

	Pages
Project cost estimates	5
Departmental budgets	30
Capital expenditure requests	0
Sub Total	35

Specification Documents

	Pages
Requirements specifications	100
Architecture specifications	39
Initial functional specifications	100
Final functional specifications	129
Program logic specifications	65
Data design specifications	22
Detailed module design	34
Sub Total	489

External Documentation

	Pages
Introduction	0
Installation guide	34
Principles of operation	0
User's guide	83
Reference manual	0
Programmer's guide	0
System programmer's guide	0
Operator's guide	50
Message and return code ref. manual	50
Maintenance manual	0
Quick reference card	0
End-user training manual	34
Sales and marketing brochures	0
Sub Total	250

Project: DEMO   Scenario: MEASURED MIS SAMPLE
Location: BOSTON, MASSACHUSETTS

Online Documentation

	Screens
Prototype input/output screens	0
Product input/output screens	100
On-line tutorial	40
Help screens	30
Icon and graphic screens	0
On-line error messages	30
Read-me file	0
Sub Total	200

Audio/Visual Materials

	Units
Audio training cassettes	0
Video marketing tapes	0
Video training tapes	0
Interactive video training discs	0
Sub Total	0

Documentation Production Grand Totals

	Count	
Written Documents	1,494	Pages
Online Documents	200	Screens
Audio/Visual Materials	0	Units

Example of an Annual Baseline Report

Introduction

The following is an example of an annual baseline report on software productivity and quality. The report is derived from the contents and formats of several actual reports produced by major corporations. The data, although abstract, is typical of the kinds of information presented. The productivity and quality rates are derived from actual studies of real projects. Reports such as this are normally produced in the first quarter of a year, and they are based on the data of all projects which the enterprise completed in the preceding year. Thus, this report for the year 1990 would have been produced in the first quarter of 1991.

In large corporations, responsibility for such reports normally resides with a permanent measurement department. The group would typically report to a vice president or director, and it would include measurement specialists, statisticians, systems analysts, and sometimes writers.

The data itself would be gathered from the individual projects in the course of the year. The very first time such a report is produced, it will usually be necessary to expend considerable effort in both collecting and validating the data. Once annual reports become standard business practices, both the speed with which the data can be gathered and the accuracy of the numerical information improve.

Although large corporations produce thousands of them, small programs are often excluded from annual reports for reasons of policy. The exclusions are especially common in European and multinational corporations because recording performance data against individual workers may violate either national law or internal work rule regulations. This example, based on typical large-company, multinational practice, omits projects smaller than 2 person-years of total effort.

The distribution of annual baseline reports will vary, but in every case it will include all of the senior executives of the enterprise. The information provided is useful at all levels, and fairly wide distribution through an enterprise is normal. This kind of information would obviously be valuable to competitors, so security classifications such as INTERNAL USE ONLY and COMPANY CONFIDENTIAL would be normal.

Finally, this example uses the hypothetical name, ABC Corporation. It is intended to be abstract, and it certainly is not intended to identify any real corporation.

ABC CORPORATION 1990 SOFTWARE BASELINE REPORT

ABSTRACT

This report contains the results of the productivity analysis of the ABC software projects which entered production in calendar year 1989. The report is the first ABC annual report to express its results in the new Function Point and Feature Point metrics. ABC made substantial productivity gains across the board, and generally good quality gains with the exceptions that are noted in the text.

PREPARED BY:
ABC Software Metrics Department
J. Doe, Director
March 30, 1991

Executive Overview of the 1990 Software Baseline Report

The ABC Corporation has four discrete software environments: 1) Real-time Military Software, 2) Real-time Commercial Software, 3) Support Software, 4) Information Systems. Since these four environments produce different kinds of software, use different tools and methods, and report to different executives, it is desirable to show their productivity and quality data separately.

The year 1990 showed continued improvements in software productivity rates for all four operating areas of the ABC Corporation and improvements in quality for all operating areas except that of internal support software. Corrective actions have been put in place to bring support software quality up to adherence of ABC's corporate quality goals.

The 1990 report introduces the use of Function Point and Feature Point metrics for normalization purposes. The older "lines of code" normalization will continue to be used for comparative and historical purposes.

Software productivity gains in 1990

Figure 1 shows the net improvement in software productivity by area between 1989 and 1990. All areas experienced improvements, with information systems having the highest overall percentage gain of 29.4%. The overall corporate gain was 19.4%, which reflects the cu-

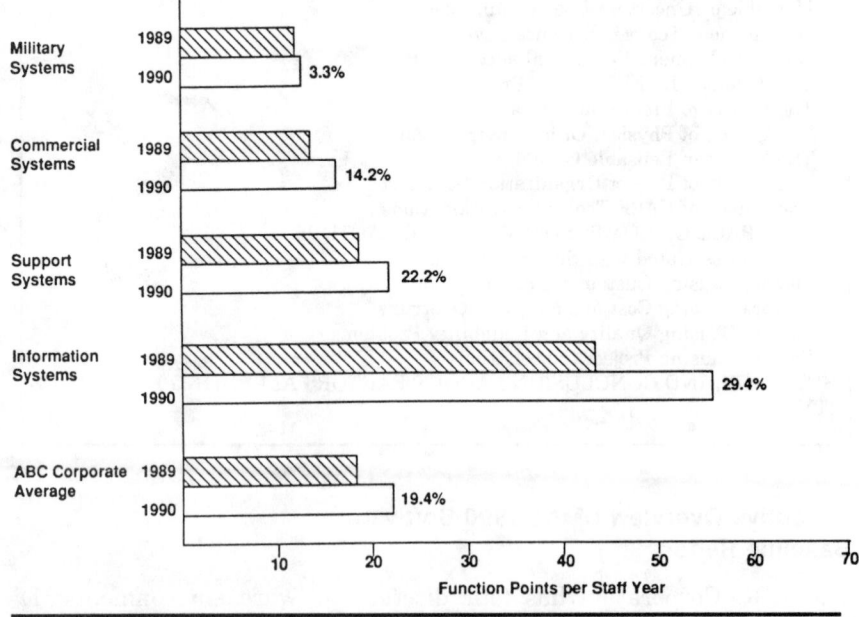

Figure 1   ABC software productivity rates in 1989 and 1990, by area.

mulative results of the last several years of ABC software technology improvements.

ABC's military projects area had the lowest gain of 3.3%. Since military specifications determine many of the deliverables and much of the kind of work which must be performed, military software is more difficult to improve than the other classes of ABC projects.

Software quality and defect levels in 1990

Figure 2 shows the net improvement in user-reported software defect rates between 1989 and 1990. All areas except that of internal support tools experienced defect reductions and quality improvements in 1990. The ABC information system area had the greatest reduction in defects at − 17.9%. The overall ABC performance reflected a reduction of − 5.5% in user-reported defects. While such a reduction is encouraging, it is desirable to reduce defect rates still further in 1991.

The unfortunate increase in defect rates for internal support tools of 16.6% in 1990 was due to schedule pressure interfering with the usage of reviews and inspections. Corrective actions have been put in place for 1991.

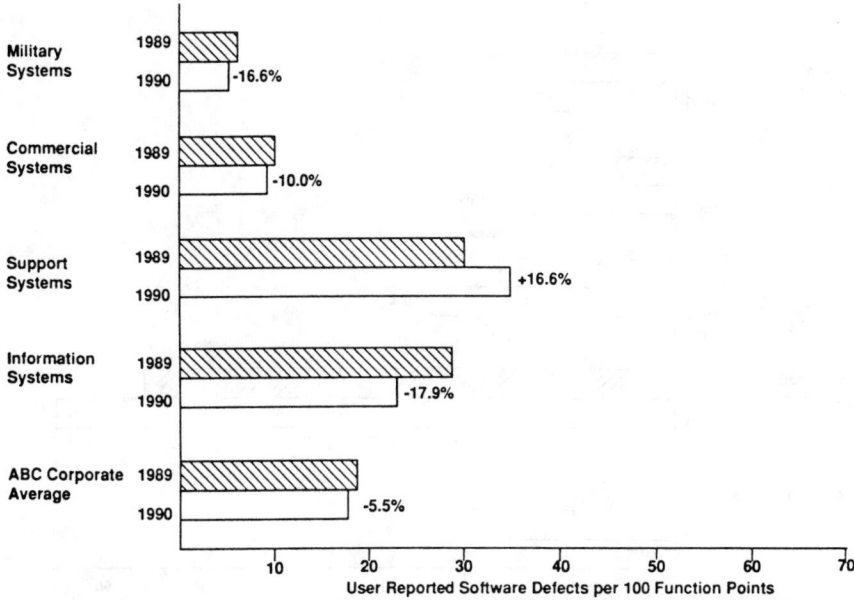

Figure 2   ABC user-reported defect rates in 1989 and 1990, by area.

Summary of overall productivity and quality results

Overall, ABC is continuing to make progress in both software productivity and quality. However, in 1991 the ABC Corporation should achieve even better results than were accomplished in 1990, due to the continued improvements in methods and to new tool sets to be installed.

ABC Productivity and Quality Targets for 1991

As the software methods and technologies at ABC continue to improve, the year 1991 should see significant gains in both productivity and quality. The improvement goals are based on the empirical observations of what major corporations have been able to accomplish. Although the goals are challenging to both managers and technical staff, they are not impossible to achieve.

Figure 3 shows the 1991 productivity improvement targets, which establish an overall goal of 14.4%. Figure 4 shows the overall 1991 quality and defect rate target, which calls for a 53.0% overall reduc-

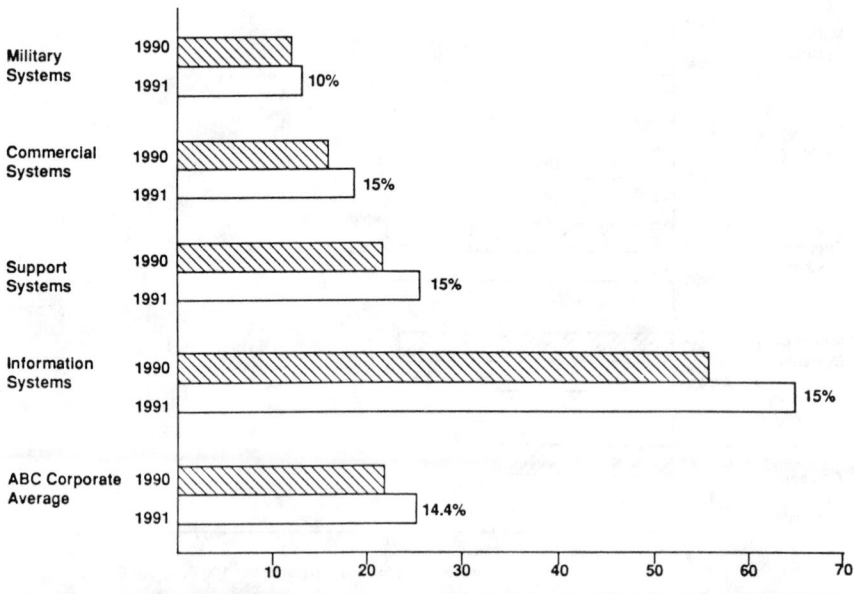

Figure 3   ABC software productivity targets for 1991, by area.

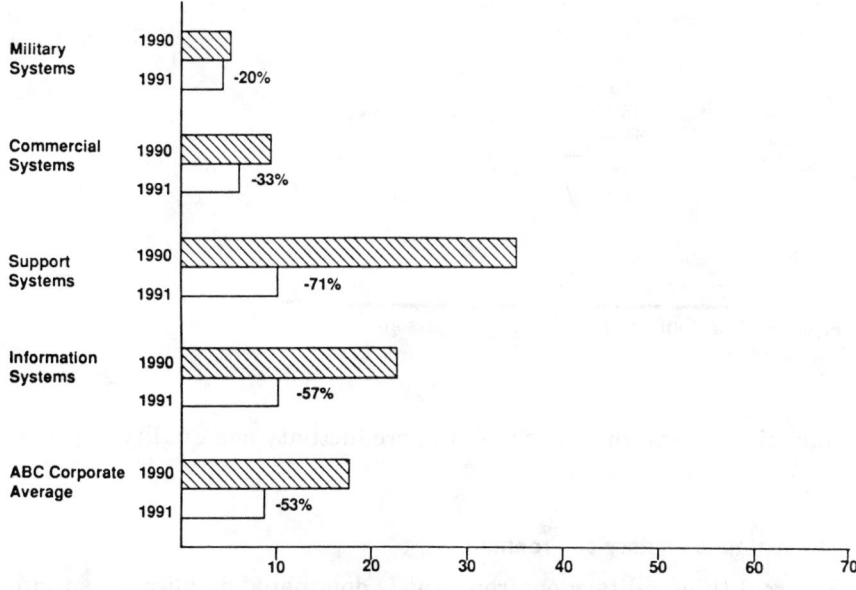

Figure 4   ABC user-reported defect targets for 1991, by area.

tion in user-reported defects. This reduction, although comparatively high, is within the capabilities of the ABC staff and technology sets.

ABC software demographics

The overall distribution of the ABC software population stayed relatively constant between 1989 and 1990. The net voluntary attrition rate of software personnel has stayed relatively constant at 4.0% per year since 1985. The new-hire growth rate of ABC personnel between 1989 and 1990 was 8.0%. When the attrition and new-hire rates are considered together, it is seen that the software staff of ABC grew by a net of 4%. The new-hire growth rate is targeted to be approximately 5% in 1991. If the attrition rate stays constant, then ABC should experience a 1% net growth next year. Net growth (new hires – (voluntary + involuntary attrition)) is now at 4%.

Figure 5 shows the overall distribution of the ABC software professional and management staff.

Analysis of the Four ABC Software Environments

The factors which cause the variations among the four software environments have been identified by multiple-regression techniques, as

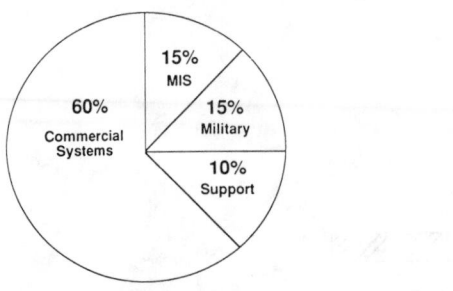

Figure 5 Distribution of ABC software personnel, by area.

have the factors which are yielding productivity and quality improvements.

The real-time military environment

The real-time military environment is dominated by military specifications, including the new 2167A Military Specification on software
quality. Military specifications require such rigorous documentation
of all phases and activities that approximately 45% of all military
software costs are associated with paperwork. In addition, the military requirements for independent verification and validation and independent testing add activities to the development chart of account
that are not present for other classes of software.

Approximately 30% of military software costs are associated with
defect removal and quality control. The code itself approximates 20%
of military software costs. The special military requirements are
placed on top of the high complexity of telecommunications software
and the known difficulties of building software on hardware that is itself unstable and being developed simultaneously. Military projects
have the lowest productivity rates of all forms of software, and this
situation will probably continue indefinitely. Military software quality, however, is often significantly better than average.

The improvements between 1989 and 1990 are attributable to the
introduction of an integrated design environment providing full
graphics and text support coupled with a data dictionary.

The real-time commercial environment

The real-time commercial environment is dominated by the impact of
highly complex algorithms, unstable hardware, and severe timing and
performance constraints. The need for high quality and reliability for

real-time commercial software is extreme. The combination of these factors requires careful development with complete specifications, full design and code inspections, exhaustive testing, and substantial modelling and simulation during the development phase.

The volume of paperwork is smaller for commercial software than for military, but it still amounts to some 30% or more of the total development expense. Quality control and the sum of all defect removal activities for real-time commercial software comprise some 35% of all development expenses. The code itself typically comprises some 30% of the development expenses for real-time commercial software.

The improvements between 1989 and 1990 are attributable to the introduction of full design and code inspections, plus the new integrated design environment offering full graphics and text support and a data dictionary.

The support environment

Internal support software, such as engineering aids or software test tools, is dominated by the need for short development cycles, since the tools are usually on the critical path for other projects. Internal systems software that is not intended for external customers is usually sparsely documented, and the major concentration of effort is found during coding, integration, and testing. Typically, paperwork for internal systems software comprises 20% or less of the total development expenses, coding comprises more than 40%, and the sum of defect removal activities would comprise some 25% or less.

The improvements in productivity between 1989 and 1990 reflect the introduction of the new integrated design environment offering full graphics and text support and a data dictionary. The small decline in software quality reflected in the increased defect levels in 1990, and the less than satisfactory quality over the past few years, implies a need to use inspections on ABC's internal systems software development. It is also suggested that internal systems software be required to achieve quality goals similar to those established for commercial and military software: less than 0.5 valid unique defect reports per KLOC per year, or the equivalent metric of no more than 10 delivered defects per 100 feature points.

The management information systems environment

The MIS environment is dominated primarily by user requirements and secondarily by the fact that the bulk of MIS work tends to be maintenance and enhancements. Because user requirements are often ambiguous and rapidly changing, the observed variations in MIS software costs are far greater than for the other three classes of software. Typical MIS projects will average 20% to 30% of all development costs in requirements, specifications, and paperwork. Coding costs will average 30% to 45%, while defect removal costs will average 15% to 35%. The large range of uncertainty is typical of the MIS environment.

The improvement in MIS productivity and quality between 1989 and 1990 is attributable to a multifaceted approach including: A) The introduction of the Joint Application Design (JAD) methodology for creating the user requirements; B) The restructuring and geriatric care given to the older applications in the ABC production library; C) The introduction of leading-edge design methods featuring integrated graphics/text support and a data dictionary; D) The introduction of application generators, query languages, and database methods on selected projects which significantly improved Function Point productivity rates. Improvements in productivity caused by very high level languages such as SQL or QBE or with application generators are not directly measurable with lines of code metrics.

However, the fact that MIS quality is still significantly worse than the other classes of software produced by ABC implies that more changes will be necessary. It is recommended that design and code inspections be introduced in 1991 for critical MIS applications, and that MIS software be required to achieve the same quality levels as our commercial software: no more than 0.5 annual defects per KLOC per year for applications in production, or the equivalent metric of achieving no more than 10 delivered defects per 100 Function Points.

This quality goal for MIS should also benefit productivity, since the target can only be achieved by minimizing one of the more expensive activities of all software; i.e., defect removal.

Overall trends and conclusions

The ABC Corporation has continued to make significant improvements in software productivity in 1990. The 1987, 1988, and 1989 investments in new design tools and methods appear to have been effective, as does the introduction of the JAD requirements method. The adoption of Function Points and Feature Points is beginning to provide new levels of economic understanding of software.

Quality, although better than industry norms, needs continued improvement in 1991. An increased emphasis on design and code inspections for support software and MIS applications will accomplish this target.

Background of the 1990 Baseline

This baseline is the fourth annual report produced by the ABC corporation, and the first to adopt the use of functional metrics. The ABC Management Committee recognized that software was becoming a critical aspect of ABC operations in 1985, and issued a request for more complete software information. The result of that request was the first ABC baseline, produced in 1987 and covering the year 1986.

As a manufacturer of telecommunications equipment and private branch exchanges (PBX), the products of the ABC corporation have software as part of the critical path leading to delivery. Once installed, the reliability of the equipment in the perception of users is significantly related to the quality of the software itself. In addition, ABC also produces much of its own test and engineering support software, and many of its own management information systems. The ABC government systems division also produces ruggedized and portable telecommunications equipment for U.S. military and defense agencies and for the NATO countries.

This corporate measurement report is produced annually at the request of ABC management committee, and it highlights the importance of achieving the highest possible levels software quality and achieving optimum productivity at the same time. By corporate policy, projects totalling less than two person-years of effort have been excluded as separate projects from this report. Small projects are handled as aggregates by summing their sizes, effort, and quantified results.

The ABC corporation has four distinct programming environments, and each environment has its own characteristic productivity and quality profile: 1) real-time telecommunications software embedded within the ABC military products; 2) real-time telecommunications software embedded within the ABC commercial and consumer products; 3) systems software produced internally to aid the ABC engineering and software engineering populations; 4) management information software produced to aid in the operation and management of ABC.

Table 1 shows the 1989 and 1990 annual productivity rates for these

TABLE 1 1989 and 1990 Annual Software Productivity Rates in Source Statements per Person-Year

Environment	1989	1990	Change	Percent
Real-time military	1500	1550	50	3.3
Real-time commercial	1750	2000	250	14.2
Systems and support	2250	2750	500	22.2
Information systems	3500	4250	750	21.4
ABC corporate average	2025	2345	320	15.8

TABLE 2 1989 and 1990 Annual User-Reported Software Defect Rates
per KLOC

Environment	1989	1990	Change	Percent
Real-time military	0.5	0.4	−0.1	(20.0)
Real-time commercial	0.8	0.7	−0.1	(12.5)
Systems and support	2.5	2.8	0.3	10.7
Information systems	3.5	3.1	−0.4	(11.4)
ABC corporate average	1.5	1.4	−0.1	(6.6)

four software environments, expressed in "source statements per person year" measured to the ABC standard chart of accounts.

Table 2 shows the 1989 and 1990 annual user-reported defect rates for the same four software environments. The unit of measure is "unique valid defects per KLOC reported by users in one calendar year."

As can be seen from Tables 1 and 2, ABC enjoyed substantial improvements in both productivity and quality with the exception of the quality levels for "Systems and Support," for which improvement plans have been made.

ABC Migration to Function Points and Feature Points

Because the four discrete ABC environments use many different programming languages and measurements based on "source code statements" are known to be paradoxical and unreliable in mixed language environments, the ABC corporate measurement department decided to adopt the IBM Function Point metrics for information systems measurements and the extended SPR Feature Point metrics for the real-time and systems measurements. This decision was made in November of 1990, and it reflects the growing international trend toward function-based metrics for software.

Previous attempts at ABC to use Function Points in 1985 had not yielded satisfactory results for real-time software, because that technique was perceived as being optimized for information systems. The extended SPR Feature Point technique, originally developed in 1986, is suitable for real-time software, however. Tables 3 and 4 contain the ABC productivity and quality rates for 1989 and 1990 expressed in these new metrics.

Because functional metrics are free of the distortions and paradox associated with "lines of code," they provide a much clearer picture of economic productivity than was previously possible. When comparing Table 3 with Table 1, note that the improvement in ABC's economic

TABLE 3 1989 and 1990 Annual Software Productivity Rates Expressed in Feature Points and Function Points per Year

Environment	1989	1990	Change	Percent
Real-time military	12.0	12.4	0.4	3.3
Real-time commercial	14.0	16.0	2.0	14.2
Systems and support	18.0	22.0	4.0	22.2
Information systems	43.8	56.6	12.8	29.4
ABC corporate average	18.6	22.2	3.6	19.4

TABLE 4 1989 and 1990 Annual User-Reported Software Defect Rates Expressed in Defects per 100 Function or Feature Points per Year

Environment	1989	1990	Change	Percent
Real-time military	6.0	5.0	−1.0	(16.6)
Real-time commercial	10.0	9.0	−1.0	(10.0)
Systems and support	30.0	35.0	5.0	16.6
Information systems	28.0	23.0	−5.0	(17.9)
ABC corporate average	18.0	17.0	−1.0	(5.5)

software productivity was substantially greater than revealed by Table 1. This was due, in part, to the expanded use of application generators and query languages by the ABC Information Systems group. The productivity impact of higher-level languages was masked and distorted by the former "lines of code" metric.

Because quality is a positive matter, the ABC Measurement Department also recommends that software quality be expressed by using the unit of measure "Feature Points Delivered per Defect." This unit expresses the number of Feature (or Function) Points which are associated with a single user-reported bug. This metric yields progressively larger values as quality improves. Table 5 shows the ABC Corporation's 1989 and 1990 quality data with this metric.

Since the overall goal of the ABC Corporation's productivity and quality improvement program is to deliver more functionality to users

TABLE 5 1989 and 1990 Annual User-Reported Software Defect Rates Expressed as Feature and Function Points per Reported Defect

Environment	1989	1990	Change	Percent
Real-time military	16.1	20.2	4.1	25.0
Real-time commercial	10.0	11.4	1.4	14.0
Systems and support	3.2	2.9	−4.0	(9.4)
Information systems	3.6	4.3	0.7	19.5
ABC corporate average	5.5	6.0	0.5	9.1

with higher quality at the same time, this new metric of Feature Points per Defect will become an auxiliary corporate quality measure.

ABC Defect Removal Efficiencies

Table 6 shows the overall defect removal efficiency rates for the four environments, using the ABC standard formula for removal efficiency:

$$\text{Removal efficiency} = \frac{\text{prerelease defects}}{\text{prerelease defects} + 1 \text{ year of user defects}}$$

The defects counted are valid unique defects. Duplicate defects and invalid defects (user errors, hardware faults, etc.) are excluded from the efficiency calculations. The efficiency calculation includes the sum of all four severity levels from Severity 1 (total failure of software) through Severity 4 (superficial error).

Because the formula requires one year of user-reported defect reports before efficiency can be calculated, Table 6 shows the overall efficiencies for 1989 rather than for 1990. The 1990 efficiencies will be included in the 1991 annual report:

Although the ABC results are within approximate industry averages as reported by Software Productivity Research, it is obvious that the systems and support environment and the IS environment are not as rigorous in defect removal as the two real-time environments. Increased utilizations of inspection technologies will be necessary to achieve significant quality increases in 1990.

Differences in the Work Content of the Four ABC Environments

Prior to the utilization of the Software Productivity Research tool set, ABC had planned to develop a single "life cycle" systems development methodology (SDM) across all of its four environments. That would

TABLE 6 1989 Defect Removal Efficiencies of ABC Environments

ABC software domain	Overall efficiency, %
Real-time military environment	96.5
Real-time commercial environment	95.0
Systems and support environment	78.0
Information systems environment	80.0
ABC corporate average	90.3

Cost Accumulators	Environment			
	MIS	Sup	Sys	Mil
1. Requirements	X	X	X	X
2. Prototyping	X		X	X
3. Architecture			X	X
4. Formal Plans and Estimates			X	X
5. Initial Analysis and Design	X	X	X	X
6. Detail Design	X		X	X
7. Formal Design Reviews			X	X
8. Coding	X	X	X	X
9. Reusable Code			X	X
10. Purchased Package Code	X	X		X
11. Formal Code Inspections			X	X
12. Independ. Verif. & Valid.				X
13. Formal Configuration Mgt.			X	X
14. Formal Integration	X		X	X
15. User Documentation	X	X	X	X
16. Unit Testing	X	X	X	X
17. Function Testing	X	X	X	X
18. Integration Testing			X	X
19. System Testing	X		X	X
20. Field Testing			X	X
21. Acceptance Testing	X	X		X
22. Independent Testing				X
23. Formal Quality Assurance			X	X
24. Installation & Training	X	X	X	X
25. Project Management	X	X	X	X
Total activities	13	10	21	25

Figure 6 Average tasks performed for MIS, support, systems, and military projects within ABC.

not have been beneficial due to the differences in work content performed across the four main classes of ABC software. Figure 6 shows the average tasks performed in each ABC environment class.

The importance of Figure 6 is significant in terms of both ABC's productivity and quality goals. The differences in tasks performed is one of the key contributors to the overall differences in productivity. MIS and support software would benefit from the utilization of additional tasks that benefit quality, while military projects are constrained to perform tasks that appear perhaps unnecessary but are required by military specifications.

In all four ABC environments, substantial flexibility exists in both the maximum and average numbers of activities performed. For MIS projects, the smallest number of activities recorded was three and the largest was 17. For support software, the smallest number was 1 and the largest number was 6. For commercial systems software, the smallest number recorded was 5 and the largest number was 23. For military projects, the smallest number recorded was 19 and the largest was of course all 25.

Variations in the number of activities performed is a significant reason for productivity rate differences between large and small projects and also between project classes.

Differences in Software Specialization at ABC

Not only are there significant differences in the tasks performed among the four ABC software environments, but there are also significant differences in the kinds of staff specialists utilized. The significance of this factor is only just starting to be researched, and this is the first time occupation groups have been included in the ABC baseline report. Figure 7 shows the various specialists identified within ABC.

	Environment			
Occupation Groups	MIS	Sup	Sys	Mil
1. Application Programmers	X	X		X
2. Systems Programmers		X	X	X
3. Systems Analysts	X		X	X
4. Database Programmers	X			X
5. Database Administrators	X			
6. Proposal Specialists				X
7. Cost-Estimating Specialists				X
8. Measurement Specialists	X		X	X
9. Purchasing Specialists	X			X
10. Integration Specialists			X	X
11. Testing Specialists			X	X
12. Configuration Specialists				X
13. Quality Assurance			X	X
14. Technical Writers			X	X
15. Network Specialists	X		X	X
16. Human Factors Specialists			X	X
17. Microcode Specialists			X	X
18. Maintenance Specialists			X	X
19. Marketing Specialists			X	X
20. Contracts Specialists			X	X
21. Education Specialists			X	X
22. Customer Support	X		X	X
23. Field Service			X	X
24. Research Specialists			X	
25. Project Managers	X	X	X	X
Total	9	3	17	23

Figure 7 Average sets of specialists utilized for MIS, support, systems, and military projects within ABC.

It is apparent from Figure 7 that both the ABC information system groups and the internal tool development might benefit from the specialist skills used elsewhere within the company. In particular, it may also be useful to make some of the special skills available for MIS projects, such as human factors and integration.

ABC Software Productivity and Quality Goals for 1991

The year 1990 marks the last year that the older "source code statements" metric will be used as the primary metric for expressing software productivity and quality goals, although data will continue to be normalized to this base for several more years as a courtesy to those not yet familiar with function points and feature points.

The 1991 productivity and quality goals will be expressed in terms of the new Function Point/Feature Point metrics. The main productivity target for 1991 will be expressed as "Function or Feature Points delivered per staff year." The main quality target for 1991 will be expressed as "User-reported defects per 100 Feature/Function Points per year." Table 7 contains the new 1991 productivity goals, and Table 8 contains the new 1991 quality goals.

The technologies and methods that will allow these goals to be achieved include the normal ramp-up in the learning curve of the new JAD requirements method and the integrated graphics/text design tools introduced in 1990. Another and major contributing factor will be increased utilization of reusable code and the creation of a library of "blueprints" or reusable designs, commencing in late 1990.

Although the overall corporate defect reduction required for 1991 exceeds 50%, the technology for accomplishing this target has been in existence for many years and has demonstrated its effectiveness: The target essentially requires that internal systems and support software and the ABC corporate information systems use formal design and code inspections.

Formal design and code inspections for internal systems and for IS

TABLE 7 1990 Actual and 1991 Target Software Productivity Rates
Expressed in Feature Points and Function Points

Environment	1990	1991	Change	Percent
Real-time military	12.4	13.6	1.2	10.0
Real-time commercial	16.0	18.4	2.0	15.0
Systems and support	22.0	25.3	4.0	15.0
Information systems	56.6	65.1	8.5	15.0
ABC corporate average	22.2	25.4	3.2	14.4

TABLE 8 1990 Actual and 1991 Target User-Reported Software Defect Rates Expressed as Unique Valid Defects per 100 Function or Feature Points

Environment	1990	1991	Change	Percent
Real-time military	5.0	4.0	−1.0	(20.0)
Real-time commercial	9.0	6.0	−3.0	(33.3)
Systems and support	35.0	10.0	−25.0	(71.0)
Information systems	23.0	10.0	−13.0	(57.0)
ABC corporate average	17.0	8.0	−9.0	(53.0)

projects had been rejected in 1985, due to the assumption that the inspection process would delay delivery of these tightly scheduled projects. The ABC corporate productivity and quality measurements since then have shown this assumption to be unjustified. The projects that use careful reviews and inspections tend to have shorter schedules than those that do not. Similar findings have been reported from other enterprises, including IBM itself.

The introduction of design and code inspections for all project classes within the ABC Corporation will allow a new corporate goal to be set: All classes of software should achieve at least a 95% cumulative defect removal efficiency rate, using the standard corporate formula of defects found prior to delivery plus defects found during the first year of production. This goal will become effective for projects delivered in 1988.

ABC Corporation Enterprise Demographics

Table 9 summarizes the 1990 ABC overall demographics in terms of software staffing, function and feature points produced, source code produced, and user-reported unique valid defects:

Table 10 gives the size distribution of the programs, systems, and applications completed in calendar year 1990. As can be seen, 90% of all projects delivered in 1990 were small or very small in size.

TABLE 9 Overall 1990 ABC Corporation Software Demographics

Environment	Staffing in 1990	Lines of source code	Function/ feature points	Defects reported by users
Real-time military	75	116,250	930	46
Real-time commercial	300	600,000	4,800	420
Systems and support	50	137,500	1,100	385
Information systems	75	318,250	4,250	988
ABC totals	500	1,712,000	11,080	1,839

TABLE 10 Size Ranges of Software Projects Completed in 1990

Size range in KLOC		Projects complete	Percent of projects
Very large	> 512 K	0	0.0
Large	256–512 K	1	0.5
Medium	64–256 K	4	2.0
Small to medium	16–64 K	15	7.5
Small	2–16 K	40	20.0
Very small	< 2 K	140	70.0
Totals		200	100.0

TABLE 11 Effort Ranges of Software Projects Completed in 1990

Size range in KLOC		Labor-years of effort	Percent of effort
Very large	> 512 K	0	0.0
Large	256–512 K	150	20.4
Medium	64–256 K	250	34.0
Small to medium	16–64 K	200	27.2
Small	2–16 K	100	13.6
Very small	< 2 K	35	4.8
Totals		735	100.0

It is surprising to compare Table 10 and Table 11. From Table 10, it would appear that the bulk of the work at ABC is concentrated on small to very small programs, since those sizes constituted some 90% of the ABC software projects in 1989. However, when Table 11 is viewed, those same sizes accumulated less than 20% of the ABC effort.

Table 11 gives the development effort distribution of the programs, systems, and applications completed in calendar year 1990. Note that, although the projects were completed in calendar 1990, or otherwise they would not be in this report, the starting dates often were prior to 1990. The single large project, for example, started in 1984. This explains why the total effort for projects installed in 1990 is larger than the total software staff in 1990.

As can be seen, some 54% or bulk of ABC's corporate programming effort, was concentrated in the large and medium categories.

Table 12 gives the volume of source code and the percentage contribution of each size range to the overall 1990 deliveries. As can be seen, 57.9% of the delivered code was concentrated in the small to medium and medium-size categories.

Table 13 gives the 1990 overall ABC Corporation's software population by job category.

Table 14 shows the net change due to attrition, plus new hiring.

TABLE 12 Volume of Source Code for Software Projects Completed in Calendar Year 1990

Size range in KLOC		Source code delivered	Percent of total code
Very large	> 512 K	0	0.0
Large	256–512 K	260,000	15.2
Medium	64–256 K	512,000	29.9
Small to medium	16–64 K	480,000	28.0
Small	2–16 K	320,000	18.7
Very small	< 2 K	140,000	8.2
Totals		1,712,000	100.0

TABLE 13 Overall 1990 ABC Software Employment Distribution

Category	Number of personnel	Percent of personnel
Director(s)	1	0.2
3rd-line management	3	0.6
2nd-line management	12	2.4
1st-line management	34	6.8
Management subtotal	50	10.0
Senior software engineers*	25	5.0
Senior systems analysts	10	2.0
Programmer/analysts	35	7.0
Software engineers*	250	50.0
Software quality assurance	15	3.0
Software technical writers	15	3.0
Technical subtotal	400	80.0
Planning/estimating	10	2.0
Measurements	15	3.0
Administration/support	25	5.0
Administrative subtotal	50	10.0
ABC 1990 total	500	100.0

*The job title "software engineer" has been utilized by ABC as a generic title for as many as 10 different subspecialties, including testing specialists, maintenance specialist, and many others. This situation is common in high-technology and telecommunication companies, but it is not adequate to meet current needs. (Indeed, some telecommunication companies use the title "member of the technical staff" for more than 50 occupations.) Expanded job descriptions and position codes are being developed by the ABC personnel department, and they will be used in the next annual report.

TABLE 14 Annual Personnel Changes in 1989

	Number	Percent
1990 Attrition	20	4.0
1990 New hires	40	8.0
1990 Net change	40	4.0

Analysis of Factors Which Cause Variations

The ABC Corporate Measurement Department has been licensed to use a set of software measurement methods and tools developed by Software Productivity Research, Inc., of Burlington, Mass. The SPR proprietary measurement technique contains two major elements:

1. A questionnaire that includes all of the known soft factors that can impact software projects by as much as 1 percent.

2. A measurement tool that collects the hard staffing, effort, cost, and schedule data by activity using a standard chart of accounts for 25 development/enhancement activities. (Supplemental charts of accounts are used for capturing user effort, commercial software maintenance effort for field service and customer support, and package evaluations).

The SPR measurement methodology generates several reports that allowed our ABC statisticians to use multiple-regression techniques to isolate the factors that cause productivity and quality variations. Our statisticians were able to derive the correlations that explained variations in hard data by using multiple-regression techniques on the soft data. This section summarizes the key findings, dealing first with individual factors and then with composite sets of factors. The results throughout are shown in two ways.

1. Lines of Source Code per Man-Year (abbreviated LOC/MY)

2. Feature Points per Man-Year (abbreviated FP/MY)

Single-Factor Influences

Following are discussions of the major individual factors which have been demonstrated to cause significant changes in productivity or quality.

Concurrent hardware and software development

This factor is very significant when it occurs, but it occurs primarily only for the real-time communications projects where the communications hardware is being built simultaneously with the software. This factor seldom or never affects MIS projects. Unstable hardware was noted on 20 of the 200 projects delivered in 1990, and yielded the results listed in Table 15.

TABLE 15 Annual Software Productivity with Stable and Unstable Hardware

Factor	Source code production (LOC/MY)	Feature Point production (FP/MY)
Stable hardware	3000	24
Unstable hardware	1500	12

Constraints on performance or memory utilization

Real-time performance constraints and tight memory requirements degrade productivity when they occur, because of the extra effort needed to tune the software. Memory and performance constraints occurred primarily on the real-time communications and military projects. This factor seldom affects MIS projects. Constrained memory and performance requirements were noted on 30 of the 200 projects delivered in 1990, and yielded the results listed in Table 16.

TABLE 16 Annual Software Production with Constrained Performance and Memory Utilization

Factor	Source code production (LOC/MY)	Feature Point production (FP/MY)
No constraints	2700	22
Severe constraints	1800	15

Volume of difficult and complex code

Complexity of software is partly subjective, but the McCabe essential complexity metric provides reasonably effective insights into code structural complexity. Highly complex or difficult code degrades productivity, as may be expected. Whether or not any given program needs to be complex, or whether the complexity is caused by inexperience or haste, is a more difficult question. Complexity occurs often in software, and 80 of the 200 projects delivered in 1990 had significant

TABLE 17 Annual Software Production with Low, Medium, and
High Volumes of Difficult, Complex Code

Factor	Source code production (LOC/MY)	Feature Point production (FP/MY)
Low complexity	4500	50
Medium complexity	2500	25
High complexity	1200	10

amounts of complex, difficult code within them. For 25 of the projects, complexity appeared to derive from the nature of the problems themselves. For 55 of the projects with high complexity, the complexity appeared to be accidental (Table 17).

Unstable or uncertain user requirements

Unstable and uncertain user requirements are a widespread phenomenon (Table 18), and prior to the introduction of the Joint Application Design (JAD) methodology in 1988, some 70% of the ABC projects cited unstable requirements. Even though the JAD method works effectively for MIS projects, it is not as easy to apply to commercial or military software where the project does not meet the needs of a single identified set of customers, and where the customers are not employees of ABC. In 1990, unstable requirements remains a problem, and 90 projects out of the 200 delivered cited this factor.

TABLE 18 Annual Software Production with Stable and Unstable
User Requirements

Factor	Source code production (LOC/MY)	Feature Point production (FP/MY)
No constraints	3500	40
Severe constraints	1700	18

Development team experience levels

The experience levels of the development teams vary from leading experts through novices. As might be anticipated, productivity rates vary accordingly. From the 1990 data, 10 projects out of 200 asserted that the development team was uniformly high in experience; 25 projects asserted that the development team was new to the application area; and 165 stated that the development team was of mixed experience levels (Table 19).

TABLE 19 Annual Software Production with Experienced, Average, and Inexperienced Development Staffs

Factor	Source code production (LOC/MY)	Feature Point production (FP/MY)
Experienced staff	4000	50
Average staff	3000	27
Inexperienced staff	1600	15

New development versus enhancement projects

As the industry and the ABC corporation mature, the quantity of aging software that needs enhancement grows larger each year. In 1990, the ABC corporation's production library consisted of some 5500 identifiable programs and 200 systems, with an aggregate total of 15,000,000 source statements in various languages. The Function/Feature Point totals for the production library is 135,000. A substantial amount of the total ABC software effort goes into the maintenance and enhancement (and replacement) of aging software. In 1990, 120 projects out of the 200 delivered involved enhancing or maintaining existing applications. Some 15 projects out of 200 were complete replacements of older programs. The observed productivity rates and curves for enhancement projects are sufficiently different from development to require their own analysis. Because of the overhead costs of analyzing the existing software, regression testing it, and recompiling it, enhancement productivity rates are normally lower than producing an equivalent amount of new code (Table 20).

TABLE 20 Annual Software Production Rates for Development and Enhancement Projects

Factor	Source code production (LQC/MY)	Feature Point production (FP/MY)
New projects	3200	37
Enhancements	2500	23

Small versus large software projects

Enhancement projects and new development projects follow different patterns when considering size. Small development projects are significantly more productive than large. However, small enhancement projects are usually low in productivity, due to overhead costs of recompiling, regression testing, etc. Small projects are less than 16 K source statements, and large projects are greater than 64 K (Table 21).

TABLE 21 **Annual Software Production Rates for Small versus Large Development and Enhancement Projects**

Factor	Source code production (LOC/MY)	Feature Point production (FP/MY)
Small development	5000	60
Large development	2500	24
Small enhancement	1750	15
Large enhancements	3000	28

The impact of programming languages

One of the primary reasons for adopting Function Points and Feature Points is that source code metrics penalize high-level languages. The penalty is caused by a well-known phenomenon that has been understood for more than 200 years by manufacturing managers, but unfortunately not by software managers. When a manufacturing process includes a significant percentage of fixed costs and there is a decline in the number of units produced, the cost per unit will go up. For software, there are many fixed and inelastic costs. When migration occurs to a higher-level language, the results are mathematically equivalent to a manufacturing process with fewer units produced, since high-level languages require fewer statements to implement functions.

The 1990 report is the first ABC measurement report to segregate productivity rates by language, and the new SPR Feature Point technique (used on real-time and military projects) and IBM Function Point technique (used on MIS projects) illustrated the hazards of "Lines of Code" metrics when projects are measured to a standard life cycle with a high percentage of paperwork and overhead costs included. In Table 22 are the 1990 data by language. At least 10 projects were developed in each of the languages shown from the 1990 data.

The impact of physical office environments

This is a new study topic included for the first time in the 1990 report. Analysis outside the ABC Corporation by Gerald McCue, Dean of Architecture at Harvard, and Tom DeMarco and Tim Lister, of the Atlantic Systems Guild, indicated that the physical office environment would have a strong impact on software development productivity. Office space of more than 78 square feet was often associated with high software productivity, while office space of less than 44 square feet or open office arrangements was often associated with low software productivity (Table 23). Since the SPR questionnaire captures data on office space, it was decided to explore this factor. The results were ambiguous in ABC, since except for 50 of the personnel working in a

TABLE 22 Annual Software Production as a Function of the Programming Language Used for Development

Language	Source code production (LOC/MY)	Feature Point production (FP/MY)
Assembly language	4000	18
C	3500	24
Cobol	3000	28
Ada	2500	33
APL	1500	45
Objective-C	1250	47
Query language(s)	1000	77

Note: This table clearly reveals why Function Points and Feature Points are superior to "Line of Source Code" metrics for economic analysis and productivity studies. The older "Lines of Source Code" metrics penalize high-level languages, and they always achieve their highest rates for the least productive languages.

TABLE 23 Annual Software Production as a Function of the Size of the Programming Office

Factor	Source code production (LOC/MY)	Feature Point production (FP/MY)
> 75 square feet	3500	37
50 to 75 square feet	3200	32
< 50 square feet	2400	27

temporary rented office building, where they averaged 75 square feet of enclosed space, and all of the other office space was between 40 and 70 square feet per technical staff member. Although trends were noted, the 0% availability of larger office environments meant that the high-end benefits could not be explored.

Since office space is a new topic in this year's survey, a total of 125 ABC software personnel were interviewed regarding their perceptions of the ABC office environment. The results were unambiguous: All occupants of crowded office space felt their performance suffered as a result. Several enjoyed the social advantages of working with colleagues, but none who had moved from smaller to larger office space wished to return to the previous environment. This is a factor which deserves more extended study in the future.

The impact of reusable code

"Reusable code" is defined as independent functional modules that can be linked or included in a program without requiring any internal

TABLE 24 **Annual Software Production Rates as a Function of the Amount of Reused Code in the Application**

Factor	Source code production (LOC/MY)	Feature Point production (FP/MY)
> 50% reusability	9500	87
25% to 50% reuse	4500	42
10% to 25% reuse	3500	32
< 10% reusability	3000	28

modification. Examples of reusable code include calendar routines, date conversion routines, square root routines, and routines for handling pull-down menus, standard input validation routines, and the like. Code that is borrowed from other applications can be classed as reusable if it does not require modification. If borrowed code does require minor or major change before use, it should be termed "modified code." Some 50 projects out of 200 reported various degrees of reusable code. Because of the very high productivity impact of reusability, this technology should be extended in 1988 (Table 24).

Since this factor had the largest impact of any factor in the baseline, it is apparent that ABC should institute an aggressive campaign to achieve higher levels of reusability in all four ABC environments.

The impact of project organization structures

This is a new topic studied for the first time in 1990. Observations from other companies such as GTE and ITT had indicated that matrix management for large software projects had a negative effect on productivity. The ABC data tends to confirm this hypothesis. Of the 200 projects reported, 20 used a matrix management organization, 25 were hierarchically organized, 65 were small team projects (2–3), and 90 were individual projects (Table 25).

TABLE 25 **Annual Software Production Rates as a Function of Project Organization Structure**

Factor	Source code production (LOC/MY)	Feature Point production (FP/MY)
One-person projects	5500	50
Small teams (2–3)	4250	39
Hierarchical	3750	34
Matrixed	2800	25

The impact of CASE tools and workstations

The acronym "CASE" stands for the term "Computer-Aided Software Engineering" and refers to loosely integrated tool sets that are intended to provide continuous support from design through development. The ABC CASE environment, experimental in 1990, includes a graphics/text design tool with an integrated data dictionary, an application generator coupled to the design engine, and a workstation optimized for these tools. (*Note:* Vendor names are deliberately omitted from this report.) Since the ABC CASE environment was experimental in 1990, it was used on only five small projects out of 200 (Table 26). To equalize the comparisons, the CASE results are reported against 10 projects of similar sizes and attributes.

TABLE 26 **Annual Software Production Rates Using Experimental CASE Tool Suites and Workstations**

Factor	Source code production (LOC/MY)	Feature Point production (FP/MY)
CASE development	6000	55
Non-CASE projects	4000	36

The Impact of Composite Multiple Factors

This section deals with the impact of simultaneous changes in several factors at once. Because of the large number of possibilities, the organizing principle for this section is in declining order of results. The factors associated with successful projects are discussed first, and then the factors associated with various problems, ending with the factors most often associated with cancelled projects and disasters.

Factors associated with successful projects

The word "successful" in the context of this report means three things: 1) The project was completed on time and within budget; 2) The first year of production revealed acceptable levels of quality and reliability; 3) Users were generally satisfied with the functionality and ease of use of the software. All three of these items must be present for a project to be considered a success. An "average" project is one where at least one and sometimes two of the criteria were met. An "unsuccessful" project is one where none of the three criteria were met but the project was finished and delivered anyway (Table 27).

The factors most often associated with success include but are not limited to the following: 1) Stable and unambiguous requirements; 2)

TABLE 27 Annual Software Production for Successful, Average, and Unsuccessful Projects

Factor	Source code production (LOC/MY)	Feature Point production (FP/MY)
Successful projects	4250	39
Average projects	2500	23
Unsuccessful projects	1100	12

Stable and well-understood hardware; 3) Well-seasoned, experienced development teams; 4) No excessive schedule pressure on the managers or developers; 5) Adequate computer availability and response time; 6) Full reviews and inspections of major deliverables; 7) Careful design and specification; 8) Automation of design and documentation.

Of the 375 projects reported over the last two years in the 1989 and 1990 reports, some 30 or 8% meet the above criteria for being termed "successful." It is interesting and statistically significant that successful projects are often record-setters for productivity and quality simultaneously.

Factors causing customer dissatisfaction

In reviewing several hundred letters and attending a number of meetings with customers and customer organizations, the major factors that cause dissatisfaction appear to be these: 1) Poor quality and reliability; 2) Inadequate functionality; 3) Hard to use or irrational commands and menus; 4) Poor user documentation; 5) Poor customer support; 6) Late delivery of promised functions.

Conversely, the factors cited most often by users who like software products are these: 1) Intuitive command and menu structure; 2) Excellent functionality; 3) Excellent quality and reliability; 4) Good or excellent user documentation; 5) Good or excellent customer support.

The controllable factors which development managers and staff can utilize to achieve high levels of user satisfaction are these: 1) Joint Application Design (JAD) requirements development where possible; 2) Prototyping where possible; 3) Reviews and Inspection; 4) Professional writers.

Of the 375 projects reported in 1989 and 1990, some 40, or 10.6%, had high levels of user satisfaction, while 65, or 17.3%, had significant user complaints after delivery. As it turns out, projects with high levels of user satisfaction are usually more productive than projects that lack this attribute, as can be seen in Table 28.

TABLE 28 Annual Software Production Rates for Projects with High and Low User Satisfaction

Factor	Source code production (LOC/MY)	Feature Point production (FP/MY)
High user satisfaction	3850	36
Low user satisfaction	3200	29

Factors causing cost and schedule overruns

The primary factor causing cost and schedule overruns is the common occurrence that the schedules and development costs were set before the project was defined. Of the 375 projects reported in 1986 and 1990, some 135, or 36%, had their schedules and budgets assigned prior to the completion of requirements while the project scopes were still unstable.

The second most common reason for cost and schedule overruns is new functionality added to a project after the requirements are nominally frozen. Some 60 out of 375 projects (16%) reported that substantial new functions were added during the design and development period. In the most extreme case, a project was initially sized at 80,000 source statements. New functionality ordered by the executive vice president, who was the customer for the project, brought the delivered size of the application up to 195,000 source statements: an increase of 144%.

The third most common reason for cost and schedule overruns is inaccurate sizing and estimating. There are more than 30 commercially available software estimating programs in the United States in 1990, but only 25 projects out of 200 (12.5%) reported using a formal estimating approach.

The fourth most common reason for cost and schedule overruns a complex of multiple factors: 1) Inexperience of the development team; 2) Unstable hardware; 3) Unexpected attrition of key project personnel; 4) Failure to consider topics such as multi-site development; 5) Poor morale; 6) Management disputes regarding the project; 7) Inadequate tools, workstations, computer availability, or response time.

As may be expected, the projects overrunning their estimated costs and schedules had lower productivity than those which met their cost and schedule estimates, as can be seen in Table 29.

Factors causing quality and reliability problems

In all major studies to date, there is an almost perfect correlation between quality and productivity. Those projects that aim at high qual-

TABLE 29 Annual Software Production Rates for Projects That Met Cost
and Schedule Estimates Versus Projects That Overran Their Cost
and Schedule Estimates

Factor	Source code production (LOC/MY)	Feature Point production (FP/MY)
Estimates met	4250	39
Estimates not met	2650	22

ity will also achieve shorter development schedules and higher productivity rates than yielded by any other target. The reasons for this phenomenon are straightforward: Defect removal has been the most expensive aspect of software development since the software industry began in 1946. Projects that utilize a well-chosen combination of defect prevention and defect removal methods will simultaneously optimize both quality and productivity.

The defect prevention methods most often associated with high quality and high productivity include but are not limited to the following: 1) JAD or Joint Application Design requirements methods; 2) Prototyping; 3) User involvement during requirements and design; 4) Fully automated design tools with graphics and text support and an integral data dictionary; 5) Formal analysis and design methods such as Warnier-Orr Design, Jackson Design, Structured Design, state transition diagramming, etc.; 6) Reusable code and standard functional modules; 7) Structured programming techniques; 8) Restructuring of aging Cobol applications via one of the commercial restructuring engines; 9) Tracking of defects and quality.

The defect removal methods most often associated with high quality and high productivity include but are not limited to the following: 1) Formal design and code inspections; 2) structured walk-throughs; 3) Formal test departments staffed by testing specialists; 4) Tracking of defects and quality (this is both a prevention and removal technique); 5) Formal test libraries; 6) Quality Assurance reviews of key deliverables.

The methodologies most often associated with low quality and low productivity include but are not limited to the following: 1) No reviews or inspections at all; 2) No significant user involvement during requirements and design; 3) No formal requirements and design methods; 4) No quality tracking at all; 5) No formal test library; 6) No Quality Assurance organization at all; 7) No quality goals for managers or key projects; 8) Corporate emphasis on schedule adherence rather than quality; 9) No testing specialists at all.

The phrase "high quality" (Table 30) means meeting or bettering the ABC corporate targets for annual user-reported defect rates plus

TABLE 30 Annual Software Production Rates for Projects That Have High Quality Versus Projects with Low Qualities

Factor	Source code production (LOC/MY)	Feature Point production (FP/MY)
High-quality projects	4000	38
Low-quality projects	2200	28

achieving good to excellent user reports on functionality and usability. Of the 375 projects reported in 1986 and 1990, some 20 (10%) had high quality, while 40 (20%) had low quality.

The phrase "low quality" means the bottom quartile of annual user-reported defects (i.e., the largest quantity of defect reports) plus achieving low to very low user satisfaction reports on functionality and usability. Of the 375 projects reported in 1989 and 1990, some 40 (20%) had low quality.

Factors causing project cancellations

In 1989 and 1990, some 375 software projects were completed and included in the two annual ABC productivity reports. There were also 40 projected cancelled over that same time period, or 10.6% of all projects begun. The factors which were associated with the cancellations are these:

1. *Change in business environment:* Closing of a business unit negated the need for projects. This factor caused 15 out of 40 cancellations.

2. *Costs exceed value:* The anticipated cost to complete of the projects versus the anticipated value of the projects did not meet the corporate requirements for internal rates of return. This factor caused 10 out of 40 cancellations.

3. *Stronger project selected:* Two similar projects were in simultaneous development. When this fact became known, one of the projects was terminated. This factor caused 5 out of 40 cancellations. This factor is not uncommon in large enterprises, and it implies a need for more careful project screening and justification.

4. *Unachievable objectives:* The project requirements were unimplementable by using available technologies, and the project was terminated by joint agreement of users and development management. This factor caused 5 out of 40 cancellations.

5. *Miscellaneous causes:* These projects were cancelled for various reasons, including A) the primary sponsor and user of the project

left the company; B) a purchased package became available that performed the same functions; C) hardware changes negated the need for project. These factors caused 5 out of 40 cancellations.

Because the projects were cancelled, their complete productivity data is not known. It is significant, however, that the accumulated effort on the 40 cancelled projects amounted to 125 person-years, or 12.5% of the available staff time for 2 years.

Summary and Conclusions about Factors Affecting Productivity

There are more than 200 individual factors that are known to affect software productivity and quality. These factors exert both an individual impact, and of course combinations of factors can exert synergistic impacts.

This report highlights some of the major and better understood factors as they relate to productivity and quality. Other topics, no less important, have been omitted in the interest of conciseness from this year's report and will be dealt with in the future.

The ABC Corporation in 1990 can be defined as a better-than-average enterprise in overall quality and productivity at present. Further, because of strong executive, management, and staff desire to improve, our rate of change is much faster than normal. The prognosis for 1991 and the future is excellent.

Example of an Executive Briefing on a New Baseline

Introduction

When software measurement programs get underway in an enterprise, the information is obviously of vital importance to senior management and executives. Not only do the software executives have an interest in the results, but so do senior corporate executives up to the levels of the CEO and indeed the board of directors.

Although printed baseline reports such as the one illustrated in Appendix D are distributed to executives, it is normal practice to supplement the printed baseline report with a presentation in either overhead or 35-mm slide format. That allows the executives to interact directly and ask questions about topics that may be outside the scope of the printed baseline.

For the example baseline shown here, a half-day working session is normally reserved to give executives a chance to fully explore the issues that are raised. It often happens that the half day expands to a full day if major issues are surfaced that need extended discussions. This presentation is normally given to management by the director or senior manager who is responsible for carrying out the baseline. In large corporations such as IBM, ITT, AT&T, and Hewlett-Packard, the executive briefing may be given many times in many different laboratories and locations. For example, the annual IBM, ITT, and Hewlett-Packard baseline presentations were given internationally at more than 20 locations within the respective companies.

The following is an example of an executive briefing on an initial software baseline. In this case the baseline was prepared by the consulting staff of Software Productivity Research. (To ensure confidentiality, excerpts from several actual baselines have been melded together rather than using data prepared for a single enterprise.)

Context of the Example

The sample baseline presentation in this appendix is typical of an annual baseline when a company first starts its measurement program. Since measurement itself is new in such a situation, the baseline presentation must provide some background information about the measurement process itself, as well as about the findings of the baseline study.

In later years, the baseline presentations may eliminate the background information on measurement and concentrate only on the findings. However, when an initial baseline is prepared, executives will have as many questions about the measurement process as they have about the findings, so it is important to include some background information. Indeed, if the executive questions about the measurement process are not answered clearly and precisely, the results of the baseline may not be credible.

The example baseline is a divisional MIS baseline for one unit of a manufacturing company, identified in the example as "XYZ company." Note that this is a hypothetical example and is not intended to represent any actual company. The initial baseline was created from the analysis of 19 MIS projects which spanned the nature, size, and scope of the division's software work. The projects were a mixture of new development, enhancement, and maintenance work. The sizes ranged from small to large, and the platforms on which the projects were developed ranged from microcomputers to mainframes.

Some of the kinds of projects included were an order entry system, an accounts receivable system, a human resources system, and a benefits tracking system. The data collected for the projects themselves was derived from structured interviews by using a proprietary questionnaire. The interviews were conducted with the project managers and teams, augmented by data from the company's project-tracking system. (Tracking system data is seldom accurate enough to be relied upon, however.)

The interview sessions averaged about $3\frac{1}{2}$ h per project, and the data collection was spread over a period of about 2 weeks. The interview process itself normally arouses some apprehension ahead of time, since the project managers and teams may be uncertain as to the intent. This apprehension disappears immediately once the sessions begin, and it becomes obvious that the purpose is to find out what the project staffs really think about the suitability of the tools, methods, and environments that are available to them.

Components of the Executive Briefing

The normal format of a baseline executive briefing includes the following sections and contents:

1. *Introduction (normally 5 to 10 pages)* Brief discussion of how measurements were taken and what projects were measured.

2. *Executive summary (normally 5 to 15 pages)* Highlights of key findings in 10 min or so.

3. *Findings (normally 10 to 30 pages)* Significant strengths and weaknesses derived from the interviews and both the soft and hard data collected.

4. *Conclusions (normally 10 to 30 pages)* How the organization stacks up in both an absolute sense and compared to other companies in the same lines of business (if known) and to U.S. norms.

5. *Opportunities (normally 10 to 20 pages)* The word "opportunity" is a polite way to point out problems that need to be fixed.

6. *Next steps (normally 5 to 20 pages)* The next step after an initial baseline report is normally to produce an improvement plan aimed at correcting the key deficiencies noted.

7. *Appendix (normally 10 to 20 pages)* Backup data in substantial amounts should detailed questions be asked.

Assuming that the baseline presentation will be given to somewhere between 3 and 10 executives at a sitting, and that there will be a normal volume of questions and dialog between the presenter and the executives, a briefing such as the following will take between 2 and 4 h to present. However, for the very first sets of briefings when a company is just getting started with measurement, it is desirable to plan on at least half a day and sometimes a full day for the session.

Preparation of the Executive Briefing

There are a number of alternative ways to reach the same end when it comes to baseline presentations and reports. ITT, for example, used Focus as the database for holding its baseline information, SAS for the statistical analysis, and Merganthaler phototypesetters for report preparation.

The baseline presentation shown in this appendix was prepared from data collected by using the proprietary CHECKPOINT® data collection tool and the associated interview questionnaire. The results of the projects were aggregated and statistically analyzed using proprietary tools developed by Software Productivity Research. The presentation itself was produced using ordinary laser printers.

In addition to the basic statistical analysis, the consultants who gathered the data discussed the findings among themselves and with both the clients and the consulting staff of SPR. It is normal when outside consultants collect the data to produce intermediate reports to apprise the clients of the early findings. The final report, included here, should not contain major surprises which no one in the client organization realized would be forthcoming.

The aggregation, statistical analysis, and report preparation took about two calendar weeks and somewhat more than 2 weeks of effort, since it involved both consulting and production personnel. The moral of the story is simple: Allow adequate time for both thoughtful analysis and for final production.

Problems Widely Reported via Executive Briefings

To the management and staff of any given company, the problems identified in a baseline presentation will no doubt seem unique. However, to management consultants who work with many different companies, certain problems occur repeatedly in many different organizations. Just as physicians tend to see quite a large number of similar medical conditions such as influenza or hay fever, consultants tend to see quite a lot of similar software problems.

The baseline presentation shown here contains a typical volume of problems that are widespread in MIS organizations throughout the United States. Following are six very common problems observed in the U.S. as a whole, and in this report in particular:

1. Quality control is not very good.
2. Schedule pressure is the strongest driving force.
3. Requirements are seldom stable, so that projects grow significantly late in development.
4. There is little consistency from project to project in the tools or methods used.
5. The physical office space is cramped and noisy.
6. Prior to the baseline itself, there was no meaningful measurement program of either quality or productivity.

Fortunately, there are available solutions for all six of these common problems, although the solution to problem 5 is normally very expensive. For example, office space in urban areas such as Boston, San Francisco, and New York is currently renting for about $35 per square foot. To double or triple the space per staff member is not a trivial expense.

However, until the impact of problems such as these six is quantified, they can exist (and have existed) for many years. When the problems and their implications are measured in a formal baseline presentation, it becomes possible to move toward their solution in a reasonable and well-planned fashion.

There will also be problems that are in fact unique to an enterprise that will require customized solutions. As a rule of thumb, about 70 percent of observed problems are fairly standard but perhaps 30 percent of the observed problems will be unique to the specific enterprise or location.

Executive Responses to the Briefings

For many years, senior management has experienced frustration that is due to an inability to bring software projects under full management control. Although there may be aspects of discomfort if some of the problems found and reported are serious, the normal response by senior management to a baseline presentation is a compound of surprise, interest, and relief. The surprise is because they may never before have seen a rational, quantified depiction of software. The interest is because they finally have something tangible that allows them to exert management judgment about needed improvements. The relief is because they can finally see the light at the end of the tunnel: Software is no longer an esoteric discipline but is now capable of being a true business function.

There is one almost universal executive reaction to an initial baseline presentation. The executives will want the same kind of information, or even more, on a continuing basis. A surprisingly large number of measurement specialists, including both A. J. Albrecht and the author, did not originally plan long-term careers in the measurement domain. The requests by IBM's senior executives for more and more quantified information on MIS projects (in the case of Albrecht) and systems software (in the case of the author) led to continuing measurement studies and eventually into new permanent careers that centered around software measurement. This same phenomenon can be observed in other large enterprises as well. Once solid, reliable, and quantified information on software becomes available, executives will never want to go back to the previous situation of "unmeasured and therefore unmanageable."

A software baseline study and the associated presentation and written report are key steps in bringing software out of the dark ages and into the light as both a true engineering discipline and a valuable component of modern business.

XYZ COMPANY

SOFTWARE
MEASUREMENT
BASELINE STUDY

Final Report

Software Productivity Research, Inc.
77 South Bedford Street
Burlington, MA 01803
(617) 273-0140
Fax: (617) 273-5176

TABLE OF CONTENTS

- Introduction

- Executive Summary

- Findings

- Conclusions

- Opportunities

- Next Steps

- Appendix

C000037/2

425

INTRODUCTION

FOUR AREAS NEED TO BE MANAGED TO IMPROVE SOFTWARE QUALITY AND PRODUCTIVITY

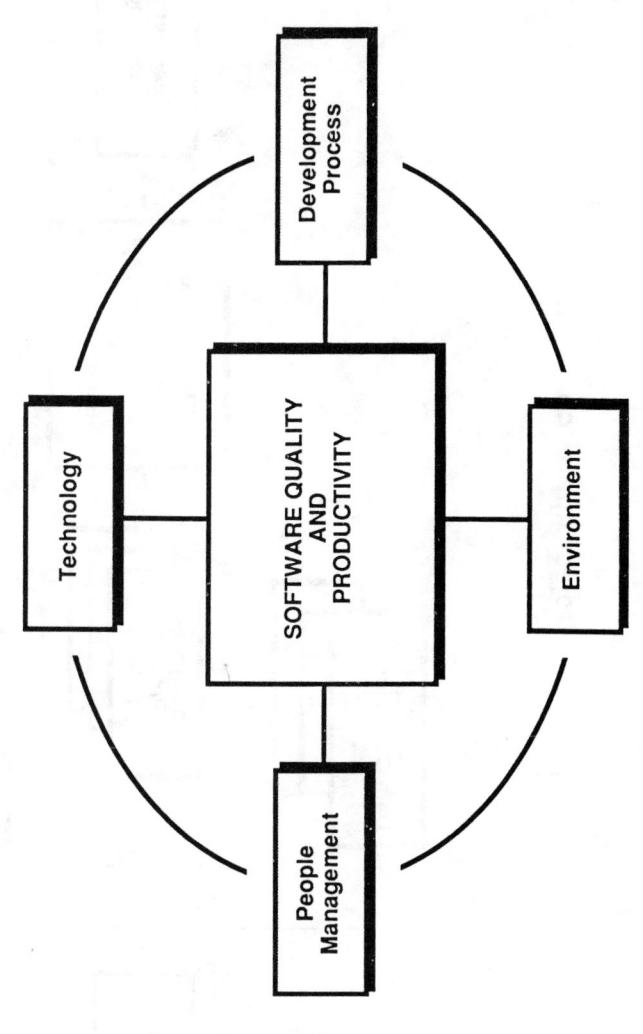

C000374

427

THE SOFTWARE MEASUREMENT BASELINE PROCESS

Project Approach

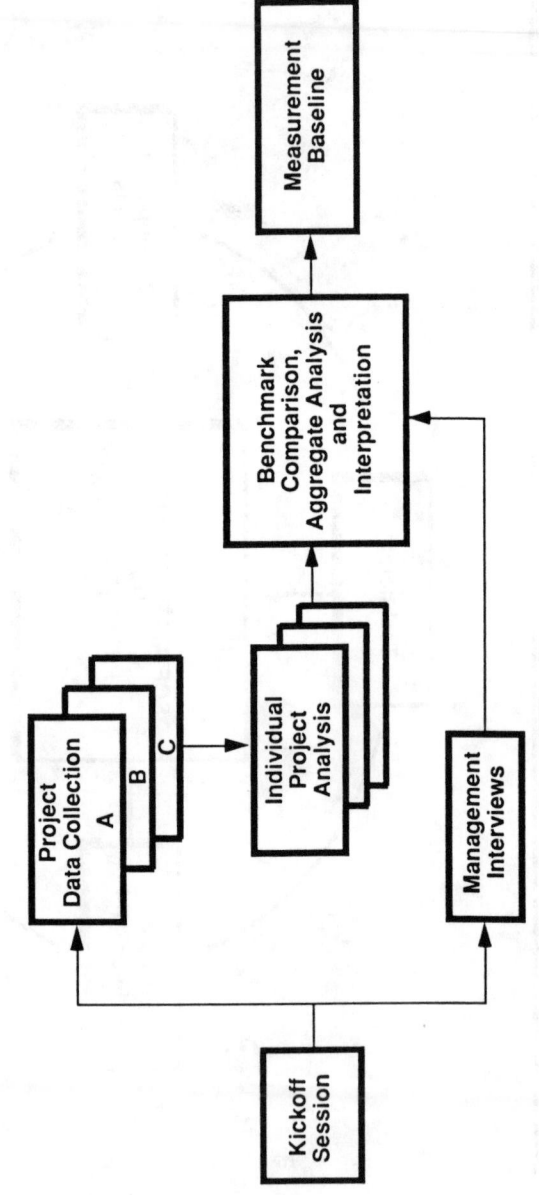

Kickoff Session → Project Data Collection (A, B, C) → Individual Project Analysis → Benchmark Comparison, Aggregate Analysis and Interpretation → Measurement Baseline

Kickoff Session → Management Interviews → Benchmark Comparison, Aggregate Analysis and Interpretation

C0003715

SOFTWARE QUALITY AND PRODUCTIVITY MEASUREMENT LEADS TO NEW STRATEGIC DIRECTION AND MANAGEMENT PLANS

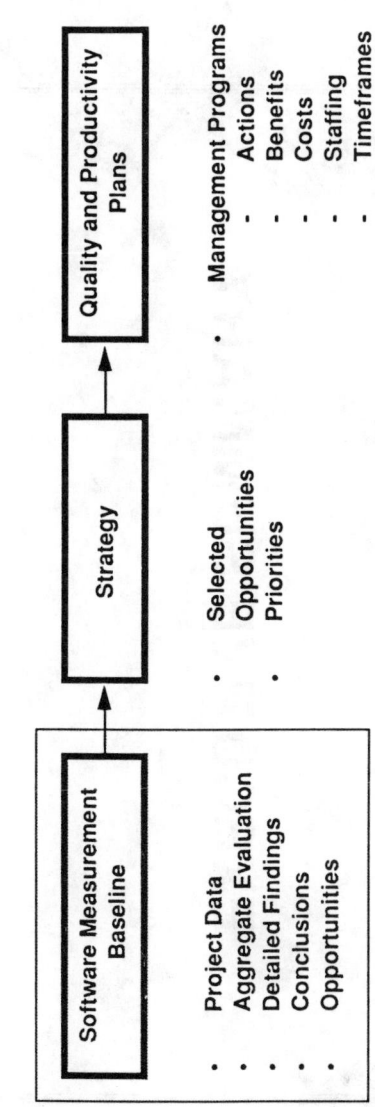

C00037/11

EXECUTIVE SUMMARY

PROJECT SCOPE

Project review included 19 applications, varying in type, size, and technology.

CODE	PROJECT I.D.	TYPE	SIZE	TECHNOLOGY
A	Purchase Order Entry	D	L	MF
B	Securities Handling	D	S	MF
C	Claims	D	S	MF
D	Automatic Teller	E	S	MF
E	Human Resources	D	S	MF
F	Payroll Front-End	D	M	MF
G	Distribution Systems	M	M	MF
H	On-Line Agent	E	L	MF
J	Merchandising Systems	D	M	PC
K	Accounts Receivable	E	M	MF
L	Benefits	E	S	MF
M	Long Term Care	E	S	PC
N	Manufacturing Systems	D	S	MF
P	Confirmation	E	L	PK
Q	Prototype	E	L	MF
R	Financial Analysis	M	L	MF
S	Systems Conversion	D	S	MF
T	Checkpoint	D	S	MF
U	On-Line Inquiry	E	M	PC

KEY:

1. TYPE	2. SIZE	3. TECHNOLOGY
D = Development	L = Large (>500 FP)	MF = Mainframe
E = Enhancement	M = Medium (200-500 FP)	PC = Micro
M = Maintenance	S = Small (<200 FP)	PK = Package

C00037/9

EXECUTIVE SUMMARY

- I/S needs to develop a greater awareness of business problems and strategies, and focus their efforts on tactically supporting those strategies.

- People Management includes an I/S staff with strong, technical expertise. High morale and company loyalty are prevalent. It is necessary to move forward in new directions:

  - The Need to Increase Business Knowledge
  - Manage Customer Expectations
  - Develop Project Management Skills

- Technology includes the lack of consistent use of development methods, techniques, and tools reducing productivity and increasing project risk. Use of tools needs to be propagated using the following:

  - Enforcement/Standards
  - Newsletters
  - Tool Assessment/Feedback

EXECUTIVE SUMMARY (CONT)

- Development Process needs to be brought up-to-date. To meet the demands for the future I/S must move ahead decisively:

  - Updated SDM's
  - QA Process
  - Measurement Program
  - Automated Design Methods

- Environment is mainly focused on I/S profession and not the overall "big picture" of the business

  - Move Culture Towards Quality
  - Customer/I/S Team Building

C00037/14

FINDINGS

HARD DATA FINDINGS

INDIVIDUAL PROJECT DATA WAS COLLECTED
AND COMPARED TO INDUSTRY STANDARDS.

- Staffing Levels

- Project Schedules

- Documentation Volumes

- Productivity Levels

- Defect Removal

PROJECT STAFFING LEVELS ARE HIGH EMPHASIZING THE PUSH FOR QUICKER SYSTEMS DELIVERY

Industry Staffing Averages

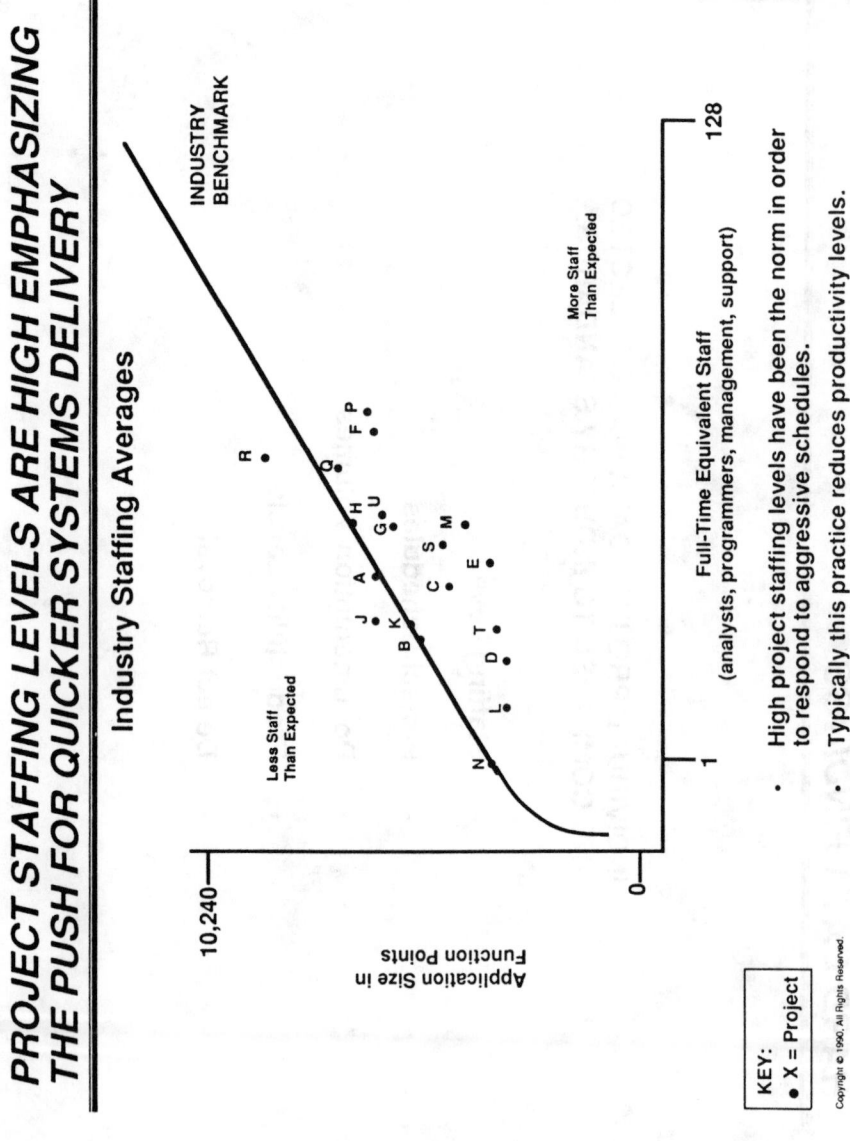

KEY:
● X = Project

- High project staffing levels have been the norm in order to respond to aggressive schedules.
- Typically this practice reduces productivity levels.

436

SHORTER SCHEDULES REFLECT THE DEADLINE DRIVEN ENVIRONMENT

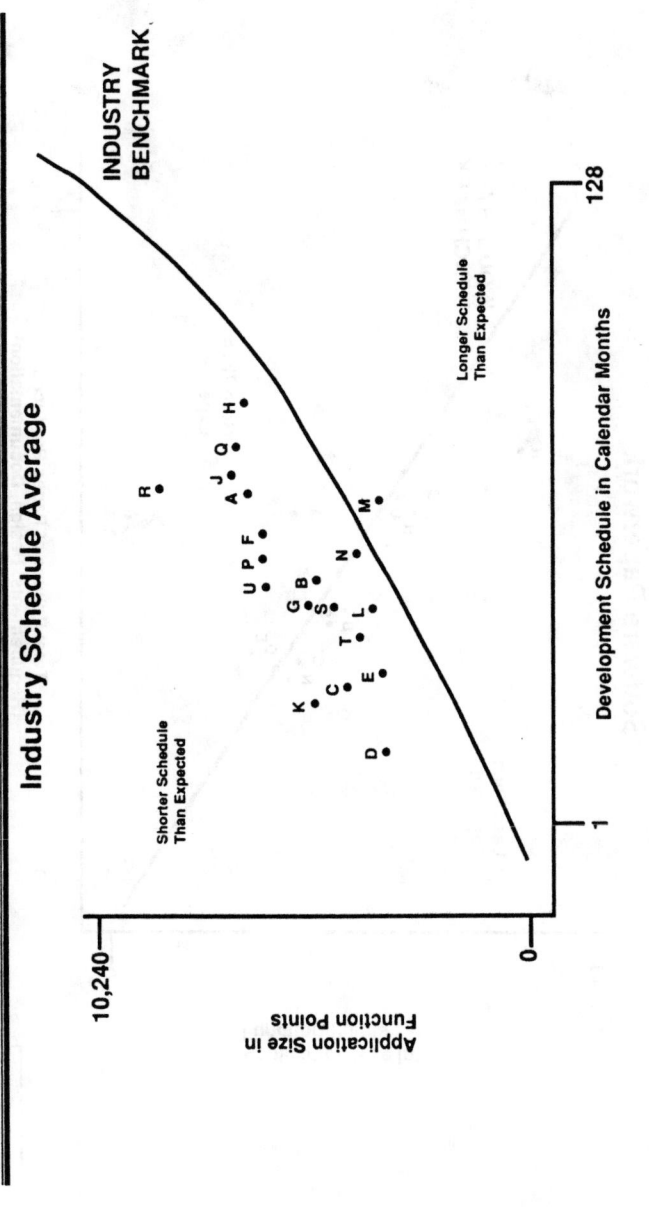

Industry Schedule Average

Application Size in Function Points

Development Schedule in Calendar Months

INDUSTRY BENCHMARK

Shorter Schedule Than Expected

Longer Schedule Than Expected

- Most projects reported scheduling pressures as a major concern.

KEY:
● X = Project

437

SOFTWARE AND USER DOCUMENTATION WAS GENERALLY LESS THAN EXPECTED

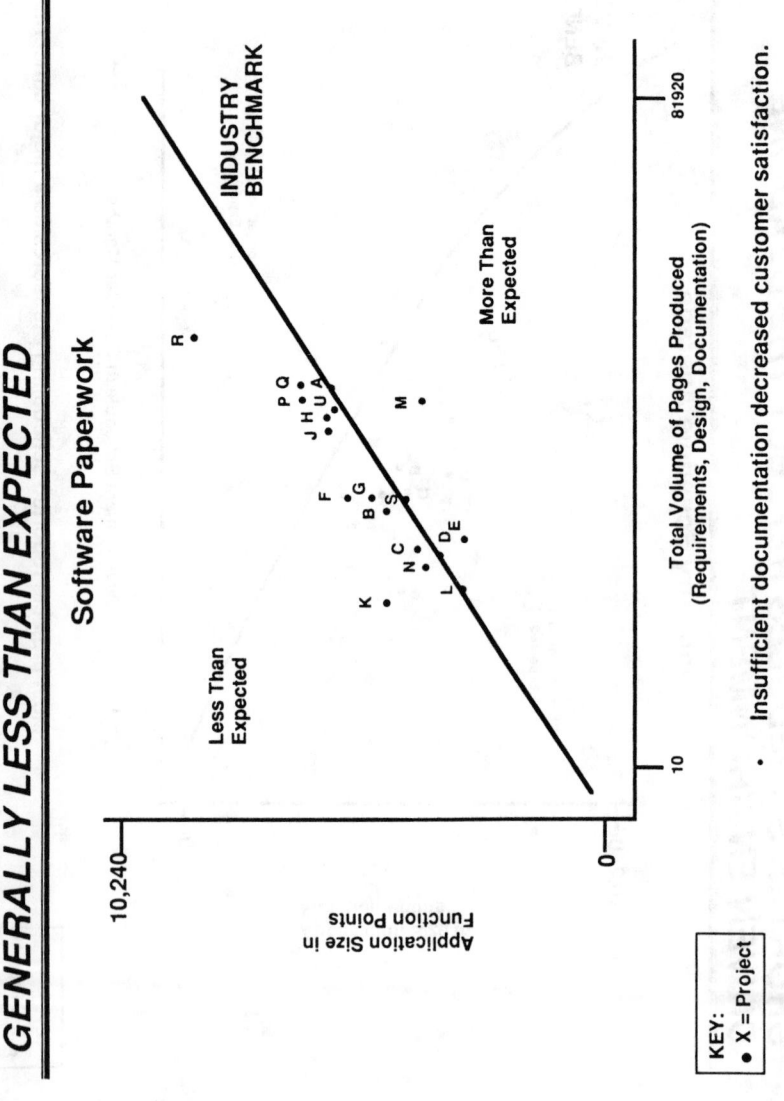

Software Paperwork

INDUSTRY BENCHMARK

Less Than Expected

More Than Expected

Application Size in Function Points

10,240

0

Total Volume of Pages Produced
(Requirements, Design, Documentation)

10   81920

- Insufficient documentation decreased customer satisfaction.

KEY:
● X = Project

OVERALL PRODUCTIVITY LEVELS VARIED SIGNIFICANTLY

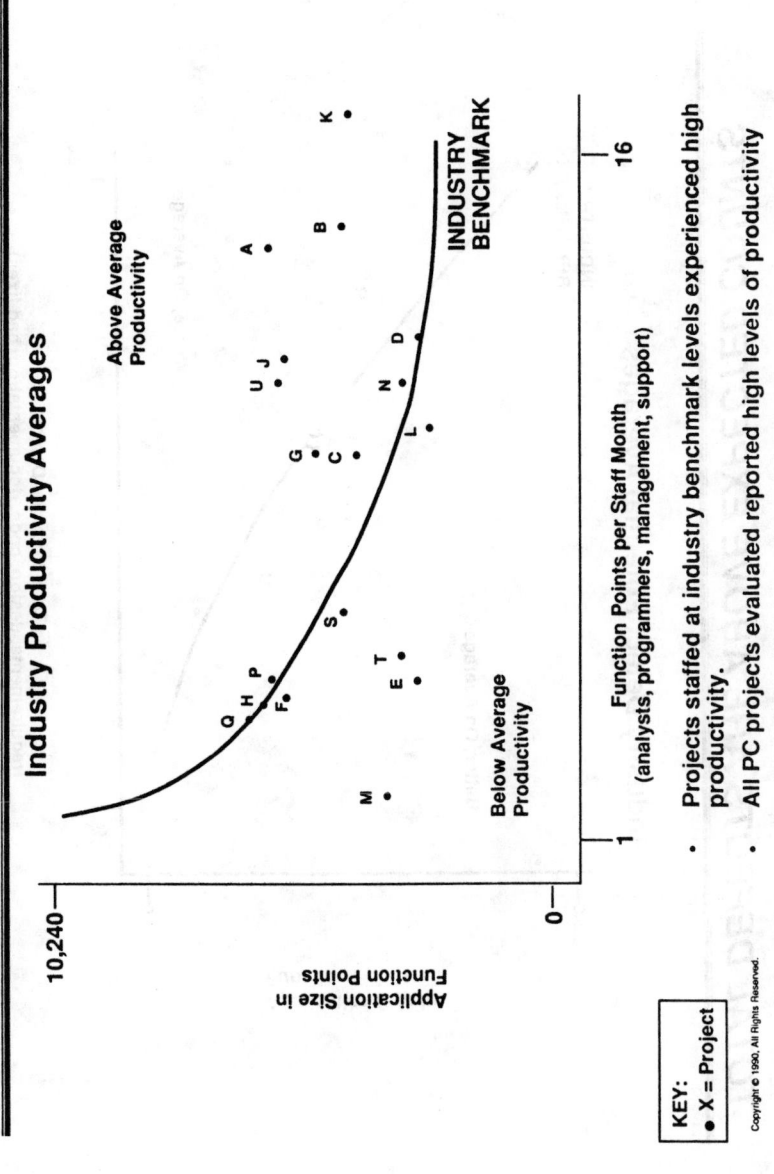

Industry Productivity Averages

Above Average Productivity

Below Average Productivity

INDUSTRY BENCHMARK

Application Size in Function Points

10,240

1

0

Function Points per Staff Month
(analysts, programmers, management, support)

16

- Projects staffed at industry benchmark levels experienced high productivity.

- All PC projects evaluated reported high levels of productivity

439

TOTAL DEFECTS ARE ABOVE EXPECTED COUNTS

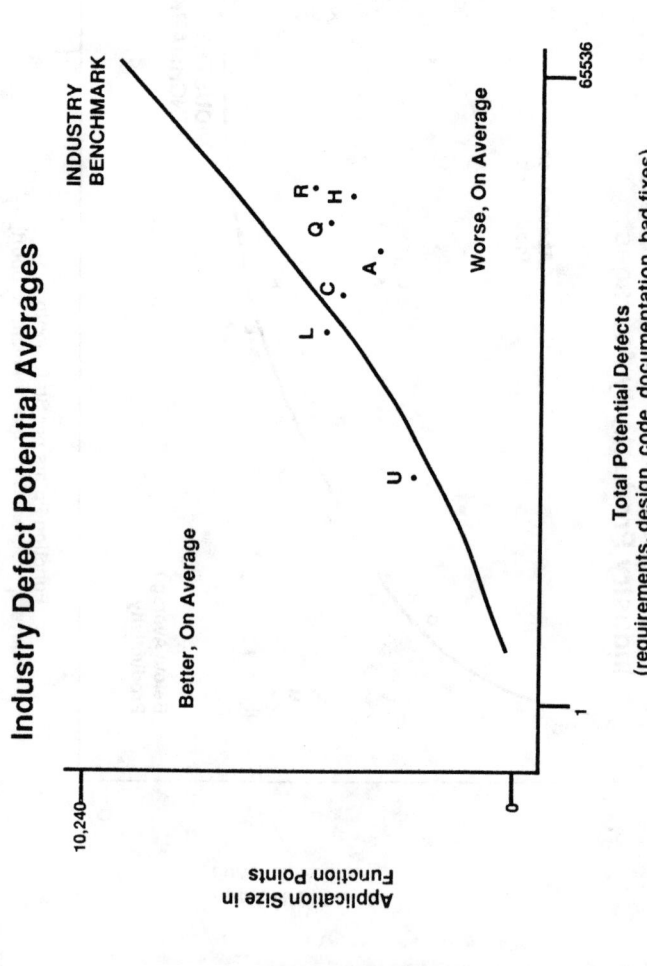

Industry Defect Potential Averages

INDUSTRY BENCHMARK

Better, On Average

Worse, On Average

L C Q R H A U

Application Size in Function Points

10,240

0

1

65536

Total Potential Defects
(requirements, design, code, documentation, bad fixes)

DEFECT FORECASTING SHOULD BE PERFORMED TO PREDICT DEFECT COUNTS

Industry Delivered Defect Averages
Expectations Based on Size Shown

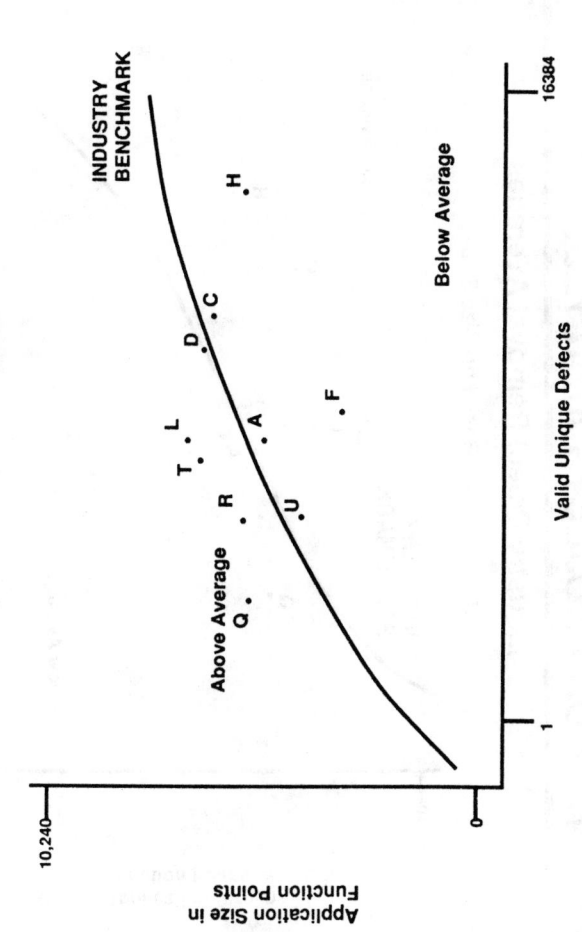

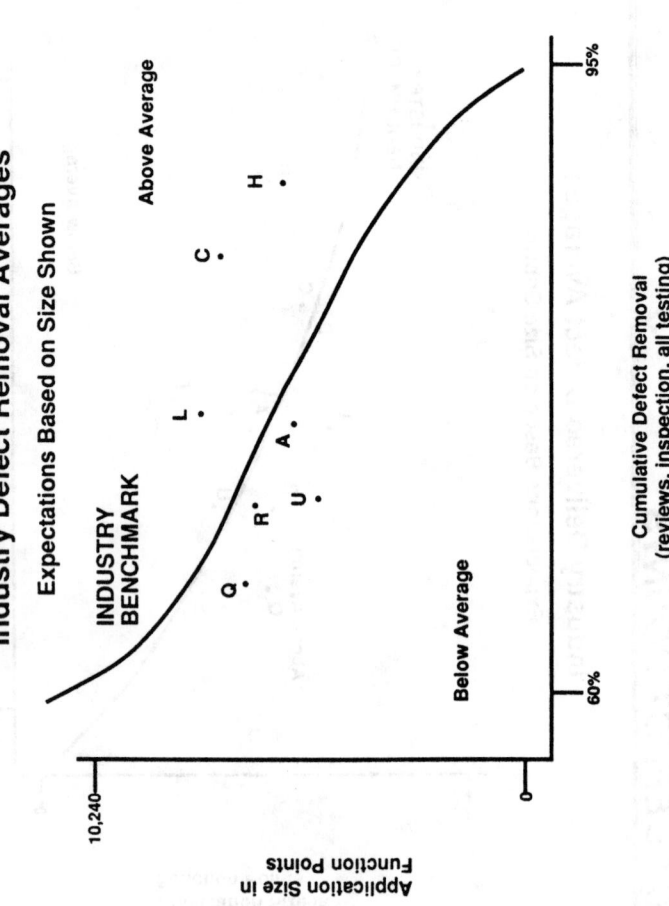

DEFECT REMOVAL EFFICIENCY RATES VARIED SIGNIFICANTLY ON PROJECTS ANALYZED.

Industry Defect Removal Averages

Expectations Based on Size Shown

Above Average

INDUSTRY BENCHMARK

Below Average

Application Size in Function Points

10,240

0

60%   95%

Cumulative Defect Removal
(reviews, inspection, all testing)

CUSTOMER PERCEPTION OF SYSTEMS QUALITY WAS SURVEYED

2 Perspectives Were Sought

	CUSTOMERS	
Survey	End User	Project Team
Data Accuracy	✓	
System Availability	✓	
Functionality	✓	
Reliability	✓	
Screens/Reports	✓	
Documentation	✓	
Training	✓	
System Design		✓
Estimating/Planning		✓
Project Controls		✓
Computer Support		✓
Development Techniques		✓
Development Tools		✓
Technical Knowledge		✓
Resource Availability		

C0003/24

443

END-USER CUSTOMERS ARE GENERALLY SATISFIED WITH DELIVERED SYSTEMS

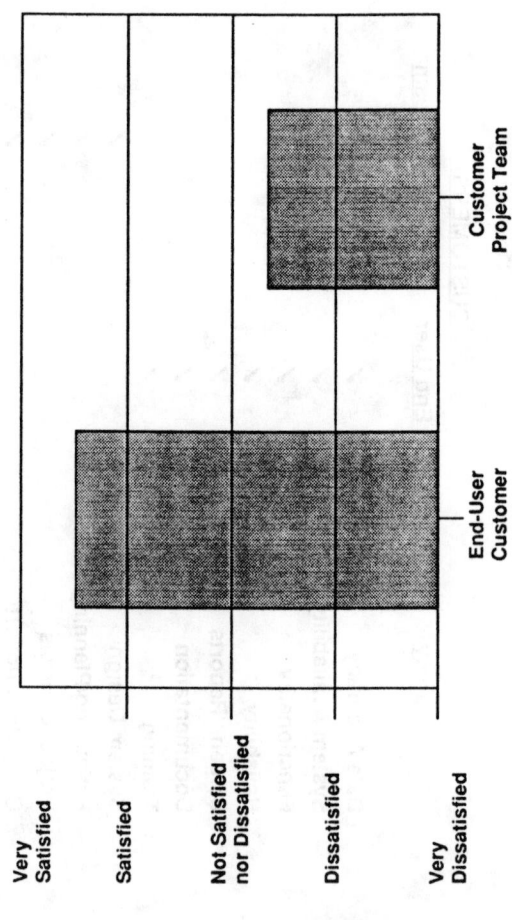

Very
Satisfied

Satisfied

Not Satisfied
nor Dissatisfied

Dissatisfied

Very
Dissatisfied

End-User
Customer

Customer
Project Team

- Customer project team members were less than satisfied with development activities.

END-USER CUSTOMER CONCERNED WITH QUALITY AND QUANTITY OF DOCUMENTATION

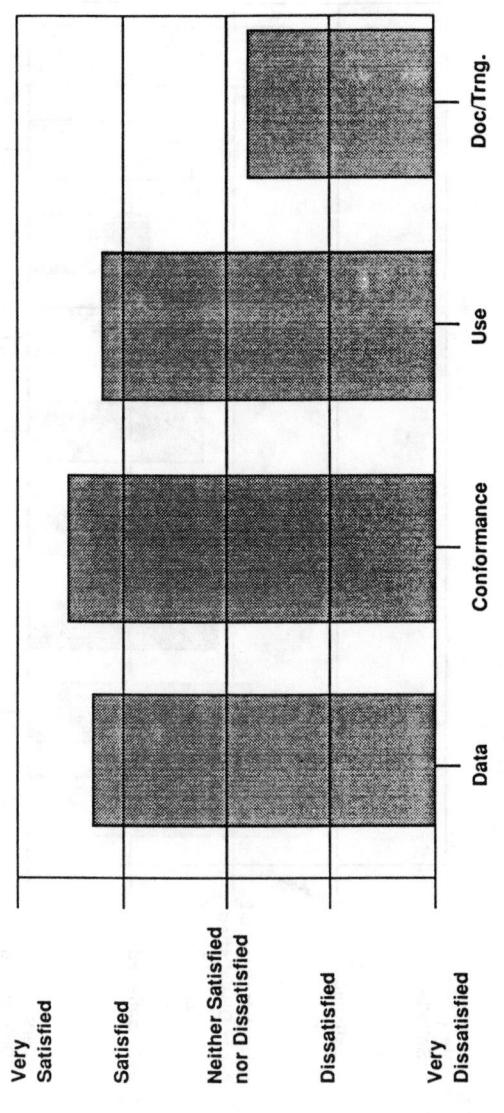

- Support documentation was of poor quality.

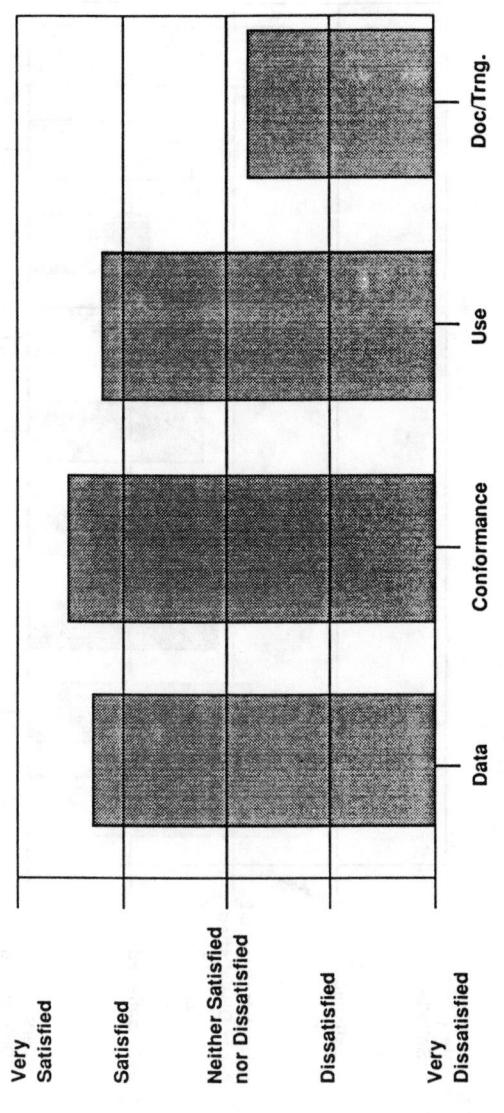

C0003726

445

PROJECT TEAM CUSTOMERS FOCUS ON PLANNING, AND DEVELOPMENT TOOLS AND TECHNIQUES, AS AREAS FOR IMPROVEMENT

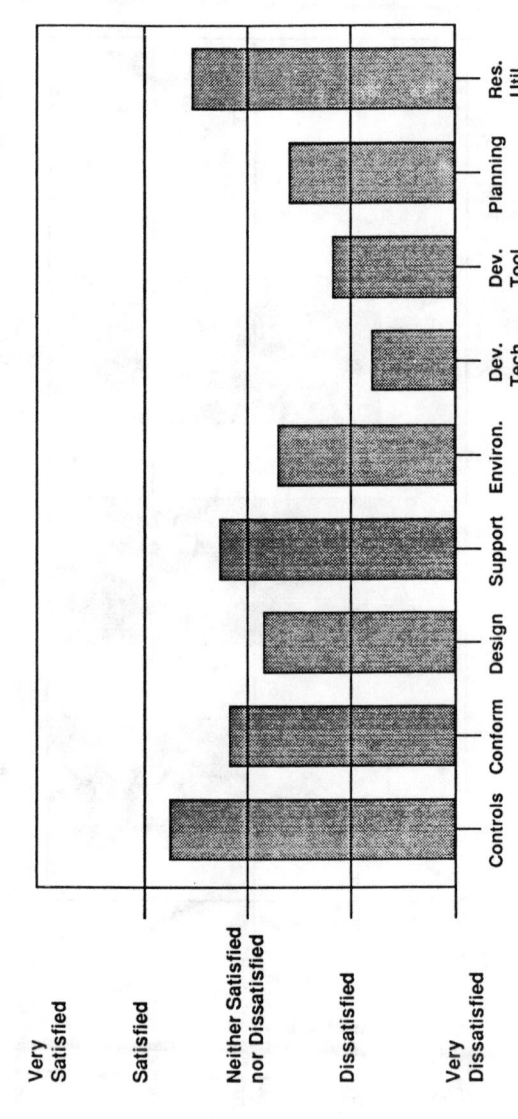

- Customers are not satisfied with the accuracy of estimates and project plans.
- System documentation and testing sign-off procedures are not adequate.
- Customers are less than satisfied with development techniques and tools.

C00037/27

446

SOFT DATA FINDINGS

PROJECT WORKSHOPS WERE CONDUCTED, FOCUSING ON A BROAD RANGE OF MEASURES.

- Experience Levels

- Tools/Methods

- Defect Removal Activity

- Project Management

- Environment

- Maintenance & Enhancement Support

C00037/28

447

A HIGH LEVEL OF DEVELOPMENT EXPERIENCE MAY BE OFFSET BY LIMITED USER INVOLVEMENT AND EXPERIENCE

Staff/Customer Experience

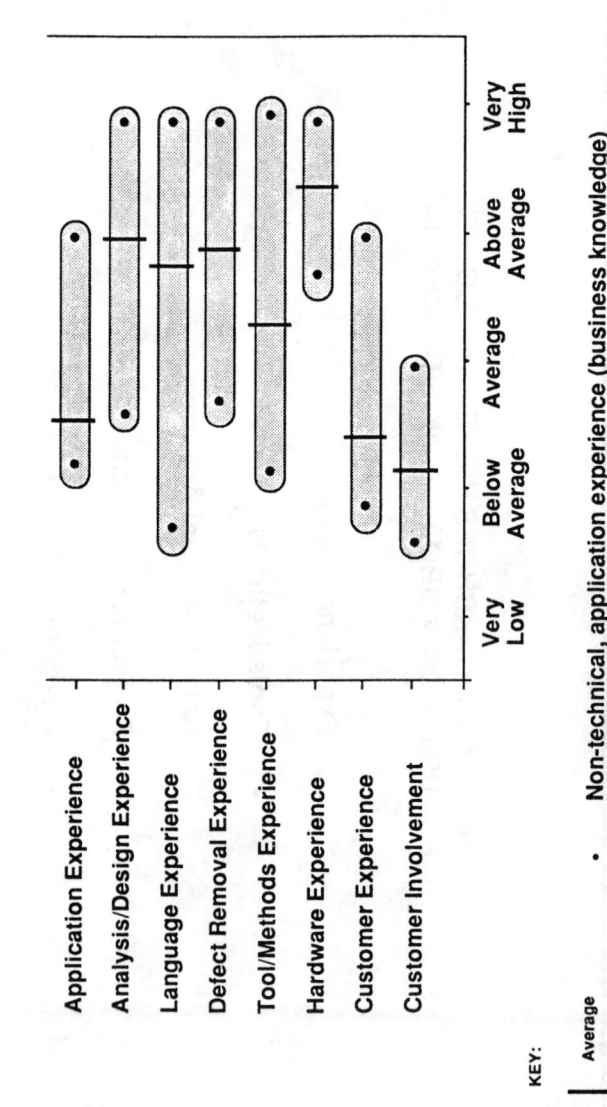

KEY:

| Average

● Project Range

● Non-technical, application experience (business knowledge) was rated lowest among skill areas.

448

C00037/29

A SYSTEMS DEVELOPMENT METHODOLOGY EXISTS BUT IS USED SPARINGLY ACROSS PROJECTS

Development Methods

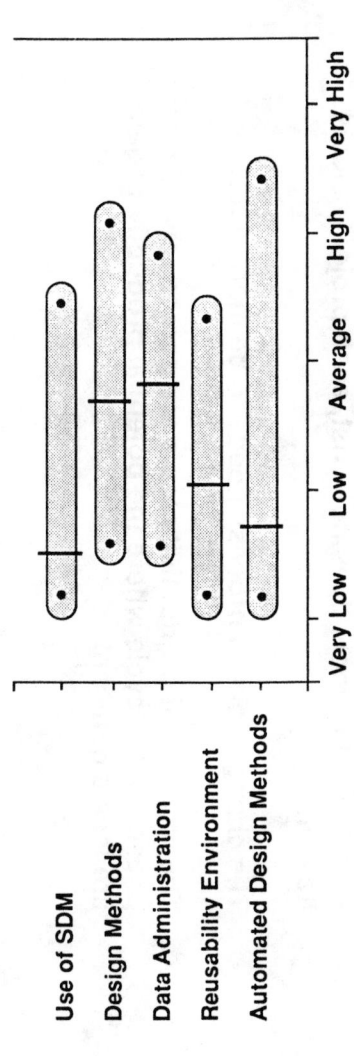

Degree of Utilization

KEY:

Average	•	Development techniques are used inconsistently from project to project.
Project Range	•	Automated methods are used infrequently.
•		Use of SDM's and automated design methods are not enforced.

C00037/30

449

DEVELOPMENT METHODS

Additional Findings

- A stable set of tools does not exist, each project selects its own.

- The change control process needs to be more rigorous.

- The majority of productivity tools are geared towards later phases of life cycle where the potential productivity gains are less significant.

BASELINE DATA

BASELINE DATA - PROJECT KEY

PROJECT I.D.

Purchase Order Entry
Securities Handling
Claims
Automatic Teller
Human Resources
Payroll Front-End
Distribution Systems
On-Line Agent
Merchandising Systems
Accounts Receivable
Benefits
Long Term Care
Manufacturing Systems
Confirmation Prototype
Financial Analysis
Systems Conversion
Checkpoint
On-Line Inquiry

EXPLANATION OF NORMALIZED SCALE

The scale used for the soft data on the following pages normalizes the Checkpoint Questionnaire Scale by exactly reversing it (e.g., 3.2 becomes 2.8).

The Normalized Scale facilitates statistical analysis and graphical representation of the data.

Checkpoint Questionnaire Scale		Normalized Scale
5.0 - 4.5	Poor	1.0 - 1.5
4.5 - 3.5	Below Average	1.5 - 2.5
3.5 - 2.5	Average	2.5 - 3.5
2.5 - 1.5	Above Average	3.5 - 4.5
1.5 - 1.0	Leading Edge	4.5 - 5.0

BASELINE DATA - END-USER CUSTOMER SATISFACTION

ATTRIBUTE

CODE	SYST. DATA	SYST. CONF.	SYST. USE	SYST. DOC/TRNG.	TOTAL
A	3.75	3.29	3.33	3.63	3.48
B	2.90	2.26	2.75	3.00	4.00
C	3.84	3.79	4.15	3.60	3.89
D	3.75	2.71	2.38	1.75	2.77
E	4.00	4.00	3.75	3.55	3.20
F	3.45	3.70	3.87	2.00	3.25
G	3.00	3.00	3.87	2.00	3.00
H	3.90	3.82	3.88	3.15	3.71
J	3.70	3.70	4.00	2.10	3.50
K	4.14	4.00	3.45	2.33	3.60
L	3.60	3.27	3.96	1.65	3.20
M	4.46	4.23	4.13	3.88	3.05
N	5.00	5.00	4.09	5.00	4.69
P	3.38	3.13	3.29	2.75	3.15
Q	4.00	3.95	3.88	3.39	3.81
R	4.05	4.17	3.93	1.73	3.00
S	4.00	3.75	3.86	3.50	3.78
T	5.00	4.86	4.92	2.00	4.00
U	4.43	4.50	4.44	1.95	3.10
CLIENT AVG.	**4.20**	**4.45**	**4.15**	**2.88**	**3.92**

453

BASELINE DATA - PRODUCTIVITY

ATTRIBUTE

CODE	TECH	TYPE	FP	EFF	SCH	FTE	DOC	FP/MO
A	MF	D	588	40.3	10.5	3.8	1969	14.58
B	MF	D	193	13.8	6.0	2.3	199	13.99
C	MF	D	145	16.0	3.5	4.6	166	9.06
D	MF	E	63	5.2	2.0	2.6	163	12.12
E	MF	D	69	16.2	3.7	4.4	174	4.26
F	MF	D	437	110.0	8.0	14.4	335	3.80
G	MF	M	288	30.8	5.3	5.9	380	9.36
H	MF	E	604	164.3	22.0	6.6	1000	3.68
J	PC	D	392	34.0	11.0	3.1	914	11.53
K	MF	E	202	12.2	2.5	3.2	67	16.50
L	MF	E	57	6.2	5.0	1.5	108	9.83
M	PC	E	80	50.0	11.3	6.3	1407	1.60
N	MF	D	79	7.1	7.0	1.0	121	11.06
P	PK	E	513	104.4	7.0	14.9	1181	4.91
Q	MF	E	671	186.9	16.0	11.7	1541	3.59
R	MF	M	3162	120.0	12.0	10.1	2136	25.98
S	MF	D	158	28.5	5.7	4.8	450	5.54
T	MF	D	63	14.2	4.3	3.3	110	4.44
U	PC	E	405	35.0	5.3	7.0	1195	10.95
CLIENT AVG.			429	52.4	7.8	6.0	716	9.30

KEY:

CODE
Identifies Projects on graphs

TYPE
D = Development
E = Enhancement
M = Maintenance

TECHNOLOGY
MF = Mainframe
PC = Micro
PK = Package

FP = Function Points
EFF = Effort (Person-Months)
SCH = Schedule (Elapsed Months)
FTE = Staff (Full-Time Equivalents)
DOC = Documentation (Pages)
FP/MO = Productivity (Function Points per Person-Month)

C0003T/55

454

BASELINE DATA - PEOPLE MANAGEMENT

ATTRIBUTE

CODE	APPL. EXP.	ANAL. DSN. EXP.	LANG. EXP.	DEF. REM. EXP.	USER EXP.	USER INVOL.	H/W EXP.	PROJ. ORG. STRCT.	MORALE	TEAM COHES.	TOOL/ METH. EXP.	MAINT. PERS.	TOTAL
A	3.0	5.0	5.0	4.5	4.0	2.0	4.5	2.0	5.0	5.0	3.0		4.1
B	2.0	2.0	4.5	2.5	4.0	2.0	4.5	4.5	4.5	4.0	4.5		3.7
C	2.0	3.0	4.0	3.0	2.5	6.5	4.0	2.0	5.0	4.5	2.5		3.3
D	2.0	3.0	3.0	4.5	3.5	2.0	5.0	2.0	4.0	5.0	4.5		3.7
E	4.0	4.0	5.0	4.5	2.3	2.0	5.0	4.0	3.0	5.0	5.0		4.1
F	3.0	3.0	3.0	3.0	4.0	2.0	4.0	1.0	1.0	3.0	3.0		2.9
G	3.5	3.5	4.0	4.0	1.8	1.7	5.0	2.5	5.0	4.5	3.0		3.7
H	3.5	4.0	3.5	3.0	4.0	41.0	3.5	3.0	3.0	5.0	3.0	3.6	3.6
J	2.0	3.0	3.0	4.0	3.0	3.0	5.0	3.0	5.0	4.0	2.0	3.7	3.4
K	4.5	5.0	4.0	5.0	4.0	2.0	5.0	4.0	5.0	5.0	5.0	4.0	4.5
L	2.0	3.0	4.0	3.5	3.0	2.0	4.0	3.0	4.0	4.0	4.0		3.5
M	2.0	4.0	4.0	3.0	4.0	3.5	4.0	3.0	4.0	3.0	2.5		3.4
N	5.0	3.0	1.5	4.0	3.5	2.0	5.0	4.0	3.5	5.0	2.0		3.7
P	3.0	4.5	4.0	3.3	3.0	2.0	4.0	1.0	3.0	1.5	3.0		3.1
Q	3.0	2.0	4.0	4.5	2.5	1.9	4.0	3.0	5.0	4.0	2.5		3.3
R	4.0	3.0	3.0	4.5	4.0	4.0	4.0	3.0	3.0	4.0	4.0	4.0	3.7
S	3.0	4.0	4.0	3.3	4.0	2.0	4.0	3.0	4.0	4.5	3.5		3.8
T	2.5	5.0	5.0	5.0	3.0	2.0	4.0	4.0	4.0	4.0	2.0		3.9
U	3.0	4.0	2.0	4.5	3.3	2.0	4.0	3.0	2.5	3.0	3.0		3.3
CLIENT AVG.	2.5	3.7	3.6	3.7	2.5	2.0	4.3	2.9	3.6	4.1	3.3	3.8	3.6

KEY:

Poor	1.0	1.5
Below Average	1.5	2.5
Average	2.5	3.5
Above Average	3.5	4.5
Leading Edge	4.5	5.0

BASELINE DATA - TECHNOLOGY

ATTRIBUTE

CODE	RESP. TIME	DEV. COMPTR. SUPPORT	PROJ. LIB./EQUIP.	MAINT. COMPTG. SUPPORT	HDWRE. NOVELTY	SUPPORT S/W NOVELTY	AUTO. METH.	TOTAL
A	3.0	4.8	2.8		5.0	1.0	1.0	2.9
B	3.0	4.8	3.5		5.0	3.8	3.0	3.8
C	3.0	4.8	2.5		4.0	3.0	4.5	3.6
D	3.0	3.8	3.5		5.0	5.0	2.0	3.7
E	3.0	4.5	2.5		5.0	5.0	1.0	3.5
F	3.0	5.0	3.0		5.0	5.0	1.0	3.7
G	3.0	4.4	3.5		5.0	4.0	3.0	3.8
H	3.5	4.8	3.0	4.0	5.0	5.0	1.0	3.8
J	5.0	4.4	3.5	5.0	5.0	4.0	1.0	4.0
K	3.0	5.0	3.0	5.0	5.0	5.0	1.0	3.9
L	3.0	5.0	3.5		4.0	4.0	1.0	3.4
M	5.0	4.3	2.5		5.0	3.0	1.0	3.5
N	3.0	4.1	3.8		4.0	3.0	1.0	3.1
P	4.0	4.5	3.0		5.0	3.0	3.0	3.8
Q	3.0	4.8	3.5		5.0	4.0	1.0	3.5
R	3.0	4.8	3.0	5.0	5.0	5.0	1.0	3.8
S	3.0	4.8	3.0		5.0	4.5	1.0	3.5
T	3.0	4.8	3.0		5.0	3.0	4.0	3.8
U	5.0	4.4	2.5		4.0	5.0	2.0	3.8
CLIENT AVG.	**3.4**	**4.6**	**3.1**	**4.8**	**4.8**	**4.0**	**1.8**	**3.6**

KEY:

Poor	1.0 -	1.5
Below Average	1.5 -	2.5
Average	2.5 -	3.5
Above Average	3.5 -	4.5
Leading Edge	4.5 -	5.0

BASELINE DATA - DEVELOPMENT PROCESS

ATTRIBUTE

CODE	PRODVTY. MEASURES	USE OF SDM	DESIGN METHODS	DATA ADMIN.	REUSEABILITY ENVIRONMENT	QA FUNCT. EXISTS	QUAL. MEAS. DB EXISTS	DEF. REM. ENVIRON.
A	1.0	2.5	4.0	3.0	2.0	1.0	1.0	3.5
B	1.0	1.5	2.3	4.5	5.0	1.0	1.0	2.0
C	1.0	3.0	4.0	2.0	2.5	2.0	2.0	3.0
D	1.0	3.0	1.7	3.0	2.0	1.0	1.0	2.0
E	1.0	1.0	2.0	4.0	1.0	1.0	1.0	3.0
F	1.0	2.0	2.3	2.0	2.0	1.0	1.0	3.5
G	1.0	2.5	3.5	2.5	5.0	1.0	1.0	3.5
H	1.0	1.0	2.0	4.0	2.0	2.0	2.5	3.8
J	1.0	3.0	2.7	3.0	2.5	2.0	1.0	3.0
K	1.0	2.5	2.3	5.0	3.0	1.0	1.0	3.0
L	1.0	1.0	2.7	5.0	1.0	1.0	1.0	3.5
M	1.0	3.0	2.7	3.0	2.5	3.0	1.0	3.0
N	1.0	2.0	3.0	1.0	4.0	3.0	1.0	2.5
P	1.0	3.0	2.0	1.0	2.5	1.0	1.0	2.5
Q	1.0	1.5	2.3	1.0	5.0	1.0	1.0	2.5
R	1.0	1.0	2.3	3.0	3.5	1.0	1.0	3.3
S	1.0	3.0	2.0	1.5	2.0	1.0	1.0	2.5
T	1.0	2.0	4.2	4.0	2.0	1.0	1.0	3.0
U	1.0	2.0	4.2	1.0	3.0	1.0	1.0	3.5
CLIENT AVG.	1.0	1.5	2.7	2.8	2.0	1.4	1.1	3.0

KEY:

Poor	1.0	-	1.5
Below Average	1.5	-	2.5
Average	2.5	-	3.5
Above Average	3.5	-	4.5
Leading Edge	4.5	-	5.0

BASELINE DATA - DEVELOPMENT PROCESS (CONT)

ATTRIBUTE

CODE	DEF. REM. SCHED.	TOOLS/ TESTING FUNCTION	CUSTOMER SUPPORT	L-R PLANNING/ STABILITY	DOC TYPE SIZE/ FORMAT	AUTO. DOC. PREP.	DOC. METHODS	DOC. OUTPUT DIST.	TOTAL
A	2.0	4.0			2.0	4.2	4.0	3.0	2.7
B	3.0	4.5			2.0	2.3	4.0	2.8	2.7
C	2.0	3.8			2.0	2.3	3.5	1.8	2.6
D	2.0	4.0			1.0	2.7	3.0	3.0	2.3
E	3.0	4.5			4.0	2.7	4.5	3.0	2.5
F	1.8	4.5			2.0	2.3	2.0	3.3	2.2
G	2.0	4.0			2.0	3.3	4.5	2.0	2.7
H	2.0	4.0	4.5	2.5	4.0	2.3	3.0	3.3	2.7
J	2.0	3.5	4.3	1.5	2.5	2.7	5.0	3.0	2.7
K	2.5	3.5	3.7	2.0	2.0	3.2	3.0	3.0	2.6
L	2.0	3.5			1.0	2.7	3.0	3.0	2.2
M	2.0	3.5			2.0	2.0	4.0	3.0	2.6
N	1.0	4.5			4.0	2.7	4.0	2.3	2.3
P	3.0	4.0			3.0	3.0	3.0	3.0	2.8
Q	3.0	4.0			2.0	2.3	3.0	2.5	2.3
R	3.0	3.5	4.5	2.0	2.0	3.2	3.0	3.0	2.6
S	1.5	4.0			3.0	2.7	3.0	3.0	2.2
T	5.0	4.0			1.0	3.7	4.0	2.5	3.0
U	2.0	3.0			1.0	2.7	3.0	3.5	2.3
CLIENT AVG.	**2.4**	**3.9**	**4.3**	**2.0**	**2.2**	**2.8**	**3.5**	**2.8**	**2.5**

KEY:

Poor	1.0 -	1.5
Below Average	1.5 -	2.5
Average	2.5 -	3.5
Above Average	3.5 -	4.5
Leading Edge	4.5 -	5.0

C00037/59

BASELINE DATA - ENVIRONMENT

ATTRIBUTE

CODE	FUNC. NOV.	PROD. REST.	LEGAL/ STAT.	PROG. COMP.	PROD. FACT.	DEV. GEO.	OFFICE ENV.	NOISE/ INTER.	MAINT. AVAIL.	TOTAL
A	1.0	5.0	5.0	3.0		4.0	2.3	3.0		3.3
B	1.5	3.0	5.0	2.3		5.0	2.3	2.0		3.0
C	5.0	3.0	5.0	3.8		4.0	2.3	3.0		3.7
D	4.0	3.0	5.0	3.0		4.0	2.3	1.0		3.2
E	3.0	2.5	5.0	2.5		5.0	2.3	2.0		3.2
F	3.0	3.0	3.0	1.5		4.0	2.3	2.0		2.7
G	4.0	3.0	5.0	4.0		5.0	2.0	2.0		3.6
H	4.0	3.3	3.0	2.5	3.5	4.5	2.3	1.0	1.0	2.8
J	2.0	2.5	5.0	2.7	2.5	5.0	2.3	3.0	3.5	3.2
K	3.0	3.0	5.0	2.0	2.5	5.0	2.3	1.5	3.0	3.0
L	4.0	2.0	5.0	3.2		5.0	2.3	5.0		3.8
M	3.0	2.5	3.0	3.5		3.0	2.3	2.3		2.8
N	4.0	2.8	3.0	3.3		4.0	1.5	1.5		2.9
P	4.0	2.8	5.0	4.2		5.0	2.3	1.0		3.5
Q	4.0	3.0	3.0	2.8		5.0	2.0	2.0		3.1
R	3.0	3.0	5.0	2.2	2.5	5.0	2.3	1.5	1.0	2.8
S	4.0	5.0	5.0	3.0		5.0	2.3	2.0		3.8
T	2.0	3.0	5.0	4.0		3.0	2.3	2.0		3.0
U	2.5	2.3	5.0	2.3		5.0	2.5	4.0		3.4
CLIENT AVG.	3.2	3.0	4.5	2.9	2.8	4.5	2.2	2.2	2.1	3.2

KEY:

Poor	1.0 -	1.5
Below Average	1.5 -	2.5
Average	2.5 -	3.5
Above Average	3.5 -	4.5
Leading Edge	4.5 -	5.0

C0003760

FINDINGS BASIS

FINDINGS BASIS - PRODUCTIVITY

ATTRIBUTE

% DEVIATION FROM INDUSTRY AVERAGE

CODE	SCH	FTE	DOC	FP/MO
A	60	-207	-51	12
B	58	-189	73	0
C	138	-260	-82	14
D	110	10	-10	266
E	-14	-50	54	-62
F	14	-340	2	-54
G	422	-52	-93	333
H	92	-15	-69	126
J	608	72	-95	N/A
K	-2	-27	-60	-12
L	41	-80	-52	-14
M	65	-136	-52	62
N	40	-197	-28	-21
P	0	-230	-20	-56
Q	48	-19	-40	144
R	76	-75	-42	180
S	49	-58	-26	46
T	70	-148	-51	8
U	-8	0	-35	16

KEY:

SCH	=	Schedule
FTE	=	Staff (Full-Time Equivalents)
DOC	=	Documentation
FP/MO	=	Productivity (Function Points per Person-Month)

FINDING

- Schedule is much shorter than expected on vast majority of projects (79%).

- Staff levels significantly higher than expected on virtually all projects (84%).

- Documentation less than expected for nearly all projects (84%).

- Productivity levels tended toward norm: half of projects within 21% of industry average.

EXPLANATION OF TABLE:

% Deviation From Industry Average indicates how much better (positive %) or worse (negative %) the measured attribute is compared to the industry average.

For example, project A in the *Baseline Data - Productivity* table was sized at 132 Function Points and had a schedule measured at 3.5 months. The industry average schedule for a project with 132 Function Points is 8.8 months. Therefore, project A's schedule is (8.8 - 3.5) ÷ 8.8 = 60% better than the industry average.

FINDINGS BASIS - CUSTOMER SATISFACTION

FINDING	SUPPORTIVE DATA
STRENGTHS	
• Customers Generally Satisfied With Systems	Interviews
- End User Customers	4.65
- Project Team Customers	2.50
WEAKNESSES	
• Project Team Customers Not Completely Satisfied With:	
- Project Controls	3.44
- System Design	3.39
- Development Techniques	3.34
- Development Tools	3.18
• Customers Express Loss of Control and Doubts About I/S Productivity	Interviews

KEY:

Very Dissatisfied	1.0 - 1.5
Dissatisfied	1.5 - 2.5
Not Completely Satisfied	2.5 - 3.5
Satisfied	3.5 - 4.5
Very Satisfied	4.5 - 5.0

FINDINGS BASIS - PEOPLE MANAGEMENT

FINDING	SUPPORTIVE DATA
STRENGTHS	
• Above Average Hardware Experience	4.3
• Above Average Team Cohesiveness	4.1
• Above Average Analysis/Design Experience	3.7
• Above Average Language Experience	3.6
• Above Average Defect Removal Experience	3.7
• Very Good Employee Loyalty	Interviews
WEAKNESSES	
• Below Average User Experience	2.0 - 2.5
• Extensive Use of Generalists vs. Specialists	Interviews
• Reluctance to Change	Interviews

KEY:

Poor	1.0 - 1.5
Below Average	1.5 - 2.5
Average	2.5 - 3.5
Above Average	3.5 - 4.5
Leading Edge	4.5 - 5.0

FINDINGS BASIS - TECHNOLOGY

	FINDING	SUPPORTIVE DATA
STRENGTHS		
•	Above Average Hardware Novelty	4.8
•	Above Average Maintenance Computer Support	4.8
•	Above Average Development Computer Support	4.6
•	Support Software Novelty Above Average	4.0
WEAKNESSES		
•	Poor Automated Design Methods	1.8
•	Maintenance Lifecycle Not Closely Managed	Interviews
•	Insufficient Technology Transfer Communications	Interviews

KEY:

Poor	1.0	1.5
Below Average	1.5	2.5
Average	2.5	3.5
Above Average	3.5	4.5
Leading Edge	4.5	5.0

FINDINGS BASIS - DEVELOPMENT PROCESS

FINDING	SUPPORTIVE DATA
STRENGTHS	
• None	
WEAKNESSES	
• Poor Productivity Measures	1.0
• Poor Quality Measurements	1.1
• Poor QA Existence	1.4
• Poor Reusability Environment	2.0
• Poor Long Range Planning Stability	2.0
• Below Average Documentation Format	2.2
• Below Average Defect Removal Scheduling	2.4
• User Generated Documentation	Interviews
• Insufficient SDM Enforcement	Interviews

KEY:

Poor	1.0	- 1.5
Below Average	1.5	- 2.5
Average	2.5	- 3.5
Above Average	3.5	- 4.5
Leading Edge	4.5	- 5.0

C00037/66

FINDINGS BASIS - ENVIRONMENT

FINDING	SUPPORTIVE DATA
STRENGTHS	
• Above Average Legal/Statutory Requirements	4.5
• Above Average Development Geography	4.5
WEAKNESSES	
• Below Average Maintenance Availability	2.1
• Below Average Office Environment	2.2
• Below Average Noise Suppression	2.2
• Culture of Quantity vs. Quality	Interviews
• Culture of Complacency and Limited Accountability	Interviews
• Higher Degree of Business Urgency than Perceived I/S Urgency	Interviews

KEY:

Poor	1.0 - 1.5
Below Average	1.5 - 2.5
Average	2.5 - 3.5
Above Average	3.5 - 4.5
Leading Edge	4.5 - 5.0

HIGH PRODUCTIVITY PROJECTS CONSISTENTLY USED A COMBINATION OF TOOLS AND METHODS

Productivity Factors

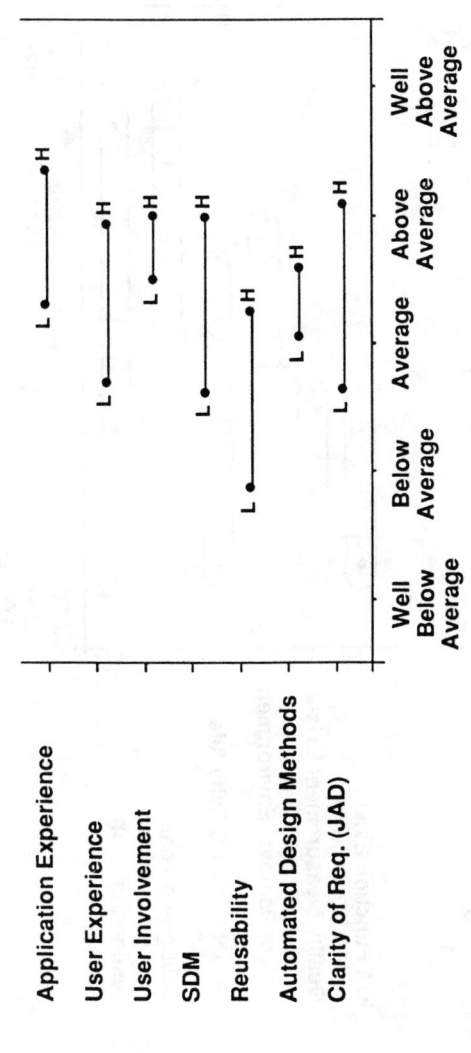

- User involvement was a key factor in productivity gains.

L = Low Productivity Projects
H = High Productivity Projects

C00037/32

467

INFORMAL QUALITY ASSURANCE ACTIVITIES ARE TYPICALLY PERFORMED BY DEVELOPMENT TEAM

Quality Assurance Management

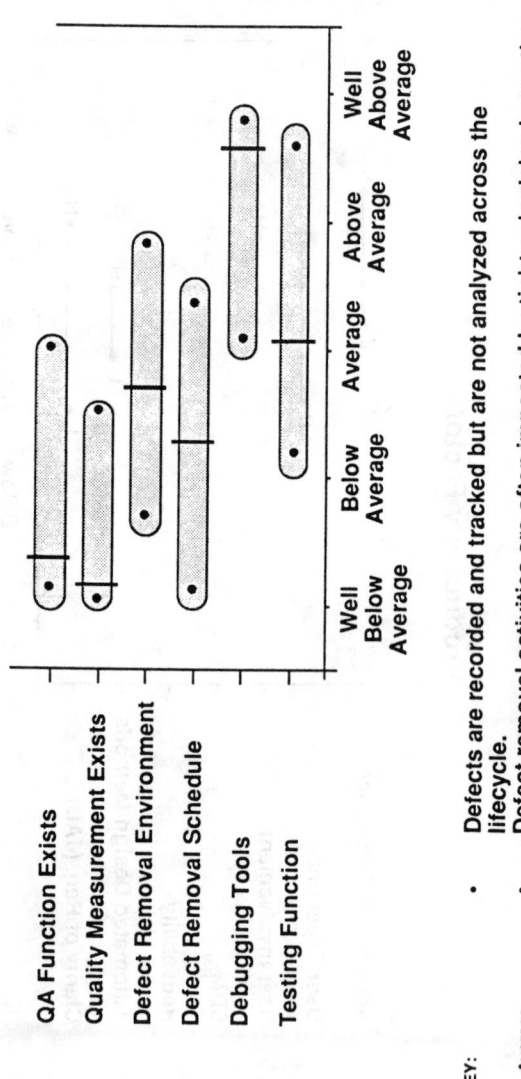

- Defects are recorded and tracked but are not analyzed across the lifecycle.
- Defect removal activities are often impacted by tight schedules impacting the ability to do adequate reviews/inspections.
- Testing is often viewed as more important than pre-test reviews.

KEY:

| Average

● Project Range

C0037/33

468

A NUMBER OF KEY DEFECT REMOVAL ACTIVITIES ARE NOT PERFORMED

Defect Removal Activity

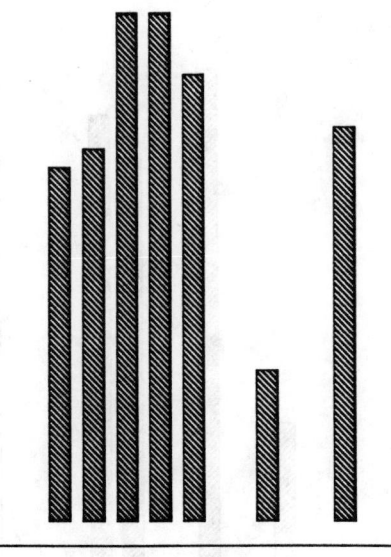

EFFECTIVENESS

Poor — Avg. — Excel

Non-Test Defect Removal

- Customer Requirements
- Prototyping
- Requirements Review
- Function Design Review
- Logic Design Review
- Data Structure Design Review
- Module Design Review
- User Documentation
- Maintenance Documentation Review
- Code Review/Inspection
- Quality Assurance Review
- Design Reviews
- Performance Reviews

KEY:

Performed
Not Performed

C00037/34

469

A NUMBER OF KEY DEFECT REMOVAL ACTIVITIES ARE NOT PERFORMED

Defect Removal Activity

EFFECTIVENESS

Testing Defect Removal

- Unit Testing
- New Function Testing
- Regression Testing
- Stress or Performance Testing
- System Testing
- Integration Testing
- Field Testing
- User Acceptance Testing

Poor   Avg.   Excel

Post-Release Defect Removal

- Error-Prone Module Analysis
- User Satisfaction Survey

Poor   Avg.   Excel

KEY:
Performed
Not Performed

C0003735

PRODUCTIVITY MEASURES ARE INCOMPLETE AND INCONSISTENT

Project Management Environment

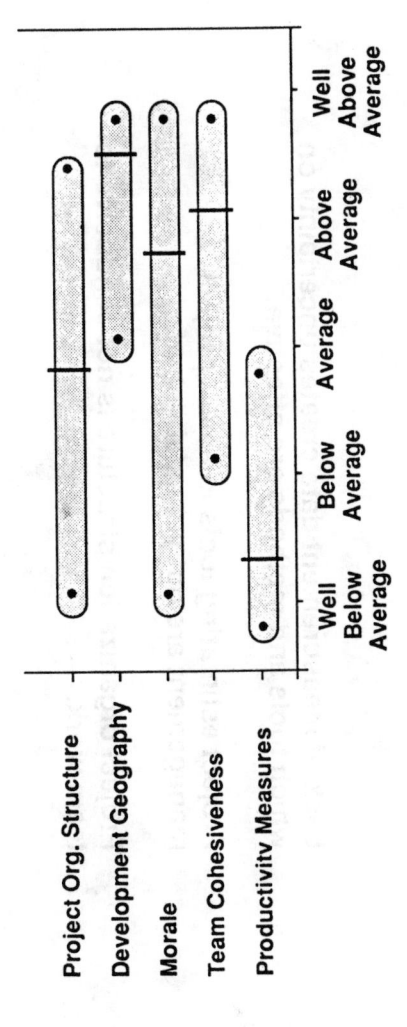

Project Org. Structure

Development Geography

Morale

Team Cohesiveness

Productivity Measures

Well Below Average — Below Average — Average — Above Average — Well Above Average

KEY:

| Average

• Project Range

- • A number of projects reported a matrix organization which can impact productivity negatively.
- • Morale varies significantly by project.

C00037/37

PROJECT MANAGEMENT ENVIRONMENT

Additional Findings

- Lack of measurement data creates uncertainty on which tools and methods are effective.

- Project estimating tools to assist project management are not yet established.

- Project organization structure is not conducive to team work.

PHYSICAL ENVIRONMENT IS NOT CONDUCIVE TO HIGH PRODUCTIVITY OR QUALITY

Environmental Factors

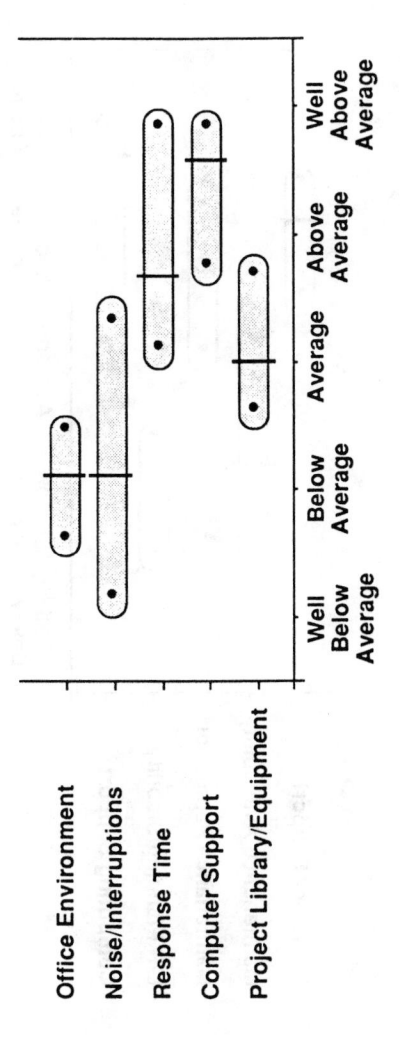

KEY:

| Average
• Project Range

- • Individual offices are not enclosed contributing to noise, distractions, and frequent interruptions.
- • Computer support and response time is reliable and effective.

C00037/39

473

LONG RANGE SYSTEMS PLANNING IS NOT YET A PART OF THE COMPANYS' OVERALL BUSINESS STRATEGY

Maintenance and Enhancement Support

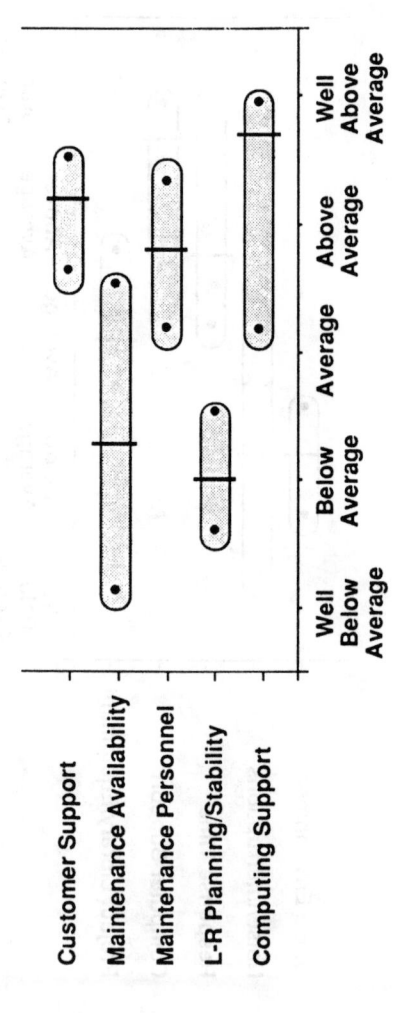

KEY:

—— Average

● Project Range

- Customer support is well staffed with experienced people.
- Frequent changes to software and limited long range planning has resulted in a low stability rating.
- Systems are not being analyzed for possible improvements through restructuring.

C00037/40

474

SCHEDULE PRESSURE AND UNCLEAR USER REQUIREMENTS WERE HIGH RISK FACTORS ON MOST PROJECTS

Project Risk Analysis

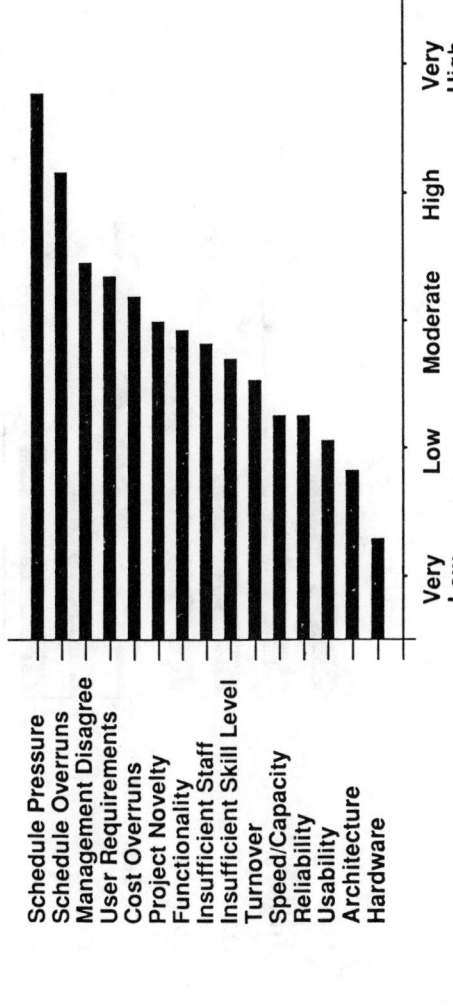

KEY:

■ AVERAGE

- User requirements are frequently unstable.
- Management disagreements on most projects should be a concern.

C00037/42

475

END-USER DOCUMENTATION IS VERY LIMITED

Percent of Expected Documents

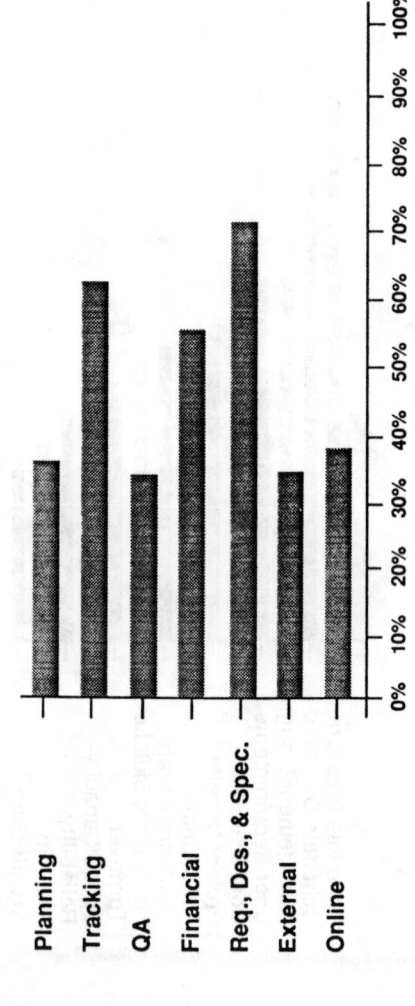

CONCLUSIONS

A MULTIFACETED IMPROVEMENT PLAN IS REQUIRED TO EFFECTIVELY ORCHESTRATE CHANGE

Kiviat Graph of Software Goals

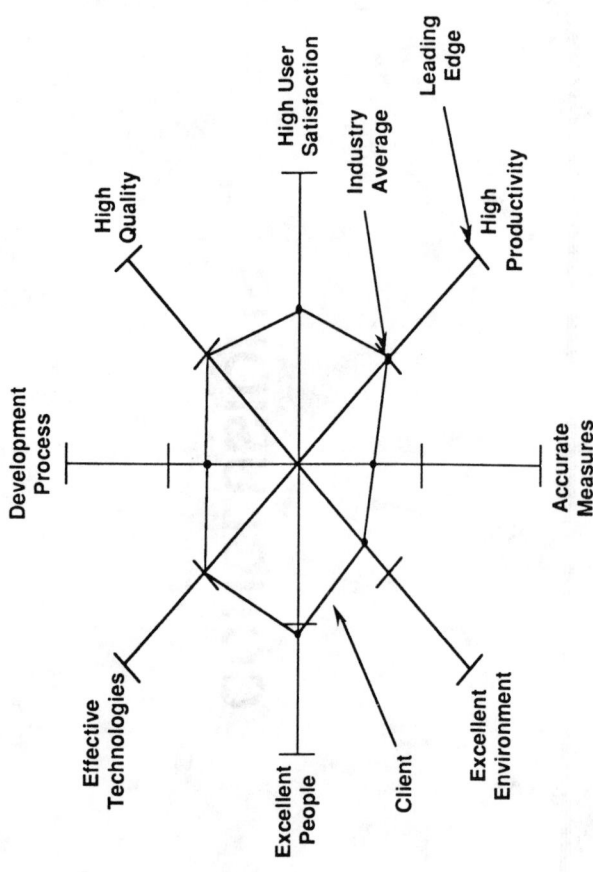

High Quality

High User Satisfaction

Industry Average

Leading Edge

High Productivity

Development Process

Accurate Measures

Effective Technologies

Excellent People

Client

Excellent Environment

OPPORTUNITIES

SUMMARY OF OPPORTUNITIES

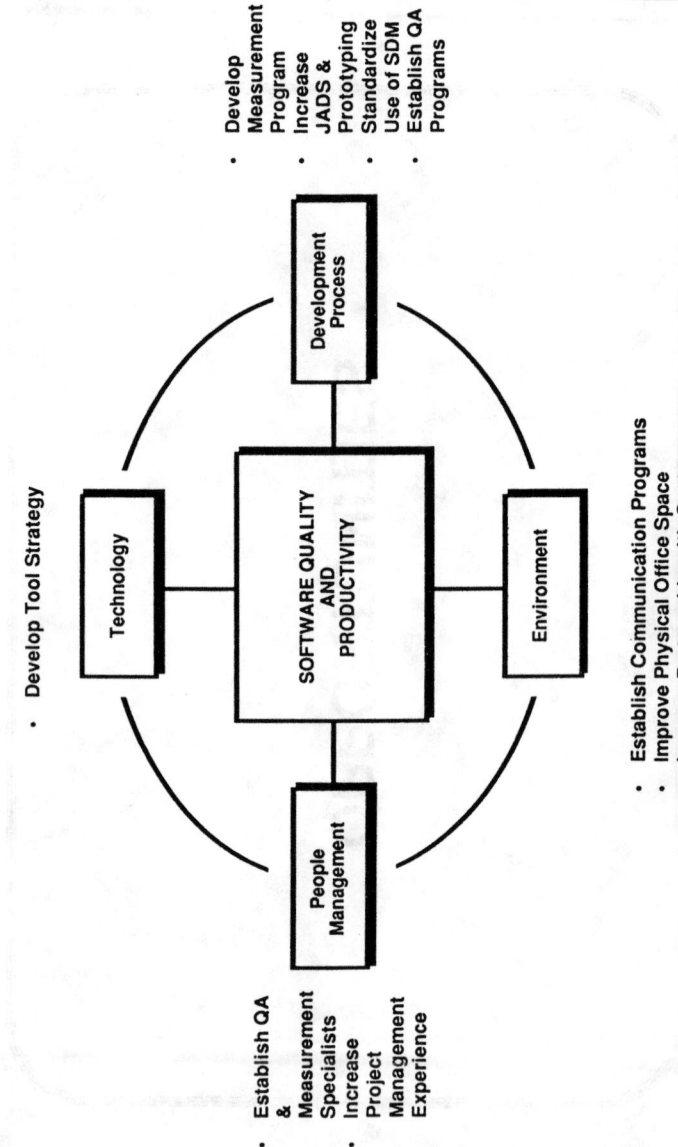

- Develop Tool Strategy

- Develop Measurement Program
- Increase JADS & Prototyping
- Standardize Use of SDM
- Establish QA Programs

- Establish Communication Programs
- Improve Physical Office Space
- Improve Partnership with Customers

- Establish QA & Measurement Specialists
- Increase Project Management Experience

C00037/46

480

NEXT STEPS

NEXT STEPS DEVELOP A QUALITY/PRODUCTIVITY PLAN

Planning Overview

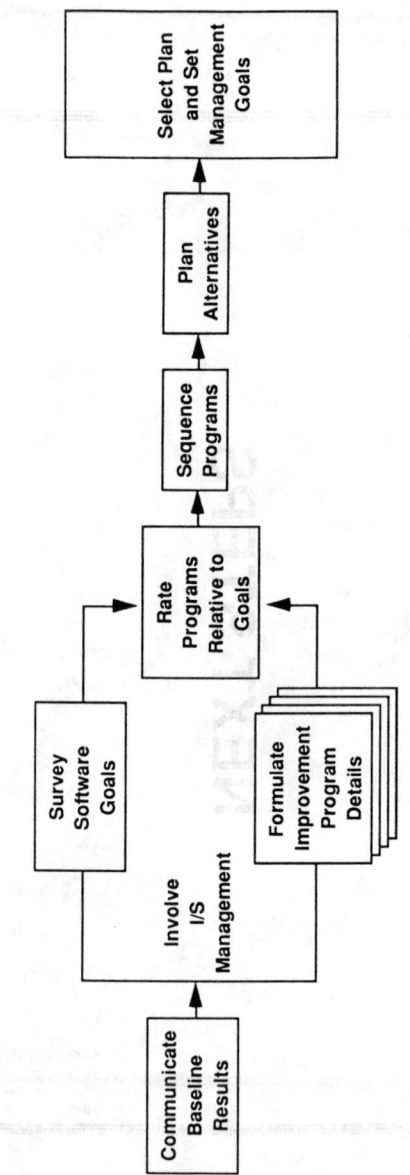

C00037/48

NEXT STEPS

- Conduct software goals survey.

- Gain management acceptance of baseline results.

- Identify and involve I/S management in program planning to formulate program details.

- Develop plans and set goals.

C0003749

APPENDIX

APPENDIX

- Baseline Data

- Findings Basis

Index

About the Author

Capers Jones is founder and chairman of Software Productivity Research, Inc., a leader in state-of-the-art software productivity management. An international speaker and author of two software engineering books, Mr. Jones has led a series of successful seminars that have been attended by employees of AT&T, IBM, Hewlett-Packard, Boeing, and many other of the world's leading corporations.